STP MATHEMATICS

NATIONAL CURRICULUM

10B

L. BOSTOCK, B.Sc.

S. CHANDLER, B.Sc.

A. SHEPHERD, B.Sc.

E. SMITH, M.Sc.

STANLEY THORNES (PUBLISHERS) LTD

First published in 1999 by
Stanley Thornes (Publishers) Ltd,
Ellenborough House,
Wellington Street,
CHELTENHAM GL50 1YW

99 00 01 02 03/ 10 9 8 7 6 5 4 3 2

A catalogue record of this book is available from the British Library.

ISBN 0-7487-3191-1

Artwork by Peters & Zabransky, Linda Jefferey.

The Publishers are grateful to the following for permission to reproduce copyright material:
Martyn Chillmaid: photograph p. 46
Sharp: photograph p. 55

Front cover image produced using material kindly supplied by I LOVE LOVE CO, makers of The Happy Cube © Laureyssens/Creative City Ltd 1986/91. Distributed in UK by: RIGHTRAC, 119 Sandycombe Road, Richmond, Surrey TW9 2ER Tel. 0181 940 3322.

The authors and publishers are grateful to the following examination boards for permission to reproduce questions from their past examination papers. (Any answers included have not been provided by the examining boards, they are the responsibility of the authors and may not necessarily constitute the only possible solutions.)

London Examinations, A division of Edexcel Foundation (London)
Northern Examinations and Assessment Board (NEAB)
University of Cambridge Local Examinations Syndicate (MEG)
The Associated Examining Board (SEG)
Welsh Joint Education Committee (WJEC)

Typeset by Tech-Set, Gateshead, Tyne & Wear.
Printed in and bound in China

CONTENTS

INTRODUCTION

To the pupil

This book continues to help you to learn, enjoy and progress through Mathematics in the National Curriculum up to intermediate level at GCSE. As well as a clear and concise text the book offers a wide range of practical and investigational work that is relevant to the mathematics you are learning.

Everyone needs success and satisfaction in getting things right. With this in mind we have divided many of the exercises into three types of question.

The first type, identified by plain numbers, e.g. **15**, helps you to see if you understand the work.

The second type, identified by an underline, e.g. **<u>15</u>**, are extra, but not harder, questions for quicker workers, for extra practice or for later revision.

The third type, identified by a coloured square, e.g. **15** , are for those of you who like a greater challenge.

Most chapters have a 'mixed exercise' after the main work of the chapter has been completed. These will help you to revise what you have done, either when you have finished the chapter or at a later date. All chapters end with some mathematical puzzles, practical and/or investigational work. For this work you are encouraged to share your ideas with others, use any mathematics you are familiar with, to use reference books and try to solve each problem using different approaches, appreciating the advantages and disadvantages of each method.

The book starts with a summary of the main results from Books 7B, 8B and 9B. At intervals throughout the book there are further summaries. These list the most important points that have been covered in the previous chapters and conclude with revision exercises that test the work covered up to that point.

At this stage you will find that you use a calculator more frequently, and for some topics its use is essential, but it is still unwise to rely on a calculator for number work that can be done in your head or easily on paper. Since you will have at least one non-calculator paper when you sit your GCSE examinations, some of the exercises in this book are designed to be worked without a calculator. They are clearly marked and will give valuable practice in the basic number skills that you need to master without the aid of a calculator. Remember, whether you use a calculator or do the working yourself, always estimate your answer and always ask yourself the question, 'Is my answer a sensible one?'.

Mathematics is an exciting and enjoyable subject when you understand what is going on. Remember, if you don't understand something ask someone who can explain it to you. If you still don't understand, ask again. Good luck with your studies.

To the teacher

This is the fourth book of the STP National Curriculum Mathematics series. It is based on the ST(P) Mathematics series but has been extensively rewritten and is now firmly based on the Programme of Study for Key Stages 3 and 4. It also contains several non-calculator exercises in preparation for the non-calculator papers at GCSE.

Most scientific calculators now on sale use direct keying sequences for entering functions such as tan 33° and this is the order used in this book.

The B series of books aims to prepare pupils for the intermediate tier at GCSE; GCSE syllabuses vary however, and a few of the topics in this book are not in all syllabuses.

SUMMARY 1

**MAIN RESULTS
FROM BOOKS 7B,
8B AND 9B**

**TYPES OF
NUMBER**

Even numbers divide exactly by 2, e.g. 6, 10, ...

Odd numbers do not divide exactly by 2, e.g. 3, 7, ...

A **prime number** has only two different factors, 1 and itself, e.g.
$7 = 7 \times 1$. (2 is the smallest prime number; 1 is not a prime number
because it does not have a factor other than 1.)

Square numbers can be drawn
as a square grid of dots, e.g. 9:
The smallest square number is 1.
Square numbers are also called **perfect squares**.

Rectangular numbers can be
drawn as a rectangular grid of dots, e.g. 6:

Triangular numbers can be
drawn as a triangular grid of dots, e.g. 6:

Negative numbers are used to describe a quantity when it goes below a
zero level.
For example, 2 °C below freezing point (0 °C) is written −2 °C and is
called 'minus' 2 °C or 'negative' 2 °C.
Positive and negative numbers are together called **directed numbers**.
They can be represented on a number line:

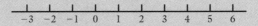

Index numbers: the small raised 2 in 3^2 is called an index and it tells
you how many 3s are multiplied together,

e.g. 3^2 means 3×3 and 3^5 means $3 \times 3 \times 3 \times 3 \times 3$.

A **factor** of a number will divide into the number exactly.
When two or more numbers have the same factor, it is called a **common
factor**,

e.g.   8 and 6 have a common factor of 2.

1

A **multiple** of a number can be divided exactly by that number,

e.g.　12 is a multiple of 3.

A **common multiple** of two or more numbers can be divided exactly by each of those numbers,

e.g.　12 is a common multiple of 2, 3, 4, 6 and 12.

CALCULATING WITH NUMBERS

The sign in front of a number refers to that number only.
The order in which you add or subtract does not matter, so $1 - 5 + 8$ can be calculated in the order $1 + 8 - 5$, i.e. $9 - 5 = 4$.
When a calculation involves *a mixture of operations*, start by calculating anything inside brackets, then follow the rule 'do the multiplication and division first',

e.g.　$2 + 3 \times 2 = 2 + 6$　　and　　$(2 + 3) \times 2 = 5 \times 2$
　　　　　　　　$= 8$　　　　　　　　　　　　　$= 10$

Division is the opposite of multiplication,

e.g.　$6 \div 3 = 2$　because　$6 = 3 \times 2$

To *add and subtract directed numbers* we use these rules:

　　　　when the signs are the same, we add.
　　　　when the signs are different we subtract.

For example,　$2 + (+3) = 2 + 3$　and　$2 - (-3) = 2 + 3$
　　　　　　　　$2 + (-3) = 2 - 3$　and　$2 - (+3) = 2 - 3$

Remember that the sign, or signs, in front of a number apply only to that number,

e.g.　$-2 + 3$　means start with -2 and then add 3; it is not the same as $2 - (+3)$.

To *multiply directed numbers* we use similar rules.
When two numbers of the same sign are multiplied together, the result is positive.
When two numbers of different signs are multiplied together, the result is negative.

For example,　$(+2) \times (+3) = +6$　and　$(-2) \times (-3) = +6$
　　　　　　　　$(+2) \times (-3) = -6$　and　$(-2) \times (+3) = -6$

The same rules apply to division,

e.g.　$(+8) \div (+2) = +4$　and　$(-8) \div (-2) = +4$
　　　　$(+8) \div (-2) = -4$　and　$(-8) \div (+2) = -4$

FRACTIONS

A fraction describes the size of a part of some quantity.

A fraction is written in the form $\frac{2}{3}$.

The *denominator* (the bottom number) tells us how many equal-sized parts the quantity is divided into.
The *numerator* (the top number) tells us the number of the equal-sized parts that are being considered.

For example, $\frac{2}{3}$ of this square is shaded.

Equivalent fractions each describe the same sized part of a quantity.

The shaded part of this square can be described as $\frac{4}{6}$ or $\frac{2}{3}$ of the square,

i.e. $\frac{4}{6}$ and $\frac{2}{3}$ are equivalent fractions.

We can find a fraction equivalent to a given fraction by multiplying or dividing the top and bottom by the same number,

e.g. $\qquad \frac{2}{3} = \frac{2 \times 2}{2 \times 3} = \frac{4}{6}$

$\qquad \frac{9}{24} = \frac{9 \div 3}{24 \div 3} = \frac{3}{8}$ (This is sometimes called *cancelling*.)

Fractions can be added or subtracted when they have the same denominator.

For example, to add $\frac{1}{2}$ to $\frac{1}{3}$ we must first change them into equivalent fractions with the same denominators, then we add the numerators,

i.e. $\qquad \frac{1}{2} + \frac{1}{3} = \frac{1}{2} \times \frac{3}{3} + \frac{1}{3} \times \frac{2}{2} = \frac{3}{6} + \frac{2}{6} = \frac{5}{6}$

A **mixed number** is a combination of a whole number and a fraction,

e.g. $\qquad 1\frac{3}{4} = 1 + \frac{3}{4}$

$\qquad\qquad = \frac{4}{4} + \frac{3}{4} = \frac{7}{4}$

$\frac{7}{4}$ is called an **improper fraction**. Any fraction whose top is larger than the bottom is an improper fraction.

To multiply one fraction by another fraction, we multiply their numerators together and multiply their denominators together,

e.g. $\qquad \frac{1}{2} \times \frac{5}{3} = \frac{1 \times 5}{2 \times 3} = \frac{5}{6}$

Mixed numbers must be changed into improper fractions before they can be multiplied,

e.g. $\qquad 1\frac{1}{2} \times \frac{3}{5} = \frac{3}{2} \times \frac{3}{5} = \frac{3 \times 3}{2 \times 5} = \frac{9}{10}$

To multiply by a whole number, treat it as a fraction by writing it over 1,

e.g. $4 \times \frac{3}{5} = \frac{4}{1} \times \frac{3}{5} = \frac{12}{5} = 2\frac{2}{5}$

To divide by a fraction, we turn the fraction upside down and multiply by it,

e.g. $\frac{1}{2} \div \frac{5}{3} = \frac{1}{2} \times \frac{3}{5} = \frac{3}{10}$

To multiply or divide with mixed numbers, first change the mixed numbers to improper fractions.

To find a fraction of a quantity, multiply the fraction by the quantity,

e.g. $\frac{3}{8}$ of £20 $= £(\frac{3}{8} \times 20)$

To express one quantity as a fraction of another, first express both quantities in the same unit and then place the first quantity over the second,

e.g. 25 p as a fraction of £3 is equal to $\frac{25}{300} = \frac{1}{12}$,

or, to put it another way, 25 p is $\frac{1}{12}$ of £3.

RATIO

Ratios are used to compare the relative sizes of quantities.
For example, if a model of a car is 4 cm long and the real car is 400 cm long, we say that their lengths are in the ratio $4:400$.

Ratios can be simplified by dividing the parts of the ratio by the same number,

e.g. $4:400 = 1:100$ (dividing both 4 and 400 by 4).

Ratios are closely related to fractions, for example, the length of the model as a fraction of the length of the car is $\frac{4}{400} = \frac{1}{100}$.

To divide a quantity in a given ratio, say $3:5$, find the fractions $\frac{3}{3+5}$ and $\frac{5}{3+5}$ of the quantity,

e.g. to divide £24 in the ratio $3:5$, find $\frac{3}{8}$ of £24 and $\frac{5}{8}$ of £24.

A *map ratio* is the ratio of a length on the map to the length it represents on the ground. When expressed as a fraction, it is called the **representative fraction**.

DECIMALS

In decimal notation, numbers to the right of a decimal point represent tenths, hundredths, ...,

e.g. $0.53 = \frac{5}{10} + \frac{3}{100}$

Decimals can be added or subtracted in the same way as whole numbers. We must remember to place the decimal points in line and, when necessary, to fill in any blank spaces with zeros, e.g.   to add 12.5 and 7.95, we can write them as

$$\begin{array}{r} 12.50 \\ +\ 7.95 \\ \hline 20.45 \end{array}$$

To multiply a decimal by 10, 100, 1000, ..., we move the point 1, 2, 3, ... places to the right,

e.g. $2.56 \times 10 = 25.6$, and $2.56 \times 1000 = 2560(.0)$

To divide a decimal by 10, 100, 1000, ..., we move the point 1, 2, 3, ... places to the left,

e.g. $2.56 \div 10 = 0.256$, and $2.56 \div 1000 = 0.002\,56$

(Moving the point to the right is equivalent to moving the figures to the left, and vice-versa.)

To multiply decimals without using a calculator, first ignore the decimal point and multiply the numbers. Then add the number of decimal places in each of the decimals being multiplied together; this gives the number of decimal places in the answer,

e.g. $2.5 \times 0.4 = 1.00 = 1$ $(25 \times 4 = 100)$
        $[(1)+(1) = (2)]$

To divide by a decimal, move the point in *both* numbers to the right until the number we are dividing by is a whole number,

e.g. $2.56 \div 0.4 = 25.6 \div 4$

Now we can use ordinary division, keeping the decimal point in the same place,

e.g. $25.6 \div 4 = 4)\overline{25.6}$ with 6.4 above

To round (i.e. to correct) a number to a specified place value or number of decimal places, look at the figure in the next place: if it is 5 or more, add 1 to the specified figure, otherwise leave the specified figure as it is,

e.g.   to write 52.564 correct to 2 decimal places, we have

$52.56|4 = 52.56$ correct to 2 decimal places

and to write 52.564 correct to 1 decimal place, we have

$52.5|64 = 52.6$ correct to 1 decimal place

Similarly, to give 52.564 correct to the nearest whole number, we write

$52|.564 = 53$ correct to the nearest whole number.

Significant figures

The first significant figure in a number is the first non-zero figure when reading from left to right.

The second significant figure is the next figure to the right, whether or not it is zero, and so on.

For example, in 0.0205, the first significant figure is 2,

the second significant figure is 0,

the third significant figure is 5.

To round (i.e. to correct) a number to a specified place value or number of significant figures, look at the figure in the next place; if it is 5 or more, add 1 to the specified place, otherwise leave the specified figure as it is.

For example, $0.020\overset{|}{5} = 0.021$ correct to 2 significant figures

$0.02\overset{|\,|}{0}5 = 0.02$ correct to 1 significant figure.

PERCENTAGES

A percentage of a quantity means the number of one hundredths of the quantity, e.g. 20% of a pie means 20 out of 100 equal-sized parts of the pie, i.e.

$20\% = \frac{20}{100}.$

INTERCHANGING PERCENTAGES, FRACTIONS AND DECIMALS

A percentage, a fraction and a decimal are different ways of describing the size of the same part of a quantity,

e.g.   the shaded part of this diagram is

$50\% = 0.5 = \frac{1}{2}$ of the area of the square.

A fraction can be changed to a decimal by dividing the bottom number into the top number,

e.g. $\frac{3}{8} = 3 \div 8 = 0.375$

A decimal can be expressed as a fraction by placing the numbers after the decimal point over '1 together with the number of zeros equal to the number of decimal places',

e.g. $0.15 = \frac{15}{100}, \ 0.7 = \frac{7}{10}, \ 0.137 = \frac{137}{1000}, \ 1.25 = 1\frac{25}{100} = 1\frac{1}{4}$

A percentage can be expressed as a fraction by placing the percentage over 100,

e.g. $33\% = \frac{33}{100}$

Reversing the process, *a fraction can be expressed as a percentage* by multiplying the fraction by 100,

e.g. $\frac{2}{5} = \frac{2}{5} \times 100\% = \frac{2}{5} \times \frac{100}{1}\% = 40\%$

We can express *a percentage as a decimal* if we divide the percentage by 100, that is we move the decimal point two places to the left,

e.g. $33\% = 0.33$

and *a decimal can be expressed as a percentage* by multiplying the decimal by 100, that is by moving the decimal point two places to the right,

e.g. $0.325 = 32.5\%$

WORKING WITH PERCENTAGES

To find one quantity as a percentage of another quantity, express the first quantity as a fraction of the second (make sure that the units are the same) and then multiply by 100,

e.g.   25 p as a percentage of £2 $= \frac{25}{200} \times 100\% = 12.5\%$
i.e.   25 p is 12.5% of £2

To find a percentage of a quantity, first change the percentage to a decimal and then multiply the decimal by the quantity.

To *increase* a quantity by 15%,
we find *the increase* by finding 15% of the quantity,
we find *the new quantity* by finding $100\% + 15\%$,
i.e.   115% of the original quantity, so we multiply by 1.15.

To *decrease* a quantity by 15%,
we find *the decrease* by finding 15% of the quantity,
we find *the new quantity* by finding $100\% - 15\%$,
i.e.   85% of the original quantity, so we multiply by 0.85.

SHAPES

The **perimeter** of a shape is the total distance all round its edge.

Angles
One complete revolution $= 4$ right angles $= 360°$.

1 *right angle* $= 90°$

An *acute angle* is less than one right angle.

An *obtuse angle* is larger than 1 right angle but less than 2 right angles.

A *reflex angle* is larger than two right angles.

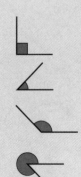

Vertically opposite angles are equal.

Angles on a straight line add up to 180°.
Two angles that add up to 180° are called
supplementary angles.

Angles at a point add up to 360°.

When two **parallel lines** are cut by a transversal,
the **corresponding angles** are equal,

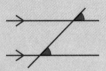

and the **alternate angles** are equal.

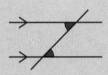

Triangles
The three angles in a triangle add up to 180°.

An equilateral triangle has all three sides equal
and each angle is 60°.
An isosceles triangle has two sides equal and the
angles at the base of these sides are equal.

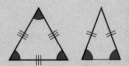

Quadrilaterals
A quadrilateral has four sides.
The four angles in a quadrilateral add up to 360°.

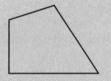

Special quadrilaterals

In a square
- all four sides are the same length
- both pairs of opposite sides are parallel
- all four angles are right angles.

In a rectangle
- both pairs of opposite sides are the same length
- both pairs of opposite sides are parallel
- all four angles are right angles.

In a rhombus
- all four sides are the same length
- both pairs of opposite sides are parallel
- the opposite angles are equal.

In a parallelogram
- the opposite sides are the same length
- the opposite sides are parallel
- the opposite angles are equal.

In a trapezium
- just one pair of opposite sides are parallel.

A **polygon** is a plane (i.e. flat) figure bounded by straight lines, e.g.

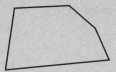

A **regular polygon** has all angles equal and all sides the same length.
This is a regular hexagon.

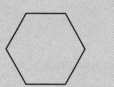

The *sum of the exterior angles of any polygon* (regular or not) is 360°.

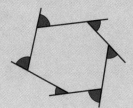

The *sum of the interior angles* of any polygon depends on the number of sides.
For a polygon with n sides, this sum is $(180n - 360)°$ or $(2n - 4)$ right angles.

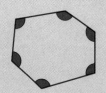

A **cube** is a solid and all of its faces are squares.
A **cuboid** is a rectangular block.

Cube

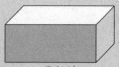

Cuboid

A **prism** is a solid with a constant cross-section.

SYMMETRY

A shape has a **line of symmetry** if, when it is folded along that line, one half of the shape fits exactly over the other half,

e.g.   this shape has one line of symmetry.

A shape has **rotational symmetry** if, when it is turned about a centre point to a new position, it looks the same,

e.g.   this shape has rotational symmetry.

CONGRUENCE

Two figures are congruent when they are exactly the same shape and size. One shape may be turned over compared with the other.

These two triangles are congruent.

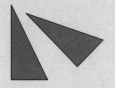

TRANSFORMATIONS

Reflection
When an object is reflected in a mirror line, the object and its image form a symmetrical shape with the mirror line as the axis of symmetry.

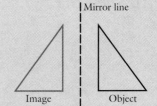

Translation
When an object is translated it moves without being turned or reflected to form an image.

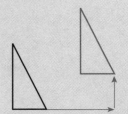

Rotation
When an object is rotated it turns about a point to form an image; the point about which it is rotated is called the *centre of rotation* and the angle it is turned through is called the *angle of rotation*.

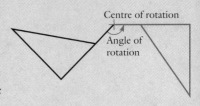

Enlargement

When an object is enlarged by a scale factor 2, each line on the image is twice the length of the corresponding line on the object.

The diagram shows an enlargement of a triangle, with scale factor 2 and centre of enlargement X.

The dashed lines are guide lines; these are drawn so that $XA' = 2XA$,
$XB' = 2XB$
and $XC' = 2XC$.

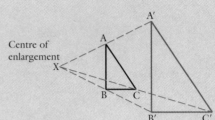

Centre of enlargement

UNITS OF LENGTH AND MASS

The *metric units of length* in common use are the kilometre, the metre, the centimetre and the millimetre, where

$$1\,km = 1000\,m, \quad 1\,m = 100\,cm, \quad 1\,cm = 10\,mm$$

The *metric units of mass* (these are the units we use for weighing) are the tonne, the kilogram, the gram and the milligram, where

$$1\,tonne = 1000\,kg, \quad 1\,kg = 1000\,g, \quad 1\,g = 1000\,mg$$

Imperial units of length in common use are the mile, yard, foot and inch, where

$$1\,mile = 1760\,yards, \quad 1\,yard = 3\,feet, \quad 1\,foot = 12\,inches$$

Imperial units of mass still in common use are the ton, stone, pound (lb) and ounce (oz), where

$$1\,ton = 2240\,lb, \quad 1\,stone = 14\,lb, \quad 1\,lb = 16\,ounces$$

For *an approximate conversion between metric and Imperial units*, use

$$5\,miles \approx 8\,km, \quad 1\,inch \approx 2.5\,cm, \quad 1\,kg \approx 2.2\,lb, \quad 1\,tonne \approx 1\,ton$$

For a quick but very rough conversion use

$$1\,km \approx \tfrac{1}{2}\,mile, \quad 1\,yard \approx 1\,m, \quad 1\,kg \approx 2\,lb$$

To *change to a smaller unit* we multiply,

e.g. to express 2 metres in centimetres, we multiply 2 by 100,
i.e. $2\,m = 2 \times 100\,cm = 200\,cm$

To *change to a larger unit* we divide,

e.g. to express 20 m in km, we divide 20 by 1000,
i.e. $20\,m = 20 \div 1000\,km = 0.02\,km$

AREA

Area is measured by standard-sized squares.
In metric units:

$$1\,\text{cm}^2 = 10\,\text{mm} \times 10\,\text{mm} = 100\,\text{mm}^2$$
$$1\,\text{m}^2 = 100\,\text{cm} \times 100\,\text{cm} = 10\,000\,\text{cm}^2$$
$$1\,\text{km}^2 = 1000\,\text{m} \times 1000\,\text{m} = 1\,000\,000\,\text{m}^2$$
$$1\,\text{hectare}\,(\,\text{ha}\,) = 100\,\text{m} \times 100\,\text{m} = 10\,000\,\text{m}^2$$

In Imperial units:

$$1\,\text{sq ft} = 12\,\text{in} \times 12\,\text{in} = 144\,\text{sq in}$$
$$1\,\text{sq yd} = 3\,\text{ft} \times 3\,\text{ft} = 9\,\text{sq ft}$$
$$1\,\text{acre} = 4840\,\text{sq yd}$$

To convert between hectares and acres, use $1\,\text{ha} \approx 2.5\,\text{acres}$.

The **area of a square** $= (\,\text{length of a side}\,)^2$.

The **area of a rectangle** $=$ length $\times$ breadth.

The **area of a parallelogram** is given by

$A = $ length $\times$ height

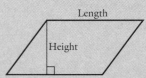

The **area of a triangle** is given by

$A = \frac{1}{2}$ base $\times$ height

The **area of a trapezium** is given by

$\frac{1}{2}$ (sum of parallel sides) $\times$ (distance between them),

i.e. $\qquad A = \frac{1}{2}(\,a+b\,) \times h$

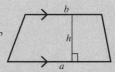

When we talk about the height of a triangle or of a parallelogram, we mean the perpendicular height.

CIRCLES

The names of the parts of a circle are shown in the diagram.
The diameter of a circle is twice the radius.

The **length of the circumference** is given by $C = 2\pi r$,

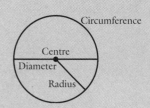

where r units is the radius of the circle and $\pi = 3.1415\ldots$
The **area of a circle** is given by $A = \pi r^2$

VOLUME AND CAPACITY

Volume is measured by standard-sized cubes.

$$1\,cm^3 = 10 \times 10 \times 10\,mm^3 = 1000\,mm^3$$
$$1\,m^3 = 100 \times 100 \times 100\,cm^3 = 1\,000\,000\,cm^3$$

The **volume of a cuboid** = length × breadth × height
The **volume of a prism** is given by
area of cross-section × length

The **volume of a cylinder** is given by $V = \pi r^2 h$

The **capacity** of a container is the volume of liquid it could hold.
The main *metric units of capacity* are the litre (1) and the millilitre (ml),
where 1 litre = 1000 ml and 1 litre = 1000 cm³ i.e. 1 ml = 1 cm³

The main *Imperial units of capacity* are the gallon and the pint, where

$$1\,gallon = 8\,pints$$

Approximate conversions between metric and Imperial units of capacity
are given by

$$1\,litre \approx 1.75\,pints \quad and \quad 1\,gallon \approx 4.5\,litres$$

DISTANCE, SPEED AND TIME

The relationship between distance, speed and time is
$$Distance = Speed \times Time$$

which can also be expressed as $Speed = \dfrac{Distance}{Time}$

or as $Time = \dfrac{Distance}{Speed}$

These relationships can be remembered from this
triangle (cover up the one you want to find).

Average speed for a journey $= \dfrac{\text{Total distance covered}}{\text{Total time taken}}$

ANGLES OF ELEVATION AND DEPRESSION

If you start by looking straight ahead,
the angle that you turn your eyes
through to look *up* at an object
is called the *angle of elevation*,
the angle you turn your eyes
through to look *down* at an object
is called the *angle of depression*.

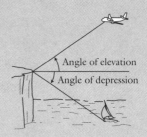

Angle of elevation
Angle of depression

THREE-FIGURE BEARINGS

A three-figure bearing of a point A from a point B gives the direction of A from B as a clockwise angle measured from the north. For example, in this diagram, the bearing of A from B is 140°.

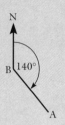

PYTHAGORAS' THEOREM

Pythagoras' theorem states that, in any right-angled triangle ABC where $\hat{B} = 90°$,

$$AC^2 = AB^2 + BC^2$$

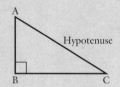

Conversely, if in a triangle the square of the longest side is equal to the sum of the squares of the other two sides, then the angle opposite the longest side is a right angle.

ALGEBRA

A **formula** is a general rule for finding one quantity in terms of other quantities,

e.g.   the formula for finding the area of a rectangle is

$$\text{Area} = \text{length} \times \text{breadth}$$

When letters are used for unknown numbers, the formula can be written more concisely,

i.e.   the area, $A\,\text{cm}^2$, of a rectangle measuring $l\,\text{cm}$ by $b\,\text{cm}$, is given by the formula $A = l \times b$.

Multiplication signs between letters, or between a number and a letter can be left out, e.g. $2x$ means $2 \times x$ and $l \times b$ can be written lb.

Divisions are usually written as fractions, e.g. $2 \div s$ is written as $\dfrac{2}{s}$

Terms such as $5n$ mean $5 \times n = n + n + n + n + n$

Like terms such as $2x + 5x$ can be simplified to $7x$.

An **equation** is a relationship between an unknown number, represented by a letter, and other numbers, for example $2x - 3 = 5$.
Solving the equation means finding the unknown number.
Provided that we do the same to both sides of an equation, we keep both sides equal; this can be used to solve the equation,

e.g.   to solve $2x - 3 = 5$,

first add 3 to both sides $2x - 3 + 3 = 5 + 3$

this gives $2x = 8$

Now divide each side by 2 $x = 4$

When an equation contains *brackets*, first multiply out the brackets,

e.g. $3x - 2(3 - x) = 6$
gives $3x - 6 + 2x = 6$ which can be solved easily.

Polynomial equations in one unknown contain terms involving powers of x,

e.g. $x^3 - 2x = 4$ and $2x^2 = 5$ are polynomial equations.

Equations containing only an x^2 term and a number can be solved by *finding square roots*. The square root of 9 can be 3, since $3 \times 3 = 9$, but it can also be -3 since $(-3) \times (-3) = 9$,

i.e.   a positive number has two square roots, one positive and one negative.

For example, if $x^2 = 9$ then $x = \pm\sqrt{9}$,

i.e. $x = +3$ and $x = -3$ are solutions.

More complex equations can be solved by **trial and improvement**, that is, by trying possible values for x until we find a value that fits the equation.

Two equations with two unknown quantities are called **simultaneous equations**. A pair of simultaneous equations can be solved algebraically by eliminating the letter which has the same number in each equation: when the signs of this letter are different, we add the equations, when the signs are the same we subtract the equations.

For example, to eliminate y from $2x + y = 5$ [1]
                            and $3x - y = 7$ [2]
we add [1] and [2] to give $5x = 12$ [3]

The value of x can be found from [3]. This value is then substituted for x in [1] or [2] to find y.

To eliminate y from $4x + y = 9$ [1]
            and $3x + y = 7$ [2]
we work out $[1] - [2]$ to give $x = 2$
Now we can substitute 2 for x in [1] (or in [2]) to find y.

Two simultaneous equations can be solved graphically by drawing two straight lines and finding the coordinates of their point of intersection.

For example, to solve $2x + y = 7$ [1]
            and $x - y = 9$ [2]

we first rearrange the equations so they are each in the form $y = \ldots$

i.e.   to $y = 7 - 2x$ [3]
            and $y = x - 9$ [4]

We then plot the lines $y = 7 - 2x$
and $y = x - 9$:

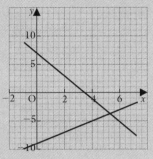

As accurately as we can read from the graph, the point of intersection is
$(5.3, -3.6)$.
So the solution is $x = 5.3$ and $y = -3.6$.

Inequalities
An inequality remains true when the same number is added to, or
subtracted from, both sides,

e.g.   if $x > 5$ then $x + 2 > 5 + 2$
         and $x - 2 > 5 - 2$

GRAPHS

Coordinates give the position of a
point on a grid. They are written as
a pair of numbers, e.g. $(2, 4)$.
The first number is the x-coordinate.
The second number is the
y-coordinate.
The x-coordinate and/or the
y-coordinate of a point can be
negative.

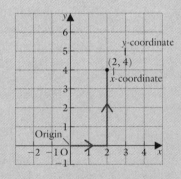

The **equation of a line or curve** gives the y-coordinate of a point in
terms of its x-coordinate. This relationship between the coordinates is
true only for points on the line or curve.

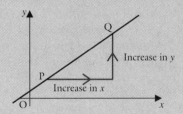

The **gradient** of a straight line can be found from two points, P and Q,
on the line, by calculating

$$\frac{\text{increase in } y \text{ in moving from P to Q}}{\text{increase in } x \text{ in moving from P to Q}} = \frac{y\text{-coordinate of Q} - y\text{-coordinate of P}}{x\text{-coordinate of Q} - x\text{-coordinate of P}}$$

When the gradient is positive, the line slopes uphill when moving from left to right.

When the gradient is negative, the line slopes downhill when moving from left to right.

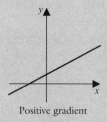

Positive gradient

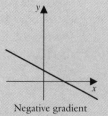

Negative gradient

The **equation of any straight line** is of the form $y = mx + c$
where m is the gradient of the line
and c is the y-intercept (where the line cuts the y-axis),

e.g.   the line whose equation is $y = 2x - 3$
has gradient 2 and y-intercept -3.

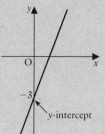

An equation of the form $y = c$ gives a line parallel to the x-axis.

An equation of the form $x = b$ gives a line parallel to the y-axis.

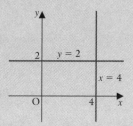

A **parabola** is a curve whose equation is in the form $y = ax^2 + bx + c$.

The shape of this curve looks like this:

When the x^2 term is positive it is the way up shown above.
When the x^2 term is negative the curve is upside down.

This, for example, is the graph of $y = x^2 - 2x$:

whereas the graph of $y = 2x - x^2$ looks like this:

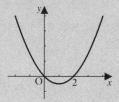

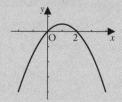

STATISTICS

A **hypothesis** is a statement which is not known to be true or untrue. We get a **scatter graph** when we plot values of one quantity against corresponding values of another quantity.

When the points are scattered about a straight line, we can draw that line by eye; the line is called the **line of best fit**.

We use the word **correlation** to describe the amount of scatter about this line.

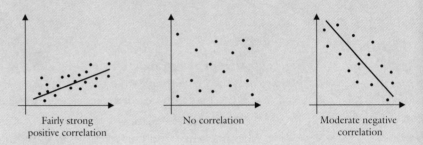

| Fairly strong positive correlation | No correlation | Moderate negative correlation |

For a list of values,

- the **range** is the difference between the largest value and the smallest value
- the **mean** is the sum of all the values divided by the number of values
- the **median** is the middle value when they have been arranged in order of size, (when the middle of the list is half way between two values, the median is the average of these two values)
- the **mode** is the value that occurs most frequently. Sometimes there is no mode, sometimes there is more than one mode.

For example, for this list of lengths

$$9 \, \text{cm}, \quad 10 \, \text{cm}, \quad 10 \, \text{cm}, \quad 12 \, \text{cm}, \quad 12 \, \text{cm}, \quad 12 \, \text{cm},$$

the range is $(12 - 9) \, \text{cm} = 3 \, \text{cm}$,

the mode is $12 \, \text{cm}$,

the mean is $(9 + 10 + 10 + 12 + 12 + 12) \div 6 \, \text{cm}$
$\qquad\qquad = 10.8 \, \text{cm}$ correct to 1 d.p.,

the median is $(10 + 12) \div 2 \, \text{cm}$, i.e. $11 \, \text{cm}$.

The mean, median and mode are together known as **measures of central tendency**.

Discrete values are exact and distinct, for example, the number of people in a queue.

Continuous values can only be given in a range on a continuous scale, for example, the length of a piece of wood.

When information is presented in an unordered form we have *raw data*.
A **frequency table** shows the number of times that each distinct value
(or category) occurs.

This frequency table shows the
distribution of scores when a dice
is rolled 20 times; it is called a
frequency distribution.

Score	Frequency
1	4
2	1
3	4
4	3
5	3
6	5

A **grouped frequency table** shows the frequencies of groups of
values.

This table, for example, shows
the distribution of the heights
of 55 tomato plants in four
groups each of width
10 centimetres.

Height, h cm	Frequency
$20 \leqslant h < 30$	5
$30 \leqslant h < 40$	15
$40 \leqslant h < 50$	25
$50 \leqslant h < 60$	10

For a grouped frequency distribution,

- the **range** is estimated as

    the upper end of the last group − the lower end of the first group

- the **modal group** is the group with the largest number of items in it.

Bar charts
A frequency distribution can be illustrated by drawing a bar for each
group (or each value for ungrouped data) whose height represents the
number of items in the group.

This bar chart illustrates the
grouped frequencies of the
heights of tomato plants in
the table above.

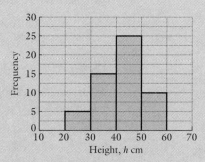

Notice that there are no gaps between the bars; heights are continuous
values so there is no value on the horizontal scale that could not be a
height. When values are discrete or in categories, there may be gaps
between the bars.

A **frequency polygon** is drawn by plotting the frequency of each group against the midpoint of that group and joining the points with straight lines.

Pie charts are used to show what fraction of the whole list each group or category is.
The size of a slice is represented by the angle at the centre of the circle.
This angle is found by first finding the number of values in the group as a fraction of all the values, and then finding this fraction of 360°.
This pie chart shows what fraction (as a percentage) the number of plants in each group is of the total number of plants given.

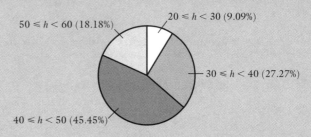

$50 \leqslant h < 60$ (18.18%)
$20 \leqslant h < 30$ (9.09%)
$30 \leqslant h < 40$ (27.27%)
$40 \leqslant h < 50$ (45.45%)

PROBABILITY

Probability is a measure of the chance that an event in the future may happen.

The probability that an event A happens is $P(A)$ where

$$P(A) = \frac{\text{the number of ways in which } A \text{ can occur}}{\text{the total number of equally likely outcomes}}$$

Probability ranges from impossibility (0), through stages of likelihood to certainty (1).
When we try to quantify probability, we need to know all the possibilities that could happen. This is called the list of all *possible outcomes*.

When we perform experiments to find out how often an event occurs, the **relative frequency** of the event is given by

$$\frac{\text{the number of times the event occurs}}{\text{the number of times the experiment is performed}}$$

Relative frequency is used to give an approximate value for probability.

The probability that an event A does not happen is equal to 1 minus the probability that it does happen,

i.e. $P(A \text{ does not happen}) = 1 - P(A \text{ does happen})$.

If p is the probability that an event will happen on one occasion, then we expect it to happen np times on n occasions. For example, the probability that a coin lands head up on one toss is $\frac{1}{2}$, so if we toss the coin 50 times, we expect (but are very unlikely to get exactly) $\frac{1}{2} \times 50$ heads, that is, 25 heads.

The exercises that follow are *not* intended to be worked through before starting the main part of this book. They are here for you to use when you need practice on the basic techniques.

Do *not* use a calculator for this exercise.

1 Find

a $349 + 276$	**e** $336 \div 6$	**i** 258×41
b $723 - 584$	**f** $560 \div 80$	**j** 64×178
c 66×80	**g** 34×76	**k** 93×485
d 48×500	**h** 351×36	**l** 732×56

  m $7 \times 63 - 249$ **q** $429 \div 21$ giving the remainder

  n $6421 - 236 \times 7$ **r** $(36 - 14) \times 3 - 49$

  p $(19 + 6) \times 5 - 96$ **s** $339 \div 23$ giving the remainder

2 **a** Write in index form **i** $3 \times 3 \times 3 \times 3$ **ii** $7 \times 7 \times 7 \times 7 \times 7 \times 7$

   b Express in index form **i** 27 **ii** 64 **iii** 36 **iv** 125

3 **a** Find the largest whole number that will divide exactly into

     i 18 and 27   **iii** 48 and 80   **v** 60, 45 and 30

    ii 48 and 72   **iv** 36 and 54   **vi** 48, 72 and 96

   b Find the smallest whole number that the given numbers will divide into exactly.

     i 8 and 7   **iii** 18 and 27   **v** 2, 6 and 18

    ii 9 and 12   **iv** 12 and 18   **vi** 3, 8 and 24

4 Find the value of

  a 2^6 **b** 3^5 **c** 5^2 **d** 3^4 **e** 2^5 **f** 5^3

5 **a** Write down the next square number after **i** 25 **ii** 49 **iii** 100

   b Write down the prime numbers between 35 and 55.

   c Which of the numbers 9, 12, 16, 22, 28, 31, 36, 37, 43, 48 are

     i prime numbers   **iii** triangular numbers

    ii rectangular numbers   **iv** square numbers?

6 Give each of the following numbers correct to

  i 2 decimal places   **ii** 2 significant figures.

a 3.756	**c** 45.094	**e** 6.996	**g** 0.0257
b 14.0088	**d** 6.083 52	**f** 1.7846	**h** 0.083 65

7 Give each of the following numbers correct to

 i 3 decimal places **ii** 3 significant figures.

 a 2.7846   **f** 0.015 076   **k** 3.2994

 b 0.1572   **g** 254.1627   **l** 0.000 925 8

 c 0.073 25   **h** 7.8196   **m** 0.009 638

 d 15.0609   **i** 3.3333   **n** 0.005 839

 e 0.000 378 4 **j** 674.8257   **p** 36.363 63

8 Find the value of

 a $3 \times 6 \div 2 + 4 \times 5$ **d** $16 \div 4 - 3 - 5 \times 2 + 6$

 b $3 \times 5 \times 7 - 5 \times 4 \times 3$ **e** $4 \times 5 \div 2 + 15 \div 3 - 2$

 c $8 \div 2 \times 3 + 9 \div 2 \times 6$ **f** $16 \div 4 \div 2 + 3 \times 4$

REVISION EXERCISE 1.2 (Fractions and decimals – the four rules)

Do *not* use a calculator for this exercise.

1 **a** Change into an improper fraction

  i $2\frac{3}{7}$ **ii** $5\frac{4}{9}$ **iii** $3\frac{3}{5}$ **iv** $9\frac{3}{4}$

 b Give as a mixed number

  i $\frac{42}{5}$ **ii** $\frac{17}{4}$ **iii** $\frac{46}{7}$ **iv** $\frac{26}{17}$

2 Express as a single fraction in its simplest form

 a $\frac{3}{4} + \frac{7}{8}$ **f** $1\frac{1}{2} + \frac{1}{5}$ **k** $\frac{5}{6} + \frac{2}{3} + \frac{1}{4}$

 b $\frac{3}{5} + \frac{3}{10}$ **g** $\frac{1}{3} + 1\frac{3}{4}$ **l** $\frac{3}{4} + \frac{13}{20} + \frac{4}{5}$

 c $\frac{1}{4} + \frac{2}{3}$ **h** $1\frac{3}{5} + 2\frac{1}{2}$ **m** $\frac{2}{7} + \frac{1}{9} + \frac{1}{6}$

 d $\frac{5}{12} + \frac{1}{4}$ **i** $\frac{2}{7} + \frac{1}{2} + \frac{3}{14}$ **n** $\frac{8}{21} + \frac{1}{2} + \frac{2}{3}$

 e $\frac{3}{10} + \frac{2}{5}$ **j** $\frac{3}{16} + \frac{3}{4} + \frac{5}{12}$ **p** $\frac{7}{12} + \frac{5}{8} + \frac{5}{6}$

3 Express as a single fraction in its simplest form

 a $\frac{1}{10} - \frac{1}{20}$ **e** $\frac{3}{10} - \frac{1}{15}$ **i** $3\frac{5}{8} - \frac{7}{8}$

 b $\frac{5}{12} - \frac{1}{12}$ **f** $\frac{7}{9} - \frac{5}{12}$ **j** $2\frac{3}{4} + 1\frac{1}{2} - 1\frac{1}{3}$

 c $\frac{3}{4} - \frac{3}{8}$ **g** $1\frac{3}{5} - \frac{1}{10}$ **k** $1\frac{3}{8} + 1\frac{1}{4} - 2\frac{1}{2}$

 d $\frac{1}{4} - \frac{2}{9}$ **h** $2\frac{1}{2} - \frac{3}{4}$ **l** $3\frac{1}{5} - 4\frac{1}{8} + 1\frac{7}{10}$

4 Express as a single fraction in its simplest form

a $\frac{2}{3} \times \frac{5}{6}$ **g** $\frac{2}{5}$ of $1\frac{3}{7}$ **m** $\frac{2}{9} \div 1\frac{2}{7}$

b $\frac{3}{4} \times \frac{2}{5}$ **h** $\frac{3}{4}$ of $2\frac{2}{5}$ **n** $\frac{3}{7} \div 1\frac{3}{4}$

c $\frac{5}{8} \times \frac{4}{5}$ **i** $\frac{5}{8}$ of $3\frac{1}{5}$ **p** $3 \div \frac{2}{3}$

d $1\frac{1}{2} \times \frac{2}{3}$ **j** $\frac{2}{5} \div \frac{3}{10}$ **q** $\frac{2}{5} \times \frac{7}{8} \times \frac{3}{7} \times \frac{10}{11}$

e $\frac{3}{5} \times 3\frac{1}{3}$ **k** $\frac{7}{8} \div \frac{1}{4}$ **r** $\frac{1}{2} \times 1\frac{1}{3} \times \frac{5}{7}$

f $\frac{3}{4} \times 1\frac{1}{3}$ **l** $\frac{7}{10} \div \frac{3}{5}$ **s** $\frac{2}{5} \times 2\frac{1}{7} \div 4$

5 Express as a single fraction in its simplest form

a $1\frac{2}{3} \times \frac{1}{2} - \frac{3}{5}$ **f** $2\frac{2}{5} \times 1\frac{7}{8} - 1\frac{2}{3}$

b $\frac{2}{7} + \frac{1}{4} \times 1\frac{1}{3}$ **g** $2\frac{1}{7} - \frac{1}{3}$ of $1\frac{2}{7}$

c $4\frac{1}{2} \div 3 + \frac{3}{4}$ **h** $(\frac{1}{2} - \frac{1}{3}) \div (\frac{3}{4} - \frac{1}{3})$

d $(2\frac{1}{5} + 1\frac{2}{3}) \div 5\frac{4}{5}$ **i** $(4\frac{1}{2} - 3\frac{3}{8}) \times 1\frac{1}{3}$

e $\frac{4}{5} \div \frac{1}{4} + \frac{1}{3} \times 4\frac{1}{2}$ **j** $2\frac{1}{2} \div 1\frac{3}{7} + 1\frac{1}{3}$

6 Find

a $1.26 + 3.75$ **e** $4.002 + 0.83$ **i** $1.07 - 0.58$

b $12.4 + 6.7$ **f** $2 - 0.17$ **j** $0.37 - 0.009$

c $5.82 + 0.35$ **g** $5.3 - 2.1$ **k** $0.000\,32 + 0.0017$

d $0.04 + 8.86$ **h** $0.16 - 0.08$ **l** $0.0127 - 0.0059$

7 Find

a 1.2×0.8 **f** 0.18×1.2 **k** $0.01 \div 0.5$

b 0.7×0.06 **g** 1.002×0.36 **l** $0.0013 \div 1.3$

c 0.4×0.02 **h** $1.08 \div 0.4$ **m** $1.876 \div 0.02$

d 0.5×0.5 **i** $0.2 \div 2.5$ **n** $27.5 \div 5$

e 3.0501×1.1 **j** 42.8×200 **p** $257.4 \div 20$

8 Fill in the blanks (marked with $\square$) in the following calculations.

a $3.7 \times \square = 14.8$ **f** $\square \times 0.85 = 1.105$

b $24.6 \div \square = 8.2$ **g** $5.9 \times \square = 0.236$

c $0.34 \times 0.06 = \square$ **h** $\square - 4.08 \div 1.7 = 0$

d $\square \div 0.45 = 1.44$ **i** $0.0018 \div 0.045 = \square$

e $0.37 \times 1.9 - \square = 0$ **j** $\square \div 0.026 = 1.4$

9 Put either $<$ or $>$ between each of the following pairs of fractions.

a $\frac{5}{8}$ $\frac{7}{10}$ **b** $\frac{2}{5}$ $\frac{1}{3}$ **c** $\frac{1}{5}$ $\frac{4}{15}$ **d** $\frac{4}{7}$ $\frac{5}{9}$

1 **a** Express as a decimal

    i $\frac{9}{25}$ **ii** $\frac{19}{20}$ **iii** 54%   **iv** $82\frac{1}{2}$%

  b Express as a fraction in its lowest terms

    i 85%   **ii** 0.42   **iii** 65%   **iv** 0.125

  c Express as a percentage

    i 0.44   **ii** $\frac{7}{25}$ **iii** 1.38   **iv** $\frac{37}{40}$

2 Copy and complete the following table.

	Fraction	Percentage	Decimal
a	$\frac{17}{20}$		
b		$37\frac{1}{2}$%	
c			0.625
d		$5\frac{3}{4}$%	
e			1.15
f	$4\frac{3}{4}$		

3 **a** Find

    i 36% of 50 kg

    ii 4.5% of 440 g

    iii 84% of 15 m

  b **i** Increase £480 by 46%

    ii Decrease £320 by 55%

    iii Increase 150 cm^2 by 56%

    iv Decrease £44 by 35%

  c Find, giving your answer correct to 3 significant figures

    i 37% of 46 km

    ii $4\frac{3}{4}$% of 12.6 m

    iii $13\frac{1}{2}$% of 245 mm

  d Express

    i 12 mm as a percentage of 6 cm

    ii 650 m as a fraction of 2 km

    iii 56 cm^2 as a percentage of 1 m^2

    iv 6 pints as a fraction of 4 gallons

4 **a** Give the following ratios in their simplest form.

   i $12:18$ **iii** $320:480$ **v** $\frac{1}{2}:\frac{5}{6}:\frac{2}{3}$

   ii $3:6:9$ **iv** $3.5:2.5$ **vi** $288:128:144$

b Simplify the following ratios.

   i $45\,\text{cm}:0.1\,\text{m}$ **iii** $340\,\text{m}:1.2\,\text{km}$ **v** $450\,\text{mg}:1\,\text{g}$
   ii $42\,\text{p}:£1.05$ **iv** $32\,\text{g}:2\,\text{kg}$ **vi** $2.2\,\text{t}:132\,\text{kg}$

c **i** Divide £45 into two parts in the ratio $4:5$.
   ii Divide 96 m into two parts in the ratio $9:7$.
   iii Divide 5 kg into three parts in the ratio $1:2:5$.
   iv Divide seven hours into three parts in the ratio $1:5:8$.

5 **a** Find the map ratio of a map on which 10 cm represents 1 km.

b The map ratio of a map is $1:200\,000$. The distance between two factories is 8 km. What distance is this on the map?

6 **a** In a sale a pair of trainers priced £35 is reduced by 30%. What is the sale price?

b Sally and Tim bought a portable CD player between them for £44.94. Sally paid $\frac{4}{7}$ of the cost and Tim paid the remainder.

   i What fraction did Tim pay?   **ii** How much did Sally pay?

7 At a concert 64% of the audience were females.

a What fraction of the audience were females?

b Express the part of the audience that was male as

   i a percentage   **ii** a decimal   **iii** a fraction in its lowest terms.

8 Estimate the value of $236.4 \div 48.7$, and then use a calculator to find its value correct to 2 decimal places.

9 A popular leisure club has 2750 members. Of these, 42% are girls, 0.3 are boys, $\frac{4}{25}$ are men and the remainder are women.

a What fraction of the members are girls?

b What decimal fraction of the members are male?

c How many of the members are female?

d What percentage of the members are women?

10 **a** Find   **i** $\frac{2}{3}$ of £36   **ii** 75% of 34 cm   **iii** $\frac{4}{9}$ of 54 kg

b Which is the smaller, $\frac{5}{12}$ of 10 or 75% of 5?

c Which is the larger, 60% of $\frac{9}{10}$ or $\frac{5}{7}$ of $\frac{3}{4}$?

1 Find the size of each marked angle.

a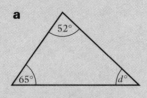

c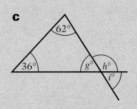

e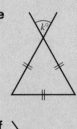

b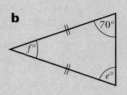

d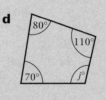

f

2 a Find the size of each exterior angle of a regular polygon with

i 15 sides **ii** 20 sides.

b Find the size of each interior angle of a regular polygon with

i 5 sides **ii** 8 sides **iii** 18 sides.

c How many sides has a regular polygon

i if each exterior angle is 15° **ii** if each interior angle is 162°?

d Is it possible for each exterior angle of a regular polygon to be

i 40° **ii** 70°?
If it is, give the number of sides.

e Is it possible for each interior angle of a regular polygon to be

i 120° **ii** 160°?

If it is, give the number of sides.

f Find the value of the angles marked $p°$.

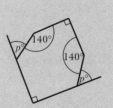

3 Find the size of each marked angle.

a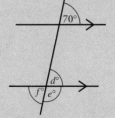

b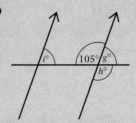

c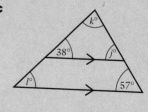

4 Find the size of each marked angle.

a

$m°$ $p°$ $44°$ $37°$ $n°$

b

$r°$ $54°$ $65°$ $q°$ $s°$

c

$75°$ $t°$ $u°$ $70°$ $v°$ $w°$

5 Find the area of each shape.

a

8 cm
5 cm

b

4 cm
2.5 cm

c

4 cm 7.1 cm
8.5 cm

d

4.3 cm 5 cm
4.5 cm

6 For each of the following figures, find the missing measurement. Draw a diagram in each case.

	Figure	Base	Height	Area
a	Triangle	8 cm		16 cm²
b	Rectangle	3 cm	15 mm	
c	Parallelogram	4 cm		20 cm²
d	Square	5 m		
e	Triangle	70 mm		14 cm²

7 Find the areas of the following shapes. Draw a diagram for each question and mark in all the measurements.

a

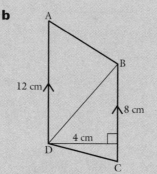

ABCD is a rhombus.
AC = 15 cm and
BD = 8 cm

b

12 cm
8 cm
4 cm

c

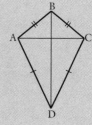

AC = 6 cm and
BD = 10 cm

8 a i Find, giving your answers in metres,
137 cm + 234 mm + 3.2 m

ii Find, giving your answers in grams,
645 g + 0.37 kg + 960 mg

iii Find, giving your answer in inches,
3 feet + 2 yards + 8 inches

b Express

i 45 mm in cm
ii 0.56 km in m
iii 48 inches in feet
iv 13 yards in feet
v 5 cm² in mm²
vi 4000 cm² in m²

vii 0.6 m² in cm²
viii 3 sq feet in sq inches
ix 5000 mm³ in cm³
x 0.002 m³ in cm³
xi 4 000 000 cm³ in m³
xii $\frac{5}{12}$ cubic feet in cubic inches

9 For the shaded part of each diagram find, correct to 3 s.f.
i the perimeter   **ii** the area.

a

c

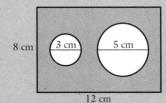

b

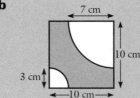

10 In this question, the cross-sections of the prisms and their lengths
are given. Find their volumes.

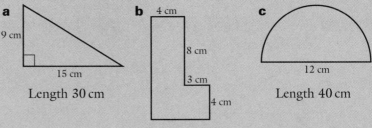

a

9 cm

15 cm

Length 30 cm

b 4 cm

8 cm

3 cm

4 cm

Length 15 cm

c

12 cm

Length 40 cm

11 a Find the volume of a rectangular metal block measuring 4.2 cm
by 3.8 cm by 1.5 cm.

b The volume of a cuboid is 136 cm³. It is 8 cm long and 3.4 cm
wide. Find its height.

12 Write down the size of each angle marked with a letter.

a

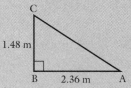

b

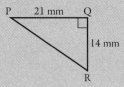

13 Give answers that are not exact correct to 3 significant figures.

a Find AC.

c Find PR.

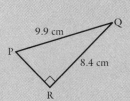

b Find PR.

d Find AB.

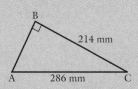

REVISION EXERCISE 1.5 (Algebra)

1 Simplify the following expressions.

a $2a + a$ **d** $7a - 3a$ **g** $10 - 3a - 4 - 5a$

b $3b + 3 - b - 2$ **e** $5b + 7 - 3b + 2$ **h** $8 + 5x - 2x - 6$

c $x + 5 + 4x - 2$ **f** $8 - 5x + 3 - 2x$ **i** $4x - 6x - 7 + 9$

2 Simplify

a $2x \times y$ **e** $a \times 2b$ **i** $2x \times 4y$

b $4a \times 3b$ **f** $3x \times x$ **j** $3a \times a \times a$

c $a \times 4c$ **g** $5a \times 2b$ **k** $a \times 5b \times b$

d $3t \times 4 \times 2t$ **h** $2n \times 4n \times 3$ **l** $3a \times 4b \times b$

3 Simplify the following expressions.

a $3(x + 7) + 2x$ **e** $8a - (2a + 3)$

b $5 + (3a - 7)$ **f** $4(a + 2) - 3(a - 4)$

c $3(2x + 3) + 4(x - 2)$ **g** $15x - 3x - 2(4x - 3)$

d $5x - 3(x + 2)$ **h** $6a - 3(2a - 5) + 3$

4 a If $P = 2(a - b)$ find P when

    i $a = 3$ and $b = 1$

    ii $a = -5$ and $b = 2$

    iii $a = -4$ and $b = -2$

b If $A = xy$ find A when

    i $x = 3$ and $y = \frac{1}{2}$

    ii $x = 4$ and $y = -2$

    iii $x = -3$ and $y = -6$

5 Solve the following equations.

a $3x = 15$

b $17 = 4x + 1$

c $7x - 3 = 2x + 7$

d $5x = 12$

e $3x - 4 = 11 - 2x$

f $4(x - 2) = 5(2x + 5)$

g $15 = x - 13$

h $6x - 3 = 18$

i $0.8x = 5.6$

j $0.03x = 0.42$

k $2 = 3 - x$

l $9 - 2x = 8$

m $7 = 3(5 - x)$

n $9 - 5x = 4 - 3x$

6 Solve the following inequalities and illustrate your solutions on a number line.

a $x - 6 < 4$

b $9 - x \geqslant 4$

c $8 > 3 - x$

d $x - 1 \leqslant 15$

e $2 > 8 + x$

f $7 > 3 - x$

g $x + 4 < 6$

h $4 - x < 9$

i $9 \geqslant 4 - x$

7 Solve the following pairs of simultaneous equations.

a $x + y = 4$
   $3x + y = 10$

b $7x - 2y = 22$
   $3x + 2y = 18$

c $3x + y = 16$
   $3x - 2y = 1$

d $5x + 3y = 25$
   $8x - 3y = 1$

e $2x - 3y = 15$
   $2x - y = 9$

f $5x + 2y = 8$
   $3x - 2y = 8$

g $x + 5y = 9$
   $x - y = 21$

h $2a + 3b = 9$
   $2a + 7b = 13$

i $2x - 3y = 13$
   $2x + y = 9$

8 Solve the following equations, giving your answers correct to 3 significant figures.

a $x^2 = 23$

b $x^2 = 0.47$

c $x^2 = 6.78$

REVISION EXERCISE 1.6 (Graphical work)

1 a Write down the gradient and y-intercept of the line whose equation is

   i $y = 3x$

   ii $y = 2x + 6$

   iii $y = 3 - \frac{1}{2}x$

   iv $y = \frac{3}{2}x + \frac{5}{2}$

b Determine whether each of the following straight lines makes an acute angle or an obtuse angle with the positive x-axis.

   i $y = -x + 2$ **ii** $y = 3 - 7x$ **iii** $y = 0.6x$ **iv** $y = 2 + 3x$

2

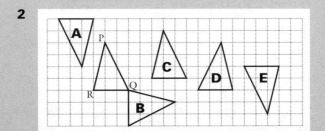

In the diagram, which images of △PQR are given by

a a translation   **b** a reflection   **c** a rotation   **d** none of these?

3

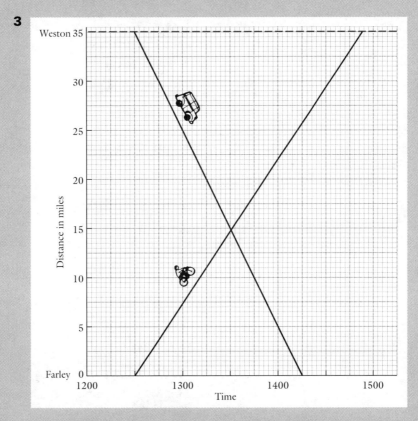

The graph shows two journeys between the villages of Farley and Weston. Molly leaves home on her bicycle to visit her friend who lives in Weston. On her way there she passes her father who is on his way from Weston to Farley by car.

a How far is it between the two places?

b How long does each journey take?

c Who has the faster average speed and by how much?

d Where and when do they pass?

4 The equation of a curve is $y = 3x^2$. Which of these sketches could be the curve?

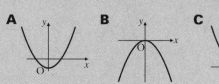

A   **B**   **C**   **D**

5 Sketch the curve whose equation is   **a** $y = -2x^2$ **b** $y = 5x^2$

6 **a** A car travels at 60 mph. How far will it travel in

    i $1\frac{3}{4}$ hours   **ii** 5 minutes?

  b How long will a train travelling at 100 mph take to travel

    i 125 miles   **ii** 240 miles?

  c Jim cycles 42 km in $3\frac{1}{2}$ hours. Find his average speed.

**REVISION
EXERCISE 1.7
(Probability and
statistics)**

1 The pie chart shows the breakdown of John Peter's bill for £120 when his car was serviced last week.

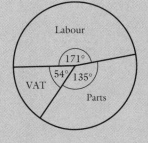

  a What fraction of the bill was labour?

  b How much was the charge for VAT?

  c What percentage of the bill was for parts?

2 **a** Find the mode, median and range of the numbers

$$9, \ 8, \ 11, \ 8, \ 9, \ 13, \ 12, \ 11, \ 8, \ 7, \ 9, \ 8, \ 12$$

  b Find the mean of the numbers given in part **a**. Give your answer correct to 3 significant figures.

3 In a sale 80 dresses are reduced. Of these, 16 are Size 8, 28 are Size 10, 24 are Size 12 and the remainder are Size 14. Ann takes a dress from the rail at random. What is the probability that the dress she takes is

  a Size 10   **b** not Size 12   **c** Size 12 or larger?

4 Two ordinary six-sided dice are rolled together 360 times.

  a Draw a table to show the equally likely outcomes of the sum of the scores on the two dice when they are rolled once.

  b About how many double threes are there likely to be?

  c About how many times should the score be 10?

5 A number is chosen at random from the first twelve non-zero whole numbers. What is the probability that the number is

a exactly divisible by 4   **b** not exactly divisible by 3   **c** a rectangular number?

6 For each scatter diagram describe the relationship between the quantities.

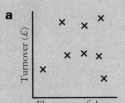  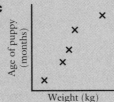

7 Given below is a list of the heights, in centimetres rounded up to the nearest centimetre, of 60 tomato plants. The list is in numerical order.

```
20   20   21   22   22   22   23   24   24   24
24   25   25   25   26   26   26   27   27   27
27   27   27   28   28   28   28   28   28   28
28   29   30   30   31   32   32   33   33   34
34   34   34   34   35   35   35   35   35   35
36   36   36   37   37   38   40   40   41   42
```

a What is the height of **i** the tallest plant **ii** the shortest plant?

b Copy and complete this frequency table.

Height, h cm	Frequency
$18 < h \leqslant 23$	
$23 < h \leqslant 28$	
$28 < h \leqslant 33$	
$33 < h \leqslant 38$	
$38 < h \leqslant 43$	

c How many plants have a height that is **i** greater than 28 cm   **ii** 33 cm or less?

d What is the modal group?

e Illustrate this information with **i** a bar chart   **ii** a frequency polygon.

8 Last Friday every pupil in Form 10W was asked how they had come to school. The results of the survey are given in the table.

Way of coming to school	Number of pupils
By bus	18
By car	4
On a bicycle	3
On foot	5

a How many pupils were there in Form 10W last Friday?

b Draw a pie chart to represent this data.

INDICES

We sometimes have to work with very large numbers and very small numbers. For example, Mary had to research some facts about the Earth and the Sun. Here is information that she found in a science dictionary.

Earth The planet that orbits the Sun between the planets Venus and Mars at a mean distance from the Sun of 149 600 000 km. It has a mass of about 5.976×10^{24} kg.

Sun The star at the centre of the Solar System. The Sun has a mass of 1.9×10^{30} kg.

In a vacuum light travels 1 km in $3.335\,609 \times 10^{-6}$ seconds.

- If Mary wants to make sense of this information, she needs to know what numbers such as 1.9×10^{30} and $3.335\,609 \times 10^{-6}$ mean.

EXERCISE 1A

Discuss what you need to know and be able to do to answer these questions.

1 Why do you think that the distance of the Earth from the Sun is written as 149 600 000 km whereas the mass of the Earth is written as 5.976×10^{24} kg?

2 It takes light $3.335\,609 \times 10^{-6}$ seconds to travel 1 km. Is this a very large or a very small interval of time?

3 Jim bought a new mechanical digger for his business. It cost £57 000. Jim needs to know what value this asset will have in 5 years time. This can be found from £57 000 $\times (2)^{-5}$.

   a If 57 000 is multiplied by 2, is the result more or less than 57 000?

   b Do you think that multiplying 57 000 by 2^{-5} will make 57 000 bigger or smaller?

Discussion of the problems in the last exercise shows that there are occasions when we need to understand and work with numbers written in the form $57\,000 \times 2^{-5}$ and 1.9×10^{30}. First we will remind ourselves of the meaning 10^{30}.

POSITIVE
INDICES

We have seen, in Book 8B, that 3^2 means 3×3

and that $2 \times 2 \times 2$ can be written as 2^3.

So 10^{30} means thirty 10s multiplied together – this is a very large number! It follows that 2 can be written as 2^1, although we do not normally do this. It also means that if a is any number then

$$a^1 = a$$

The small raised number is called the *index* or *power*. The lower number is called the *base*. We sometimes describe a^4 as a raised to the power 4.

EXERCISE 1B

Do not use a calculator for this exercise.

Find the value of 2^5.

$2^5 = 2 \times 2 \times 2 \times 2 \times 2$
$\quad = 32$

$\begin{aligned} 2 \times 2 \times 2 \times 2 \times 2 &= 4 \times 2 \times 2 \times 2 \\ &= 8 \times 2 \times 2 \\ &= 16 \times 2 \\ &= 32 \end{aligned}$

Find the value of

1 a 3^2 **b** 5^3 **c** 2^7 **d** 10^4 **e** 1.2^2 **f** 5^1

2 a 4^1 **b** 10^3 **c** 10^1 **d** 10^6 **e** 1.1^2 **f** 7^3

3 a 2^4 **b** 8^2 **c** 4^3 **d** 20^2 **e** 0.1^2 **f** 0.2^2

Find the value of 3.6×10^2.

$3.6 \times 10^2 = 3.6 \times 100$
$\qquad\qquad = 360$

Remember that numbers can be multiplied in any order,

so $3.6 \times 10^2 = 3.6 \times 10 \times 10 = 3.6 \times 100$

and to multiply by 100, we move the decimal point 2 places to the right and fill in gaps with zeros.

4 Find the value of

a 7.2×10^3 **d** 3.82×10^3 **g** 4.63×10^1

b 8.93×10^2 **e** 2.75×10^1 **h** 5.032×10^2

c 6.5×10^4 **f** 5.37×10^5 **i** 7.09×10^2

5 Find the value of

a $2^2 \times 3$ **d** $2 \times 3^3 \times 10$ **g** 4×5^2

b $3^2 \times 4^2$ **e** $5^2 \times 2^1 \times 3^2$ **h** $2^2 \times 5^2$

c $5^3 \times 2^2$ **f** $2^3 \times 3^2 \times 5$ **i** $7^2 \times 10 \times 2^2$

6 Write in index notation

a $3 \times 3 \times 3 \times 3$ **g** $0.5 \times 0.5 \times 0.5$

b $8 \times 8 \times 8$ **h** $10 \times 10 \times 10 \times 10 \times 10$

c 7 **i** $4 \times 4 \times 4 \times 4$

d 0.1×0.1 **j** $1.5 \times 1.5 \times 1.5$

e $5 \times 5 \times 5 \times 5 \times 5$ **k** 7×7

f 12 **l** 15

Write $2 \times 5 \times 2 \times 5 \times 7$ in index form.

> Remember that we can multiply numbers in any order, so we can rearrange the product to bring the same numbers together.

$2 \times 5 \times 2 \times 5 \times 7 = 2 \times 2 \times 5 \times 5 \times 7$
$$= 2^2 \times 5^2 \times 7$$

---

7 Write in index form

a $3 \times 5 \times 3$ **d** $3 \times 3 \times 5 \times 3$

b $7 \times 2 \times 2 \times 7 \times 7$ **e** $2 \times 13 \times 3 \times 13$

c $5 \times 3 \times 2 \times 2 \times 5 \times 7$ **f** $3 \times 17 \times 5 \times 17 \times 17$

Simplify $3a \times 5a$.

> Remember that we use leters to represent unknown numbers.
> The letter a appears twice in this product; it represents the same number each time it appears.
> Remember also that we can multiply numbers in any order, so we rearrange this to bring the numbers together and the letters together.

$3a \times 5a = 3 \times a \times 5 \times a$
$$= 3 \times 5 \times a \times a$$
$$= 15 \times a^2 = 15a^2$$

8 Simplify

   a $2x \times 5x$ **e** $4a \times a \times 2a$ **i** $(2t)^4$

   b $t \times t$ **f** $3y \times y \times y$ **j** $10x \times 4x \times 2x$

   c $2p \times p$ **g** $4p \times 2p \times 2p$ **k** $2s^2 \times 2s$

   d $3s \times 2s$ **h** $(3s)^3$ **l** $5t \times t^2$

9 Simplify

   a $3b \times 4b$ **e** $2w \times 5w \times w$ **i** $60a \times 2a \times a$

   b $5t \times t$ **f** $a \times 2a \times a$ **j** $(5s)^3$

   c $y \times y$ **g** $3v \times 5v \times 2v$ **k** $3x^2 \times 2x$

   d $7x \times 3x$ **h** $(2x)^3$ **l** $6y \times y^2$

10 Write these numbers as powers of 10.

   a 100 **b** 1000 **c** $1\,000\,000$ **d** $10\,000\,000\,000$

11 At the beginning of this chapter we are told that the mass of the Earth is about 5.976×10^{24} kg. Write down the mass of the Earth, as an ordinary number.

12 Why do you think that the mass of the Sun is written in the form 1.9×10^{30} kg and not as an ordinary number?

13 Margaret invested £1000 in a savings bond. The value of the bond increases each year. She can work out the value of the bond after a number of years by calculating $1000 \times (1.1)^t$ where t is the number of years for which the investment has been made. Without using a calculator find

   a the value of the bond after 1 year

   b the value of the bond after 3 years.

14 Bill bought a computer for his business. It cost £2000. He can claim tax relief against depreciation each year.
Bill can work out the amount allowed for tax relief t years after buying the computer by calculating $2000 \times 0.25 \times (0.75)^{t-1}$. Without using a calculator find the amount allowed for tax relief when $t = 2$.

15 The mass of the moon is 7.38×10^{22} kg. How many tonnes is this?

**EXPRESSING A
NUMBER AS A
PRODUCT OF ITS
PRIME FACTORS
IN INDEX FORM**

We saw how to give a number as a product of its prime factors in Book 8B. We repeat this to give more practice in using indices.

The prime numbers are 2, 3, 5, 7, 11, 13, …

A number that is not too large can be expressed as a product of prime numbers by first writing it as the product of any two factors,

e.g. $48 = 4 \times 12,$

then each factor can be written as the product of two factors, and so on until all the factors are prime numbers.

For example,
$$48 = 4 \times 12$$
$$= 2 \times 2 \times 3 \times 4$$
$$= 2 \times 2 \times 3 \times 2 \times 2$$
$$= 2 \times 2 \times 2 \times 2 \times 3 = 2^4 \times 3$$

We can use a more organised approach for larger numbers: start by trying to divide by 2 and carry on dividing by 2 until we can no longer divide exactly by 2; then try 3, then 5 and so on for each prime number until we are left with 1.

> Remember: a number is divisible by 2 if it is even
> divisible by 3 if the sum of the digits is divisible by 3
> divisible by 5 if the last digit is 0 or 5.

EXERCISE 1C

Do not use a calculator for this exercise.

Write 405 as a product of prime numbers in index form.

3	405
3	135
3	45
3	15
5	5
	1

405 is odd so it will not divide by 2.
$4 + 0 + 5 = 9$ so 405 will divide by 3.

Therefore 405 = 3 × 3 × 3 × 3 × 5
$$= 3^4 \times 5$$

Write as a product of prime numbers in index form.

1 **a** 36   **b** 525   **c** 78   **d** 264   **e** 315

2 **a** 100   **b** 240   **c** 300   **d** 154   **e** 121

3 **a** 63   **b** 112   **c** 111   **d** 44   **e** 441

4 A satellite is orbiting the Earth at a constant speed of $2^5 \times 5^4$ km/h. Find, as a product of prime numbers in index form, how far it travels in $2^3 \times 3^2 \times 5^3$ hours (about 1 year).

What is the smallest number that 405 needs to be multiplied by to become a square number?

> Any number that can be written as a^2 is a square number,
> e.g. 6^2 ($= 36$) is a square number.
> Therefore a square number must contain an even number of each of its prime factors.
> We will start by expressing 405 as a product of its prime factors.

$405 = 3^4 \times 5$

> Now we see that we need to multiply by 5 to get an even number of each prime factor.

$405 \times 5 = 3^4 \times 5 \times 5$
> $= (3^2 \times 5) \times (3^2 \times 5) = 45 \times 45$

Therefore 5 is the smallest number that 405 needs to be multiplied by to change it into a square number.

5 Find the smallest number that each given number needs to be multiplied by to change it into a square number.

a 24	**c** 45	**e** 180	**g** 108
b 32	**d** 48	**f** 240	**h** 1080

6 Express each number as a product of its prime factors and hence find its square root.

a 225	**b** 625	**c** 256	**d** 1764

MULTIPLYING NUMBERS WRITTEN IN INDEX FORM

If you did question **4** in the exercise above, you may have started it by multiplying $2^5 \times 5^4$ by $2^3 \times 3^2 \times 5^3$. Less work is involved if we can find $2^5 \times 2^3$ as a single power of 2 without having to write down all the twos, and similarly for $5^4 \times 5^3$.

$$\text{Now} \quad 2^5 \times 2^3 = (2 \times 2 \times 2 \times 2 \times 2) \times (2 \times 2 \times 2)$$
$$= 2 \times 2 \times 2 \times 2 \times 2 \times 2 \times 2 \times 2$$
$$= 2^8$$
$$\therefore \quad 2^5 \times 2^3 = 2^{5+3} = 2^8$$

But we cannot do the same with $2^5 \times 5^4$ because the numbers multiplied together are not all 2s (nor are they all 5s).

> We can multiply together different powers of the *same base* by adding the indices

but we cannot multiply together powers of different bases in this way.

EXERCISE 1D   **Do not use a calculator for this exercise.**

> Write $5^3 \times 5^4$ as a single expression in index form.
>
> $5^3 \times 5^4 = 5^{3+4}$
> $\qquad\quad = 5^7$

Write as a single expression in index form

1 a $3^5 \times 3^2$ **b** $2^2 \times 2^7$ **c** $5^4 \times 5^4$ **d** $13^2 \times 13^3$

2 a $7^5 \times 7^3$ **b** $10^4 \times 10^3$ **c** $12^4 \times 12^5$ **d** $4^7 \times 4^9$

3 a $9^2 \times 9^8$ **b** $10^9 \times 10^8$ **c** $2^5 \times 2^8$ **d** $3^4 \times 3^2$

> Write $a^4 \times a^5$ as a single expression in index form.
>
> $a^4 \times a^5 = a^{4+5}$ The base is the same for both numbers
> $\qquad\quad = a^9$ so we can add the powers.

Write as a single expression in index form

4 a $b^3 \times b^2$ **b** $r^5 \times r^3$ **c** $p^6 \times p^8$ **d** $v^2 \times v^3$

5 a $x^2 \times x$ **b** $a^5 \times a^2$ **c** $t \times t^3$ **d** $d \times d^5$

6 a $s^3 \times s^2$ **b** $x^4 \times x^2$ **c** $y \times y^4$ **d** $x^4 \times x^7$

DIVIDING NUMBERS WRITTEN IN INDEX FORM

To write $2^5 \div 2^2$ as a single number in index form we have

$$2^5 \div 2^2 = \frac{2^5}{2^2} = \frac{2 \times 2 \times 2 \times \cancel{2} \times \cancel{2}}{\cancel{2} \times \cancel{2}} = 2^3$$

i.e.

$$\frac{2^5}{2^2} = 2^{5-2} = 2^3$$

> We can divide different powers of the *same* base
> by subtracting the indices

but we cannot divide powers of different bases in this way.

EXERCISE 1E   **Do not use a calculator for this exercise.**

Write $a^7 \div a^3$ as a single expression in index form.

$$a^7 \div a^3 = a^{7-3}$$
$$= a^4$$

Write as a single expression in index form

1 a $4^4 \div 4^2$ **c** $5^6 \div 5^5$ **e** $q^9 \div q^5$
  b $7^9 \div 7^3$ **d** $10^8 \div 10^3$ **f** $15^8 \div 15^4$

2 a $6^{12} \div 6^7$ **c** $9^{15} \div 9^{14}$ **e** $3^6 \div 3^2$
  b $b^7 \div b^5$ **d** $p^4 \div p^3$ **f** $13^8 \div 13^5$

3 a $3^4 \div 3^2$ **c** $5^6 \div 5^2$ **e** $3^3 \div 3^2$
  b $2^7 \div 2$ **d** $p^3 \div p$ **f** $x^8 \div x^4$

4 a $11^3 \div 11$ **c** $2^6 \div 2^3$ **e** $5^9 \div 5^3$
  b $s^8 \div s^7$ **d** $a^5 \div a^3$ **f** $x^9 \div x^8$

5 a $6^4 \times 6^7$ **c** $7^5 \div 7$ **e** $a^9 \div a^3$
  b $3^9 \div 3^6$ **d** $x^3 \div x^2$ **f** $5^2 \times 5^2$

6 a $2^8 \times 2^7$ **c** $2^3 \div 2$ **e** 3×3^4
  b $a^9 \times a^3$ **d** $10^5 \div 10$ **f** $p^4 \div p$

7 a $c^6 \div c^3$ **c** $3^2 \times 3$ **e** $a^{12} \div a^6$
  b $5^{10} \div 5$ **d** $b^3 \times b^{10}$ **f** $10^{12} \div 10^3$

**NEGATIVE
INDICES**

When we use the rule for dividing numbers in index form, we may find we have a negative index.

Consider $2^3 \div 2^5$

Subtracting the indices gives $2^3 \div 2^5 = 2^{3-5} = 2^{-2}$

But, as a fraction, $2^3 \div 2^5 = \dfrac{\cancel{2} \times \cancel{2} \times \cancel{2}}{\cancel{2} \times \cancel{2} \times \cancel{2} \times 2 \times 2} = \dfrac{1}{2^2}$

Therefore 2^{-2} means $\dfrac{1}{2^2}$ and $\dfrac{1}{2^2}$ can be written as 2^{-2}.

In the same way, 5^{-3} means $\dfrac{1}{5^3}$,

If a and b are any two numbers, $a^{-b} = \dfrac{1}{a^b}$

EXERCISE 1F   **Do not use a calculator for this exercise.**

Find the value of 5^{-2}.

$$5^{2} = \frac{1}{5^{2}} = \frac{1}{25}$$

Find the value of

1 **a** 2^{-2} **c** 2^{-4} **e** 7^{-1} **g** 3^{-4} **i** 3^{-2}
      b 3^{-3} **d** 3^{-1} **f** 4^{-2} **h** 5^{-1} **j** 4^{-1}

2 **a** 4^{-3} **c** 15^{-1} **e** 7^{-2} **g** 10^{-2} **i** 10^{-1}
      b 6^{-2} **d** 6^{-1} **f** 5^{-3} **h** 2^{-3} **j** 8^{-2}

Find the value of 1.7×10^{-2}.

$$1.7 \times 10^{-2} = 1.7 \times \frac{1}{10^{2}}$$

$$= \frac{1.7}{100} = 0.017$$

Remember: to divide by 100 move the decimal point two places to the left.

Find the value of

3 **a** 3.4×10^{-3} **c** 6.2×10^{-2} **e** 5.38×10^{-4}
      b 2.6×10^{-1} **d** 8.21×10^{-3} **f** 74×10^{-2}

4 **a** 4.67×10^{-5} **c** 2.805×10^{-2} **e** 30.04×10^{-1}
      b 3.063×10^{-1} **d** 51.73×10^{-4} **f** 82.6×10^{-3}

5 Write these numbers as fractions
       a 10^{-3} **b** 10^{-5} **c** 10^{-4} **d** 10^{-7}

6 Write these numbers as decimals
       a 10^{-4} **b** 10^{-2} **c** 10^{-3} **d** 10^{-6}

Write $2 \div 2^{3}$ as a single number in index form.

$$2 \div 2^{3} = 2^{1} \div 2^{3}$$
$$= 2^{1-3} = 2^{-2}$$

Write as a single number in index form

7 a $5^2 \div 5^4$ **b** $3 \div 3^4$ **c** $6^4 \div 6^7$ **d** $2^5 \div 2^3$

<u>8</u> a $10^3 \div 10^6$ **b** $b^5 \div b^9$ **c** $4^8 \div 4^3$ **d** $2^a \div 2^b$

Express $\dfrac{1}{3^2}$ as a power of 3.

$\dfrac{1}{3^2} = 3^{-2}$ $\dfrac{1}{3^2}$ is the reciprocal of 3^2 and the reciprocal of 3^2 can be written as 3^{-2}.

---

9 Express as a power of a whole number

   a $\dfrac{1}{5^3}$ **b** $\dfrac{1}{2^3}$ **c** $\dfrac{1}{10^2}$ **d** $\dfrac{1}{3^3}$ **e** $\dfrac{1}{2^5}$ **f** $\dfrac{1}{10^4}$

10 Write these numbers as powers of 10.   **a** $\dfrac{1}{100}$ **b** $\dfrac{1}{1000}$

11 Write these numbers as powers of 10   **a** 0.001 **b** $0.000\,000\,01$

RECIPROCALS

If the product of two numbers is 1 then each number is called the *reciprocal* of the other.

We know that $\frac{1}{3} \times 3 = 1$ so $\frac{1}{3}$ is the reciprocal of 3   and   3 is the reciprocal of $\frac{1}{3}$.

To find the reciprocal of $\frac{3}{4}$ we require the number which, when multiplied by $\frac{3}{4}$ gives 1.

Now $\frac{4}{3} \times \frac{3}{4} = 1$ so $\frac{4}{3}$ is the reciprocal of $\frac{3}{4}$.

In all cases *the reciprocal of a fraction is obtained by turning the fraction upside down.*

Any number can be written as a fraction, e.g. $3 = \frac{3}{1}$, $2.5 = \frac{2.5}{1}$, and so on.

The reciprocal of $\frac{3}{1}$ is $\frac{1}{3}$ or $1 \div 3$, and the reciprocal of $\frac{2.5}{1}$ is $\frac{1}{2.5}$ or $1 \div 2.5$.

The reciprocal of a number is 1 divided by that number.

For a number a, we know that $a^{-1} = \dfrac{1}{a}$, i.e. a^{-1} is the reciprocal of a.

We also know that $a^{-b} = \dfrac{1}{a^b}$, i.e.

a^{-b} is the reciprocal of a^b.

DIVISION BY A FRACTION

Consider $\frac{2}{5} \div \frac{3}{7}$

This is the same as $\frac{2}{5} \times 1 \div \frac{3}{7}$

Now $1 \div \frac{3}{7}$ is the reciprocal of $\frac{3}{7}$, i.e. $\frac{7}{3}$

Therefore $\frac{2}{5} \div \frac{3}{7} = \frac{2}{5} \times \frac{7}{3} = \frac{14}{15}$

i.e.

> to divide by a fraction we multiply by its reciprocal.

EXERCISE 1G

Do not use a calculator for this exercise.

Write down the reciprocals of the following numbers.

1 **a** 4   **b** $\frac{1}{2}$ **c** $\frac{2}{5}$ **d** 10   **e** $\frac{1}{8}$ **f** $\frac{3}{11}$

2 **a** 100   **b** $\frac{2}{9}$ **c** $\frac{15}{4}$ **d** 2.5   **e** 3.2   **f** 1.6

3 Find   **a** $\frac{2}{3} \div \frac{1}{2}$ **c** $2\frac{1}{2} \div 4$ **e** $\frac{2}{9} \div 1\frac{2}{7}$ **g** $\frac{3}{7} \div 1\frac{3}{4}$

          b $1\frac{2}{3} \div \frac{5}{6}$ **d** $5 \div 1\frac{4}{5}$ **f** $\frac{1}{2} \div \frac{3}{4}$ **h** $3 \div \frac{2}{3}$

Find $2\frac{1}{2} + \frac{3}{5} \div 1\frac{1}{2}$

$2\frac{1}{2} + \frac{3}{5} \div 1\frac{1}{2} = 2\frac{1}{2} + \frac{3}{5} \div \frac{3}{2}$

$= 2\frac{1}{2} + \frac{3}{5} \times \frac{2}{3}$

$= 2\frac{1}{2} + \frac{2}{5}$

$= 2 + \frac{5}{10} + \frac{4}{10} = 2\frac{9}{10}$

> Remember that, for a mixture of operations, brackets are worked out first, then multiplication and division and lastly addition and subtraction.

$\frac{{}^{1}\cancel{3}}{5} \times \frac{2}{\cancel{3}_{1}} = \frac{2}{5}$

---

4 Find   **a** $1\frac{2}{3} \times \frac{1}{2} - \frac{2}{5}$ **b** $\frac{3}{7} + \frac{1}{4} \div 1\frac{1}{3}$ **c** $\frac{2}{5} \div \left(\frac{1}{2} + \frac{3}{4} \right)$

5 Find   **a** $5\frac{1}{2} \div 3 + \frac{2}{9}$ **b** $\frac{4}{5} \div \frac{1}{6} + \frac{1}{3} \times 1\frac{1}{2}$ **c** $\frac{9}{11} - \frac{2}{5} \times \frac{3}{4}$

6 Find   **a** $2\frac{1}{2} \div \frac{7}{9} + 1\frac{1}{3}$ **b** $\frac{3}{5} \left(1\frac{1}{4} - \frac{2}{3} \right)$ **c** $3\frac{1}{2} - \frac{2}{3} \times 6$

7 Find   **a** $\dfrac{2\frac{1}{2}}{1\frac{1}{2}}$ **b** $\dfrac{1\frac{1}{3}}{\frac{3}{4}}$ **c** $\dfrac{\frac{7}{8}}{3\frac{1}{2} - \frac{2}{3}}$

THE MEANING OF a^0

Consider $2^3 \div 2^3$; subtracting indices gives $2^3 \div 2^3 = 2^0$

and simplifying $\dfrac{2^3}{2^3}$ gives $\dfrac{\not{2} \times \not{2} \times \not{2}}{\not{2} \times \not{2} \times \not{2}} = 1$

So 2^0 means 1.

In the same way, $a^3 \div a^3 = a^0$ by subtracting indices

but $a^3 \div a^3 = \dfrac{a \times a \times a}{a \times a \times a} = 1$ by simplifying the fraction.

> Any number (except 0) to the power zero is equal to 1,
> i.e. $a^0 = 1$

The next exercise contains a mixture of questions involving indices.

EXERCISE 1H

Do not use a calculator for this exercise.

Find the value of

1 a 2^2 **b** 5^{-2} **c** 4^3 **d** 3^{-1} **e** 7^0 **f** 5^3

2 a 3^4 **b** 2^0 **c** 4^1 **d** 6^{-2} **e** 10^{-3} **f** 8^{-1}

3 a $2^4 \times 3$ **c** $2^0 \times 2^3$ **e** $4 \times 3^2 \times 5^2$

   b 5×3^2 **d** $2^2 \times 3 \times 5^2$ **f** $3^2 \times 3^5 \times 3^{-2}$

4 a $\left(\frac{1}{2}\right)^{-1}$ **c** $\left(\frac{1}{8}\right)^{-2}$ **e** $3^3 \times 3^{-3}$

   b $\left(\frac{2}{3}\right)^{-1}$ **d** $4 \div 2^{-2}$ **f** $5^5 \div 5^3$

Write as a single number or letter in index form

5 a $2^3 \times 2^4$ **c** $3^{-2} \times 3^4$ **e** $a^7 \div a^3$

   b $4^6 \div 4^3$ **d** $a^4 \times a^3$ **f** $a^5 \div a^5$

6 a $5^4 \times 5^{-2}$ **c** $b^3 \div b^3$ **e** $5^3 \div 5^9$

   b $3^5 \div 3^5$ **d** $4^{-2} \times 4^6$ **f** $a^{-2} \times a^{-3}$

7 a $3^3 \times 3^{-3}$ **b** $2^{-3} \times 2^{-2}$ **c** $t^3 \div t^4$ **d** $\dfrac{4^2 \times 4^6}{4^3}$

8 a $a^2 \times a^0$ **b** $x^{-5} \times x^4$ **c** $k^0 \times k^3$ **d** $p^2 \times p^3 \times p^5$

9 Which of these numbers is the larger?

    a 10^2 or 10^5 **b** 10^2 or 10^{-2} **c** 10^0 or 10^{-1}

10 Write these numbers in order of size with the smallest first.

$$10^4, \ 10^{-3}, \ 10^1, \ 10^0, \ 10^3, \ 10^{-2}$$

11 The first five terms of a sequence are 2, 4, 8, 16, 32.

    a Write down   **i** the next three terms.

                     ii the tenth term in index form.

    b Find an expression for the nth term.

12 You need a calculator for this question.

Cars and lorries can run out of control on steep hills. On some roads there are escape lanes; these are sand filled tracks designed to stop vehicles quickly. One of these is to be designed so that, if a vehicle enters it with a speed of 100 miles per hour, after t seconds its speed is $(100 \times 3^{-t} - 1)$ miles per hour.

    a What speed is expected   **i** after 1 second

                                ii after 3 seconds?

    b About how long does it take to stop a vehicle?

    c What is the value of $(100 \times 3^{-t} - 1)$ when $t = 6$? Does this mean anything in relation to the speed of a vehicle? Explain your answer.

MIXED EXERCISE   Do not use a calculator for this exercise.

EXERCISE 1I   **1** Write these as ordinary numbers.

        a 4^3 **b** 2^{-3} **c** $\left(\frac{1}{4}\right)^{-2}$ **d** 5^0

    2 Which is the larger

        a 2^5 or 5^2 **b** 3^{-2} or 2^{-3}?

3 **a** Express 176 as a product of its prime factors in index form.

b What is the smallest number that 176 needs to be multiplied by to change it to a square number?

4 Write the following numbers in order of size with the smallest first.

a 2^{-2}, -4, 0.3, 10^{-1} **b** 2^3, 3^2, 2×3, 23

5 Given that $504 = 2^x \times 3^y \times 7^z$, find the values of x, y and z.

INVESTIGATION

a Everyone has two biological parents.
Going back one generation, each of your parents has two biological parents.
Copy, extend and complete the tree – fill in the number of ancestors for five generations back. Do not fill in names!

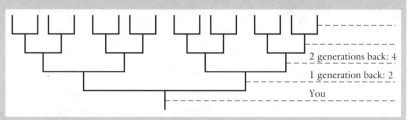

2 generations back: 4

1 generation back: 2

You

b How many ancestors does this table suggest you have

i five generations back
ii six generations back
iii ten generations back?

Give each answer as a power of 2.

c If we assume that each generation spans 25 years, how many generations are needed to go back 1000 years?

d Find the number of ancestors the table suggests that you would expect to have 6000 years back.
Give your answer as a power of 2.

e About 6000 years ago, according to the bible, Adam and Eve were the only people on the Earth. This contradicts the answer from **d**.
Suggest some reasons for this contradiction.

USING A CALCULATOR

Gordon is a student nurse. He is asked to weigh and measure a new patient and then to use the information to work out the patient's Body Mass Index.

This is $\dfrac{\text{weight in kilograms}}{(\text{height in metres})^2}$ and,

for this patient, it is $\dfrac{70.5}{1.63^2}$.

Gordon uses a calculator and writes down 265 in the patient's notes, but this is ten times larger than the correct answer.

- This is a case where accuracy really matters because the Body Mass Index is used to work out some drug doses. If this mistake goes unnoticed, the patient could die.

- Being able to recognise immediately and instinctively that answers are obviously wrong, will help you to avoid such errors.

EXERCISE 2A

1 Some calculations together with answers are given below. Some of the answers are correct and the others are very wrong.
Without using a calculator, find the wrong answers and make a note of those that you spotted immediately.

a $2 + 2 = 4$ **e** $20 \div 4 = 50$ **i** $\frac{1}{2} \times 12 = 60$

b $1 + 3 = 10$ **f** $300 \div 50 = 6$ **j** $12 \div \frac{1}{2} = 24$

c $2 \times 5 = 1$ **g** $0.1 \times 0.2 = 0.3$ **k** $50 \div (0.2)^2 = 2$

d $20 \times 4 = 800$ **h** $40 \div 0.1 = 400$ **l** $0.3 \div 0.6 = 5$

2 Consider those answers that you noted in question **1**. Discuss what it is that you know which enabled you to spot these wrong answers.

3 This is a group exercise.

Each of you should use a calculator to find the value of $\dfrac{70.5}{1.63^2}$.

Do it once only and write down the answer on the display, even if you know that it is wrong.

Now compare answers. Some of you will almost certainly have written down the wrong answer. Discuss what may have caused those wrong answers.

MENTAL ARITHMETIC

All of us are capable of making mistakes when we use a calculator. Sometimes we are at fault, at other times errors may be caused by a calculator not working properly, for example having a sticky key. Whatever the problem, if the use of a calculator gives the wrong answer, it is usually so wrong that it should be obvious.

We have also seen that there are situations where it is vital that such errors are recognised instinctively. To be able to do this we need to know (that is not have to think about)

- the addition and multiplication facts for all whole numbers from 1 to 10
- that multiplying by a number greater than 1 causes an increase and multiplying by a number less than 1 causes a decrease
- that dividing by a number greater than 1 causes a decrease and dividing by a number less than 1 causes an increase
- how to multiply and divide by powers of 10 mentally.

The next exercise gives practice in these skills.

EXERCISE 2B

Mandy calculated $\dfrac{34.5}{1.23^2}$ as 228. Is her answer too big or too small?

> 1.23^2 is bigger than 1, so $34.5 \div 1.23^2$ must be less than 34.5.

228 is too big.

1 The answers given to these calculations are all wrong. Decide, mentally, whether each answer is too big or too small.

a $278 \div 37 = 751$	**e** $4.73 \times 0.29 = 12.8$
b $72 + 85 = 83$	**f** $4.73 \times 2.9 = 1.28$
c $5.62 \times 1.15 = 4.16$	**g** $4.7 - 2.9 = 5.4$
d $0.36 \div 0.22 = 0.16$	**h** $0.28 \div 0.03 = 0.07$

2 The answers given to these calculations are all wrong. Decide, mentally, whether each answer is too big or too small.

a $\dfrac{2+7}{11} = 8.2$ **e** $\dfrac{47.8}{0.23^2} = 9.03$

b $0.45 - 0.25 \times 0.5 = 0.55$ **f** $2.66 \times 1.56 + 0.44 = 0.32$

c $(0.5)^2 = 2.5$

g $\dfrac{(1.9)^2}{0.97} = 2.1$

d $\dfrac{2.66}{5.7 - 2.3} = 7.6$ **h** $\dfrac{0.24 \times 5.6}{1.12} = 12$

Find 200×50 mentally.

> If you cannot do a calculation in one step in your head, break it down. In this case, remember that to multiply 200 by 50 we can multiply 200 first by 5 and then multiply the result by 10, i.e. $200 \times 5 = 1000$, then $1000 \times 10 = 10\,000$.

$200 \times 50 = 10\,000$

---

3 Working mentally, write down the value of

a 50×30 **d** $(40)^2$ **g** 20×300 **j** 70×200

b 40×20 **e** 12×20 **h** 40×700 **k** 400×300

c 90×60 **f** 60×40 **i** 300×60 **l** 200×500

4 Working mentally, write down the value of

a 40×30 **d** $(80)^2$ **g** 30×500 **j** $(200)^2$

b 50×70 **e** 9×70 **h** 600×30 **k** 800×500

c 80×50 **f** 20×90 **i** 700×20 **l** 1200×50

Working mentally, write down the value of $200 \div 50$.

> To divide by 50 we can divide first by 10 and then divide the result by 5, i.e. $200 \div 10 = 20$, then $20 \div 5 = 4$.

$200 \div 50 = 4$

---

5 Working mentally, write down the value of

a $500 \div 10$ **d** $180 \div 30$ **g** $5000 \div 400$ **j** $1500 \div 30$

b $600 \div 20$ **e** $120 \div 60$ **h** $2000 \div 50$ **k** $2400 \div 300$

c $400 \div 20$ **f** $500 \div 20$ **i** $1200 \div 400$ **l** $1800 \div 90$

6 Working mentally, write down the value of

a $400 \div 80$ **d** $450 \div 90$ **g** $8000 \div 200$ **j** $5500 \div 110$

b $900 \div 20$ **e** $270 \div 30$ **h** $4900 \div 70$ **k** $6300 \div 90$

c $150 \div 30$ **f** $200 \div 40$ **i** $3200 \div 800$ **l** $1600 \div 800$

Working mentally, write down the value of 0.2×0.03.

> Remember that to multiply decimals, first ignore the decimal point and multiply the numbers, i.e. $2 \times 3 = 6$.
> Now add together the number of decimal places in the numbers being multiplied; i.e. $1+2=3$: this gives the number of decimal places in the answer, i.e. 0.006.

$0.2 \times 0.03 = 0.006$

---

7 Working mentally, write down the value of

a 0.4×0.2 **d** 0.4×0.04 **g** $(0.1)^3$ **j** 50×0.1

b 0.5×0.1 **e** $(0.5)^2$ **h** 2.5×0.02 **k** 0.01×25

c 0.3×0.4 **f** 0.03×0.3 **i** 1.2×0.3 **l** 0.02×2.2

8 Working mentally, write down the value of

a 0.2×0.2 **d** 0.2×0.02 **g** 3.5×0.01 **j** 500×0.04

b 0.4×0.1 **e** $(0.8)^2$ **h** $(0.01)^2$ **k** 0.7×40

c 0.3×0.5 **f** 0.05×0.5 **i** 0.02×7 **l** $0.1 \times 0.2 \times 0.3$

Write down the answers to the following problems. Do all the working mentally.

9 The pattern printed on curtain material repeats every 0.5 m. What length of material is needed for 250 pattern repeats?

10 When Tony goes to Dusseldorf he can exchange £1 for 2.8 Deutschmarks. How many Deutschmarks will he get for £100?

11 A soap dispenser dispenses 15 ml of liquid soap each time it is used. How many litres of liquid soap does the dispenser hold if it can be used 600 times between refills?

12 Jocelyn is paid 1.2 pence for every leaflet she delivers. How much does she earn when she delivers 4000 leaflets?

ROUGH ESTIMATES

We would almost certainly use a calculator to find 1.397×62.57 but it is essential first to make a rough estimate of the answer. You will then know whether the answer you get from your calculator is reasonable or not. (An estimate cannot tell you whether your answer is right. To do this you need to check the calculation by another method.)

One way of estimating the answer to a calculation is to write each number correct to 1 significant figure.

So $\qquad 1.|397 \times 6|2.57 \approx 1 \times 60 = 60$

EXERCISE 2C

You do not need to work entirely in your head to find an estimate.
You can write down intermediate steps but do not use a calculator.

Correct each number to 1 significant figure and hence give a rough answer to $54.72 \div 0.761$

$$\frac{5|4.72}{0.7|61} \approx \frac{50}{0.8} = \frac{500}{8}$$

$$\approx 60$$

Remember that $\frac{500}{8}$ means $500 \div 8$.

For an estimate we round $500 \div 8$ to 1 significant figure.

Correct each number to 1 significant figure and hence give a rough answer for each calculation.

1 **a** 4.78×23.7 **c** $82.8 \div 146$ **e** 1.889×0.0498

     b 56.3×0.573 **d** 0.632×0.845 **f** $0.079 \div 28.9$

2 **a** $0.0674 \div 5.24$ **d** 0.0062×574

     b 354.6×0.0475 **e** $7.835 \div 6.493$

     c 576×256 **f** 4736×729

3 **a** 34.7×21 **d** $0.0326 \div 12.4$

     b 8.63×0.523 **e** $0.007\,24 \times 0.783$

     c $21.78 + 12.98$ **f** $0.094 + 0.024$

4 **a** $3.1445 - 2.301$ **d** $1.1147 - 0.0914$

     b $0.051\,66 + 0.023$ **e** $5569 \div 7705$

     c 26.8×0.058 **f** $0.000\,27 \times 5.59$

> Correct each number to 1 significant figure and hence estimate
> $$\frac{0.048 \times 3.275}{0.367}$$
>
> $$\frac{0.048 \times 3.275}{0.367} \approx \frac{0.05 \times 3}{0.4} = \frac{0.15}{0.4} = \frac{1.5}{4}$$
> $$= 0.4 \ (\text{correct to 1 s.f.})$$

Correct each number to 1 significant figure and hence give a rough answer for each calculation.

5 a $\dfrac{3.87 \times 5.24}{2.13}$

d $\dfrac{975 \times 0.636}{40.78}$

b $\dfrac{0.636 \times 2.63}{5.47}$

e $\dfrac{29 \times 315}{62}$

c $\dfrac{89.03 \times 0.079\,37}{5.92}$

f $\dfrac{(85.3 - 5.7) \times 100}{5.86}$

6 a $\dfrac{21.78 \times 4.278}{7.96}$

d $\dfrac{0.527}{6.41 \times 0.738}$

b $\dfrac{6.38 \times 0.185}{0.628}$

e $\dfrac{5.37 \times 2.49^2}{27.5 + 39.2}$

c $\dfrac{8.735}{5.72 \times 5.94}$

f $\dfrac{4937 + 5216}{(2.8 + 5.9) \times 100}$

7 a $\dfrac{(23.7)^2}{47.834}$

c $\dfrac{[(52.1)^2 + (83.7)^2] \times 1.1}{0.94}$

b $\dfrac{57.8}{(0.57)^2 \times (3.94)^2}$

d $\dfrac{5.83^2 + 1.09^2}{5.83^2 - 1.09^2}$

8 The area of this metal machine part is given by calculating $\dfrac{3.142 \times (0.2954)^2}{2.26}$ cm^2.

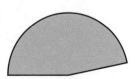

Estimate this area to 1 significant figure.

9 A bullet is fired into a block of wood. The depth that it penetrates into the block is $\dfrac{0.5 \times 0.023 \times (126.4)^2}{1567}$ metres.

Estimate this depth to 1 significant figure.

10 £1537 was put into a savings account 2 years ago. The amount now in the account is calculated using

$$£1537 \times 1.057 \times 1.5 \times 1.049 \times 0.5.$$

a Estimate the amount in the account.

b Explain whether you think your estimate is more or less than the actual amount.

11 Estimate the value of $x^3 + 3x$ when $x = 1.92$.

12 The braking distance for a car is the distance it travels from the time that the brakes are applied until the car comes to a stop.
If the car is travelling at v m/s when it starts to brake, the braking distance, in metres, is given by $\dfrac{v^2}{4g}$.
Estimate the braking distance when $v = 74$ and $g = 9.81$.

13 a Estimate 0.44×1.49.
Now find the true value.
By how much does your estimate differ from the true value?

b Repeat part **a** for 0.41×1.01.

c Suggest a way in which you could improve your estimate for part **a**.

14 500 circles are stamped out of a rectangular sheet of metal that is 215 mm wide and 418 mm long.
The diameter of each circle is 12.8 mm.

a Write down an expression from which the area of one of these circles can be calculated.

b Write down an expression from which the area of metal left can be found. Hence estimate the area of metal left.

15

The number of rabbits on Chessle Island is now estimated at 24 500. It is expected that the numbers will increase to $24\,500 \times 1.25^3$ in three years.

a Estimate the size of the rabbit population in three years.

b How accurate do you judge your estimate to be?

USING A CALCULATOR

Remember that a scientific calculator works out multiplications and divisions before additions and subtractions.

If you key in $\boxed{2 + 3 \times 4 =}$ your calculator will work out 3×4 before adding it to 2, i.e. $2 + 3 \times 4 = 2 + 12 = 14$.

If you want to add 2 and 3 and multiply the result by 4, either use brackets, i.e. press $\boxed{(2 + 3) \times 4 =}$ or do it in two stages, i.e. $\boxed{2 + 3 = \times 4 =}$

EXERCISE 2D

> Use your calculator to find 0.025×3.981, giving the answer correct to 3 significant figures.
>
> Estimate: $0.025 \times 3.981 \approx 0.03 \times 4 = 0.12$
> Calculator: $0.025 \times 3.981 = 0.099\,52\ldots$
> $\qquad\qquad\qquad\qquad = 0.0995$ (correct to 3 s.f.)
>
> > There is no need to write down all the figures in the display.
> > For an answer correct to 3 s.f., it is enough to write down the first 4 significant figures.
> > If your answer is 10 or more times larger or smaller than your estimate, check both calculations.

First make a rough estimate of the answer without using a calculator. Then use your calculator to give the answer correct to 3 significant figures.

1 a 2.16×3.28 **c** 1.48×4.74 **e** 2.304×3.251

   b 2.63×2.87 **d** 6.053×1.274 **f** 8.426×1.086

2 **a** 4.035×2.116 **d** 5.839×3.618
　 b 3.142×2.925 **e** 6.834×4.382
　 c 0.59×0.489 **f** 0.0213×2.055

3 **a** $9.571 \div 2.518$ **d** $23.4 \div 56.7$
　 b $5.393 \div 3.593$ **e** $384 \div 21.8$
　 c $7.384 \div 2.51$ **f** $0.29 \div 0.17$

4 **a** $4.931 \div 3.204$ **d** $537.8 \div 34.6$
　 b $8.362 \div 5.823$ **e** $45.35 \div 6.82$
　 c $13.05 \div 0.0506$ **f** $45.8 \div 143.7$

5 **a** 63.8×2.701 **d** $5703 \div 154.8$
　 b $40.3 \div 2.74$ **e** 39.03×49.94
　 c $400 \div 35.7$ **f** $2000 \div 52.66$

6 **a** 34.2×30.7 **d** 36.8×41.5
　 b 5007×2.51 **e** $29\,006 \div 2.015$
　 c $0.279 \div 0.521$ **f** $0.000\,59 \div 4.791$

7 **a** $0.366 - 0.37 \times 0.52$ **d** $0.0826 - 0.348 \times 0.582$
　 b $0.526 \times 0.372 + 0.027$ **e** $24.78 \times 0.0724 + 8.25$
　 c $6.924 + 1.56 \div 0.007\,93$ **f** $0.008\,35 \times 0.617 - 0.002\,47$

8 **a** $0.638 \times 825 + 54.3$ **d** $0.5824 + 1.054 \times 6.813$
　 b $52 \times 0.0895 - 0.489$ **e** $0.74 + 8.42 \div 0.56$
　 c $0.561 + 27.21 \div 5.77$ **f** $0.025 \times 2.25 \div 0.245$

Use your calculator to find $(2.486 - 1.295) \times 3.057$ giving the answer correct to 3 significant figures.

Estimate: $(2.486 - 1.295) \times 3.057 \approx (2 - 1) \times 3 = 1 \times 3 = 3$

> This can be done in one stage using the brackets buttons:
>
> press　$(2.486 - 1.295) \times 3.057 =$
>
> It can also be done in two stages:
>
> press　$2.486 - 1.295 =$　and write down the result but do not clear the display
>
> Then press　$\times 3.057 =$

Calculator: $(2.486 - 1.295) \times 3.057 = 3.640\ldots$
$$= 3.64 \text{ (correct to 3 s.f.)}$$

9 First make an estimate of the answer. Then use your calculator to find, correct to 3 significant figures

a $54.6 \times (22.05 - 8.17)$

c $32.03 \times (17.09 - 16.9)$

b $6.04 \div (1.958 - 0.872)$

d $0.51 \div (0.45 + 0.327)$

10 First make an estimate of the answer. Then use your calculator to find, correct to 3 significant figures

a $(0.824 + 0.057) \times 27.45$

c $(1.033 + 0.29) \times 4.47$

b $(2.798 - 21.25) \div 12.099$

d $(0.029 - 0.0084) \div 1.88$

Use your calculator to find $\dfrac{533 + 287}{14.7^2 + 9.35^2}$

Estimate: $\dfrac{533 + 287}{14.7^2 + 9.35^2} \approx \dfrac{500 + 300}{10^2 + 10^2} = \dfrac{800}{200} = 4$

Calculator: $\dfrac{533 + 287}{14.7^2 + 9.35^2} = 2.701\ldots$

$= 2.70 \ (\text{correct to 3 s.f.})$

We can use brackets to enter $\frac{533 + 287}{14.7^2 + 9.35^2}$ in one step:

$\boxed{(533 + 287) \div (14.7x^2 + 9.35x^2) =}$

Alternatively we can use the memory, i.e. first calculate the bottom of the fraction:

enter $\boxed{14.7x^2 + 9.35x^2 =}$ then press $\boxed{M+}$ to place the result in the memory and then clear the display. (Make sure the memory is empty before you start.) Next enter $\boxed{533 + 287 =}$ to work out the top of the fraction and then without clearing the display, enter $\boxed{\div RCL =}$ to divide the top by the bottom.

---

11 First make an estimate of the answer, then use your calculator to find, correct to 3 significant figures.

a $\dfrac{0.014}{1.53 - 0.9889}$

d $\dfrac{24.5 + 9.992}{101.7}$

b $\dfrac{0.034 + 1.3667}{1.3142}$

e $\dfrac{24.6^2}{297}$

c $\dfrac{57.2}{1.113 \times 5.906}$

f $\dfrac{57.99}{94.55 - 37.75}$

12 First make an estimate of the answer.
Then use your calculator to find, correct to 3 significant figures

a $\dfrac{5.011}{2.23 - 1.889}$ **c** $\dfrac{5.92^2}{3.908 \times 69.9}$ **e** $\dfrac{4.556}{3.07^2}$

b $\dfrac{29.304 + 18.37}{189.3}$ **d** $\dfrac{0.9502 - 0.8992}{10.3}$ **f** $\dfrac{57.99}{94.55 + 37.75}$

13 Find each value correct to 3 significant figures.

a $\dfrac{3.87 \times 5.24}{2.13}$ **e** $\dfrac{975 \times 0.636}{40.78}$ **i** $\dfrac{(85.3 - 5.7) \times 100}{5.86}$

b $\dfrac{0.636 \times 2.63}{5.47}$ **f** $\dfrac{8.735}{5.72 \times 5.94}$ **j** $\dfrac{5.37 \times 2.49^2}{27.5 + 39.2}$

c $\dfrac{6.38 \times 0.185}{0.628}$ **g** $\dfrac{0.527}{6.41 \times 0.738}$ **k** $\dfrac{4937 + 5216}{(2.8 + 5.9) \times 100}$

d $\dfrac{(23.7)^2}{47.834}$ **h** $\dfrac{57.8}{(0.57)^2 \times (3.94)^2}$ **l** $\dfrac{[(52.1)^2 + (83.7)^2] \times 1.1}{0.94}$

14 Alia had to calculate $5.87 \times (27.4 + 4.82)$ to find the area, in square metres, of a paved patio.
Find the area, giving your answer correct to 2 significant figures.

15 Tony needed to calculate $2.57 + 8.36 \times 0.19$.
He used his calculator and wrote down the result as 2.08 correct to 3 significant figures.
Without using your calculator explain how you know that Tony's answer is wrong.

16 Olive estimated 2.49×1.49 as roughly 2.

a Calculate 2.49×1.49 and find the difference between your answer and Olive's estimate of the answer.

b Suggest how Olive could improve the accuracy of her estimate.

17 Without calculating the answer, decide which of these estimates is likely to be nearest to the value of $\dfrac{1.29 \times 0.59}{(1.45)^2}$.

A $\dfrac{1 \times 0.6}{1}$ **B** $\dfrac{1 \times 1}{1}$ **C** $\dfrac{1 \times 0.6}{2}$

Give reasons for your choice.

18 Jerry travelled 5618 miles in his car on holiday and his average petrol consumption was 37 miles/gallon. Petrol cost him 68 p per litre.

a Estimate the cost of petrol for his holiday.
(Use 1 gallon $\approx$ 4.5 litres.)

b Calculate, to the nearest pound, the cost of petrol for his holiday.

USING A CALCULATOR TO FIND POWERS AND ROOTS

The y^x key is used to work out powers of numbers (if y^x is written above a key, first press 2nd F or SHIFT),

e.g. to find 2.56^3, press 2.56 y^x 3 =

The (−) key is used to change the sign of a number from positive to negative, or vice-versa.

To find the value of 1.94^{-3}, we use this key to change the index to a negative number,

i.e. press 1.94 y^x (−) 3 =

Note *that the instructions given here apply to many but not to all calculators.* You need to use the manual that comes with your calculator.

EXERCISE 2E

Use your calculator to find $(0.405)^{-3}$.

Estimate: $(0.405)^{-3} \approx (0.4)^{-3} = \dfrac{1}{0.4^3} \approx \dfrac{1}{0.06} = \dfrac{100}{6} \approx 16$

> We round each step in the estimation to one significant figure, unless the second significant figure is 4, 5 or 6, in which case it may be better to round to 2 significant figures.

Calculator: $(0.405)^{-3} = 15.05\ldots = 15.1$ (correct to 3 s.f.)

First find an estimate, then use your calculator to find, correct to 3 significant figures

1 **a** $(2.37)^3$ **d** $(2.95)^4$ **g** $(4.225)^3$

    b $(0.209)^5$ **e** $(280)^3$ **h** $(0.497)^3$

    c $(5.03)^{-2}$ **f** $(0.0219)^{-2}$ **i** $(4)^{-3}$

2 **a** $27.5 \times (2.156)^3$ **d** $518 \times (40.5)^{-2}$

    b $512 \times (0.267)^{-4}$ **e** $(1.96)^{-2} \div 2.97$

    c $108 \div (1.66)^{-3}$ **f** $(147)^4 \div (51.5)^5$

3 **a** Estimate the value of $2.37 \times (1.2)^{-t}$ when $t = 2$.

    b Calculate the value $2.37 \times (1.2)^{-t}$ when $t = 2$ giving your answer correct to 3 significant figures.

4 Copy and complete the table for values of $2x^5$ giving those values correct to 2 significant figures.

x	1.1	1.4	2.7	2.9	3.5
$2x^5$					

MIXED EXERCISES

EXERCISES 2F   **Do not use a calculator for this exercise.**

1 Andy worked out that he could get 250 cups of coffee from a 300 g jar of instant coffee powder by using 0.8 grams of powder per cup. Explain how you know that he is wrong.

2 Working mentally, write down the value of

   a 80×300 **c** $300 \div 50$ **e** 0.8×0.5

   b 70^2 **d** $1500 \div 300$ **f** 1.6×0.2

3 Give a rough estimate for each calculation.

   a 59.3×2.8 **c** $4915 - 389$ **e** $\dfrac{1.56 + 3.34}{0.125}$

   b $26.7 \div 0.78$ **d** $0.0772 + 0.2912$ **f** $\dfrac{3.77 + 9.36}{(8.45 - 4.57) \times 100}$

EXERCISE 2G   **1** Use your calculator to find the answer to each part of question **3** in **Exercise 2F**. Give your answers correct to 3 significant figures.

2 First find an estimate, then use your calculator to find, correct to 3 significant figures,

   a $(2.08)^4$ **b** $(3.56)^{-2}$ **c** $(0.96)^3$ **d** $(0.728)^{-4}$

3 Plant cells are grown in a laboratory. When conditions are perfect, the number, N, of cells after t hours is given by $N = 25 \times (1.005)^t$. Find N when $t = 72$.

PRACTICAL WORK

How accurate are calculators?

a Use your calculator to perform these instructions.

Enter 5×10^{-13} on your calculator.

Now add 2.

Next subtract 1.

Multiply the result by 10^{13}.

b Repeat the instruction given in part **a** without using a calculator. How accurate is your calculator?

c Try using a computer program, a spreadsheet for example, to see if you can find an electronic method that will give an accurate answer for part **a**.

STANDARD FORM

We come across very large numbers in news items.

For example, 'Consumer credit now stands at £52.6 billion.'

'£55 165 million was raised from personal income tax last year.'

We know that £52.6 billion is a very large number, but many of us are unsure what a billion means because there is no unambiguous definition. Most people use one billion to mean one thousand million although some people use one billion to mean one million million. It is also very difficult to compare the size of a number in billions with the size of a number in millions.

- If we need to work with very large numbers, or very small numbers, it helps if they are given in the same way and in a form that cannot have different meanings.

EXERCISE 3A

1 The mass of the Earth is 5 976 000 000 000 000 000 000 000 kg. This mass can also be written as **5.976** million trillion kg
or as 5.976×10^{24} kg

  a Find out what 'one trillion' means.

  b Discuss the advantages and disadvantages of each of these three ways of giving the mass of the Earth.

2 The mass of the Sun is

   1.9×10^{30} kg or 1 900 000 000 000 000 000 000 000 000 000 kg

  a Which of these two ways of writing the mass of the Sun would you prefer to write down and why?

  b You want to find how many times bigger the mass of the Sun is than the mass of the Earth. Discuss which way of expressing the masses of the Earth and the Sun is easier to use.

3 For this question, take one billion to mean one thousand million.

a Without doing any working, write down whether you think that
£52.6 billion is much larger or much smaller than £55.165 million.

b Express £52.6 billion as a number of millions. Do you still agree
with your answer to part **a**?

**STANDARD
FORM**

When a number is written as 5.976×10^{24} it is written in *standard
form*. The advantages of standard form over other ways of writing a
number are that

it is easier to judge the size of the number
it is quicker to write down
it does not use terms such as 'billion' which are ambiguous.

The same advantages apply to very small numbers. For example, the
time light takes to travel 1 km is

$3.335\,609 \times 10^{-6}$ seconds, i.e. $0.000\,003\,335\,609$ seconds

> A number written in standard form
> is a number between 1 and 10 multiplied by a power of 10.

So 1.3×10^{2} and 3.72×10^{-3} are in standard form,
but 13×10^{5} and 0.26×10^{-3} are not in standard form because the
first number is not between 1 and 10.

**CHANGING
NUMBERS INTO
STANDARD
FORM**

To write 6800 in standard form, the decimal point has to be placed
between the 6 and the 8 to give a number between 1 and 10. Counting
then tells us that, to change 6.8 to 6800, we must move the decimal
point three places to the right (that is, multiply by 1000, i.e. 10^{3}).

Therefore $\qquad 6800 = 6.8 \times 1000 = 6.8 \times 10^{3}$

To give 0.019 34 in standard form, the decimal point has to go between
the 1 and the 9 to give a number between 1 and 10.
This time counting tells us that, to change 1.934 to 0.019 34, we have to
move the decimal point two places to the left, that is we have to divide by
100, i.e. 10^{2}.

Remember that $1 \div 10^{2} = \dfrac{1}{10^{2}}$ and that $\dfrac{1}{10^{2}} = 10^{-2}$.

so $\qquad 0.019\,34 = 1.934 \div 100 = 1.934 \times 10^{-2}$

EXERCISE 3B   **Do not use a calculator for this exercise.**

Write 3.07×10^5 as an ordinary number.

$$3.07 \times 10^5 = 3.07 \times 100\,000$$
$$= 307\,000$$

Remember, to multiply by 100 000, we move the decimal point 5 places to the right and fill in the gaps with zeros.

1 Write as ordinary numbers

a 5.5×10^3	**e** 9.15×10^3	**i** 7.402×10^3
b 1.3×10^4	**f** 2.04×10^7	**j** 5.778×10^2
c 7.4×10^6	**g** 4.155×10^6	**k** 2.004×10^8
d 3.16×10^5	**h** 8.022×10^4	**l** 3.101×10^{11}

Write 6.13×10^{-4} as an ordinary number.

$$6.13 \times 10^{-4} = 6.13 \times \frac{1}{10^4}$$
$$= 0.000\,613$$

Remember that multiplying by $\frac{1}{10^4}$ is the same as dividing by 10^4, i.e. dividing by 10 000; so we move the decimal point 4 places to the left and fill in the gaps with zeros.

2 Write as ordinary numbers

a 4.7×10^{-3}	**e** 8.01×10^{-4}	**i** 6.027×10^{-6}
b 2.9×10^{-5}	**f** 6.35×10^{-2}	**j** 7.71×10^{-1}
c 5.1×10^{-4}	**g** 3.103×10^{-4}	**k** 2.052×10^{-8}
d 1.35×10^{-5}	**h** 5.008×10^{-2}	**l** 3.889×10^{-10}

3 Write these numbers as ordinary numbers.

a 3.78×10^3	**d** 7.4×10^{14}	**g** 4.77×10^{-4}
b 1.26×10^{-3}	**e** 6.43×10^{-8}	**h** 9.08×10^{-7}
c 5.3×10^6	**f** 4.25×10^{12}	**i** 8.15×10^{-5}

> Write $307\,000\,000\,000$ in standard form.
>
> > $$307\,000\,000\,000 = 3.07 \times 100\,000\,000\,000$$
> > $$= 3.07 \times 10^{11}$$
>
> $307\,000\,000\,000 = 3.07 \times 10^{11}$

4 Write the following numbers in standard form.

a 2500	**d** 39 070	**g** 26 030
b 630	**e** 4 500 000	**h** 547 000
c 15 300	**f** 530 000 000	**i** 30 600

5 Write the following numbers in standard form.

a 260 000	**d** 40 000	**g** 4 060 000
b 9900	**e** 80 000 000 000	**h** 704
c 246 700	**f** 4 004 000	**i** 330 400

> Write $0.006\,043$ in standard form.
>
> > $$0.006\,043 = 6.043 \div 1000$$
> > $$= 6.043 \times \frac{1}{10^3} = 6.043 \times 10^{-3}$$
>
> $0.006\,043 = 6.043 \times 10^{-3}$

6 Write the following numbers in standard form.

a 0.026	**d** 0.79	**g** 0.907
b 0.0048	**e** 0.0069	**h** 0.805
c 0.053	**f** 0.000 007 5	**i** 0.088 08

7 Write the following numbers in standard form.

a 0.000 018	**d** 0.000 000 000 4	**g** 0.000 704 4
b 0.52	**e** 0.684	**h** 0.000 000 000 073
c 0.0011	**f** 0.0535	**i** 0.001 005

8 Write the following numbers in standard form.

a 88.92	**f** 84	**k** 5090
b 0.000 050 6	**g** 351	**l** 268 000
c 0.000 000 057	**h** 0.09	**m** 30.7
d 503 000 000	**i** 0.007 05	**n** 0.005 05
e 99 000 000	**j** 36	**p** 0.000 008 8

9 Write these numbers in standard form and then place them in order of size, with the smallest first.

    a 576 000 000, 20 000 000 000, 997 000 000, 247 000, 37 500

    b 0.005 27, 0.600 05, 0.9906, 0.000 000 050 2, 0.003 005

    c 0.0705, 7.080 000, 79.3, 0.007 008 09, 560 800

10 a Without using a calculator, find $1\,200\,000 \times 400\,000$ and write your answer in standard form.

    b Now use your calculator to find $1\,200\,000 \times 400\,000$. Write down exactly what is showing on the display of your calculator. What do you think it means?

WORKING WITH NUMBERS IN STANDARD FORM

Kevin is using the special theory of relativity in a series of experiments. The theory states that a mass m is equivalent to a quantity of energy E, given by the formula $E = mc^2$

where c m/s is the speed of light and $c = 2.998 \times 10^8$.

In one set of experiments, he uses the formula to calculate the energy equivalent to some very large masses.

- To find the energy equivalent to a mass of 5.075×10^6 kg, Kevin has to calculate $(5.075 \times 10^6) \times (2.998 \times 10^8)^2$, that is, he needs to know how to work with numbers in standard form.

Calculations involving numbers in standard form can be done on a calculator. For example, to enter 1.738×10^{-6}, the number 1.738 is entered normally followed by the **EXP** button and then the power of 10.

Hence, to calculate $(1.738 \times 10^{-6}) \times (4.093 \times 10^{-4})$, we enter

> **1 . 7 3 8 EXP (−) 6 × 4 . 0 9 3 EXP (−) 4 =**

giving 7.114×10^{-10} corrected to 4 significant figures.
(Check your manual to find the key on your calculator equivalent to **EXP** .)

However, as with all calculations, it is important to know whether the answer is about right; this means that we need to be able to estimate results using non-calculator methods.

Now $(1.738 \times 10^{-6}) \times (4.093 \times 10^{-4})$
$\approx 2 \times 10^{-6} \times 4 \times 10^{-4}$
$= 8 \times 10^{-10}$ so the answer given above is reasonable.

EXERCISE 3C   Do not use a calculator for questions **1** to **6**.

Find ab when $a = 1.2 \times 10^{-2}$ and $b = 6 \times 10^{-4}$

$ab = (1.2 \times 10^{-2}) \times (6 \times 10^{-4})$

$= 7.2 \times 10^{-6}$

> Remember that numbers can be multiplied in any order,
>
> so $1.2 \times 10^{-2} \times 6 \times 10^{-4} = 1.2 \times 6 \times 10^{-2} \times 10^{-4}$
>
> $= 7.2 \times 10^{-2+(-4)}$

---

1 Write down the value of ab in standard form if

    a $a = 2.1 \times 10^2$, $b = 4 \times 10^3$

    b $a = 5.4 \times 10^4$, $b = 2 \times 10^5$

    c $a = 7 \times 10^{-2}$, $b = 2.2 \times 10^{-3}$

    d $a = 5 \times 10^{-4}$, $b = 2.3 \times 10^{-2}$

    e $a = 1.6 \times 10^{-2}$, $b = 2 \times 10^4$

    f $a = 6 \times 10^5$, $b = 1.3 \times 10^{-7}$

Find $\dfrac{a}{b}$ when $a = 1.2 \times 10^{-2}$ and $b = 6 \times 10^{-4}$

$$\frac{a}{b} = \frac{1.2 \times 10^{-2}}{6 \times 10^{-4}} = \frac{1.2}{6} \times 10^{-2-(-4)}$$

$$= 0.2 \times 10^2 = 2 \times 10^1$$

---

2 Write down the value of $\dfrac{p}{q}$ in standard form when

    a $p = 6 \times 10^5$, $q = 3 \times 10^2$

    b $p = 1.4 \times 10^8$, $q = 2 \times 10^3$

    c $p = 9 \times 10^3$, $q = 3 \times 10^5$

    d $p = 7 \times 10^{-3}$, $q = 5 \times 10^2$

    e $p = 1.8 \times 10^{-3}$, $q = 6 \times 10^{-4}$

    f $p = 2.5 \times 10^4$, $q = 2 \times 10^{-4}$

Find $a + b$ when $a = 1.2 \times 10^{-2}$ and $b = 6 \times 10^{-4}$.

$a + b = 1.2 \times 10^{-2} + 6 \times 10^{-4}$

> Multiplication must be done before addition, so each number must be written in full.

$= 0.012 + 0.0006$

$= 0.0126 = 1.26 \times 10^{-2}$

3 Write down the value of $x + y$ in standard form when

   a $x = 2 \times 10^2$, $y = 3 \times 10^3$

   b $x = 3 \times 10^{-2}$, $y = 2 \times 10^{-3}$

   c $x = 2.1 \times 10^4$, $y = 3.1 \times 10^5$

   d $x = 1.3 \times 10^{-4}$, $y = 4 \times 10^{-3}$

   e $x = 1.9 \times 10^{-3}$, $y = 2.4 \times 10^{-2}$

   f $x = 3 \times 10^5$, $y = 2.5 \times 10^6$

4 If $x = 1.2 \times 10^5$ and $y = 5 \times 10^{-2}$ find, in standard form, the value of   **a** xy **b** $x \div y$ **c** $x + 1000y$

5 If $m = 7.2 \times 10^{-7}$ and $n = 1.2 \times 10^{-5}$ find, in standard form, the value of   **a** mn **b** $m \div n$ **c** $n - m$

6 If $u = 2.6 \times 10^5$ and $v = 5 \times 10^{-3}$ find, in standard form, the value of

   a uv **b** $u \div v$ **c** $\dfrac{u}{100} + 100v$ **d** $\dfrac{u}{10} - 1000v$

7 If $p = 1.1 \times 10^4$ and $q = 2.2 \times 10^6$ find, in standard form, the value of

   a $p + q$ **b** $\dfrac{q}{p}$ **c** $q - p$ **d** $\dfrac{p + q}{p}$

8 $a = 3 \times 10^{-3}$ and $b = 4 \times 10^{-4}$. Find, in standard form, the value of   **a** $a + 2b$ **b** $100b - a$ **c** $\dfrac{a}{b}$ **d** b^2

9 $P = 4 \times 10^{-2}$ and $T = 5 \times 10^3$. Find, in standard form, the value of

   a PT **b** $\dfrac{T}{P}$ **c** $T + 3P$ **d** $\dfrac{T - 50P}{T}$

10 $S = 8 \times 10^{-3}$ and $r = 1.5 \times 10^{-2}$. Find, in standard form, the value of

   a $S + 2r$ **b** $r - 2S$ **c** $\dfrac{r}{S}$ **d** $\dfrac{4r + S}{S}$

Use your calculator to find $3.057 \times 2.485 \times 10^{-5}$, giving the answer in standard form correct to 3 significant figures.

Estimate: $3.057 \times 2.485 \times 10^{-5} \approx 3 \times 2 \div 100\,000$
$$= 6 \div 100\,000 = 0.000\,06$$

Calculator: $3.057 \times 2.485 \times 10^{-5} = 0.000\,075\,966$

Press   `3.057×2.485 EXP (−)5 =`

$$= 7.60 \times 10^{-5} \ (\,3 \text{ s.f.}\,)$$

This is reasonbly close to the estimate (which we can see is too small because both numbers were rounded down), so it is probably correct.
Notice that the answer is written with a zero at the end. This is to show that the third significant figure is zero.

For questions **11** to **25**, first estimate the answer and then use a calculator to give the answer correct to 3 significant figures.

11 a $6 \times 1.57 \times 10^4$

   b $12.5 \times 5.027 \times 10^3$

   c $0.45 \times 1.39 \times 10^{-4}$

   d $2988 \times 1.05 \times 10^{-3}$

   e $2.5 \div (\,3.1 \times 10^{-5}\,)$

   f $6.78 \div (\,2.05 \times 10^5\,)$

   g $0.055\,75 \div (\,4.035 \times 10^{-3}\,)$

   h $525 \times 2.95 \times 10^{-9}$

   i $36.9 \div (\,1.03 \times 10^5\,)$

   j $205\,000 \div (\,5.8 \times 10^{-10}\,)$

12 Light travels 1 km in about 3.3×10^{-6} seconds.
How long does light take to travel 24.5 kilometres?

13 The distance travelled by light in a vacuum during one year is equal to 9.4650×10^{15} metres. (This is called a light-year.) How far does light travel in 1 second? (1 year $= 365$ days)

14 The special theory of relativity states that a mass m is equivalent to a quantity of energy, E, where $E = mc^2$.
c m/s is the speed of light and $c = 2.998 \times 10^8$.
Find E when $m = 1.66 \times 10^{-27}$.

15 The quantity of nitrate in one bottle of mineral water is 1.5×10^{-3} g. The quantity of nitrate in another bottle of mineral water is 7.3×10^{-4} g.
The two bottles are emptied into the same jug. How much nitrate is there in the water in the jug?

16 At a time when Jupiter, Pluto and the Sun are in line, the distance of Jupiter and Pluto from the Sun are respectively 7.88×10^8 km and 5.95×10^9 km.
What is the distance between Jupiter and Pluto when the two planets and the Sun are in line and the planets

   a are on opposite sides of the Sun

   b are on the same side of the Sun?

17 Two planets A and B are respectively 1.8×10^{11} km and 8.9×10^{10} km from the Sun.

   a How much further is one planet from the Sun than the other?

   b Find the ratio of the distances of A and B from the Sun in the form $1 : n$.

   c If light travels at 3.00×10^5 km/s, find how long it takes to travel from the Sun to the more distant planet.

18 A cylinder of radius r units and length h units has a total surface area, A square units, given by $A = 2\pi r^2 + 2\pi rh$

The individual links in a chain are gold-plated cylinders of radius 2×10^{-4} m and length 8×10^{-4} m.
Find the surface area of gold-plating on

   a one link   **b** 20 000 links.

19 When an amount of money, £P, is invested at compound interest of $r\%$ p.a., the formula $A = P\left(1 + \dfrac{r}{100}\right)^t$ is used to predict the value, £A, of the investment after t years.
The trustees of a pension fund invest $£1.37 \times 10^8$.
Use the formula to predict the value of this fund after 10 years with interest assumed constant at 7.8% p.a.

20 A wire of length L cm, whose cross-section has an area of A cm^2, has a resistance R ohms given by

$$R = \frac{L \times 1.5 \times 10^{-6}}{A}$$

Find R when $L = 54$ and $A = 2.5 \times 10^{-2}$.

21 In 1997, Bestmill Bakery baked 45 million loaves of bread and used 33 700 tonnes of flour.

   a Write 45 million in standard form.

   b Write in standard form the quantity of flour used, in grams.

   c Calculate the average weight of flour used in one loaf.

22 In 1992, 16 million people paid a total of £62 billion in income tax.

   a If 1 billion = 1000 million, give £62 billion in standard form.

   b Find the average amount of tax paid per person.

23 The planet Xeron is 5.87×10^7 km from its sun. The planet Alpha is 2.71×10^8 km from the same sun.

   a Light travels at 3.0×10^5 km/s. Find, to the nearest minute, the time that light takes to travel to Alpha from is sun.

   b Find the difference between the distances of Xeron and Alpha from their sun.

   c Explain why the answer to part **b** does not necessarily give the distance between Xeron and Alpha. Could it give the distance between them? Explain your answer.

24 The mass of a proton is 1.67×10^{-24} grams and the mass of an electron is 9.11×10^{-28} grams.

   a Which has the greater mass, an electron or a proton?

   b Find, in the form $1:n$, the ratio of the mass of an electron to the mass of a proton.

25 The formula $f = \dfrac{1}{2\pi}\sqrt{\dfrac{k}{m}}$ can be used to find the frequency of vibrations in, for example, tuning forks.

   Calculate f when $k = 135$ and $m = 1.5 \times 10^5$.

PUZZLES

1 How long will it take a clock to tick 1 billion seconds if it ticks once every second?

2 If the number $10^{10^{10}}$ is written in full, how many 0s does it have?

3 10^{100} is called a googol. 10^{googol} is called a googolplex. If a googolplex is written out in full, how many zeros does it have?

4 What is the largest number you can write down using just three digits?

PROBABILITY

Fruit machines are a popular way of
losing money. You put a coin in
the machine and push the start button.
This makes three drums rotate
quickly, then slow down and
finally stop. On each drum there
are several fruits. When the
drums stop, three fruits are
shown in the centre of the display.
Depending on what they are,
there may be a prize.

Chris is attracted to fruit machines but has never played them. He will
win a prize on the machine he is looking at if cherries appear on two of
the three drums or lemons show on two of the three drums. Before he
parts with his money, he would like an idea of his chances of winning.

- To do this, he needs to know how to find the probability of combined
  events occuring, such as
    getting either a cherry or a lemon on the first drum,
    getting a cherry on both the first and the second drum.
  Both these examples involve two events, but in different ways.

- The first example concerns either one or the other event occurring,
  whereas the second example concerns both events happening.

EXERCISE 4A   Each sentence describes a situation where two events are involved.
Discuss what the events are and whether they fall into the 'either . . . or'
category or into the 'both . . . and' category.

1   An ordinary six-sided dice is rolled and scores five or six.

2   Two dice are rolled and a double six is scored.

3   Tim picked a box from a lucky dip; some boxes contain a prize and
the others are empty.

4   The England cricket captain tosses a coin to find out who has the
choice to bat or to field.

**MUTUALLY
EXCLUSIVE
EVENTS**

When an ordinary dice is rolled, it is possible to score either a five or a six. It is not possible to score both a five and a six. Such events, where it is not possible for both to happen on the same occasion, are called *mutually exclusive*.

**INDEPENDENT
EVENTS**

When two ordinary dice are rolled, it is possible to score any number from 1 to 6 on the first dice and any number from 1 to 6 on the second dice. The score obtained on the second dice is not affected in any way by the score on the first dice. Such events, where both may happen on the same occasion but each has no influence on the outcome of the other, are called *independent events*.

EXERCISE 4B

Decide whether the events described cannot both happen or can both happen independently of each other.

1 **a** Mona and Clive each buy a ticket for a raffle.

 b One of them wins first prize.

2 Two coins are tossed.

 a The first coin lands head up or tail up.

 b Both coins land head up.

3 A 10 pence coin is tossed and a dice is rolled.

 a The coin lands head up and an even number is scored on the dice.

 b A three or a six is scored on the dice.

4 A blue bag and a red bag each contain a large number of coins, some of which are counterfeit. One coin is selected at random from each bag.

 a The coin taken from the blue bag is counterfeit or not counterfeit.

 b Both coins are counterfeit.

5 Sax Airport has 100 scheduled flights due to depart on Saturday.

   a Two or three flights are cancelled.

   b One flight is cancelled because the plane is faulty and another flight is cancelled because of a hurricane at its destination.

ADDING PROBABILITIES

When two events cannot both happen at the same time, we find the probability that one or the other may happen by adding the probabilities that each happens on its own.

For example, if we select a card at random from a pack of 52, the probability of drawing an ace is $\frac{4}{52}$ and the probability of drawing a black king is $\frac{2}{52}$.

Now drawing either an ace or a black king involves two events that cannot both happen since it is impossible to draw one card which is both an ace and a black king.

There are 4 aces and 2 black kings so if we want to find the probability of drawing either an ace or a black king there are 6 cards that we would count as 'successful', therefore

$$P(\text{ace or a black king}) = \frac{6}{52}$$

> Remember that the probability that an event A will happen is $P(A)$
>
> where $P(A) = \dfrac{\text{the number of ways in which } A \text{ can occur}}{\text{the total number of equally likely outcomes}}$

$P(\text{ace}) = \frac{4}{52}$ and $P(\text{black king}) = \frac{2}{52}$

Since $\frac{6}{52} = \frac{4}{52} + \frac{2}{52}$ it follows that

$$P(\text{ace or black king}) = P(\text{ace}) + P(\text{black king})$$

Now consider the probability of scoring 5 or 6 when a dice is rolled once.

$$P(\text{score 5 or 6}) = \frac{2}{6}$$

From one roll of a dice, a score of 5 and a score of 6 cannot both happen, and $P(\text{score 5}) = \frac{1}{6}$ and $P(\text{score 6}) = \frac{1}{6}$

i.e. $\quad P(\text{score 5 or 6}) = \frac{2}{6} = \frac{1}{6} + \frac{1}{6}$

$$= P(\text{score 5}) + P(\text{score 6}).$$

From these examples we see that

> if A and B cannot both happen at the same time
> then $P(A \text{ or } B) = P(A) + P(B)$

EXERCISE 4C   Do not use a calculator.

1 A card is drawn at random from an ordinary pack of 52 playing cards. What is the probability that the card is

   a a red ace   **b** a black king   **c** a red ace or a black king?

2 Gemma rolls an ordinary dice once. What is the probability that the number shown will be

   a 2   **b** 3 or 4   **c** 2, 3 or 4?

3 A card is drawn at random from the 12 court cards (jacks, queens and kings). What is the probability that the card will be

   a a black jack

   b a red queen

   c either a black jack or a red queen?

4 Graham is looking for his house key. The probability that he left it in his office is $\frac{5}{9}$, while the probability that he left it in the car is $\frac{1}{13}$. What is the probability that

   a the key is either in his office or in the car

   b the key is somewhere else?

5 When Mrs George goes shopping the probability that she returns by bus is $\frac{3}{7}$, in a taxi $\frac{1}{7}$, on foot $\frac{5}{14}$. What is the probability that she returns

   a by bus or taxi   **b** by bus or on foot?

6 Jo has a bag containing some coloured discs. When a disc is drawn from the bag the probability that it will be a red disc is $\frac{2}{7}$, a white disc $\frac{2}{9}$ and a blue disc $\frac{1}{4}$. Jo offers the bag to Nia who draws one disc.
Find the probability that the colour of this disc will be

   a red or white   **c** red, white or blue

   b white or blue   **d** some other colour.

7 Maarit rolls an ordinary dice. What is the probability that the number on the dice will be

   a an even number   **b** a prime number   **c** either even or prime?

   Your answer to part **c** should not be the sum of the answers to parts **a** and **b**. Why not?

MULTIPLICATION OF PROBABILITIES

When two events can both happen, but neither has any effect on the outcome of the other, we find the probability that both happen by multiplying the probabilities that each happens on its own.

For example, when a coin is tossed and a dice is rolled, we can use a table to list all the possible outcomes:

Dice

		1	2	3	4	5	6
Coin	H	H,1	H,2	H,3	H,4	H,5	H,6
	T	T,1	T,2	T,3	T,4	T,5	T,6

From the table we can see that

$$P(\text{a head and an even number}) = \tfrac{3}{12} = \tfrac{1}{4}$$

Now a head from one toss of the coin and an even number from one throw of the dice can both happen independently of each other, where

$$P(\text{a head}) = \tfrac{1}{2} \quad \text{and} \quad P(\text{an even number}) = \tfrac{3}{6} = \tfrac{1}{2}$$

But

$$P(\text{a head and an even number}) = \tfrac{1}{4} = \tfrac{1}{2} \times \tfrac{1}{2}$$
$$= P(\text{a head}) \times P(\text{an even number})$$

From this example we see that

> if A and B can both happen independently of each other then
> $$P(A \text{ and } B) = P(A) \times P(B)$$

EXERCISE 4D

Do not use a calculator.

1 Two coins are tossed. What is the probability that they will both land head up?

2 Two dice are tossed. Find the probability of getting a double six.

3 Peter has two tubes of Smarties. Each tube contains 10 red Smarties and 30 Smarties of other colours. Peter takes one Smartie, chosen at random, from each tube. Find

 a the probability that a red Smartie is taken from a tube

 b the probability that a Smartie other than a red one is taken from a tube

 c the probability that both Smarties removed are not red.

4 The probability that Heather will win the girls' 100 m is $\frac{2}{5}$ and the probability that Colin will win the boys' 100 m is $\frac{3}{5}$. What is the probability that

    a both of them will win their events

    b neither of them will win their event?

5 A mother has an equal chance of giving birth to a boy or a girl. Jane plans to have two children. What is the probability that

    a the first will be a girl

    b both will be boys

    c neither will be a boy?

6 A bag contains 3 red sweets and 2 green sweets. Camilla takes one sweet at random and eats it. She then takes another sweet, also at random.

    a Find the probability that both sweets removed are red.

    b Explain why, in this case, the multiplication rule does not give the correct answer to part **a**.

EXERCISE 4E

Do not use a calculator.
Some of the events described in this exercise cannot both happen and others can, but independently of each other.

1 A red dice and a blue dice are rolled. Find the probability of getting

    a a 5 or a 6 on the red dice   **c** a 2 on both dice

    b a 1 or a 2 on the blue dice   **d** an even number on both dice.

2 A card is drawn at random from an ordinary pack of 52 playing cards. What is the probability that the card will be

    a a 2   **b** a red ace   **c** a 2 or a red ace?

3 When Kim goes to Weightwatchers the probability that she will return on foot is $\frac{1}{3}$, by bus $\frac{1}{5}$ and in a friends' car $\frac{1}{5}$. What is the probability that she will return

    a by bus or in a friends' car   **b** on foot or by bus?

4 A pack of cards is cut, reshuffled and cut again. What is the probability that

    a the first card cut is an ace or a king

    b the second card cut is an ace or a king

    c both cards cut are aces?

5 The probability that Sam will complete the 5000 m race is 0.9 and the probability that Mike will complete it is 0.6. What is the probability that both Sam and Mike will complete the 5000 m race?

6 An ordinary dice is weighted so that when it is rolled, it is not equally likely that it will show 1, 2, 3, 4, 5 or 6. The table shows the probabilities for each score.

Score	1	2	3	4	5	6
Probability	0.2	0.2	0.3	0.1	0.1	0.1

The dice is rolled once. What is the probability that it will show either 3 or 4?

7 When David throws a dart at this board,
the probability that he hits the bull's eye is 0.1,
the probability that he misses the bull's eye but hits the board is 0.7,
the probability that he misses the board completely is 0.2.

David throws two darts. Find the probability that

a with his first dart, he hits the board somewhere

b he misses the board completely with both darts.

8 Two fair dice are to be rolled. What is the probability that the total score shown by the two dice is 12?

9 Harry has a choice of three ways of going to work. He can either go by bus or by train or he can cycle. The bus journey takes 20 minutes if there is no delay. The train journey takes 30 minutes if there is no delay. It takes 25 minutes for Harry to cycle to work and he is never delayed. The probability that Harry will go by bus is $\frac{2}{3}$ and the probability that he will be delayed is $\frac{1}{4}$. The probability that Harry goes by train is $\frac{1}{6}$ and the probability that he is delayed is $\frac{1}{8}$.

a What is the probability that Harry goes to work by bus and is delayed?

b What is the probability that Harry goes to work by bus or by train?

c What is the probability that Harry is delayed on his journey to work?

TREE DIAGRAMS   When two coins are tossed, one possible outcome is a head and a tail. This outcome involves two events but they do not fit neatly into the 'either...or' category or the 'both...and' category.

This is because a head and a tail can be obtained by getting

> **either** a head on the first coin **and** a tail on the second,
> **or** a tail on the first coin **and** a head on the second.

So getting a head and a tail when two coins are tossed involves a mixture of 'both...and' and 'either...or' events and we need an organised method to deal with such a combination. One such method is to draw up a table showing all the equally likely outcomes, but this method cannot be used if all the possible outcomes are not equally likely; for example, the possible outcomes when two people take a driving test.

Suppose next that three coins are tossed and we want the probability of getting 2 heads and a tail. Three events are involved here so, again, we cannot use a table to list all the outcomes because a table can only cope with two events.

These examples show that we need a different way of listing outcomes and finding probabilities. We saw, in Book 9B, that we can use a tree diagram to list outcomes. A tree diagram can also be used to find probabilities. We will illustrate this method with a simple example.

Suppose that we have two discs, a red one marked A on one side and B on the other, and a blue one marked E on one side and F on the other. Tossing the red disc, the probability that we get A is $\frac{1}{2}$ and the probability that we get B is also $\frac{1}{2}$.

This information can be shown in the following diagram: the event is written at the end of the branch and the probability that it will happen is written on the branch.

Suppose that the red disc shows A and we go on to toss the blue disc. The probability of getting E is $\frac{1}{2}$ and the probability of getting F is $\frac{1}{2}$.

We can add this information to the diagram.

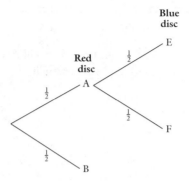

We complete the diagram by considering what the probabilities are if the red disc shows a B before we toss the blue disc.

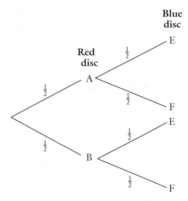

Diagrams like this are called *tree diagrams*.

To use the tree diagram to find the probability that we get first an A and then an E, follow the path from left to right for an A on the first branch and an E on the second. The two probabilities we find there are $\frac{1}{2}$ and $\frac{1}{2}$. The blue disc landing showing E is independent of the letter obtained on the red disc so we multiply the probabilities together to get $\frac{1}{4}$.

To find the probability that we get a B on the red disc and an F on the blue one, follow the B and F path and multiply the probabilities,

i.e. $P(B \text{ and } F) = \frac{1}{2} \times \frac{1}{2}$

$$= \frac{1}{4}$$

In general

we multiply probabilities when we follow a path along branches.

EXERCISE 4F

A coin is tossed and a dice is thrown. Find the probability that

a the coin will land head up and the dice will not show a six
b the coin will land tail up and the dice will show a six.

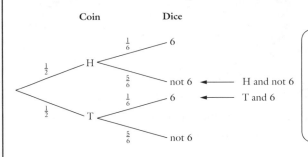

There are only 2 possible outcomes when the coin is tossed; so we need two 'branches' to show these. There are six possible outcomes when the dice is thrown, but we only need to consider these in two groups, throwing a six or not throwing a six, and we need only two branches to show these.

a $P(H \text{ and not } 6) = \frac{1}{2} \times \frac{5}{6} = \frac{5}{12}$ **b** $P(T \text{ and } 6) = \frac{1}{2} \times \frac{1}{6} = \frac{1}{12}$

1 The probability that Mark gets to work on time is $\frac{7}{8}$ and the probability that he leaves work on time is $\frac{3}{5}$.

a Find the probability that he does not leave work on time.

b Copy and complete the given probability tree.

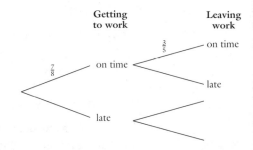

What is the probability that

c Mark gets to work on time but does not leave on time

d Mark is late for work but leaves on time?

2 The first of two boxes of tennis balls contains one white and two yellow balls; the second box contains three yellow and two lime green balls. A ball is taken at random from each box.

a Copy and complete the tree diagram.

Find the probability that

b both balls are yellow

c one is white and one is lime green.

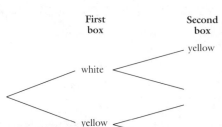

3 When a drawing pin falls to the ground the probability that it will land point up is 0.2.

a Find the probability that a pin does not land point up.

Two drawing pins fall one after the other.

b Copy and complete the tree diagram.

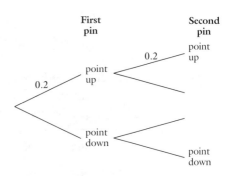

Find the probability that

c both drawing pins land point up

d both drawing pins do not land point up.

4 Two soldiers fire at a target. The probability that Becker will hit the target is 0.5 and the probability that Crossley will not hit the target is 0.3. Becker fires at the target first, then Crossley fires.
Draw a tree diagram to show the possibilities and use it to find the probability that

a both Becker and Crossley will hit the target

b neither will hit the target

c Becker will hit the target but Crossley will miss

d Crossley will hit the target but Becker will miss.

Two coins are tossed. Find the probability that they land showing a head and a tail.

We start by drawing a tree diagram.

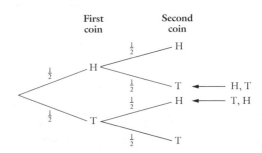

We can see that there are two paths through the tree that give a head and a tail where

$$P(\text{H on first coin and T on the second}) = P(H, T) = \tfrac{1}{2} \times \tfrac{1}{2} = \tfrac{1}{4}$$

$$P(\text{T on first coin and H on the second}) = P(T, H) = \tfrac{1}{2} \times \tfrac{1}{2} = \tfrac{1}{4}$$

Now the coins can land showing either H, T or T, H but these cannot both happen at the same time. Therefore we can find $P(H, T \text{ or } T, H)$ by adding the probabilities at the ends of the two paths, i.e. $P(H \text{ and } T) = \tfrac{1}{4} + \tfrac{1}{4} = \tfrac{1}{2}$.

$$P(H \text{ and } T) = (\tfrac{1}{2} \times \tfrac{1}{2}) + (\tfrac{1}{2} \times \tfrac{1}{2}) = \tfrac{1}{4} + \tfrac{1}{4} = \tfrac{1}{2}$$

The worked example illustrates the general rule that

> we *multiply* the probabilities when we follow a path along the branches and *add* the results of following several paths.

5 The probability that my bus has to wait at the traffic lights in the morning on the way to school is $\frac{1}{5}$. Draw a probability tree to show the possibilities that the bus has to wait or can drive through the traffic lights on two consecutive mornings.
Find the probability that, on two consecutive mornings, the bus

a will have to wait at the lights on both occasions

b will not have to wait on either morning

c will have to wait on just one morning.

6 a If a dice is rolled what is the probability of getting

   i a six   **ii** a number other than six?

b Two dice, a red and a blue, are rolled. Draw a tree diagram to show the possibilities of getting a six or not getting a six on each dice.
Find the probability that

   i both dice show sixes

   ii the red dice gives a six but the blue dice does not

   iii the blue dice gives a six but the red dice does not

   iv just one six appears.

7 In a group of six girls, four are fair and two are dark. Of five boys, two are fair and three are dark. One boy and one girl are picked at random. What is the probability, that of the two pupils picked, one is fair and one is dark?

8 In a class of 20, four pupils are left-handed. In a second class of 24, six pupils are left-handed. One pupil is chosen at random from each class. What is the probability that one of the pupils is left-handed and one is not?

9 Derek and Alexis keep changing their minds about whether to send Christmas cards to each other. In any one year, the probability that Derek sends a card is $\frac{3}{4}$ and that Alexis sends one is $\frac{5}{6}$.
Draw a probability tree and use it to find the probability that next year

a they will both send cards

b only one of them will send a card

c neither will send a card.

What should the three answers add up to and why?

10 Copy the probability tree in the worked example on page 81 and, by adding more branches to the right, extend it to show the following information: three unbiased coins are tossed, one after the other. Find the probability that

a three heads appear   **b** three tails appear

c two heads and one tail appear in any order.

11 The weather forecast suggests that the probability that it will rain on Saturday is 0.07 and the probability that it will not rain on Sunday is 0.89.

a On which of these two days is it more likely to rain? Give a reason for your answer.

b Copy and complete this tree diagram.

c Use your tree diagram to find the probability, correct to 3 d.p., that it will rain on

  i both days   **ii** just one of the days.

d The probability that it will rain on Monday is 0.3. Add more branches to your tree to include Monday.

e Use your new tree to find the probability, correct to 3 d.p., that it will rain on

  i none of the three days   **ii** at least one of the three days.

12 In a group of 120 girls, 24 have blue eyes, 48 have hazel eyes, 36 have green eyes and the remainder have brown eyes. All the girls have either long hair or short hair and the probability that a given girl has long hair is 0.25. The probability that a girl has freckles is 0.65. Assume that each attribute is independent of the others.

a Copy and complete this tree diagram.

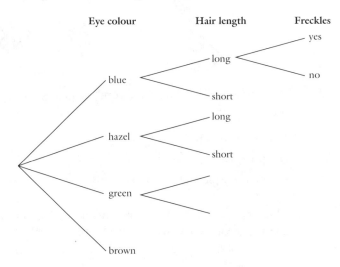

b What is the probability that a girl chosen at random from this group has

  i brown eyes, freckles and short hair

  ii long hair, no freckles and either blue or green eyes?

The next exercise contains mixed problems on probability. Some of the questions can be answered directly from the basic definition of probability and some can be answered using the sum and product rules; draw a tree diagram or a possibility table only when you think it is needed.

EXERCISE 4G

1 A letter is picked at random from the word CATASTROPHE. Find the probability that

a the letter is a vowel   **b** the letter is A or T.

2 A knitting wool sample card has 1 green, 1 black, 4 blue and 2 red samples. If one sample is picked at random, what is the probability that it is

a yellow   **b** black, green, red or blue?

3 The score on a four-sided spinner is 1, 2, 3 or 4. On a second spinner the score is 5, 6, 7 or 8. If the two are spun, find the probability that

a the score on both spinners is odd

b the score on both spinners is even

c the score on neither spinner is prime.

4

A sector is chosen at random from each circle. What is the probability that

a both sectors picked are purple

b both sectors picked are white

c one is purple and the other not?

5 There are two bags. The first contains 2 white and 3 black marbles and the second contains 1 red and 2 blue marbles. Two marbles are drawn, one from each bag. Find the probability that

a a white and a blue marble are drawn

b a black and a red marble are drawn

c neither a white marble nor a red marble is drawn.

6 In a game of skittles the probability that Ted scores more than 5 is $\frac{2}{7}$ and the probability that George scores more than 5 is $\frac{2}{9}$. Ted goes first followed by George. Use a probability tree to find the probability that

a both Ted and George score more than 5

b Ted scores more than 5 but George does not

c both score 5 or less

d one scores more than 5 but the other does not.

7 The table shows the distribution of the colours of sweets in a tube.

Yellow	Green	Red
6	4	10

The sweets are in random order in the tube.
Alison opens the tube and takes out the first sweet.
What is the probability that it is not green?

8 Twenty cards are placed face down on a table. The backs of the cards are all plain white. The fronts of the cards are either blue, purple or yellow and each has the number 1, 2, 3, 4 or 5 printed on it.
One card is chosen at random and turned over.
The tables give the probability that it is purple, blue or yellow and that the number on it is 1, 2, 3, 4 or 5.

Colour	Probability
purple	0.3
yellow	0.4
blue	0.3

Number	Probability
1	0.1
2	0.2
3	0.4
4	0.1
5	0.2

Six of these cards are purple. The diagram shows the number printed on each of the purple cards.

What is the probability that the first card turned over is

a not purple   **b** has the number 5 printed on it

c purple or has the number 5 on it or both?

9 The diagram shows two bags of sweets.
Vejay takes one sweet out of each bag.
Use a tree diagram to find the probability
that he takes out one white sweet and
one purple sweet in any order.

10 A manufacturer makes light bulbs. The probability that one of these
light bulbs is faulty is 0.01.

a Two thousand of these light bulbs are made each day.
Approximately, how many of them are expected to be faulty?
Explain why your answer is not certain to be the exact number
that are faulty.

b Three of these light bulbs are taken at random and inspected.
Use a tree diagram to find the probability that just one of them is
faulty.

11 Peter and Rajiv sold tickets for a raffle. No one else sold tickets.
Peter had a blue book of tickets numbered 1 to 500 and Rajiv had a
yellow book of tickets also numbered 1 to 500.
When the selling stopped, Peter had sold all of his tickets and Rajiv
had sold the first 400 of his tickets.

a What is the probability that blue ticket number 1 wins first prize?
Give your answer as a decimal correct to 3 decimal places.

b What is the probability that either the blue or yellow ticket
number 1 wins first prize? Give your answer as a decimal correct
to 3 decimal places.

c Peter said to Rajiv, 'The winning ticket has got to be either blue
or yellow, so the probability that a yellow ticket wins is $\frac{1}{2}$'. Why
is he wrong?

12 Give answers as decimals, correct to
3 decimal places where necessary.
This roulette wheel has the numbers
0 to 35 marked round the inside edge.
A ball is spun inside the wheel and finally
comes to rest against one of the numbers.
The wheel is used for a game in a school fair. A fee of 20 pence is
charged to have a go at spinning the wheel. A prize of £1 is given if
the ball comes to rest against a number ending in 5.

a John has one turn. What is the probability that he will win a prize?

b Amy has two turns. What is the probability that she will not win
a prize?

c There are 740 turns at this game. How much profit should the
school make?

13 A company selling cans of a cola drink has a special promotion.
If, when the can is opened, the ring-pull has a blue circle on its underside, there is a prize. Grant bought a 'six-pack' and won a prize with one of the six cans. He said, 'This shows that the probability of winning a prize is 1 in 6'. Is he right? Explain your answer.

14 Sally and Debbie play a game with two coins.
Sally tosses the two coins. If they both land the same way up, she wins. Otherwise Debbie wins. Who is more likely to win and why?

INVESTIGATION

An agricultural society wishes to hold a two-day show in September at one of four possible venues. The table shows the number of days it rained each week in September, at the four different places, over the last four years.

Venue	A				B				C				D			
Year	1995	1996	1997	1998	1995	1996	1997	1998	1995	1996	1997	1998	1995	1996	1997	1998
Week 1	2	3	2	1	2	2	0	2	2	3	1	2	2	3	3	2
Week 2	1	2	2	0	3	1	0	2	1	2	1	1	1	2	2	2
Week 3	2	3	1	1	2	0	1	2	2	2	1	1	2	3	2	1
Week 4	2	3	0	1	2	2	1	2	1	2	2	1	1	3	2	2

a Investigate the probability that it will be dry at venue A on any one day during the first week of September.

b What about a day during the second, third or fourth week?

c Repeat parts **a** and **b** for the other three venues.

d What is the probability that it will be dry on two consecutive days at venue A during the first week in September?

e Repeat part **d** for other weeks and other venues.

f What is the probability that at venue A, on two consecutive days during the first week in September, it will be
  i dry on the first day but not on the second
  ii dry on one of the two days but not on the other?

g Repeat part **f** for other weeks and venues.

h Which week and venue would you recommend to the organisers? Justify your answer. Would they be certain to get at least one dry day?

i Investigate the increased chance that it will be dry for two consecutive days during the driest week at the chosen venue than during the wettest week anywhere.

SEQUENCES

5

Rory King designs patterns
for gardens using square
paving slabs of side 50 cm.
He has slabs of different
colours and colour
codes them C1,
C2, C3 .... One

of the simplest designs he uses has a stone urn or statue on the centre of a
square area. First he lays one slab, colour C1, at the centre of the design,
then one slab of colour C2 at each side of slab C1, followed by one slab
of colour C3 at each outside edge of the slabs of colour C2, and so on.
The sketches show the patterns when the design uses 3 colours and when
it uses 5 colours.

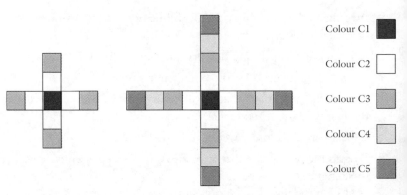

Colour C1

Colour C2

Colour C3

Colour C4

Colour C5

Rory has to adapt this design for square lawns of different sizes. To do
this he needs to know

- whether the number of slabs needed to go from one edge of the
  square lawn to the other can be either even or odd
- how many different colours are needed if exactly N slabs are required
  to go from one side of the lawn to the other
- how many slabs are needed altogether
- how many slabs of each colour are needed.

To solve these problems Rory needs to extend his knowledge of
sequences.

FINDING TERMS
IN A SEQUENCE
A sequence can be formed by starting with a number and then following a rule.

For example, the instruction could be

add 3 to the previous term, then multiply by 2.

If the first number in the sequence is 3, the next term is $(3+3) \times 2 = 12$, the following term is $(12+3) \times 2 = 30$, and so on. The first 5 terms are $3, 12, 30, 66, 138, \ldots$

EXERCISE 5A

1 The rule for giving a sequence is 'add 1 to the previous term, then multiply by 3'. If the first term is 2 write down the next four terms.

2 The rule for giving a sequence is 'subtract 1 from the previous term, then multiply by 3'. If the first term is 3 write down the next four terms.

3 A sequence obeys the rule 'multiply the previous term by 2, then add 3'. The first term is 2. Write down the first five terms of the sequence.

4 The first two terms of a sequence are 1, 1, and rule for generating this sequence is 'add the previous two terms together'. Write down the first seven terms of this sequence.

The rule for giving a sequence is 'multiply the previous term by 2, then subtract 1'.

The second term in the sequence is 9. What is the first term?

To find the first term, or starting number, the rule must be applied in reverse to the second number, 9.

i.e.   we must add 1, then divide by 2.

∴ the first term, or starting number,
   is $(9+1) \div 2 = 5$

(Check by applying the rule to the first number. Second number is $5 \times 2 - 1 = 9$)

> Alternatively we can use algebra.
> If the first term is x, the next term is $2x - 1$,
>
> i.e. $2x - 1 = 9$
> $2x = 10 \Rightarrow x = 5$
>
> ∴ the first term is 5.

5 The rule for giving a sequence is 'add 1 to the previous term, then multiply by 3'. The second number in this sequence is 12. Find the first number.

6 The rule for giving a sequence is 'add 2 to the previous term, then multiply by 2'. The second number in this sequence is 14. Find the first number.

7 The second term of a sequence is 18 and the rule for giving the sequence is 'subtract 1 from the previous term, then multiply by 3'. Find the first number.

8 The second number in a sequence is 11. The sequence is given by the rule 'multiply the previous term by 2, then add 3'. Find the first number.

9 The rule for giving a sequence is 'multiply the previous term by 3, then subtract 4'. Using this rule the third term in a sequence is 20.
Find **a** the second term **b** the first term.

10 The rule for giving a sequence is 'add the two previous terms'. The fourth term is 8 and the fifth term is 13. Find the first three terms of the sequence.

Give the first four terms of the sequence in which the nth term is $(n+2)(n+3)$.

The first term in the sequence is the value of $(n+2)(n+3)$
when $n=1$, i.e. $3 \times 4 = 12$
Similarly the second term is $4 \times 5 = 20$
    the third term is $5 \times 6 = 30$
   and the fourth term is $6 \times 7 = 42$.
The sequence is $12, 20, 30, 42, \ldots$

---

11 Give the first four terms of the sequence in which the nth term is

  a $2n+1$ **c** $(n-1)(n+1)$ **e** $(n+1)(2n-1)$

  b $2n$ **d** n^2-1 **f** $\dfrac{n}{(n+1)}$

12 A boy is given a large bar of chocolate and decides to make it last by eating half of what is left each day. This means that he eats half the bar on the first day; half of half of the bar on the second day; half of a quarter of the bar on the third day, and so on.
Write down the sequence giving the fraction of the bar that is left at the end of the first, second, third, fourth and fifth days.
In theory, how long will the bar last?

FINDING THE PATTERN IN A SEQUENCE

In the last exercise, each question gave a rule for continuing a sequence. When you need to find a rule for continuing a sequence, look for similar rules. Asking yourself the following questions may help.

- Is the next term obtained by always adding the same number to the previous term or subtracting the same number from the previous term?
- Is the next term always obtained by multiplying the previous term by the same number?
- Is every term obtained by adding the two previous terms?
- Are squares of numbers involved?

EXERCISE 5B

1 Write down, in words, a rule to give each sequence.

a $5, 11, 17, 23, 29, \ldots$ **c** $3, 9, 27, 81, \ldots$

b $12, 5, -2, -9, \ldots$ **d** $40, 20, 10, 5, 2.5, \ldots$

2 Find the next two terms in the following sequences.

a $3, 7, 11, 15, \ldots$ **d** $24, 19, 14, 9, \ldots$

b $3, -6, 12, -24, \ldots$ **e** $1, \frac{1}{3}, \frac{1}{9}, \frac{1}{27}, \ldots$

c $4, 9, 16, 25, \ldots$ **f** $2, 4, 6, 10, 16, 26, \ldots$

DIFFERENCES

Sometimes the rule or formula to find the next few terms in a sequence is not easy to spot. In this case a difference table may be helpful.
We start with a simple example that you can probably 'spot' but it illustrates the difference method.

Consider the sequence $5, \quad 9, \quad 13, \quad 17, \quad 21, \ldots$
The differences between the terms are $4 \quad 4 \quad 4 \quad 4$

The difference between consecutive terms is 4 so the sequence continues $25, 29, 33, \ldots$

Now consider the sequences $5, 6, 9, 14, 21, \ldots$ which is not as easy to 'spot'.

The terms are	5	6	9	14	21
1st difference		1	3	5	7
2nd difference			2	2	2

> These differences are not all equal so we continue the process one step further.

We can now rewrite these three lines, add more 2s to the third line and work back to the first line.

$$5 \quad 6 \quad 9 \quad 14 \quad 21 \quad 30 \to 41 \to 54$$
$$\nearrow \quad \nearrow \quad \nearrow$$
1st difference $1 \quad 3 \quad 5 \quad 7 \to 9 \to 11 \to 13$
$$\searrow\nearrow \quad \nearrow \quad \nearrow$$
2nd difference $2 \quad 2 \quad 2 \quad 2 \to 2 \to 2$

We now see that the sequence is $5, 6, 9, 14, 21, 30, 41, 54, \ldots$

EXERCISE 5C   In the questions that follow use differences, if necessary, to find the next two terms in each sequence.

1 a 5, 7, 9, 11, 13, ...   **d** −3, 0, 5, 12, 21, ...

   b 2, 5, 8, 11, 14, ...   **e** 2, 6, 12, 20, 30, ...

   c 2, 7, 12, 17, ...   **f** 0, 2, 6, 12, 20, ...

2 a 11, 15, 19, 23, ...   **d** 7, 13, 23, 37, 55, ...

   b 4, 7, 12, 19, 28, ...   **e** 0, 4, 10, 18, 28, ...

   c 1, 7, 17, 31, 49, ...   **f** 3, 4, 7, 12, 19, ...

3 a 8, 11, 16, 23, 32, ...   **d** 9, 15, 27, 45, 69, ...

   b 4, 5, 10, 19, 32, ...   **e** 1, 2, 5, 10, 17, ...

   c 2, 7, 15, 26, 40, ...   **f** 5, 0, −4, −7, −9, ...

Look at this sequence of numbers

$$9, 12, 18, 30, 54, \ldots$$

Write down, in words, a rule for getting this sequence.

This pattern is not obvious so we would try differences.

$$\begin{array}{ccccccccc} 9 & & 12 & & 18 & & 30 & & 54 \ldots \\ & 3 & & 6 & & 12 & & 24 & \end{array}$$

> Each term in the difference row is twice the previous one, i.e. the difference is doubled each time so, starting with 9 we add 3 to get 12, then double 3 added to 12 gives 18; double 6 and added to 18 gives 30, and so on.

The rule for getting this sequence is

start with 9, add 3, and then double the amount added each time.

> As an alternative we can get any term by doubling the previous term and subtracting 6, i.e. starting with 9, the terms are $2 \times 9 - 6 = 12$, $2 \times 12 - 6 = 18$, $2 \times 18 - 6 = 30, \ldots$

---

4 In this question write down, in words, a rule for getting the sequence.

   a 3, 7, 15, 31, 63, ...   **c** 3, 5, 9, 17, 33, 65, ...

   b 4, 5, 7, 11, 19, 35, ...   **d** 2, 5, 11, 23, 47, ...

5 In this question write down the next two terms in each sequence. The difference method will not help you to find the next two terms for some of these sequences.

a $5, 9, 16, 26, \ldots$ **d** $1 + 3, 1 + 3 + 5, 1 + 3 + 5 + 7, \ldots$

b $4, 5, 9, 14, 23, \ldots$ **e** $6, 9, 14, 21, 30, \ldots$

c $3, 10, 18, 27, \ldots$ **f** $\frac{7}{5}, \frac{4}{3}, \frac{9}{7}, \frac{5}{4}, \frac{11}{9}, \ldots$

6 The numbers $31, 45, 3, 17, 25, 10, 38$ when written in order of size, smallest first, would form a sequence if the value of one of them was changed. Find which one should be changed and give its correct value.

7 The numbers $97, 7, 2, 19, 137, 64, 35, 184$ when written in order of size, smallest first, would form a sequence if the value of one of them was changed. Find which one should be changed and give its correct value.

8 In a sequence the nth term is given by the expression $3n - 4$.

a Find the 50th term.

b Find the value of n if the nth term is 293.

c What is the largest value of n if the nth term is less than 1000?

9 In a sequence the nth term is given by the expression $5n + 3$.

a Find the 75th term.

b Find the value of n if the nth term is 188.

c What is the smallest value of n if the nth term is greater than 500?

10 Consider the sequence $2, 7, 12, 17, \ldots$

a Write down the next two terms and give the rule used to obtain them.

b Give the first five terms of the sequence formed by multiplying each term of the given sequence by the term following it. (The first term is 2×7, i.e. 14.)

c Use differences on the first five terms of the new sequence formed in the previous part of this question, to find the sixth and seventh terms.
Check that you are correct by using the rule given in parts **a** and **b**.

d Give the first five terms of the sequence formed by adding each term of the original sequence to the term following it.

11 The rule for giving a sequence is

each term is the sum of the two previous terms.

Using this rule write down the first six terms of a sequence if the first two terms are

a 1, 3   **b** 2, 3   **c** 3, 4

12 Find the first and second differences for the sequence you obtained in question **11** part **a**. What do you notice?
Does the same thing happen if you use the sequence obtained for question **11** part **b**?

FINDING A FORMULA FOR THE nTH TERM

When the pattern in a sequence is recognised, an expression for the nth term can often be found.
Consider the sequence $5, 7, 9, 11, \ldots$
We need to find the relationship between each term and the number n that gives its position.
It is helpful to start by making a table of values of n, and the corresponding terms in the sequence.

n	1	2	3	4	$\ldots$
nth term	5	7	9	11	
1st difference		2	2	2	2

Since the first difference is always 2, the nth term is of the form $2n + b$.
If $n = 1$ the 1st term is $2 \times 1 + b$

But the 1st term is 5

so $2 + b = 5$
i.e. $b = 3$
so nth term $= 2n + 3$

Check: $n = 1$, 1st term $= 2 \times 1 + 3 = 5$
        $n = 2$, 2nd term $= 2 \times 2 + 3 = 7$
        $n = 3$, 3rd term $= 2 \times 3 + 3 = 9$
        $n = 4$, 4th term $= 2 \times 4 + 3 = 11$

> When the first differences have the same value, a, the expression for the nth term is always of the form $an + b$ where b is a number to be found.

An expression for the nth term of some sequences can be seen easily by inspection. For example, the nth term of the sequence
$1 \times 2, 2 \times 3, 3 \times 4, 4 \times 5, \ldots$ is obviously $n \times (n + 1)$

EXERCISE 5D

Find a formula for the nth term of the sequence

a $5, 8, 11, 14, \ldots$ **b** $2 \times 3, \ 3 \times 4, \ 4 \times 5, \ldots$

a We can draw up a table for this sequence.

n	1	2	3	4
nth term	5	8	11	14
1st difference		3	3	3

Since the first differences are 3 the expression for the nth term is $3n + b$.

But the 1st term is 5

Hence $3 \times 1 + b = 5$

i.e. $b = 2$

$\therefore \quad n$th term $= 3n + 2$

Check: 1st term $= 3 \times 1 + 2 = 5$, 2nd term $= 3 \times 2 + 2 = 8$

b

n	1	2	3
nth term	2×3	3×4	4×5

Each term is the product of the two integers that follow the position numbers.

Hence nth term $= (n + 1)(n + 2)$

Check: 1st term $= (1 + 1) \times (1 + 2) = 2 \times 3$

2nd term $= (2 + 1) \times (2 + 2) = 3 \times 4$

Find a formula for the nth term of each of the following sequences.

1 a $5, 7, 9, 11, \ldots$ **d** $9, 16, 23, 30, \ldots$

    b $0, 3, 6, 9, 12, \ldots$ **e** $2, 11, 20, 29, \ldots$

    c $7, 11, 15, 19, \ldots$ **f** $3 \times 5, \ 4 \times 6, \ 5 \times 7, \ldots$

2 a $1 \times 3, \ 2 \times 4, \ 3 \times 5, \ldots$ **d** $\frac{1}{2}, \frac{2}{3}, \frac{3}{4}, \frac{4}{5}, \ldots$

    b $1, 6, 11, 16, \ldots$ **e** $\frac{1}{3}, \frac{1}{4}, \frac{1}{5}, \frac{1}{6}, \ldots$

    c $1, 5, 9, 13, \ldots$ **f** $0, -2, -4, -6, \ldots$

3 This is a sequence of pairs of numbers:

$$(1, 4), (2, 5), (3, 6), (4, 7), \ldots$$

Find

    a the next pair in the sequence   **b** the nth pair in the sequence.

Sometimes we find that the first differences are not all the same. In this case add another row and find the second differences.

> If the second differences are all the same, we can use the fact that the expression for the nth term involves n^2.

Find an expression for the nth term of the sequence 2, 6, 12, 20, 30, ...

If we use n for the position number of a term we can arrange the terms in a table and find the 1st differences.

n	1	2	3	4	5
nth term	2	6	12	20	30
1st difference		4	6	8	10
2nd difference			2	2	2	2

The 1st differences are not constant so we find the 2nd differences. When the 2nd difference is constant but the 1st difference is not, the nth term involves n^2.
Make another table, without the differences but adding values of n^2.

n	1	2	3	4	5
nth term	2	6	12	20	30
n^2	1	4	9	16	25

We can now see that each term in the sequence is greater than the value of n^2 by an amount n.

i.e. nth term $= n^2 + n$

---

4 Find a formula for the nth term of the sequence in terms of n.

    a 2, 5, 10, 17, 26, ...   **c** 3, 8, 15, 24, 35, ...   **e** 0, 3, 8, 15, 24, ...

    b 7, 10, 15, 22, 31, ...   **d** 2, 8, 18, 32, 50, ...   **f** 0, 9, 24, 45, 72, ...

5 Look at this tile arrangement.

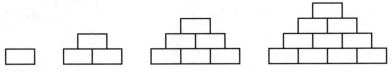

    a Draw the next arrangement in the sequence.

    b Copy and complete this table.

Arrangement number	1	2	3	4	5	6	7
Number of tiles							

    c Find an expression for the number of tiles in the nth arrangement.

6 Here is another tile arrangement.

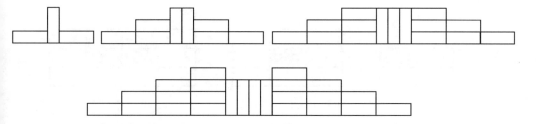

  a Draw the next arrangement in the sequence.

  b Copy and complete this table.

Arrangement number	1	2	3	4	5	6	7
Number of tiles							

  c Find an expression for the number of tiles in the nth arrangement.

7 Consider this tile arrangement.

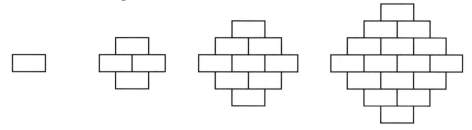

  a Draw the next arrangement in the sequence.

  b Copy and complete this table.

Arrangement number	1	2	3	4	5	6	7
Number of tiles							

  c Find an expression for the number of tiles in the nth arrangement.

8 Write down the 10th term, and an expression for the nth term, of each sequence.

  a $1, 3, 9, 27, \ldots$

  b $1, \frac{1}{4}, \frac{1}{9}, \frac{1}{16}, \ldots$

  c $1, 1 + 2, 1 + 2 + 3, 1 + 2 + 3 + 4, \ldots$

9 Find an expression for the number of purple tiles in the nth diagram in each sequence of diagrams.

a

b

c

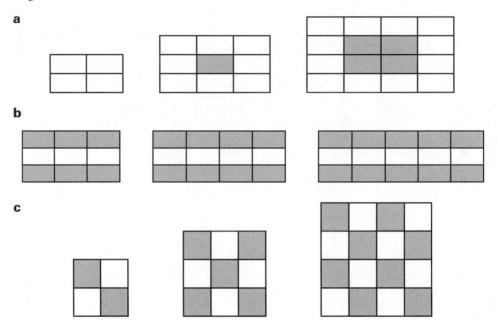

10 Dylan makes fences in different lengths built up in units. A single unit fence needs 5 pieces of wood whereas a two-unit fence needs 9 pieces. All the pieces are the same length.

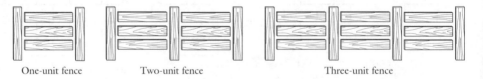

One-unit fence   Two-unit fence   Three-unit fence

   a Sketch a five-unit fence.

   b How many extra pieces are needed each time Dylan increases the length of the fence by one unit?

   c Dylan counted how many pieces he needed to make each fence length. He then drew this table.

Fence length in units	1	2	3	4	5	6
Number of pieces	5	9	13			

Copy and complete the table to show how many pieces are needed for a fence of 4, 5 and 6 units.

   d Explain how to work out the number of pieces needed for a fence length of 25 units.

   e Write down, in terms of n, an expression for the number of pieces needed for a fence of length n units.

11 John made these patterns with sticks.

 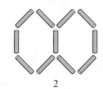 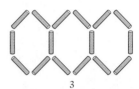

1　　　　　2　　　　　　　3

a Write down the number of sticks required for each of the first five patterns in the sequence.

b How many sticks are needed in this sequence for

  i the nth term   **ii** the 30th term?

c John has a batch of 50 sticks. How many patterns can he make in this sequence? How many more sticks does he need to make the next pattern in the sequence?

12

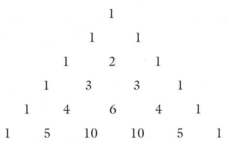

```
            1
          1   1
        1   2   1
      1   3   3   1
    1   4   6   4   1
  1   5  10  10   5   1
```

a Copy this pattern and write down the next three rows.

b Add the numbers in each row and write them down to give the first seven terms of a sequence.

i.e.   1st term $= 1$, 2nd term $= 2$, 3rd term $= 4$, ...

c Use this sequence to find the sum of all the numbers in the 9th row of the triangular pattern given above. What is the sum of the numbers in the 12th term?

d Write each term of the sequence in part **b** as a power of 2. Hence write down, as a power of 2, the sum of the numbers in the nth row of the pattern.

13 a The nth term of a sequence is equal to the sum of the first n terms of the sequence $2, 7, 12, 17, \ldots$ (e.g. the third term is $2 + 7 + 12$, i.e. 21). Write down the first five terms.

b A new sequence is formed when the nth term of the sequence you found in part **a** is divided by n. Write down the first five terms of this new sequence using fractions where necessary.

c Find, in terms of n, an expression for the nth term of the sequence found in part **b**.

d Hence give an expression, in terms of n, for the nth term of the sequence you found in part **a**.

14 Find a formula, in terms of n, for the nth term in the sequence

$$2, 6, 12, 20, 30, \ldots$$

15 Give an expression for the nth term of the sequence

$$4, 10, 18, 28, \ldots.$$

16 Find a formula, in terms of n, for the number of sticks in the nth shape of this sequence.

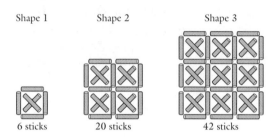

Shape 1	Shape 2	Shape 3
6 sticks	20 sticks	42 sticks

17

One of the races at a school sports day is set out with bean bags placed at 1 metre intervals along the track.
A competitor starts at S, runs to the first bag, picks it up and returns to S. Then she runs to the second bag, picks it up and returns to S, and so on.
How far has a competitor run when she has returned

a 1 bean bag   **b** 4 bean bags   **c** n bean bags?

18 In a sequence the nth term is found by working out the value $\frac{1}{2}n(n+1)$. Find

a the first five terms of the sequence

b the 20th term of the sequence

c an expression for the term before the nth term.

19 Repeat question **18** when the expression for the nth term is $\frac{n}{6}(n+1)(2n+1)$.

20 Solve the problems Rory encountered at the beginning of the chapter.

Do not use a calculator for this exercise.

1 **a** Look at the sequence of numbers 4, 10, 22, 46, ...
The rule that has been used to get each number from the one
before it is 'add 1, then multiply by 2'.
Write down the next two numbers in the sequence.

b Using the same rule, but a different first term, the second term
is 20. Find the first term.

2 Write down the first four terms and the 20th term of the sequence
whose nth term is

a $4n + 7$ **b** $5n - 4$ **c** $n^2 + 3$ **d** $(n+2)(n+3)$

3 Find the next two terms in the sequence

a 6, 11, 18, 27, ...   **b** $1, -\frac{1}{2}, \frac{1}{4}, -\frac{1}{8}, \ldots$
c $1 \times 3, \ 2 \times 4, \ 3 \times 5, \ 4 \times 6, \ldots$

4 This is a sequence of pairs of numbers
$(1, 8), (2, 9), (3, 10), (4, 11), \ldots$

a Write down the next pair of numbers in the sequence.

b Find   **i** the 50th pair.   **ii** the nth pair.

5 Look at this sequence of numbers 2, 5, 8, 11, 14, ...

a Write down the next two numbers in the sequence.

b Work out   **i** the 19th term   **ii** the 30th term.

c Write down a rule for finding the nth term in the sequence.
You may give the answer in words or as a formula.

6 **a** Write down the next two numbers in the number pattern
3, 8, 13, 18, 23, ...

b Write down, in words, the rule for finding the next number from
the one before it.

c Write down the rule for finding the nth number in the pattern.

7 A number pattern begins 1, 2, 3, 5, 8, 13, ...

a What is the next number in this pattern?

b The number pattern is continued. Explain how to find the 8th
number in the pattern. Find the 9th and 10th numbers.

8 The porter at a cattle market is setting up pens to hold sheep. Each pen is formed by fitting panels together.

  a When the number of sheep expected is not large, the pens are erected in one row as shown in the diagram.

    How many panels are needed to make

    i 5 pens   **ii** 8 pens   **iii** n pens?

  b For a larger number of sheep the pens are built in pairs, back to back as shown.

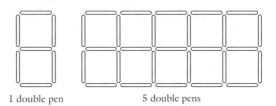

       1 double pen   5 double pens

    How many panels are needed to make

    i 1 double pen   **ii** 4 double pens   **iii** n double pens?

  c The porter thinks that fewer panels might be used if the pens were erected as shown.

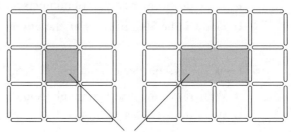

                  To be kept empty of sheep

    i What is the smallest number of pens that can be built in this way?
    ii How many panels are needed to erect 14 pens?

  d Which of the layouts given in parts **a**, **b** and **c** will use the least number of panels to provide

    i 8 pens   **ii** 16 pens   **iii** 20 pens?

INVESTIGATION

> When Jo was asked for the next term in the sequence 3, 9, 27, ...
> she said 81, whereas when Sally was asked the same question she said
> 57. The teacher accepted both answers as correct.
> Investigate how this can be possible.

ALGEBRAIC FRACTIONS

Algebraic expressions occur in many different contexts; in geography you may meet a formula for working out the connectivity of a transport system, in business it could be a formula to find the accumulated interest paid on a loan after a number of repayments have been made, while in medicine it could be a formula for working out the dose rate of a drug, and so on.

All these involve letters and numbers; to be able to work effectively with them, we need skill in handling algebraic expressions. In this chapter we continue building up that skill.

It is important to remember that letters are used to represent numbers, so when dealing with algebraic expressions the ordinary rules of arithmetic apply.

SIMPLIFYING FRACTIONS

We simplify a fraction such as $\frac{10}{50}$ by recognising that 10 is a common factor of the numerator and denominator and then cancelling that common factor,

i.e.
$$\frac{10}{50} = \frac{\cancel{10}^{1}}{5 \times \cancel{10}_{1}} = \frac{1}{5}$$

To simplify an algebraic fraction, we do exactly the same thing: we find, and then cancel, the common factors of the numerator and denominator.

Note that we do not have to write the number 50 as 5×10 but when the factors are letters it helps at this stage to put in the multiplication sign.

For example xy can be written as $x \times y$

and $2(a+b)$ can be written as $2 \times (a+b)$

EXERCISE 6A

Simplify   **a** $\dfrac{2xy}{6y}$ **b** $\dfrac{2a}{a^2b}$

a $\dfrac{2xy}{6y} = \dfrac{\cancel{2} \times x \times \cancel{y}}{\cancel{6} \times \cancel{y}} \,{}_{3}\,{}_{1}$

$\quad = \dfrac{x}{3}$

b $\dfrac{2a}{a^2b} = \dfrac{2 \times \cancel{a}}{\cancel{a} \times a \times b}$

$\quad = \dfrac{2}{ab}$

Simplify

1 **a** $\dfrac{2x}{8}$ **b** $\dfrac{ab}{2b}$ **c** $\dfrac{p^2}{pq}$ **d** $\dfrac{xy}{y^2}$ **e** $\dfrac{3}{6a}$

2 **a** $\dfrac{2ab}{4bc}$ **b** $\dfrac{6p}{3pq}$ **c** $\dfrac{xz}{2x}$ **d** $\dfrac{3pq}{6p}$ **e** $\dfrac{10x}{15xy}$

3 **a** $\dfrac{5p^2q}{10p}$ **b** $\dfrac{a^2b}{abc}$ **c** $\dfrac{b^2}{bd}$ **d** $\dfrac{m^2n}{kmn}$ **e** $\dfrac{5s^2}{20st}$

FACTORS

We know that $3 \times 2 = 6$ but neither $3 + 2$ nor $3 - 2$ is equal to 6. We can write a number as the product of its factors but, in general, we cannot write a number as the sum or difference of its factors.

Thus $\begin{cases} p \text{ and } q \text{ are factors of } pq \\ a \text{ and } (a - b) \text{ are factors of } a(a - b) \end{cases}$

but in general $\begin{cases} p \text{ is } not \text{ a factor of } p + q \\ b \text{ is } not \text{ a factor of } a - b \end{cases}$

This means that in the fraction $\dfrac{p + q}{pq}$ we *cannot* cancel q because q is not a factor of the numerator.

Sometimes the common factors in a fraction are not very obvious.

Consider $\dfrac{x - 2}{y(x - 2)}$

Placing the numerator in brackets and using the multiplication sign

gives $\dfrac{(x - 2)}{y \times (x - 2)}$

Now we can see clearly that $(x - 2)$ is a common factor, so

$$\dfrac{\cancel{(x - 2)}}{y \times \cancel{(x - 2)}} \,{}_{1} = \dfrac{1}{y}$$

EXERCISE 6B

> Simplify where possible   **a** $\dfrac{2a(a-b)}{a-b}$ **b** $\dfrac{pq}{p-q}$
>
> **a** $\dfrac{2a(a-b)}{a-b} = \dfrac{2 \times a \times (a-b)^{1}}{(a-b)_{1}} = 2a$
>
> **b** $\dfrac{pq}{p-q} = \dfrac{p \times q}{(p-q)}$ which cannot be simplified.

Simplify where possible

1 a $\dfrac{x-y}{x(x-y)}$ **b** $\dfrac{p+q}{2p}$ **c** $\dfrac{(p-q)(p+q)}{p+q}$

2 a $\dfrac{st}{s(s-t)}$ **b** $\dfrac{4x}{8(x-y)}$ **c** $\dfrac{(4+a)}{(4+a)(4-a)}$

3 a $\dfrac{2a}{a-b}$ **b** $\dfrac{3(a+b)}{6ab}$ **c** $\dfrac{a-b}{3(a+b)}$

4 a $\dfrac{u-v}{v(u-v)}$ **b** $\dfrac{10a}{15(a-b)}$ **c** $\dfrac{(u+v)(u-v)}{u+v}$

5 a $\dfrac{s-t}{2(s-t)}$ **b** $\dfrac{s-t}{3s}$ **c** $\dfrac{s+6}{(s+6)(s-6)}$

**MULTIPLICATION
AND DIVISION OF
FRACTIONS**

Remember that to multiply fractions, the numerators are multiplied together and the denominators are multiplied together,

i.e. $\dfrac{3}{4} \times \dfrac{5}{7} = \dfrac{3 \times 5}{4 \times 7} = \dfrac{15}{28}$,   so $\dfrac{x}{y} \times \dfrac{z}{2} = \dfrac{x \times z}{y \times 2} = \dfrac{xz}{2y}$

Remember also that $\dfrac{1}{6}$ of x means $\dfrac{1}{6} \times x$ and

$\dfrac{1}{6} \times x = \dfrac{1}{6} \times \dfrac{x}{1} = \dfrac{x}{6}$, so $\dfrac{1}{6}$ of $x = \dfrac{x}{6}$ [1]

To divide by a fraction we multiply by the reciprocal of that fraction,

i.e. $\dfrac{2}{3} \div \dfrac{5}{7} = \dfrac{2}{3} \times \dfrac{7}{5} = \dfrac{14}{15}$

and $x \div 6 = \dfrac{x}{1} \div \dfrac{6}{1} = \dfrac{x}{1} \times \dfrac{1}{6} = \dfrac{x}{6}$ [2]

Comparing [1] and [2] we see that

> $\dfrac{1}{6}$ of x, $\dfrac{1}{6}x$, $x \div 6$ and $\dfrac{x}{6}$ are all equivalent.

EXERCISE 6C

1   Simplify

   a $\dfrac{a}{b} \times \dfrac{c}{d}$ **b** $\dfrac{a}{b} \div \dfrac{c}{d}$ **c** $\dfrac{a}{b} \times c$ **d** $\dfrac{(a-b)}{4} \div \dfrac{(a+b)}{3}$

Simplify

2 a $\dfrac{x-y}{2} \times \dfrac{5}{x}$

   c $\dfrac{(x-2)}{3} \times (x+3)$

   b $\dfrac{x-y}{2} \div \dfrac{5}{x}$

   d $\dfrac{(x-2)}{3} \div (x+3)$

3 a $\dfrac{a}{b} \div c$

   c $\dfrac{x}{y} \div \dfrac{2}{3}$

   b $\dfrac{p}{q} \div \dfrac{1}{r}$

   d $\dfrac{3}{4}$ of $\dfrac{x}{y}$

It is sometimes possible to simplify fractions before multiplying, in the same way as with numerical fractions.

Simplify   **a** $12 \times \dfrac{x}{3}$ **b** $\dfrac{2x}{3} \div 8$

a $12 \times \dfrac{x}{3} = \dfrac{\cancel{12}^{\,4}}{1} \times \dfrac{x}{\cancel{3}_{\,1}} = 4x$

b $\dfrac{2x}{3} \div 8 = \dfrac{2x}{3} \div \dfrac{8}{1} = \dfrac{\cancel{2x}^{\,1}}{3} \times \dfrac{1}{\cancel{8}_{\,4}} = \dfrac{x}{12}$

> Remember that $2x = 2 \times x$

Simplify

4 a $4 \times \dfrac{x}{8}$ **b** $\dfrac{1}{5}$ of $10x$ **c** $\dfrac{5x}{2} \div 4$ **d** $\dfrac{3}{4} \times \dfrac{2x}{5}$

5 a $\dfrac{1}{2} \times \dfrac{x}{3}$ **b** $\dfrac{2}{5} \times \dfrac{3x}{4}$ **c** $\dfrac{4x}{9} \div 8$ **d** $\dfrac{4x}{9} \div \dfrac{2}{3}$

6 a $9 \times \dfrac{x}{6}$ **b** $\dfrac{3}{4} \times 2x$ **c** $\dfrac{x}{3} \div \dfrac{1}{6}$ **d** $\dfrac{3}{5}$ of $15x$

7 a $\dfrac{1}{3}$ of $2x$ **b** $\dfrac{2}{3}$ of $9x$ **c** $\dfrac{x}{4} \div \dfrac{1}{2}$ **d** $\dfrac{3x}{2} \div \dfrac{1}{6}$

8 a $\dfrac{2x}{3} \times \dfrac{6}{5}$ **b** $\dfrac{x}{2} \times \dfrac{2}{3}$ **c** $\dfrac{2x}{3} \div \dfrac{5}{6}$ **d** $\dfrac{5x}{3} \times \dfrac{6}{25}$

Simplify   **a** $\dfrac{3x}{5} \times \dfrac{10x}{13}$ **b** $\dfrac{5x}{9} \div \dfrac{20x}{3}$

a $\dfrac{3x}{\cancel{5}_{\,1}} \times \dfrac{\cancel{10x}^{\,2}}{13} = \dfrac{3 \times 2 \times x \times x}{13} = \dfrac{6x^2}{13}$

b $\dfrac{5x}{9} \div \dfrac{20x}{3} = \dfrac{\cancel{5x}^{\,1}}{\cancel{9}_{\,3}} \times \dfrac{\cancel{3}^{\,1}}{\cancel{20x}_{\,4}} = \dfrac{1}{12}$

> Remember that to divide by a fraction, we turn it upside down and multiply.

Simplify

9 a $\dfrac{x}{2} \times \dfrac{x}{3}$ **d** $\dfrac{4b}{9} \times 18b$ **g** $\dfrac{9x}{4} \div \dfrac{9x}{8}$

b $\dfrac{3x}{2} \times \dfrac{x}{4}$ **e** $\dfrac{25x}{7} \times \dfrac{21x}{5}$ **h** $12b \div \dfrac{4b}{5}$

c $\dfrac{4a}{7} \times \dfrac{a}{8}$ **f** $\dfrac{x}{2} \div \dfrac{x}{3}$ **i** $\dfrac{16x}{3} \div \dfrac{4x}{9}$

Simplify $\dfrac{ab}{4} \times \dfrac{8}{a^2}$

$$\dfrac{ab}{4} \times \dfrac{8}{a^2} = \dfrac{\overset{1}{\cancel{ab}}}{\cancel{4}_1} \times \dfrac{\cancel{8}^2}{\cancel{a^2}_a} = \dfrac{2b}{a}$$

Simplify

10 a $\dfrac{2a}{b} \div \dfrac{a^2}{3b^2}$ **c** $\dfrac{4xy}{3} \times \dfrac{9}{x^2}$ **e** $\dfrac{1}{b^2} \div \dfrac{2}{b}$

b $\dfrac{pq}{6} \times \dfrac{3}{p^2}$ **d** $\dfrac{x^2}{4} \div \dfrac{xy}{2}$ **f** $\dfrac{7p}{5q} \times \dfrac{10q}{21p^2}$

11 a $\dfrac{2ab}{5} \div \dfrac{a}{b}$ **c** $\dfrac{2p^2 \times q}{4pq}$ **e** $\dfrac{a}{b} \times \dfrac{2a}{3b} \div \dfrac{2b}{3a}$

b $\dfrac{2p^2}{3} \times \dfrac{q}{4p}$ **d** $\dfrac{a^2}{2b} \div 2a$ **f** $\dfrac{5xy \times y}{10x^2y}$

12 a $\dfrac{6x \times 5y}{10xy^2}$ **c** $\dfrac{ab \times 12b}{18ab}$ **e** $\dfrac{4s^2}{3t^2} \times \dfrac{6t^2}{2s}$

b $\dfrac{12pq^2}{3p^2 \times 2p}$ **d** $\dfrac{xy}{3} \div \dfrac{2x^2}{3y^2}$ **f** $\dfrac{4pq}{9} \div \dfrac{6p^2}{5q}$

LOWEST COMMON MULTIPLE

Before we can simplify $\frac{2}{3} + \frac{1}{5}$ we must change both $\frac{2}{3}$ and $\frac{1}{5}$ into equivalent fractions with the same denominator. This common denominator must contain both 3 and 5 as factors; there are many numbers we could choose but 15 is the lowest such number.
In this case 15 is called the *lowest common multiple* (LCM) of 3 and 5.

To simplify $\dfrac{3}{x} + \dfrac{2}{y}$ we follow the same pattern. We need a common denominator with both x and y as factors. Again there are many we could use, but the simplest is xy; this is the LCM of x and y, because it is the simplest expression that x and y both divide into exactly.

EXERCISE 6D

> Find the LCM of ab and c.
>
> > a, b and c all divide into abc.
>
> The LCM is abc.

1 Find the lowest common multiple of

a p, q **c** $2, 3, 5$ **e** x, y, wz **g** v, uw

b r, st **d** a, b, c **f** a, d **h** p, q, r

> Find the LCM of **a** $4, 10$ **b** ab, a^2 **c** $2x, 6x$
>
> **a** $\qquad\qquad 4 = 2 \times 2 \quad$ and $\quad 10 = 2 \times 5$
>
> > The LCM is the *lowest* number that 4 and 10 divide into exactly, so the factors it must include are 2×2 from 4 and 5 from 10
> >
> > The factor of 2 from 10 is not needed as 2 is already included.
>
> $\qquad \therefore$ the LCM of 4 and 10 is $2 \times 2 \times 5 = 20$
>
> **b** $ab = a \times b \quad$ and $\quad a^2 = a \times a$
>
> $\qquad \therefore$ the LCM is $a \times b \times a = a^2 b$
>
> **c** $2x = 2 \times x \quad$ and $\quad 6x = 2 \times 3 \times x$
>
> $\qquad \therefore$ the LCM is $2 \times 3 \times x = 6x$

Find the lowest common multiple of

2 a x, xy **c** $pq, 3p$ **e** ab, bc **g** $5a, ab$

  b $x^2, 2x$ **d** $x^2, 2xy$ **f** $3p, p^2$ **h** $3pq, q^2$

3 a $2x, 3x$ **c** $6a, 9a$ **e** a, ab, a^2 **g** $3y, 5y$

  b $4x, 8x$ **d** $6, 4, 10$ **f** $10x, 15x$ **h** $2x, 3x, 4x$

ADDITION AND SUBTRACTION OF FRACTIONS

To add or subtract fractions we first have to change them into equivalent fractions with a common denominator.

Thus to find $\frac{2}{3} + \frac{1}{5}$, we choose a common denominator of 15 which is the lowest number that 3 and 5 both divide into exactly.

Now $$\frac{2}{3} = \frac{2 \times 5}{3 \times 5} = \frac{10}{15} \quad \text{and} \quad \frac{1}{5} = \frac{1 \times 3}{5 \times 3} = \frac{3}{15}$$

Therefore $$\frac{2}{3} + \frac{1}{5} = \frac{10 + 3}{15} = \frac{13}{15}$$

To simplify $\dfrac{3}{x} + \dfrac{2}{y}$ we follow the same pattern:

xy is the LCM of x and y.

$$\frac{3}{x} = \frac{3 \times y}{x \times y} = \frac{3y}{xy} \quad \text{and} \quad \frac{2}{y} = \frac{2 \times x}{y \times x} = \frac{2x}{xy}$$

$$\therefore \qquad \frac{3}{x} + \frac{2}{y} = \frac{3y + 2x}{xy}$$

EXERCISE 6E

Simplify **a** $\dfrac{1}{2a} + \dfrac{1}{b}$ **b** $\dfrac{3}{4x} - \dfrac{1}{6x}$

a $\dfrac{1}{2a} + \dfrac{1}{b} = \dfrac{(1) \times (b) + (1) \times (2a)}{2ab}$

> $2ab$ is the simplest expression that $2a$ and b each divide into exactly.

$$= \frac{b + 2a}{2ab}$$

b $\dfrac{3}{4x} - \dfrac{1}{6x} = \dfrac{(3) \times (3) - (1) \times (2)}{12x}$

$$= \frac{9 - 2}{12x} = \frac{7}{12x}$$

> $12x$ is the simplest expression that $4x$ and $6x$ divide into exactly.

Simplify

1 a $\dfrac{1}{x} + \dfrac{1}{y}$ **b** $\dfrac{3}{p} + \dfrac{2}{q}$ **c** $\dfrac{2}{x} - \dfrac{3}{y}$ **d** $\dfrac{4}{3p} + \dfrac{2}{q}$

2 a $\dfrac{2}{y} - \dfrac{3}{4y}$ **b** $\dfrac{3}{8p} - \dfrac{1}{4p}$ **c** $\dfrac{2}{s} - \dfrac{1}{t}$ **d** $\dfrac{3}{a} + \dfrac{1}{2b}$

3 a $\dfrac{3}{x} - \dfrac{2}{y}$ **b** $\dfrac{5}{7a} + \dfrac{3}{4b}$ **c** $\dfrac{1}{a} + \dfrac{5}{8a}$ **d** $\dfrac{1}{3x} - \dfrac{1}{7x}$

4 a $\dfrac{1}{3x} - \dfrac{2}{5y}$ **b** $\dfrac{1}{a} + \dfrac{5}{2b}$ **c** $\dfrac{1}{2x} + \dfrac{1}{3x}$ **d** $\dfrac{3}{7x} - \dfrac{2}{5x}$

Simplify $\dfrac{4a}{3b} - \dfrac{b}{6a}$

$$\frac{4a}{3b} - \frac{b}{6a} = \frac{(4a) \times (2a) - (b) \times (b)}{6ab}$$

$$= \frac{8a^2 - b^2}{6ab}$$

> $3b = 3 \times b$ and
> $6a = 2 \times 3 \times a$,
> $\therefore$ LCM $= 6ab$

Simplify

5 a $\dfrac{1}{2a} + \dfrac{3}{4b}$ **c** $\dfrac{s}{t^2} + \dfrac{s^2}{2t}$ **e** $\dfrac{5}{7x} - \dfrac{3}{14xy}$

b $\dfrac{a}{2b} - \dfrac{a^2}{b^2}$ **d** $\dfrac{5}{2a} + \dfrac{2}{3ab}$ **f** $\dfrac{9}{a^2} - \dfrac{3}{2ab}$

6 a $\dfrac{3}{x} - \dfrac{4}{xy}$ **c** $\dfrac{1}{x^2} + \dfrac{2}{3x}$ **e** $\dfrac{3x}{2y} - \dfrac{3y}{2x}$

b $\dfrac{2}{p^2} - \dfrac{3}{2p}$ **d** $\dfrac{2y}{3x} - \dfrac{3x}{2y}$ **f** $\dfrac{7}{9p} - \dfrac{5}{6q}$

7 a $\dfrac{3a}{4b} + \dfrac{b}{6a}$ **c** $\dfrac{5}{8x} + \dfrac{2}{4y}$ **e** $\dfrac{a^2}{b^2} + \dfrac{4a}{5b}$

b $\dfrac{5}{2p} - \dfrac{3}{4q}$ **d** $\dfrac{p}{3q} + \dfrac{p^2}{q^2}$ **f** $\dfrac{7}{5pq} + \dfrac{8}{15q}$

Simplify $\dfrac{x-2}{3} - \dfrac{x-4}{2}$

> We place brackets round the numerators *before* putting the fractions over a common denominator. This keeps each numerator together so that the signs are not confused. If you need reminding about how to multiply out brackets go to page 146.

$$\frac{(x-2)}{3} - \frac{(x-4)}{2} = \frac{2(x-2) - 3(x-4)}{6}$$

$$= \frac{2x - 4 - 3x + 12}{6}$$

$$= \frac{-x + 8}{6} = \frac{8 - x}{6}$$

Simplify

8 a $\dfrac{x+2}{5} + \dfrac{x-1}{4}$ **b** $\dfrac{x+3}{4} - \dfrac{x+1}{3}$ **c** $\dfrac{x+3}{7} - \dfrac{x+2}{5}$

9 a $\dfrac{2x-1}{3} + \dfrac{x+2}{5}$ **b** $\dfrac{2x+3}{4} - \dfrac{x-2}{6}$ **c** $\dfrac{2x-1}{7} - \dfrac{x-2}{5}$

Remember that $\dfrac{1}{5}(x-2) = \dfrac{(x-2)}{5}$

10 a $\dfrac{1}{7}(2x-3) - \dfrac{1}{3}(4x-2)$ **c** $\dfrac{2x+3}{5} - \dfrac{3x-2}{4}$

    b $\dfrac{1}{4}(5x-1) - \dfrac{1}{3}(2x-3)$ **d** $\dfrac{3-x}{2} + \dfrac{1-2x}{6}$

11 a $\dfrac{5-2x}{3} + \dfrac{4-3x}{2}$ **c** $\dfrac{2+5x}{8} - \dfrac{3-4x}{6}$

    b $\dfrac{1}{4}(3-x) + \dfrac{1}{6}(1-2x)$ **d** $\dfrac{1}{5}(4-3x) + \dfrac{1}{10}(3-x)$

12 a $\dfrac{1}{8}(5x+4) - \dfrac{1}{3}(4x-1)$ **c** $\dfrac{1}{9}(4-x) - \dfrac{1}{6}(2+3x)$

    b $\dfrac{1}{3}(x+5) + \dfrac{1}{6}(2x-1)$ **d** $\dfrac{1}{4}(3-x) - \dfrac{1}{3}(2+x)$

Simplify $\dfrac{2(x+1)}{3} - \dfrac{3(x-2)}{5}$

$$\dfrac{2(x+1)}{3} - \dfrac{3(x-2)}{5} = \dfrac{5 \times 2(x+1) - 3 \times 3(x-2)}{15}$$

$$= \dfrac{10(x+1) - 9(x-2)}{15}$$

$$= \dfrac{10x + 10 - 9x + 18}{15}$$

$$= \dfrac{x + 28}{15}$$

Simplify

13 a $\dfrac{4(x+2)}{3} + \dfrac{2(x-1)}{5}$ **c** $\dfrac{3(x-1)}{2} + \dfrac{3(x+4)}{7}$

    b $\dfrac{3(x-1)}{4} + \dfrac{2(x+1)}{3}$ **d** $\dfrac{7(x-3)}{3} - \dfrac{2(x+5)}{9}$

14 a $\dfrac{2(x-2)}{3} - \dfrac{3(x-1)}{7}$ **c** $\dfrac{2(3x-1)}{5} + \dfrac{4(2x-3)}{15}$

    b $\dfrac{5(2x-1)}{2} - \dfrac{4(x+3)}{5}$ **d** $\dfrac{3(x-2)}{5} - \dfrac{7(x-4)}{6}$

Simplify $\dfrac{2}{x} - \dfrac{1}{x+2}$

$$\dfrac{2}{x} - \dfrac{1}{(x+2)} = \dfrac{(2)(x+2)-(1)(x)}{x(x+2)}$$

> We place the two-term denominator in brackets. We do not multiply out the bracket in the denominator.

$$= \dfrac{2x+4-x}{x(x+2)}$$

$$= \dfrac{x+4}{x(x+2)}$$

Simplify

15 a $\dfrac{2}{a} + \dfrac{1}{a+3}$ **b** $\dfrac{4}{x+2} + \dfrac{2}{x}$ **c** $\dfrac{3}{x-1} + \dfrac{4}{x}$

16 a $\dfrac{3}{x-4} + \dfrac{1}{2x}$ **b** $\dfrac{2}{2x+1} - \dfrac{3}{4x}$ **c** $\dfrac{3}{2x+1} + \dfrac{1}{3x}$

EXERCISE 6F

Give each expression as a single fraction in as simple a form as possible.

1 a $\dfrac{2}{a} - \dfrac{b}{c}$ **b** $\dfrac{pq}{r} \times \dfrac{r^3}{p^2}$ **c** $\dfrac{2p}{q} \div \dfrac{p^2}{4}$ **d** $\dfrac{5x^2 y}{10x \times xy^2}$

2 a $\dfrac{x+2}{4} + \dfrac{x-5}{3}$ **b** $\dfrac{2ab \times b^2}{6a^2 \cdot}$ **c** $\dfrac{4}{x^2} - \dfrac{2}{3x}$ **d** $\dfrac{M}{2} - \dfrac{M+1}{3}$

3 a $\dfrac{3}{4x} - \dfrac{2}{3x}$ **b** $\dfrac{2}{5x} \div \dfrac{3}{4x}$ **c** $\dfrac{a^2}{bc} \div \dfrac{a}{b^2}$ **d** $\dfrac{5}{4x} \div \dfrac{5}{6x}$

4 a $\dfrac{2}{5x} + \dfrac{3}{4x}$ **b** $\dfrac{2}{5x} \times \dfrac{3}{4x}$ **c** $\dfrac{1}{3x} + \dfrac{6}{x-1}$ **d** $\dfrac{1}{3x} \times \dfrac{6}{x-1}$

5 a $\dfrac{x+4}{5} + \dfrac{2x-1}{10}$ **b** $\dfrac{x+4}{5} \times \dfrac{2x-1}{10}$ **c** $\dfrac{3}{2a} - \dfrac{2}{a-1}$

6 a $\dfrac{5}{4x} + \dfrac{5}{6x}$ **b** $\dfrac{5}{4x} \times \dfrac{5}{6x}$ **c** $\dfrac{3}{4y-3} \div \dfrac{y}{4y-3}$

EXPRESSIONS AND EQUATIONS

When we write $x + x = 2x$ we are showing the equivalence between two forms of the *same* expression. The equality between two forms of the same expression is called an *identity*. An identity is true for any value of x,

e.g.   when $x = 6$, $x + x = 12$ and $2x = 12$

when $x = 3$, $x + x = 6$

and $2x = 6$.

If, on the other hand, we are given $x + 2 = 2x$, we find that when $x = 6$, LHS $= 6 + 2 = 8$ and RHS $= 2 \times 6 = 12$,

i.e. $x + 2$ and $2x$ are not equal for all values of x.

$x + 2 = 2x$ is called an *equation*; we can find the values of x (if any) for which the equality is valid by solving the equation.

> Note that LHS means left-hand side and RHS means right-hand side.

EXERCISE 6G

Determine which of these are identities and which are equations.

1 $2x + 3x = 5x$ **4** $2p + 8 = 3p$ **7** $2(x + 1) = 4$

2 $2x + 3x = 5$ **5** $\dfrac{x}{3} + \dfrac{x}{3} = \dfrac{2x}{3}$ **8** $3x + 6 = 3(x + 2)$

3 $y + 5y = 6y$ **6** $\dfrac{1}{x} + \dfrac{3}{x} = 4$ **9** $2(x + y) = 2x + 2y$

EQUATIONS CONTAINING FRACTIONS

Peter doesn't know the capacity of his fuel tank. When the gauge shows that it is quarter full, he empties the contents into a measuring container. This shows 7.25 litres. Peter can find the capacity of his tank by multiplying 7.25 by 4; he can also form an equation and find out how to solve it.

This second method will help with more complicated situations that cannot be sorted out by using simple arithmetic.

If the capacity of the tank is x litres, then $\frac{1}{4}$ of $x = 7.25$

Now $\frac{1}{4}$ of x is $\frac{x}{4}$ so the equation is $\dfrac{x}{4} = 7.25$

To solve this equation, we need to find x.

We know what $\frac{1}{4}$ of x is, so to find x we make $\dfrac{x}{4}$ four times larger,

i.e.   we need to multiply both sides by 4.

$$\dfrac{x}{\cancel{4}_{1}} \times \dfrac{\cancel{4}^{1}}{1} = 7.25 \times 4 = 29$$

The capacity of Peter's tank is 29 litres.

EXERCISE 6H

Solve the equation $\dfrac{x}{3} = 2$

> As $\dfrac{x}{3}$ means $\dfrac{1}{3}$ of x, to find x we need to make $\dfrac{x}{3}$ three times larger.

$$\dfrac{x}{3} = 2$$

Multiply each side by 3 $\qquad \dfrac{x}{\cancel{3}_{\,1}} \times \dfrac{\cancel{3}^{\,1}}{1} = 2 \times 3$

$$x = 6$$

Note We can remove fractions from an equation by multiplying both sides by the same quantity.

Solve the following equations.

1 a $\dfrac{x}{5} = 3$ **b** $\dfrac{x}{8} = 9$ **c** $\dfrac{x}{3} = 6$

2 a $\dfrac{x}{2} = 4$ **b** $7 = \dfrac{x}{9}$ **c** $\dfrac{x}{4} = 4$

3 a $\dfrac{x}{6} = 8$ **b** $\dfrac{x}{7} = 8$ **c** $8 = \dfrac{x}{12}$

Solve the equation $\dfrac{3x}{4} = 12$

$$\dfrac{3x}{4} = 12$$

Multiply both sides by 4 $\qquad \dfrac{3x}{\cancel{4}_{\,1}} \times \dfrac{\cancel{4}^{\,1}}{1} = 12 \times 4$

$$3x = 48$$

Divide both sides by 3 $\qquad\qquad x = 48 \div 3$

$$= 16$$

Check: LHS $= \dfrac{3x}{4} = \dfrac{3}{\cancel{4}_{\,1}} \times \dfrac{\cancel{16}^{\,4}}{1} = 12 =$ RHS

Solve the equations.

4 a $\dfrac{2x}{3} = 8$ **c** $\dfrac{5x}{7} = 1$ **e** $\dfrac{4x}{7} = 12$

   b $\dfrac{3x}{5} = 9$ **d** $\dfrac{5x}{8} = 20$ **f** $\dfrac{2x}{9} = 5$

Solve the equation $\dfrac{2x}{5} = \dfrac{1}{3}$

$$\dfrac{2x}{5} = \dfrac{1}{3}$$

Multiply each side by 5

$$\dfrac{2x}{\cancel{5}} \times \dfrac{\cancel{5}^{\,1}}{1} = \dfrac{1}{3} \times \dfrac{5}{1}$$

$$2x = \dfrac{5}{3}$$

Divide each side by 2

$$x = \dfrac{5}{3} \div 2$$

$$x = \dfrac{5}{3} \times \dfrac{1}{2}$$

$$x = \dfrac{5}{6}$$

Check: LHS $= \dfrac{2x}{5} = \dfrac{\cancel{2}^{\,1}}{\cancel{5}_{\,1}} \times \dfrac{\cancel{5}^{\,1}}{\cancel{6}_{\,3}} = \dfrac{1}{3} =$ RHS

Solve the following equations.

5 a $\dfrac{3x}{2} = \dfrac{1}{4}$ **d** $\dfrac{2x}{3} = \dfrac{4}{5}$ **g** $\dfrac{5x}{7} = \dfrac{3}{4}$

b $\dfrac{4x}{3} = \dfrac{1}{5}$ **e** $\dfrac{6x}{5} = \dfrac{2}{3}$ **h** $\dfrac{3x}{7} = \dfrac{2}{5}$

c $\dfrac{2x}{9} = \dfrac{1}{3}$ **f** $\dfrac{3x}{8} = \dfrac{1}{2}$ **i** $\dfrac{4x}{7} = \dfrac{3}{14}$

Answer questions **6** to **11** by forming equations and solving them.

6 Tim Silcocks came first in the local Tennis Tournament and won £200. What was the total prize money if Tim won two-thirds of it?

7 The width of a rectangular flower-bed is 18 m. This is $\dfrac{5}{6}$ of its length. Find the length of the bed.

8 The width of a rectangle is $\dfrac{2}{3}$ its length.
If the rectangle is $\dfrac{5}{6}$ of a foot wide, how long is it?

9 The capacity of a can of oil is x gallons. It is $\dfrac{3}{4}$ full.
When this oil is poured into a separate container it is found to measure $\dfrac{1}{2}$ gallon. Find the capacity of the can.

10 When a $\frac{5}{8}$ inch-long screw is screwed into a piece of wood until the top of its head is flush with the surface of the wood, it has penetrated through $\frac{7}{8}$ of the thickness of the wood. If the wood is w inches thick, form an equation in w and solve it. How thick is the wood?

11 The length of a rectangle is $1\frac{1}{3}$ times its width. Find the perimeter of the rectangle if the length is 160 mm.

HARDER EQUATIONS INVOLVING FRACTIONS

Some problems result in an equation involving the sum or difference of two or more fractions.

Angela took part in the Vosper Tennis Tournament. She won the Singles title and, with a partner, also won the Mixed Doubles. Her prize money for the Singles was $\frac{1}{6}$ of the total prize money and her share of the prize money for the Mixed Doubles was $\frac{1}{24}$ of the total prize money. Altogether she won £1500. What was the total prize money awarded to all the winners?

Let the total prize money be £x.

Then the amount, in pounds, that Angela won in the Singles was

$$\frac{1}{6} \times \frac{x}{1} = \frac{x}{6}$$

The amount, in pounds, that Angela won in the Mixed Doubles was

$$\frac{1}{24} \times \frac{x}{1} = \frac{x}{24}$$

But the sum of her prize money was £1500

$$\therefore \qquad \frac{x}{6} + \frac{x}{24} = 1500$$

Both 6 and 24 divide into 24, so multiplying both sides by 24 eliminates all fractions from the equation. Notice that there are three terms, *each of which* is multiplied by 24.

i.e.
$$\frac{\overset{4}{\cancel{24}}}{1} \times \frac{x}{\cancel{6}_1} + \frac{\overset{1}{\cancel{24}}}{1} \times \frac{x}{\cancel{24}_1} = 24 \times 1500$$

$$4x + x = 24 \times 1500$$

$$5x = 24 \times 1500$$

Dividing both sides by 5
$$x = \frac{24 \times \overset{300}{\cancel{1500}}}{\cancel{5}_1}$$

$$= 7200$$

The total prize money for the tournament was therefore £7200.

EXERCISE 6I

Solve the equation $\dfrac{x}{5} + \dfrac{1}{2} = 1$

$$\frac{x}{5} + \frac{1}{2} = 1$$

> The terms in an equation are separated by a plus sign or by a minus sign. Multiplying both sides of an equation by a number means that each term must be multiplied by that number. For this equation we must multiply $\dfrac{x}{5}$, $\dfrac{1}{2}$ and 1, by 10.

Multiply both sides by 10 $\dfrac{\cancel{10}^{2}}{1} \times \dfrac{x}{\cancel{5}_{1}} + \dfrac{\cancel{10}^{5}}{1} \times \dfrac{1}{\cancel{2}_{1}} = 10$

$$2x + 5 = 10$$

Take 5 from each side $2x = 5$

Divide each side by 2 $x = 2\dfrac{1}{2}$

Solve the following equations.

1 a $\dfrac{x}{4} - 1 = 4$ **b** $\dfrac{x}{3} - \dfrac{1}{3} = 4$ **c** $\dfrac{x}{6} + 2 = 3$

2 a $\dfrac{x}{3} + \dfrac{1}{4} = 1$ **b** $\dfrac{x}{5} - \dfrac{3}{4} = 2$ **c** $\dfrac{x}{3} - \dfrac{2}{9} = 4$

3 a $\dfrac{P}{3} + 2 = \dfrac{3P}{5}$ **b** $\dfrac{A}{4} + \dfrac{A}{5} = 9$ **c** $\dfrac{t}{3} + 4 = \dfrac{t}{5}$

4 a I think of a number and add $\dfrac{1}{3}$ of it to $\dfrac{1}{2}$ of it.
If x is the number I think of, write an expression in terms of x for adding $\dfrac{1}{3}$ of it to $\dfrac{1}{2}$ of it.

   b The result for part **a** is 10. Form an equation in x and solve it.

5 I think of a number x. When $\dfrac{3}{7}$ is subtracted from $\dfrac{3}{4}$ of the number the result is 1. Form an equation in terms of x and solve it to find the number.

6 Benjamin Findley won the singles competition of a local bowls tournament, for which he got $\dfrac{1}{5}$ of the total prize money. He also won the pairs competition for which he got $\dfrac{1}{20}$ of the prize money. He won £250 altogether. How much was the total prize money?

Solve the equation $\dfrac{x}{2} = \dfrac{1}{6} + \dfrac{x}{3}$

$$\frac{x}{2} = \frac{1}{6} + \frac{x}{3}$$

> 2, 3 and 6 all divide into 6, so multiplying each side by 6 will eliminate all fractions from this equation.

Multiply each side by 6 $\quad \dfrac{x}{2_{,}} \times \dfrac{6^{3}}{1} = \dfrac{1}{6_{,}} \times \dfrac{6^{1}}{1} + \dfrac{x}{3_{,}} \times \dfrac{6^{2}}{1}$

$$3x = 1 + 2x$$

Take $2x$ from each side $\qquad x = 1$

Check: LHS $= \dfrac{1}{2}$ $\qquad$ RHS $= \dfrac{1}{6} + \dfrac{1}{3}$

$$= \frac{1}{6} + \frac{2}{6} = \frac{3}{6} = \frac{1}{2}$$

Solve the following equations.

7 a $\dfrac{x}{3} + \dfrac{1}{4} = \dfrac{1}{2}$ $\qquad$ **c** $\dfrac{3x}{5} + \dfrac{2}{9} = \dfrac{11}{15}$

$\quad$ **b** $\dfrac{x}{5} - \dfrac{x}{6} = \dfrac{1}{15}$ $\qquad$ **d** $\dfrac{x}{3} - \dfrac{x}{12} = \dfrac{1}{4}$

8 a $\dfrac{x}{4} + \dfrac{2}{3} = \dfrac{x}{3}$ $\qquad$ **c** $\dfrac{2x}{5} - \dfrac{3}{10} = \dfrac{x}{4}$

$\quad$ **b** $\dfrac{5x}{6} + \dfrac{x}{8} = \dfrac{3}{4}$ $\qquad$ **d** $\dfrac{5x}{12} - \dfrac{1}{3} = \dfrac{x}{8}$

9 A square was reduced in size, more in one direction than the other, to give a rectangle. The length of the rectangle was $\frac{5}{8}$ of the length of the square and its width was $\frac{3}{5}$ of the width of the square. The perimeter of the rectangle was $2\frac{3}{4}$ inches. Find the length of the sides of the square.

10 Solve the following equations.

$\quad$ **a** $\dfrac{3x}{4} + \dfrac{1}{3} = \dfrac{x}{2} + \dfrac{5}{8}$ $\qquad$ **c** $\dfrac{3}{5} - \dfrac{x}{9} = \dfrac{2}{15} - \dfrac{2x}{45}$

$\quad$ **b** $\dfrac{2x}{7} - \dfrac{3}{4} = \dfrac{x}{14} + \dfrac{1}{4}$ $\qquad$ **d** $\dfrac{4}{7} + \dfrac{2x}{9} = \dfrac{15}{9} - \dfrac{4x}{21}$

Sometimes the unknown letter is the denominator.

Solve the equation $\dfrac{1}{x} + \dfrac{1}{2x} = \dfrac{5}{6}$

$\therefore \quad \dfrac{6x}{1} \times \dfrac{1}{x} + \dfrac{6x}{1} \times \dfrac{1}{2x} = \dfrac{6x}{1} \times \dfrac{5}{6}$

> The simplest expression that x, $2x$ and 6 all divide into exactly is $6x$ so we multiply both sides of the equation by $6x$; this means multiplying each of the three terms by $6x$.

$\therefore \quad 6 + 3 = 5x$

$\qquad 9 = 5x$

$\qquad \frac{9}{5} = x \quad \text{i.e.} \quad x = 1\frac{4}{5}$

Solve the following equations.

11 a $\dfrac{3}{x} = \dfrac{1}{2}$ **b** $\dfrac{2}{3x} = \dfrac{1}{2}$ **c** $\dfrac{5}{A} = \dfrac{2}{3}$ **d** $\dfrac{3}{2t} = \dfrac{4}{9}$

12 a $\dfrac{1}{2} + \dfrac{4}{x} = 1$ **b** $\dfrac{2}{3} - \dfrac{1}{x} = \dfrac{13}{15}$ **c** $\dfrac{3}{x} + \dfrac{3}{10} = \dfrac{9}{10}$ **d** $\dfrac{3}{8} - \dfrac{2}{x} = \dfrac{1}{6}$

13 a $\dfrac{3}{4} - \dfrac{2}{x} = \dfrac{5}{12}$ **b** $\dfrac{1}{x} - \dfrac{1}{3x} = \dfrac{1}{2}$ **c** $\dfrac{3}{2x} + \dfrac{1}{4x} = \dfrac{1}{3}$ **d** $\dfrac{1}{x} - \dfrac{1}{2} = \dfrac{3}{2x}$

Solve the equation $\dfrac{x-2}{4} - \dfrac{x-3}{6} = 2$

> Place brackets round the top of each fraction to keep the two terms in the numerator together.

$\qquad \dfrac{(x-2)}{4} - \dfrac{(x-3)}{6} = 2$

Multiply each side by 12

$\qquad \dfrac{12}{1} \times \dfrac{(x-2)}{4} - 12 \times \dfrac{(x-3)}{6} = 24$

$\qquad 3(x-2) - 2(x-3) = 24$

$\qquad 3x - 6 - 2x + 6 = 24$

$\qquad x = 24$

Solve the following equations.

14 a $\dfrac{x+1}{4} = \dfrac{1}{2}$ **b** $\dfrac{x-2}{3} = 5$ **c** $7 = \dfrac{2x-1}{3}$ **d** $\dfrac{4x+5}{2} = 9$

15 a $\dfrac{x+2}{4} + \dfrac{x-3}{2} = \dfrac{1}{2}$ **b** $\dfrac{x}{4} - \dfrac{x+3}{3} = \dfrac{1}{2}$ **c** $\dfrac{2}{3} - \dfrac{x+1}{9} = \dfrac{5}{6}$

16 a $\dfrac{x}{5} + \dfrac{x+1}{4} = \dfrac{8}{5}$ **b** $\dfrac{2x}{5} - \dfrac{x-3}{8} = \dfrac{1}{10}$ **c** $\dfrac{3x}{20} + \dfrac{x-2}{8} = \dfrac{3}{10}$

17 a $\dfrac{x-4}{3} - \dfrac{x+1}{4} = \dfrac{1}{6}$ **b** $\dfrac{x+3}{5} + \dfrac{x-2}{4} = \dfrac{3}{10}$ **c** $\dfrac{2x-1}{7} + \dfrac{3x-3}{4} = \dfrac{1}{7}$

18 a $\dfrac{1}{x+1} = \dfrac{1}{2}$ **b** $\dfrac{2}{x-1} = \dfrac{1}{4}$ **c** $8 = \dfrac{3}{x-2}$ **d** $\dfrac{4}{x-5} = \dfrac{1}{3}$

MIXED EXERCISE

EXERCISE 6J   **Do not use a calculator for this exercise.**

1 Simplify   **a** $\dfrac{6xy}{3y^2}$ **b** $\dfrac{2x(x-y)}{4x^2}$ **c** $\dfrac{3(x-y)}{(x-y)(x+y)}$

2 Simplify   **a** $\dfrac{1}{2p} - \dfrac{1}{3p}$ **b** $\dfrac{15xy \times 3y}{9xy^2}$ **c** $\dfrac{2y^2}{3} \times \dfrac{9}{4xy}$

3 Solve the equations

   a $\dfrac{3x}{4} = 5$ **c** $\dfrac{x}{4} + \dfrac{3x-2}{6} = \dfrac{1}{3}$ **e** $\dfrac{1}{x} + \dfrac{1}{2} = 3$

   b $\dfrac{3}{4x} = \dfrac{5}{2}$ **d** $\dfrac{x}{2} + \dfrac{3x}{4} = 7$ **f** $\dfrac{5}{x+1} = 6$

4 a Simplify $\dfrac{x-2}{4} + \dfrac{x}{3}$ **b** Solve the equation $\dfrac{x}{2} - \dfrac{2x-4}{3} = \dfrac{1}{4}$

5 a Simplify $\dfrac{x+1}{2} + \dfrac{x-3}{4}$ **b** Solve the equation $\dfrac{x+1}{2} = \dfrac{x-3}{4}$

INVESTIGATION

You now know how to express the sum of two fractions such as $\dfrac{1}{x+1} + \dfrac{1}{x-1}$ as a single fraction,

i.e. $\dfrac{1}{x+1} + \dfrac{1}{x-1} = \dfrac{(x-1)+(x+1)}{(x-1)(x+1)} = \dfrac{2x}{(x-1)(x+1)}$

Therefore starting with a single fraction such as $\dfrac{2x}{(x-1)(x+1)}$ it must be possible to reverse the process and express it as the sum (or difference) of two fractions.

Investigate how $\dfrac{2}{(x+1)(x-1)}$ can be expressed as the sum or difference of two fractions.

If you think you have found a method that will work with any such fraction, try it by expressing $\dfrac{4}{(x+2)(2x-1)}$ as the sum or difference of two fractions.

SUMMARY 2

INDICES

When a number is written in the form 3^4, 3 is called the base and the raised 4 is called the index or power.

3^4 means $3 \times 3 \times 3 \times 3$.

Negative indices

For any number a, $a^{-b} = \dfrac{1}{a^b}$, so 3^{-4} means $\dfrac{1}{3^4}$,

Zero index

$3^0 = 1$, in fact $a^0 = 1$ for all values of a except 0.

Rules of indices

We can multiply different powers of the same base by adding the indices,

e.g. $3^4 \times 3^2 = 3^{4+2} = 3^6$ and $a^5 \times a^7 = a^{5+7} = a^{12}$

We can divide different powers of the same base by subtracting the indices,

e.g. $3^4 \div 3^2 = 3^{4-2} = 3^2$ and $y^5 \div y^7 = y^{5-7} = y^{-2}$

RECIPROCALS

The reciprocal of a number is 1 divided by that number, for example, the reciprocal of 4 is $\frac{1}{4} = 0.25$

the reciprocal of $\frac{3}{5}$ is $\frac{5}{3}$

and the reciprocal of 0.8 is $1 \div 0.8 = 1.25$

In general, a^{-1} is the reciprocal of a.

STANDARD FORM

A number written in standard form is a number between 1 and 10 multiplied by a power of ten, e.g. 1.2×10^5.

To change 32 700 to standard form, we place the decimal point between 3 and 2 to give a number between 1 and 10. Counting then tells us that, to change 3.27 to 32 700, we must move the decimal point 4 places to the right (that is multiply by 10 000, i.e. 10^4).

So $32\,700 = 3.27 \times 10^4$.

PROBABILITY

We *add probabilities* when we want the probability that one or the other of two (or more) events will happen, provided that only one of the events can happen at a time.

Events such that only one of them can happen on any one occasion are called *mutually exclusive*.

For example, when one dice is rolled,

$$\text{P(scoring 5 or 6)} = \text{P(scoring 5)} + \text{P(scoring 6)}$$

We *multiply probabilities* when we want the probability that two (or more) events both happen, provided that each event has no influence on whether or not the other occurs.
Events such that each has no influence on whether the other occurs are called *independent events*.
For example, when two dice A and B are rolled,

P(scoring 6 on A and on B) = P(scoring 6 on A) × P(scoring 6 on B)

Tree diagrams
Tree diagrams can be used to illustrate the outcomes when two or more events occur.

This tree, for example, shows the possible outcomes when two coins are tossed.

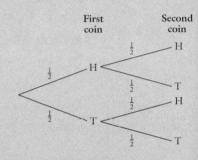

We *multiply* the probabilities when we follow a path along the branches and *add* the results of following several paths.

SEQUENCES

A sequence can be formed when we have a rule.
This rule may be an instruction giving one term and how to find the next term from the previous one,

e.g   the first term is 2 and the next term is double the previous term; then the sequence is 2, 4, 8, 16, 32, ...

A sequence can also be generated when we know the *nth term* expressed in terms of *n*, the position number of the term. Any term of the sequence can then be found by giving *n* a numerical value.
For example, when the *n*th term = $3n - 2$,
the 10th term is given by substituting 10 for *n*,
i.e.   by $3(10) - 2 = 28$

To find the *n*th term from the first few terms of a sequence, we first try to spot the pattern. If we cannot, a *difference table* may help;
the first row of the table lists the terms of the sequence,
the second row gives the differences between successive terms: if the numbers in this row are all equal, the *n*th term is $an + b$ where *a* is equal to the difference between the terms and *b* is a number that can be found by looking at the first term.

When the numbers in the second row are not equal, we can add another row to give the difference between them; if this row of second differences are all equal, then the nth term involves n^2.

ALGEBRAIC FRACTIONS

The same rules apply to fractions with letter terms as are used for fractions with numbers only,

i.e.   *fractions can be simplified* by cancelling common factors of the numerator and denominator,

e.g. $$\frac{2xy}{4y \times (2y - x)} = \frac{{}^1\!\cancel{2xy}{}^1}{{}_2\!\cancel{4y} \times (2y - x)} = \frac{x}{2(2y - x)}$$

To *add or subtract fractions*, first change them into equivalent fractions with a common denominator,

e.g. $$\frac{3}{2x} - \frac{5}{4y} = \frac{6y}{4xy} - \frac{5x}{4xy} = \frac{6y - 5x}{4xy}$$

To *multiply fractions*, multiply the numerators and multiply the denominators,

e.g. $$\frac{2x}{3y} \times \frac{5y^2}{7x} = \frac{2\cancel{x}^{\,1}}{3\cancel{y}_{\,1}} \times \frac{5\cancel{y}^{\,y}}{7\cancel{x}_{\,1}} = \frac{2 \times 5y}{3 \times 7} = \frac{10y}{21}$$

and to *divide by a fraction*, turn it upside down and multiply,

e.g. $$\frac{x}{x - 2} \div \frac{2x^2}{3x - 1} = \frac{{}^1\cancel{x}}{x - 2} \times \frac{3x - 1}{2\cancel{x^2}_{\,x}} = \frac{3x - 1}{2x(x - 2)}$$

To *solve an equation that contains fractions*, multiply each term in the equation by the lowest number that each denominator divides into exactly. This will eliminate all fractions from the equation,

e.g.   if $\dfrac{x}{2} + 1 = \dfrac{2}{3}$

multiplying each term by 6 gives

$$\frac{6}{1} \times \frac{x}{2} + 6 \times 1 = \frac{6}{1} \times \frac{2}{3}$$

which simplifies to $3x + 6 = 4$ which can be solved easily.

REVISION EXERCISE 2.1 (Chapters 1, 2 and 3)

1 a Find the value of **i** 4.72×10^2 **ii** 4^3 **iii** 1.2^2

   b Express as a single expression in index form
   i $2^3 \times 2^5$ **ii** $10^7 \times 10^{10}$ **iii** $2^{10} \div 2^8$

2 Find the value of

a 3^{-2} **c** 5.9×10^{-2} **e** 2^{-4}

b 12^{-1} **d** 7.23×10^{4} **f** 5^{-3}

3 a Which is the larger

   i 10^{3} or 10^{6} **ii** 10^{-2} or 10^{-3} **iii** 10^{0} or 10^{-2} ?

b Write as an ordinary number   **i** 2.14×10^{3} **ii** 5.21×10^{-2}

4 Use your calculator to find, correct to 3 significant figures

a 27.34×0.0893 **c** $\dfrac{54.39 \times 4.873}{54.39 - 4.873}$

b $16.84^{2} \div 0.5632$ **d** $\dfrac{1}{(0.4463)^{2}}$

5 The answers given to the following calculations are all wrong. Decide, in your head, whether each answer is too large or too small.

a $\dfrac{3+8}{9} = 0.12$ **c** $\dfrac{(1.8)^{2}}{0.93} = 0.35$

b $(0.72)^{-1} = 13.9$ **d** $\dfrac{20.4}{0.58^{2}} = 6.06$

6 Use your calculator to find the value of πr^{2} when $r = 8.47 \times 10^{-4}$ cm. Give your answer in the standard form $a \times 10^{n}$ where a is correct to 4 significant figures.

7 a Write in standard form

   i 0.00926 **ii** $730\,000$

b Write as an ordinary number

   i 2.47×10^{-5} **ii** 6.24×10^{2} **iii** 3.47×10^{-2}

8 a Write the following numbers in standard form and then place them in order of size with the smallest first.

          $324\,000, \ 99\,000, \ 1\,270\,000, \ 8700$

b Which is the larger and by how much

         3.56×10^{-2} or 8.43×10^{-2} ?

9 Given that $a = 7.5 \times 10^{6}$ and $b = 5 \times 10^{7}$ find, in standard form, the value of

a $a + b$ **b** ab **c** $\dfrac{a}{b}$ **d** $10a + b$

10 A light year is the distance travelled by light in a solar year (approximately 365 days). If the speed of light is approximately 3×10^8 metres per second, calculate a light year in metres, giving your answer in standard form.

11 a Work out the value of n in each of the following:

    i $3^4 + 2^n = 97$
    ii $y^9 \div y^3 = y^n$

  b Saturn is approximately 1.43×10^9 km from the Sun.
    Venus is approximately 1.08×10^8 km from the Sun.
    How much further from the Sun is Saturn than Venus?
    Give your answer in standard form.   (SEG)

12 Calculate, giving your answer in standard form correct to 3 significant figures

$$\frac{1.52 \times 10^5 - 4.6 \times 10^4}{4.56 \times 10^{-2}}$$

      (London)

13 a Use your calculator to work out the value of

$$\frac{6.08 \times (9.72)^2}{581 + 237}$$

  Write down the full calculator display.

  b **i** Write down a calculation that could be done mentally to check the answer to part **a**, using numbers rounded to one significant figure.
    ii Write down the answer to your calculation in part **i**. (MEG)

REVISION EXERCISE 2.2 (Chapters 4, 5 and 6)

1 A card is drawn at random from an ordinary pack of 52 playing cards. A second card is drawn at random from another ordinary pack of 52 cards. What is the probability that

  a the first card is a red 2

  b the second card is a black queen

  c the first card is a red 2 and the second card is a black queen?

2 The probability that Simon completes his maths homework is $\frac{7}{8}$ and that Hilary completes her maths homework is $\frac{3}{4}$. What is the probability that

  a Simon does not complete his maths homework

  b both Simon and Hilary complete their maths homework

  c neither Simon nor Hilary complete their maths homework?

3 When the post arrived Val had 3 first-class letters and 4 second-class letters while Dirk had 5 first-class letters and 2 second-class letters. A letter is taken at random from each batch.

a Copy and complete the tree diagram by writing in the probabilities on each branch.

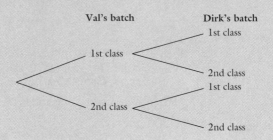

Find the probability that

b both letters are first class

c one is first class and one is second class.

4 Crisps of several different flavours are on sale in the school tuck shop. At any given time it is known that the probability that the next sale will be 'plain' is $\frac{1}{5}$ and the probability that the next sale will be 'salt and vinegar' is $\frac{1}{2}$. Find the probability that the next sale will be either a packet of plain crisps or a packet that is flavoured with salt and vinegar.

5 Jo can go to work by car, on a bus, by train or on a bicycle. The probability that she goes by car is $\frac{1}{3}$, on the bus $\frac{1}{10}$ and by train $\frac{1}{5}$. What is the probability that next week

a she goes by car or on the bus on Monday

b she goes by car on Monday and on the bus on Tuesday

c she cycles on Wednesday?

6 a Write down, in words, the rule for getting the sequence

$$2, 5, 11, 23, 47, \ldots$$

b Find the next two terms in the sequence $5, 8, 11, 14, \ldots$

c The rule for giving a sequence is

add 3 to the previous term, then multiply by 2.

i If the first term is 4 write down the first five terms of the sequence.

ii Using the same rule, but starting with a different first term, the third term in a sequence is 26. Find the first two terms.

7 a Write down the first four terms and the 30th term of the sequence whose nth term is $n^2 + n$.

b Find a formula for the nth term of the sequence
$$0, 2, 6, 12, 20 \ldots .$$

8

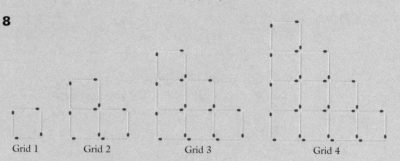

Grid 1   Grid 2   Grid 3   Grid 4

Phil is making a pattern with matchsticks.

a How many matchsticks are used to make the figure in

i Grid 1   **ii** Grid 2   **iii** Grid 3   **iv** Grid 4

b Without drawing any more grids write down

i the number of matchsticks in Grid 5
ii an expression, in terms of n, for the number of matchsticks in the nth grid.

9 a Simplify

i $5 \times \dfrac{x}{10}$ **iii** $\dfrac{3x}{2} \div \dfrac{5}{8}$ **v** $\dfrac{pqr}{p^2 q}$

ii $\dfrac{2}{5}$ of $25x$ **iv** $\dfrac{3p}{12}$ **vi** $\dfrac{p+4}{(p-4)(p+4)}$

b Write as a single fraction in its simplest form

i $\dfrac{a-b}{3} \times \dfrac{5}{a}$ **ii** $\dfrac{3ab}{4} \div \dfrac{a}{b}$ **iii** $\dfrac{6p}{5q} \times \dfrac{15q}{9p^2}$ **iv** $\dfrac{x^2}{4} \times \dfrac{12}{3xy}$

10 Solve the equations.

a $\dfrac{x}{4} = 5$ **c** $\dfrac{2x}{3} = \dfrac{5}{7}$ **e** $\dfrac{3}{x} = \dfrac{1}{5}$

b $\dfrac{x}{3} - 1 = 5$ **d** $\dfrac{5x}{12} - \dfrac{7}{4} = \dfrac{x}{8}$ **f** $\dfrac{x+1}{3} = \dfrac{x-1}{2}$

11 $2, 5, 8, 11, 14, \ldots, \ldots, 23$

a Write in the missing numbers in the sequence.

b Work out the 12th number in the sequence.

c Work out an algebraic expression for the nth term in the sequence.

(London)

12 When you drop a match box on to a table, there are three ways it can land.

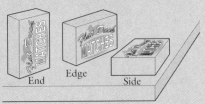

Jane has found that the probability of it landing on one end is approximately 0.1 and the probability of it landing on one side is approximately 0.6.

a Estimate the probability that the matchbox will land on one edge. Show your method clearly.

b Jane drops two identical matchboxes.
What is the probability that both boxes will land on one end?

c Jane and Sarah are playing a game.

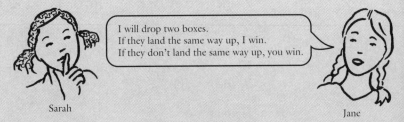

> I will drop two boxes.
> If they land the same way up, I win.
> If they don't land the same way up, you win.

Sarah   Jane

Who is more likely to win the game?
Show all your working.   (NEAB)

13 Solve the equation $\dfrac{2x + 3}{3} - \dfrac{x - 1}{4} = 5$ (WJEC)

**REVISION
EXERCISE 2.3
(Chapters 1 to 6)**

Do not use a calculator for this exercise.

1 a Find the value of   **i** 5.97×10^3 **ii** 10^5 **iii** 4^{-2} **iv** 5^0

  b Write as a single expression in index form

  i $2^3 \times 2^5$ **ii** $5^2 \times 5^7$ **iii** $a^3 \times a^4$ **iv** $b^7 \div b^5$

2 a Express 1225 as the product of its prime factors and hence find its square root.

  b Write, as a single number in index form

  i $5^3 \times 5^2$ **ii** $4^{-5} \times 4^{-2}$

  c Find the smallest number that 252 needs to be multiplied by to change it to a square number.

3 a Write in index form

   i $3 \times 3 \times 7 \times 7 \times 7$ **ii** $2 \times 5 \times 2 \times 2 \times 5 \times 5$

b Find the value of

   i 3.4×10^5 **ii** 8.6×10^{-2}

c Write as a power of 10

   i $100\,000$ **ii** $\frac{1}{10\,000}$ **iii** 0.01 **iv** $0.000\,01$

4 a Write in standard form   **i** $47\,000$ **ii** $0.000\,008\,2$

b Write as an ordinary number

   i 5.5×10^4 **ii** 7.24×10^{-4} **iii** 3.72×10^0

c Estimate the value of $\dfrac{1.793}{5.026 + 0.9943}$

5 Given that $a = 1.5 \times 10^{-2}$ and $b = 5 \times 10^{-3}$ find, in standard form

  a $a + b$ **b** ab **c** $a - b$ **d** $\dfrac{a}{b}$

6 When Mrs Hussain needs to buy bread, the probability that she buys it in the supermarket is $\frac{4}{9}$, while the probability that she buys it at the local bakery is $\frac{1}{3}$. What is the probability that

  a she buys bread either at the supermarket or at the local bakery

  b she buys bread somewhere else.

7 Celia has two bags. Bag A contains 4 sweet apples and 5 sour apples while bag B contains 6 sweet apples and 4 sour apples. Ian takes one apple from each bag.

  a Copy and complete the tree diagram by filling in the probabilities on the branches.

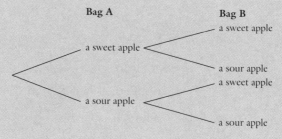

  b Find the probability that

    i both apples are sweet

   ii one apple is sweet and the other is sour.

8 a Find the next two terms in each sequence.

    i $3, 7, 13, 21, 31, \ldots$ **ii** $3, 9, 21, 39, 63, \ldots$

  b In a sequence the nth term is given by the expression $5n - 7$.

    i Find the 45th term.

    ii Find the value of n if the nth term is 293.

    iii What is the largest value of n if the nth term is less than 500?

9 Look at the sequence of numbers $5, 13, 21, 29, 37, \ldots$

  a Write down, in words, the rule for getting each number from the one before it.

  b Write down a formula, in terms of n, for the nth term of this sequence.

10 a Simplify **i** $\dfrac{3b}{8} \times 16b$ **ii** $\dfrac{8x}{5} \div \dfrac{4x}{15}$ **iii** $\dfrac{(a+b)(a-b)}{(a-b)}$

  b Solve these equations.

    i $\dfrac{3x}{4} = 21$ **ii** $\dfrac{x}{2} + \dfrac{1}{3} = 2$ **iii** $\dfrac{3x}{4} = \dfrac{x}{2} + \dfrac{3}{4}$

REVISION EXERCISE 2.4 (Chapters 1 to 6)

1 a Write the following in order of size with the smallest first

$$3^{-2}, \ -9, \ 0.3, \ 10^{-1}$$

  b Write as a single expression in index form

    i $3^4 \times 3^2$ **ii** $5^9 \div 5^6$ **iii** $a^3 \times a^3 \times a^5$ **iv** $b^4 \div b^4$

2 Use a calculator to find, correct to 3 significant figures

  a 0.047×6.421 **c** 1.2^5

  b $4703 \div 2423$ **d** $34.67 \div (0.873)^2$

3 a Give the number 67.039 correct to

    i 3 significant figures   **ii** 2 significant figures.

  b Use a calculator to find, correct to 3 significant figures, the value of

    i 53.8×2.835 **iii** $0.8846 \div 16.77$

    ii 9.427×3.293 **iv** $\dfrac{1}{0.4735}$

4 a Give $0.007\,396$ correct to

    i 2 significant figures   **ii** 2 decimal places.

  b Simplify **i** $\dfrac{7}{12} \times \dfrac{2}{21}$ **ii** $3\dfrac{1}{3} \times 2\dfrac{1}{4}$ **iii** $8\dfrac{1}{8} \div 7\dfrac{3}{7}$

  c Use your calculator to find, correct to 3 significant figures, the value of

    i $\dfrac{78.42 - 35.96}{78.42 + 35.96}$ **ii** $\dfrac{(7.974)^2}{0.6429}$

5 a Give 1.9057 correct to

   i 2 decimal places **ii** 3 significant figures **iii** 1 significant figure.

  b Use a calculator, giving your answers correct to 3 significant figures, to find

   i 0.846×12.55 **ii** $16.87 \div 24.66$ **iii** $\dfrac{1}{39.4}$

6 a Write in standard form **i** $0.000\,004\,23$ **ii** $8\,790\,000$

  b Write as an ordinary number

   i 7.92×10^{-3} **ii** 5.96×10^{3} **iii** 8.2×10^{5} **iv** 2×10^{-4}

  c Use the formula $E = mc^2$ to find E when $m = 1.4 \times 10^{-25}$ and $c = 2.998 \times 10^{8}$.

7 If $x = 2.4 \times 10^4$ and $y = 5.57 \times 10^3$ find, in standard form

  a $x + y$ **b** xy **c** $x \div y$ **d** $x^2 y$

8 An ordinary dice is weighted so that when it is rolled it is not equally likely that it will show 1, 2, 3, 4, 5 or 6.

The table shows the probability for scoring 1, 2, 3, 4 or 5.

Score	1	2	3	4	5	6
Probability	0.2	0.2	0.2	0.1	0.2	

The dice is rolled once. What is the probability of scoring

  a 6   **b** either a 3 or a 4   **c** an odd number?

9 Two minibuses are used for a school trip to the theatre. In the blue minibus there are 9 girls and 6 boys while in the yellow minibus there are 7 girls and 8 boys. A student is chosen at random from each minibus to distribute the tickets for the show.

  a Copy and complete the tree diagram.

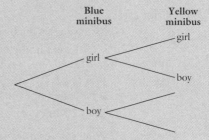

  b Find the probability that

   i both students are boys

   ii one student is a girl and the other student is a boy.

10 Find a formula for the nth term of the sequence

  a $11, 15, 19, 23, \ldots$ **b** $\frac{1}{2}, \frac{1}{4}, \frac{1}{6}, \frac{1}{8}, \ldots$ **c** $3 \times 5, \, 5 \times 7, \, 7 \times 9, \ldots$

DIRECT AND INVERSE PROPORTION

7

Richard has a new scooter.

The instructions state that the tank must be filled with fuel mixed from oil and petrol in the ratio 1 : 50. If Richard puts 20 ml of oil in the tank, the ratio 1 : 50 tells him he needs to add 50 times as much petrol, that is 1000 ml, which is 1 litre. The ratio also tells him that 100 ml of oil has to be mixed with 100×50 ml of petrol, and so on.

- Although we can vary the amount of oil and petrol, the relationship between them is always the same, i.e. 1 : 50.
  Any two quantities that are always in the same ratio to each other, behave in the same way.
  For example, if one quantity is doubled, so is the other;
  if one quantity is quadrupled, so is the other, and so on.
  Quantities that are related in this way are said to be *directly proportional*.

Richard uses his moped to travel to work. The distance is 10 miles. If he leaves home at 8 a.m. the journey takes him 40 minutes. Using average speed $= \dfrac{\text{distance}}{\text{time}}$ gives his average speed as 15 mph. If he leaves at 7.30 a.m. he avoids the rush hour and the journey only takes 20 minutes. In this case his average speed is 30 mph.

- As the distance is fixed, there is a relationship between the average speed and the time the journey takes. In this case however, when the speed doubles, the time halves. So the relationship between the speed and the time is not one where they are in the same ratio.
  Quantities that are related this way, that is when one trebles, the other decreases to a third, when one quadruples, the other decreases to a quarter, and so on, are said to be *inversely proportional*.

In this chapter we are going to work with these two forms of relationship. First however, you need to be able to recognise when quantities are related in either of these two ways and, equally importantly, when they are not.

EXERCISE 7A

In each question discuss how the quantities are related. Some may be directly proportional, some may be inversely proportional. Some may be related in a different way from either of these and others may not be related in any way.

1 Jane's pay for working an 8-hour day and her pay for working a 37-hour week assuming the rate of pay per hour is constant.

2 Simon's pay for working an 8-hour day and his pay for working a 45-hour week when this includes overtime pay at a higher rate than the standard rate of pay per hour.

3 The age of a woman and her weight.

4 The number of £1 coins in a pile and the height of the pile.

5 The time it takes to fill a swimming pool and the number of hoses used to fill it, assuming that the rate of flow of water from each hose is the same.

6 The number of sweets that can be bought for £1 and the cost per kilogram of those sweets.

7 The number of towels in a washing machine and the time it takes to wash them.

8 The size of a telephone bill and the number of calls made from the telephone.

9 The size of an electricity bill including the standard charge and the number of units used.

10 The area of a square and the length of its side.

11 The size of an interior angle of a regular polygon and the number of sides.

12 The number of boxes needed to store 60 bottles and the number of bottles in each box.

13 The number of pencils bought at 50 p each and their total cost.

14 The number of items bought in a supermarket and their total cost.

15 The number of people attending a meeting and the number of biscuits allowed per person when there are 100 biscuits in total.

16 The time it takes to build a wall and the number of bricklayers building it, assuming that they all work at the same rate.

17 The number of tea towels hanging on a washing line and the time it takes them to dry.

18 The number of loaves of bread made and the total weight of flour used.

19 The time it takes a mechanical digger to dig a trench and the size of the trench.

SIMPLE DIRECT PROPORTION

If we know the cost of one article, we can easily find the cost of ten similar articles or, if we know what someone is paid for one hour's work, we can find what the pay is for five hours.

EXERCISE 7B

> If $1 \, cm^3$ of lead weighs $11.3 \, g$, what is the weight of
>
> **a** $6 \, cm^3$ **b** $0.8 \, cm^3$?
>
> $1 \, cm^3$ weighs $11.3 \, g$
>
> **a** $6 \, cm^3$ weigh $6 \times 11.3 \, g = 67.8 \, g$
>
> **b** $0.8 \, cm^3$ weigh $0.8 \times 11.3 \, g = 9.04 \, g$

1 The cost of 1 kg of sugar is 90 p.
What is the cost of   **a** 3 kg   **b** 12 kg?

2 In one hour an electric fire uses $1\frac{1}{2}$ units. Find how much it uses in
a 4 hours   **b** $\frac{1}{2}$ hour.

3 One litre of petrol takes a car 18 km. At the same rate, how far does it travel on
a 4 litres   **b** 6.6 litres?

4 The cost of 1 kg of mushrooms is £3.30. Find the cost of
a 500 g   **b** 2.4 kg.

We can reverse the process and, for instance, find the cost of one article if we know the cost of three similar articles.

$18 \, \text{cm}^3$ of copper weigh $162 \, \text{g}$. What is the weight of $1 \, \text{cm}^3$?

$18 \, \text{cm}^3$ weigh $162 \, \text{g}$

$1 \, \text{cm}^3$ weighs $\dfrac{162}{18} \, \text{g} = 9 \, \text{g}$

---

5 Six pens cost £7.20. What is the cost of one pen?

6 A car uses eight litres of petrol to travel 124 km. At the same rate, how far can it travel on one litre?

7 A carpet costs £117.60. Its area is $12 \, \text{m}^2$. What is the cost of $1 \, \text{m}^2$?

We can use the same method even if the quantities given are not whole numbers of units.

The mass of $0.6 \, \text{cm}^3$ of a metal is $3 \, \text{g}$. What is the mass of $1 \, \text{cm}^3$?

The mass of $0.6 \, \text{cm}^3$ is $3 \, \text{g}$

The mass of $1 \, \text{cm}^3$ is $\dfrac{3}{0.6} \, \text{g} = 5 \, \text{g}$

---

8 $8.6 \, \text{m}^2$ of carpet cost £71.38. What is the cost of $1 \, \text{m}^2$?

9 The cost of running a refrigerator for 3.2 hours is 4.8 p. What is the cost of running the refrigerator for one hour?

10 A piece of webbing is 12.4 cm long and its area is $68.2 \, \text{cm}^2$. What is the area of a piece of this webbing that is 1 cm long?

DIRECT PROPORTION

When two varying quantities are always in the same ratio, they are said to be *directly proportional* to one another (or sometimes simply *proportional*).

For example, when buying pads of paper which all cost the same amount, the total cost is proportional to the number of pads. The ratio of the number of pads bought to their total cost stays the same, and if we know the cost of 11 pads, we can find the cost of 14 pads.

One method for solving problems involving direct proportion uses ratio. Another, which uses the ideas in the last exercise, is called the unitary method because it makes use of the cost of one article or the time taken by one man to complete a piece of work, and so on.

EXERCISE 7C

The mass of $16\,\text{cm}^3$ of a metal alloy is $24\,\text{g}$. What is the mass of $20\,\text{cm}^3$ of the same alloy?

First method (using ratios)
Let the mass of $20\,\text{cm}^3$ be x grams.

Then $x : 20 = 24 : 16$

> The ratio of mass to volume stays the same. Write it starting with x.

i.e. $\dfrac{x}{20} = \dfrac{24}{16}$

$\cancel{20} \times \dfrac{x}{\cancel{20}} = \cancel{20}^{5} \times \dfrac{\cancel{24}^{6}}{\cancel{16}}$

so $x = 30$

The mass of $20\,\text{cm}^3$ is 30 grams.

Second method (unitary method)

> Rewrite the first sentence so that it *ends* with the quanity you want, i.e. the mass.

$16\,\text{cm}^3$ has a mass of $24\,\text{g}$

$\therefore$ $1\,\text{cm}^3$ has a mass of $\dfrac{24}{16}\,\text{g}$

> There is no need to work out the value of $\frac{24}{16}$ yet.

so $20\,\text{cm}^3$ has a mass of $\cancel{20}^{5} \times \dfrac{\cancel{24}^{6}}{\cancel{16}}\,\text{g} = 30\,\text{g}$

For this exercise use whichever method you prefer.

1 At a steady speed a car uses four litres of petrol to travel $75\,\text{km}$. At the same speed how much petrol is needed to travel $60\,\text{km}$?

2 A hiker walked steadily for four hours, covering $16\,\text{km}$. How long did he take to cover $12\,\text{km}$?

3 An electric fire uses $7\frac{1}{2}$ units in three hours. How many units does it use in five hours?

4 How long does the electric fire in question **3** take to use 9 units?

5 A rail journey of 300 miles costs £84. At the same rate per mile

   a what would be the cost of travelling 250 miles

   b how far could you travel for £63?

6 A machine in a soft drinks factory fills 840 bottles in six hours. How many could it fill in five hours?

7 A 6 kg bag of sprouts costs 396 p. At the same rate, what would an 8 kg bag cost?

8 A scale model of a ship is such that the mast is 9 cm high and the mast of the original ship is 12 m high. The length of the original ship is 27 m. How long is the model ship?

Either method will work, whether the numbers are complicated or simple. Even if the problem is about something unfamiliar, we can solve it if we know that the quantities are proportional.

In a spring balance the extension in the spring is proportional to the load. If the extension is 2.5 cm when the load is 8 newtons, what is the extension when the load is 3.6 newtons?

Ratio method

Let the extension be x cm.

$$x : 3.6 = 2.5 : 8$$

> As the extension is proportional to the load, the ratio extension : load stays the same.

i.e. $$\frac{x}{3.6} = \frac{2.5}{8}$$

so $$3.6 \times \frac{x}{3.6} = 3.6 \times \frac{2.5}{8} \text{ giving } x = 1.125$$

The extension is 1.125 cm.

Unitary method

> Remember to rewrite the sentence so that we end with the extension.

A load of 8 newtons gives an extension of 2.5 cm.

A load of 1 newton gives an extension of $\frac{2.5}{8}$ cm.

So a load of 3.6 newtons gives an extension of

$$3.6 \times \frac{2.5}{8} \text{ cm} = 1.125 \text{ cm}$$

---

9 It costs £392 to hire scaffolding for 42 days. How much would it cost to hire the same scaffolding for 36 days at the same daily rate?

10 The rates of currency exchange published in the newspapers on a certain day showed that 14 kroner could be exchanged for 210 pesos. How many pesos could be obtained for 32 kroner?

11 At a steady speed, a car uses 15 litres of petrol to travel 164 km. At the same speed, what distance can be travelled if 6 litres were used?

12 If a 2 kg bag of sugar contains 9×10^6 crystals, how many crystals are there in   **a** 5 kg   **b** 1.8 kg   **c** 0.03 kg?

13 The current flowing through a lamp is proportional to the voltage across the lamp. When the voltage across the lamp is 10 volts the current is 0.6 amps. What voltage is required to make a current of 0.9 amps flow?

14 The amount of energy carried by an electric current is proportional to the number of coulombs. If 5 coulombs carry 19 joules of energy, how many joules are carried by 6.5 coulombs?

15 Ten grains of rice weigh 1.5×10^{-3} kg. What is the weight of 1000 grains of rice?

16 The compression in a spring is proportional to the load placed on it.
A load of 5 kg compresses a spring by 25 mm.
How far will a load of 12.5 kg compress the same spring?

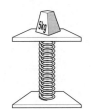

17 The air resistance of a moving car is proportional to the speed at which the car is travelling. When a car is moving at 50 km/h, it is subject to air resistance of 2500 newtons. If the car is subject to air resistance of 3500 newtons at what speed must it be moving?

18 Two varying quantities, x and y, are directly proportional.
Copy and complete this table.

x	2	4	6	8
y	10			

19 Two quantities, R and S, are directly proportional. Copy and complete the table giving corresponding values of R and S.

R	2.5	5	6.6	10.9
S	21.3			

20 A recipe for date squares lists the following quantities:

Ingredients	Costs
125 g of brown sugar	500 g cost 76 p
75 g of oats	750 g cost 102 p
75 g of flour	1.5 kg cost 88 p
100 g of margarine	250 g cost 36 p
100 g of dates	250 g cost 84 p
Pinch of bicarbonate of soda	–
Squeeze of lemon juice	1 p

Find the cost of making these date squares as accurately as possible, then give your answer correct to the nearest penny.

INVERSE PROPORTION

At the start of this chapter we found that some quantities are not directly proportional to one another, although there is a connection between them. When we considered the relationship between Richard's average speed and the time taken to travel 10 miles, we saw that when the average speed doubled, the time halved. This means that the reciprocal, or inverse, of the time is proportional to the average speed. We also saw that

when the speed is 15 mph, the time taken is 40 minutes

and   when the speed is 30 mph, the time taken is 20 minutes.

If we multiply the speed and the corresponding time together, the result is 600 in both cases.

As another example, suppose that a fixed amount of food is available for several days. If each person eats the same amount each day, the more people there are, the shorter is the time that the food will last.

In fact, if the food will last 2 people for 6 days,

it will last 6 people for 2 days,

i.e. when we treble the number of people, the number of days the food will last decreases to a third. Hence the number of days the food will last is inversely proportional to the number of people eating it.

Again, we see that the product of the number of days and the number of people it will feed is 12 in both cases.

These examples illustrate the fact that

> when two quantities are inversely proportional,
> their product remains constant.

EXERCISE 7D   In this exercise, assume that the rates are constant.

> Four bricklayers can build a certain wall in ten days. How long
> would five bricklayers take to build it?
>
> **Constant product method**
> Suppose that 5 bricklayers take x days to build the wall,
>
> then $5 \times x = 4 \times 10$
>
> i.e. $5x = 40$ giving $x = 8$
>
> It would take them 8 days.
>
> **Unitary method**
> 4 bricklayers take 10 days.
> 1 bricklayer would take 40 days.
> 5 bricklayers would take $\frac{40}{5}$ days = 8 days

For this exercise use whichever method you prefer.

1 Eleven taps fill a tank in three hours. How long would it take to fill
the tank if only six taps are working?

2 Nine children share out equally the chocolates in a large tin and get
eight each. If there were only six children, how many would each get?

3 The length of an essay is 174 lines with an average of 14 words per
line. If it is rewritten with an average of 12 words per line, how
many lines will be needed?

4 A field of grass feeds 24 cows for six days. How long would the
same field feed 18 cows?

5 The dimensions of a block of stamps are 30 cm wide by 20 cm high.
The same number of stamps could also have been arranged in a
block 24 cm wide. How high would this second block be?

6 A batch of bottles were packed in 25 boxes taking 12 bottles each.
If the same batch had been packed in boxes taking 15 each, how
many boxes would be filled?

7 When knitting a scarf 48 stitches wide, one ball of wool gives a
length of 18 cm. If the scarf had been 54 stitches wide instead, how
long a piece would the same ball give?

8 In a school, 33 classrooms are required if each class has 32 pupils. How many classrooms would be required if the class size was reduced to 22?

9 A factory needs 42 machines to produce a given number of articles in 63 days. How many machines would be required to produce the same number of articles in 54 days?

10 A swimming pool can be filled in 3 hours when 6 hoses are used. How long will it take to fill the same pool when 4 hoses are used?

11 An ink cartridge in a printer will last 20 days when an average of 50 sheets of paper are printed each day.
How long will a cartridge last when the average number of sheets printed per day is increased to 80?

12 It is estimated that a two-mile trench for an underground water pipe can be dug in 72 hours when 2 mechanical diggers are used.
About how long will it take to dig the trench if 5 mechanical diggers can be used?

13 Two quantities, p and q, that can vary in value are inversely proportional.
Copy and complete the table.

p	20	5	0.5	0.01
q	0.5			

14 Two quantities, f and w, that can vary in value are inversely proportional.
Copy and complete the table.

f	12.5	3		0.01
w	6		70	

EXERCISE 7E

This exercise contains a mixture of questions, some of which cannot be answered because the quantities are in neither direct nor inverse proportion. In these cases give a reason why there is no answer. For those questions that can be solved, give answers correct to three significant figures where necessary.

1 A man earned £30.60 for an eight-hour day. How much would he earn at the same rate for a 38-hour week?

2 A typist typed 3690 words in $4\frac{1}{2}$ hours. How long would it take the typist to type 2870 words at the same rate?

3 The list of exchange rates states that £1 = 7 French francs and £1 = 2300 lira, so that 7 francs = 2300 lira.

a How many lira can 54 francs be exchanged for?

b How many francs are 1000 lira worth?

4 At the age of twelve, a boy is 1.6 m tall. How tall will he be at the age of eighteen?

5 A ream of paper (500 sheets) is 6.2 cm thick. How thick is a pile of 360 sheets of the same paper?

6 If I buy balloons at 14 p each, I can buy 63 of them. If the price of a balloon increases to 18 p, how many can I buy for the same amount of money?

7 A boy's mark for a test is 18 out of a total of 30 marks? If the test had been marked out of 40 what would the boy's mark have been?

8 Twenty-four identical mathematics text books occupy 60 cm of shelf space. How many of these books will fit into 85 cm?

9 A lamp post 4 m high has a shadow 3.2 m long cast by the Sun. A man 1.8 m high is standing by the lamp post. At the same moment, what is the length of his shadow?

10 A contractor decides that he can build a barn in nine weeks using four men. If he employs two more men, how long will the job take? Assume that all the men work at the same rate.

11 A twelve-year-old girl gained 27 marks in a competition. How many marks did her six-year-old sister gain?

12 For a given voltage, the current flowing is inversely proportional to the resistance. When the current flowing is 2.5 amps the resistance is 0.9 ohms. What is the current when the resistance is 1.5 ohms?

In questions **13** to **18** the tables give some corresponding values of two variables. Decide whether the variables are directly proportional, inversely proportional or neither.

13

x	2	4	7	8	9	12
y	6	12	21	24	30	36

14

p	2	3	6	7	9	10
q	20	10	5	6	6.5	10

15

w	1	2	4	8	10	20
p	18	9	4.5	2.25	1.8	0.9

17

l	1	2	4	5	8	10
b	4	2	1	0.8	0.5	0.4

16

s	2	5	6	10	15	20
t	18	45	54	90	135	180

18

x	1	2	4	8	10	20
y	2	8	32	126	200	800

MIXED EXERCISES

EXERCISE 7F   Do not use a calculator for this exercise.

1 A car uses 7 gallons of petrol for a 280 km journey.
At the same rate, how far could it go on 8 gallons?

2 Eight typesetters together could complete a task in five hours. If all the typesetters work at the same rate, how long would it take six of them?

3 A wordprocessor operator charges £40 for work which took her six hours. How much would she charge for nine hours' work at the same rate?

4 James Bond takes 4 minutes to complete a Grand Prix circuit when driving at an average speed of 90 mph. How long will it take him to complete one circuit if he increases his average speed to 120 mph?

5 A ream of paper (500 sheets) is 7 cm thick. How thick is a pile of 400 sheets of the same paper?

6 Jo spent £5.50 on cat food and it fed her cat for 9 days.

  a How much a week does it cost Jo to feed her cat?

  b Jo spends £10 next time she buys cat food. How many days will it last?

7 An agricultural feed merchant delivers a quantity of pignuts to a farm. This quantity lasts 200 pigs for 9 days. The farm reduced the number of pigs to 180. How many days will the same quantity of pignuts last for?

8 The school hall was set up for examinations with 14 rows of 8 desks. The layout is to be changed next year so that there will be only 7 desks in each row. How many rows of desks will there be then?

9 It costs £1.50 a day to keep an electric heater on for 2 hours in the morning and 4 hours in the evening. How much will it cost to keep the heater on for a full day of 24 hours?

10 'Artco' carpet costs £216 to cover a floor area of $12\,m^2$.

    a How much would it cost to cover a floor area of $14\,m^2$ with this carpet?

    b What floor area would this carpet cover for a cost of £144?

EXERCISE 7G   Use a calculator for this exercise and use your common sense to decide how accurate your answers should be.

1

A coffee bar usually has 24 pints of milk delivered daily and this is just enough to make 348 cups of cappuccino coffee. On Monday only 15 pints of milk were delivered. How many cups of cappuccino coffee would this make?

2 Mrs Andrews has a fixed budget to buy text books. She can afford up to 250 books that cost £8.60 each. How many books costing £10.50 each can she afford?

3 A book with 750 pages is 3.5 cm thick not counting the cover. How many pages would you expect in a book that is 2 cm thick excluding covers, assuming that it uses the same paper?

4 A charity finds that the amount it spends on fund raising and the income this generates is in the ratio 2:25.

    a In 1995, £2480 was spent on fund raising. How much income did this generate?

    b In 1997, the amount spent on fund raising was increased to £4500. How much income should this have generated?

5 An aeroplane takes 2 hours 34 minutes to fly from Corby to Aristos at an average speed of 720 km/h. How long will the same journey take at an average speed of 650 km/h?

6 Light takes 8 seconds to travel from the Sun to the Earth, a distance of 149 600 000 km. How long does it take light to travel from the Sun to Venus which is 108 000 000 km from the Sun?

7 The current flowing through an electrical component is proportional to the voltage across the component. When the voltage across the component is 1.7 volts the current is 0.2 amps. What voltage is required to make a current of 0.7 amps flow?

8 It is estimated that a bag of sand weighing 1.3 kg holds 2.4×10^5 grains. Estimate the number of grains in a bag of sand weighing 1.8 kg.

9 The length of a newspaper article is 26 column inches when it is set with an average of 14 words per line. How many column inches will the article take if it is set at an average of 12 words per line?

10 A manufacturer uses 250 tonnes of straw to make 720 000 sun hats. What weight of straw is needed to make 25 000 sun hats?

INVESTIGATION

Sweets at a 'Pick and Mix' counter are sold by weight at £0.56 per 100 grams.

a If x grams cost y pence, copy and complete this table giving values of y corresponding to values of x.

x	20	50	100	200	500	1000
y						

b Use a scale of 1 cm for 50 units on the x-axis and a scale of 2 cm for 50 units on the y-axis to plot these points on a graph.

c What do you notice about these points. Can you use your graph to find the cost of 162 grams?

d The cost and weight of these sweets are directly proportional. Investigate the graphical relationship between other quantities that are directly proportional. What do you notice? Is this always true?

e Extend your work to investigate the graphical relationship between two quantities that are inversely proportional. You can use some of the questions in **Exercise 7D** as examples of quantities that are inversely proportional.

EXPANDING BRACKETS

The area of this rectangle can be found by multiplying its length by its width,

i.e.   the area $= (x + 3)(x + 2)$

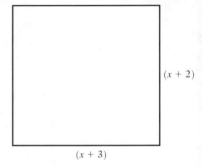

$(x + 2)$

$(x + 3)$

The area can also be found by dividing the rectangle into sections as shown opposite. Adding these four sections together gives the area as

$$x^2 + 3x + 2x + 6.$$

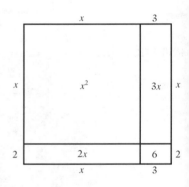

- This means that $(x + 3)(x + 2)$ and $x^2 + 3x + 2x + 6$ are two forms of the same expression. Being able to write $(x + 3)(x + 2)$ as $x^2 + 3x + 2x + 6$ *without* having to draw a diagram is clearly an advantage. This chapter shows you how it is done.

We begin with a reminder about multiplying out simpler brackets.

BRACKETS   Remember that $4(x + 2)$ means multiply every term inside the bracket by 4, i.e. $4(x + 2) = 4x + 8$

For directed numbers

when the signs are the same (both $+$ or both $-$), the product is positive, when the signs are different (one $+$ and one $-$), the product is negative

i.e. $(+3) \times (+4) = 12$ and $(-4) \times (-2) = 8$
whereas $(-3) \times 2 = -6$ and $3 \times (-4) = -12$

EXERCISE 8A   Multiply out the brackets.

1 a $4(x+1)$ **d** $2(3+4x)$ **g** $3(5-3x)$

  b $3(5x-2)$ **e** $2(5+6a)$ **h** $7(x-1)$

  c $5(x+4)$ **f** $8(2-5b)$ **i** $5(3-x)$

2 a $-5(x-3)$ **d** $-7(2-3x)$ **g** $-2(5+2x)$

  b $-2(3a+5)$ **e** $-3(2x-5)$ **h** $-(4-3x)$

  c $-(3x-11)$ **f** $-4(3b+2)$ **i** $-3(7x-2)$

Simplify

a $6x+5(x-4)$ **b** $9+(2x-5)$ **c** $6x-3(2+x)$

a $6x+5(x-4)=6x+5x-20$

        $=11x-20$

> First multiply out the bracket then collect like terms.

b

> $9+(2x-5)$ means 9 add $2x$ and add -5.

$9+(2x-5)=9+2x-5$

        $=4+2x$

> Numbers can be added and subtracted in any order so $9+2x-5=9-5+2x$

c

> $6x-3(2+x)$ means $6x$ take away 3 twos and 3 xs

$6x-3(2+x)=6x-6-3x$

        $=3x-6$

> $6x-6-3x=6x-3x-6$

Simplify the following expressions.

3 a $3x+5(x+1)$ **d** $3(x+2)+5$

  b $5+3(2x+3)$ **e** $3x+2(x-6)$

  c $4(x+3)+3(2x+5)$ **f** $5(3x-2)+2(3x-1)$

4 a $7x-(2x+3)$ **d** $5x-(5+x)$

  b $4-3(3+x)$ **e** $10-3(2x+3)$

  c $9a-(3a+7)$ **f** $6b-4(2b+1)$

Multiply out   **a** $-3(4x-7)$ **b** $8-(2-3x)$ **c** $2a(b-2a)$

a $-3(4x-7)=-12x+21$

> $-3(4x-7)=-3\times 4x$ and -3×-7
> $\qquad\qquad\quad = -12x+21$

b $8-(2-3x)=8-2+3x$
$\qquad\qquad = 6+3x$

> $-(2-3x)$ means take away 2 and take
> away $-3x$
> i.e. -2 and $-(-3x)$

c $2a(b-2a)=2ab-4a^2$

> $2a\times b=2ab$ and
> $2a\times 2a=2\times 2\times a\times a=4a^2$

Multiply out the following brackets.

5 a $-4(x-3)$ **c** $3-(6x-7)$ **e** $-(2b-4)$ **g** $-3(5+3x)$

  b $3a(b-a)$ **d** $-7(3-2x)$ **f** $12-3(2y-5)$ **h** $-6(2-5x)$

6 a $x(3x+5)$ **c** $2y(5y-2)$ **e** $-2p(p+q)$ **g** $-4a(5a-3)$

  b $-5(3a+4)$ **d** $a(2a-3b)$ **f** $-4a(b-2a)$ **h** $-x(4x-1)$

Simplify   **a** $2x-3(3x-7)$ **b** $3(x-4)-2(5-3x)$ **c** $4x(x-2)-3x(x+7)$

a $2x-3(3x-7)=2x-9x+21$
$\qquad\qquad\qquad = -7x+21$
$\qquad\qquad\qquad = 21-7x$

> Write the positive term first.

b $3(x-4)-2(5-3x)=3x-12-10+6x$

> Multiply out the brackets first.

$\qquad\qquad\qquad\qquad = 9x-22$

> Collect like terms: $3x-12-10+6x=3x+6x-12-10$

c $4x(x-2)-3x(x+7)=4x^2-8x-3x^2-21x$

> $4x\times x=4\times x\times x=4x^2$

$\qquad\qquad\qquad\qquad = x^2-29x$

Simplify

7 a $7x-3(2x-5)$ **b** $5x-4(3x-2)$ **c** $2a-4(2a-7)$ **d** $12-5(2a-3)$

8 a $8x-(3-x)$ **b** $7-2(5x-4)$ **c** $8-5(5b-4)$ **d** $c-(3c-2)$

9 a $(p-3q)-4q$ **b** $7x-3(3x-1)$ **c** $3a-4(3-5a)$ **d** $-3(x+3y)-5y$

10 a $x^2 - 2x(2x - 1)$

  b $x^2 - 3x(y - 3x)$

  c $4p^2 - 3q(p - q)$

  d $4a^2 - 3a(3 - 4a)$

  e $4a^2 + 3a(3a - 4)$

  f $3x^2 - 2y(x - 3y)$

11 a $3x(x - 4) - 6x$

  b $-5a(4 - 3a) + 10a^2$

  c $-7a(2a - 1) - 3a^2$

  d $4a(3 - a) + 2a$

  e $2x(3x + 2) - 4x^2$

  f $-5x(2 - x) + 10x^2$

12 a $4(2x - 5) - (x - 4)$

  b $3(3x + 4) + (x - 6)$

  c $7(4 - x) - (5 - 3x)$

  d $15x - 3(4 + 3x)$

  e $3(x + 2) + 7(x + 3)$

  f $5(2x - 1) - 3(3x + 5)$

13 a $4(x - 2) - 3(3x + 2)$

  b $2x(3x - 1) - 3x(x + 4)$

  c $6x(2x - 1) - (x - 7)$

  d $9 - 4(3x + 2) - 6x$

  e $4x(x + 3) - 3x(4 - x)$

  f $3(x - 4) + 6x(3x - 2)$

14 a $2x(2x + 3) - x(x + 5)$

  b $4x(x - 2) - 3x(x + 3)$

  c $-x(3x - 2) + 5x(x + 1)$

  d $5x(5x - 4) + 3x(x + 2)$

  e $7x(x + 3) + 4x(x - 6)$

  f $-4x(3 - 2x) + 3x(x - 4)$

THE PRODUCT OF TWO BRACKETS

Sometimes we have to find the product of two brackets, each of which contains two terms, for example $(a + b)(c + d)$.

$(a + b)(c + d)$ means that each term in the second bracket has to be multiplied by each term in the first bracket

i.e. $(a + b)(c + d) = a \times (c + d) + b \times (c + d)$

The multiplication can be done in any order but it is easier if you always use the same pattern.

Multiply the brackets together in the following order

1 the first terms in the brackets
2 the outside terms
3 the inside terms
4 the second terms in the brackets.

Thus $(a + b)(c + d) = ac + ad + bc + bd$

This process is called *expanding* the brackets.

EXERCISE 8B

Expand **a** $(x+3y)(2y+z)$ **b** $(3x-4y)(x+z)$

a $(x+3y)(2y+z) = x \times 2y + x \times z + 3y \times 2y + 3y \times z$

$$= 2xy + xz + 6y^2 + 3yz$$

> When a combination of numbers and letters are multiplied together we usually write the numbers first and the letters in alphabetical order. Remember that numbers can be multiplied in any order
>
> i.e. $x \times 2y = x \times 2 \times y = 2 \times x \times y = 2xy$
>
> Similarly $3y \times 2y = 3 \times y \times 2 \times y = 3 \times 2 \times y \times y = 6y^2$

b $(3x-4y)(x+z) = 3x^2 + 3xz - 4xy - 4yz$

Remember that the product of two numbers with the same sign gives a positive result and the product of two numbers with different signs gives a negative result.

Expand

1 a $(a+b)(c+d)$ **b** $(a-b)(c+d)$ **c** $(p+q)(s+t)$

2 a $(x+y)(y+z)$ **b** $(2a+b)(c+2d)$ **c** $(2a+b)(3c+d)$

3 a $(5x+2y)(z+3)$ **b** $(5x+4y)(z+2)$ **c** $(x+y)(z-4)$

4 a $(3x-2y)(5-z)$ **b** $(p+q)(2s-3t)$ **c** $(3p-q)(4r-3s)$

5 a $(a-2b)(c-d)$ **b** $(3a-4b)(3c+4d)$ **c** $(6u-5v)(w-5r)$

6 a $(7x-2y)(3-2z)$ **b** $(3a+4b)(2c-3d)$ **c** $(2a+b)(5c-2)$

We get a slightly simpler form when we find the product of two brackets such as $(x+2)$ and $(x+3)$,

i.e.   using the order we chose earlier

$$(x+2)(x+3) = x^2 + 3x + 2x + 6$$

$$= x^2 + 5x + 6$$

> Since $2x$ and $3x$ are like terms they can be collected.

i.e. $(x+2)(x+3) = x^2 + 5x + 6$

EXERCISE 8C   In this exercise expand and simplify the products.

1 a $(x+3)(x+4)$ **b** $(a+4)(a+5)$

2 a $(x+2)(x+4)$ **b** $(b+2)(b+7)$

3 a $(x+1)(x+6)$ **b** $(c+4)(c+6)$

4 a $(x+5)(x+2)$ **b** $(p+3)(p+12)$

5 a $(x+8)(x+3)$ **b** $(q+7)(q+10)$

Expand and simplify $(x-3)(x-8)$

$$(x-3)(x-8) = x^2 - 8x - 3x + 24$$ Remember $(-3)\times(-8) = +24$

$$= x^2 - 11x + 24$$

---

6 a $(x-2)(x-3)$ **b** $(x-3)(x-4)$

7 a $(x-5)(x-7)$ **b** $(x-4)(x-8)$

8 a $(a-2)(a-8)$ **b** $(b-4)(b-2)$

9 a $(x-10)(x-3)$ **b** $(a-4)(a-4)$

10 a $(b-5)(b-5)$ **b** $(p-7)(p-8)$

Expand $(x-7)(x+4)$

$$(x-7)(x+4) = x^2 + 4x - 7x - 28$$

$$= x^2 - 3x - 28$$

---

11 a $(x+3)(x-2)$ **b** $(x+7)(x-2)$

12 a $(x-4)(x+5)$ **b** $(x-5)(x+6)$

13 a $(x-7)(x+4)$ **b** $(x+10)(x-1)$

14 a $(a+3)(a-10)$ **b** $(b-8)(b+7)$

FINDING THE PATTERN

You may have noticed in the previous exercise, that when you expanded the brackets and simplified the answers, there was a definite pattern.

e.g. $(x+4)(x+7) = x^2 + 7x + 4x + 28$
$= x^2 + 11x + 28$

We could have written it

$(x+4)(x+7) = x^2 + (7+4)x + (4) \times (7)$
$= x^2 + 11x + 28$

Similarly $(x+3)(x-5) = x^2 + (-5+3)x + (3) \times (-5)$
$= x^2 - 2x - 15$

and $(x-5)(x-2) = x^2 + (-2-5)x + (-5) \times (-2)$
$= x^2 - 7x + 10$

In each case there is a pattern:
the *product* of the two numbers in the brackets gives the number term in the expansion, while *collecting* the two numbers gives the number of xs.

EXERCISE 8D

Use the pattern given above to expand and simplify the following products.

1 a $(x+4)(x+5)$ **b** $(x+8)(x+6)$

2 a $(a+2)(a+5)$ **b** $(a+10)(a+7)$

3 a $(x-4)(x-5)$ **b** $(x-8)(x-6)$

4 a $(a-2)(a-5)$ **b** $(a-10)(a-7)$

5 a $(a+2)(a-5)$ **b** $(a-10)(a+7)$

6 a $(y-6)(y+3)$ **b** $(y+10)(y-2)$

7 a $(z+4)(z-10)$ **b** $(z-12)(z+1)$

8 a $(p+5)(p-8)$ **b** $(p+2)(p-13)$

9 a $(p+6)(p+7)$ **b** $(z+4)(z-3)$

10 a $(x+7)(x-3)$ **b** $(p-8)(p-4)$

The pattern is similar when the brackets are slightly more complicated.

EXERCISE 8E

Expand and simplify the product $(2x + 5)(x + 3)$

$$(2x + 5)(x + 3) = 2x^2 + 6x + 5x + 15$$
$$= 2x^2 + 11x + 15$$

In this exercise expand and simplify the products.

1 a $(2x + 1)(x + 1)$ **b** $(3x + 2)(x + 1)$

2 a $(x + 2)(5x + 2)$ **b** $(x + 3)(3x + 2)$

3 a $(5x + 2)(x + 3)$ **b** $(4x + 3)(x + 1)$

4 a $(3x + 4)(x + 5)$ **b** $(7x + 2)(x + 3)$

Expand and simplify the product $(2x - 3)(3x + 5)$

$$(2x - 3)(3x + 5) = 6x^2 + 10x - 9x - 15$$
$$= 6x^2 + x - 15$$

5 a $(3x + 2)(2x + 3)$ **b** $(5x + 3)(2x + 5)$

6 a $(4x - 3)(3x - 4)$ **b** $(7x - 2)(3x - 2)$

7 a $(5x + 6)(2x - 3)$ **b** $(3x - 2)(4x + 1)$

8 a $(7a - 3)(3a - 7)$ **b** $(3b + 5)(2b - 5)$

9 a $(2a + 3)(2a - 3)$ **b** $(4x + 3)(4x - 3)$

10 a $(3b + 7)(3b - 7)$ **b** $(5y - 2)(5y + 2)$

11 a $(7y - 5)(7y + 5)$ **b** $(3x - 1)(3x + 1)$

12 a $(5a + 4)(4a - 3)$ **b** $(4x - 7)(4x + 5)$

Expand and simplify $(5+x)(2-x)$

$$(5+x)(2-x) = 10 - 5x + 2x - x^2$$
$$= 10 - 3x - x^2$$

The terms can be written in any order,
e.g. $-3x - x^2 + 10$.
However it is usual to put the x term in the middle.

13 a $(2-x)(4+x)$ **b** $(7+x)(3-x)$ **c** $(4+3x)(2-x)$

14 a $(1+4x)(2-x)$ **b** $(x-1)(1-x)$ **c** $(x-3)(2-x)$

15 a $(5-y)(4+y)$ **b** $(4-2p)(5+2p)$ **c** $(2-3x)(2+x)$

Expand and simplify $(2x-3)(6-5x)$

$$(2x-3)(6-5x) = 12x - 10x^2 - 18 + 15x$$
$$= -10x^2 + 27x - 18$$

We could also write this as $-18 + 27x - 10x^2$.

16 a $(2x+1)(1+3x)$ **b** $(5x+2)(4+3x)$ **c** $(5x+2)(2-x)$

17 a $(7x+4)(3-2x)$ **b** $(6x-1)(3-x)$ **c** $(4x-3)(3-5x)$

18 a $(5a-2)(3-7a)$ **b** $(3-p)(4+p)$ **c** $(3x+2)(4-x)$

IMPORTANT PRODUCTS

Three very important products are:

$$(x+a)^2 = (x+a)(x+a)$$
$$= x^2 + xa + ax + a^2$$
$$= x^2 + 2ax + a^2 \quad (\text{since } xa \text{ is the same as } ax)$$

i.e. $(x+a)^2 = x^2 + 2ax + a^2$ so $(x+3)^2 = x^2 + 6x + 9$

$$(x-a)^2 = (x-a)(x-a)$$
$$= x^2 - xa - ax + a^2$$
$$= x^2 - 2ax + a^2$$

i.e. $(x-a)^2 = x^2 - 2ax + a^2$ so $(x-4)^2 = x^2 - 8x + 16$

$$(x-a)(x+a) = x^2 + xa - ax - a^2 = x^2 - a^2$$

i.e. $$(x-a)(x+a) = (x+a)(x-a) = x^2 - a^2$$

so $$(x+5)(x-5) = x^2 - 25$$

It is worthwhile learning these results thoroughly. Given the left-hand side you should know what the right-hand side is or given the right-hand side you should know the left-hand side.

EXERCISE 8F

Expand $(x+7)^2$

> Comparing $(x+7)^2$ with $(x+a)^2$ tells us that in this case $a = 7$.
> So $x^2 + 2ax + a^2$ becomes $x^2 + 2(7)x + (7)^2$.

$$(x+7)^2 = x^2 + 14x + 49$$

> Also, we can write $(x+7)^2$ as $(x+7)(x+7)$ and multiply out in the usual way.

In this exercise expand the given expressions.

1 a $(x+1)^2$ **b** $(b+4)^2$ **c** $(c+d)^2$

2 a $(x+2)^2$ **b** $(x+z)^2$ **c** $(m+n)^2$

3 a $(a+3)^2$ **b** $(y+x)^2$ **c** $(a+9)^2$

4 a $(t+10)^2$ **b** $(p+7)^2$ **c** $(e+f)^2$

5 a $(x+12)^2$ **b** $(p+q)^2$ **c** $(u+v)^2$

6 a $(x+8)^2$ **b** $(a+b)^2$ **c** $(M+m)^2$

Expand $(3x+2)^2$

$$(3x+2)^2 = (3x)^2 + 2(2)(3x) + (2)^2$$

i.e. $$(3x+2)^2 = 9x^2 + 12x + 4$$ $\begin{array}{l}(x+a)^2 = x^2 + 2ax + a^2 \\ \text{Replace } x \text{ by } 3x \text{ and } a \text{ by } 2.\end{array}$

7 a $(2x+1)^2$ **b** $(6c+1)^2$ **c** $(3a+4)^2$

8 a $(4b+1)^2$ **b** $(3a+1)^2$ **c** $(4y+3)^2$

9 a $(5x+2)^2$ **b** $(2x+5)^2$ **c** $(3W+2)^2$

Expand $(3x + 2y)^2$

$(3x + 2y)^2 = (3x)^2 + 2(3x)(2y) + (2y)^2$
$(3x + 2y)^2 = 9x^2 + 12xy + 4y^2$

> Note: $2(3x)(2y)$ is the same as $2(2y)(3x)$.

10 a $(x + 2y)^2$ **b** $(3a + 2b)^2$ **c** $(7x + 2y)^2$ **d** $(3x + y)^2$

11 a $(3a + b)^2$ **b** $(3s + 4t)^2$ **c** $(2x + 5y)^2$ **d** $(3s + t)^2$

Expand $(x - 5)^2$

$(x - 5)^2 = x^2 - 10x + 25$

12 a $(x - 2)^2$ **b** $(x - 3)^2$ **c** $(x - 1)^2$ **d** $(x - 6)^2$

13 a $(x - 7)^2$ **b** $(x - 4)^2$ **c** $(a - 10)^2$ **d** $(a - b)^2$

14 a $(M - n)^2$ **b** $(x - y)^2$ **c** $(u - v)^2$ **d** $(s - t)^2$

Expand $(3x - 7)^2$

$(3x - 7)^2 = (3x)^2 + 2(3x)(-7) + (-7)^2$
$ = 9x^2 - 42x + 49$

15 a $(3x - 1)^2$ **b** $(2a - 1)^2$ **c** $(6x - 1)^2$ **d** $(4x - 3)^2$

16 a $(5z - 1)^2$ **b** $(4y - 1)^2$ **c** $(2x - 3)^2$ **d** $(5x - 3)^2$

17 a $(10y - 9)^2$ **b** $(7b - 2)^2$ **c** $(3p - 4)^2$ **d** $(6M - 5)^2$

Expand $(5a - 6b)^2$

$(5a - 6b)^2 = (5a)^2 + 2(5a)(-6b) + (-6b)^2$
$(5a - 6b)^2 = 25a^2 - 60ab + 36b^2$

18 a $(2y - x)^2$ **b** $(a - 3b)^2$ **c** $(3x - 2y)^2$ **d** $(7x - 3y)^2$

19 a $(5x - y)^2$ **b** $(m - 8n)^2$ **c** $(A - 2b)^2$ **d** $(3p - 5q)^2$

20 a $(3m - 2n)^2$ **b** $(5a - 2b)^2$ **c** $(4x - 3y)^2$ **d** $(2M - 5m)^2$

EXERCISE 8G

> Expand **a** $(a+3)(a-3)$ **b** $(2x+5)(2x-5)$
>
> **a** $(a+3)(a-3) = a^2 - 9$
>
> **b** $(2x+5)(2x-5) = 4x^2 - 25$ $\boxed{(2x+5)(2x-5) = (2x)^2 - (5)^2}$

In this exercise expand the given products.

1 a $(x+4)(x-4)$ **b** $(x+5)(x-5)$

2 a $(b+6)(b-6)$ **b** $(a-7)(a+7)$

3 a $(c-3)(c+3)$ **b** $(q+10)(q-10)$

4 a $(x+12)(x-12)$ **b** $(R-r)(R+r)$

5 a $(2x-1)(2x+1)$ **b** $(5x+1)(5x-1)$

6 a $(3x+1)(3x-1)$ **b** $(2a-3)(2a+3)$

7 a $(7a+2)(7a-2)$ **b** $(10m-1)(10m+1)$

8 a $(5a-4)(5a+4)$ **b** $(6a+5)(6a-5)$

> Expand $(4x+3y)(4x-3y)$
>
> $$(4x+3y)(4x-3y) = (4x)^2 - (3y)^2$$
> $$= 16x^2 - 9y^2$$

9 a $(3x+4y)(3x-4y)$ **b** $(10a-9b)(10a+9b)$

10 a $(2a-5b)(2a+5b)$ **b** $(R+2r)(R-2r)$

11 a $(1-2a)(1+2a)$ **b** $(1+3x)(1-3x)$

12 a $(7y+3z)(7y-3z)$ **b** $(3-5x)(3+5x)$

The results from this exercise are very important when written the other way round, i.e. $x^2 - a^2 = (x-a)(x+a)$

We refer to this as 'factorising the difference between two squares' and we will deal with it in Chapter 14.

SUMMARY

The following is a summary of the most important types of examples considered in this chapter that will be required in future work.

1 $2(3x + 4) = 6x + 8$

2 $(x + 3)(x + 4) = x^2 + 7x + 12$

3 $(x - 2)(x - 3) = x^2 - 5x + 6$

4 $(x - 2)(x + 3) = x^2 + x - 6$

5 $(3x + 1)(2x + 3) = 6x^2 + 11x + 3$

6 $(3x - 1)(2x - 3) = 6x^2 - 11x + 3$

7 $(3x + 1)(2x - 3) = 6x^2 - 7x - 3$

8 $(2 + x)(3 - x) = 6 + x - x^2$

Note that
a) if the signs in the brackets are the same, i.e. both $+$ or both $-$, then the number term is $+$ (examples **2, 3, 5** and **6**)

whereas
b) if the signs in the brackets are different, i.e. one $+$ and one $-$, then the number term is $-$ (examples **4** and **7**)

c) the middle term is given by collecting the product of the outside terms in the brackets and the product of the inside terms in the brackets, i.e.

in **2** the middle term is $4x + 3x$ i.e. $7x$

in **3** the middle term is $-3x - 2x$ i.e. $-5x$

in **4** the middle term is $3x - 2x$ i.e. x

in **5** the middle term is $9x + 2x$ i.e. $11x$

in **6** the middle term is $-9x - 2x$ i.e. $-11x$

in **7** the middle term is $-9x + 2x$ i.e. $-7x$

in **8** the middle term is $-2x + 3x$ i.e. x

Most important of all we must remember the general expansions

$$(x + a)^2 = x^2 + 2ax + a^2$$
$$(x - a)^2 = x^2 - 2ax + a^2$$
$$(x + a)(x - a) = x^2 - a^2$$

MIXED EXERCISE

EXERCISE 8H

Do not use a calculator for this exercise.

Expand

1 a $5(x+2)$

   b $8p(3q-2r)$

   c $(x-8)(x-12)$

   d $(4y+3)(4y-7)$

2 a $(3a+b)(2a-5b)$

   b $(4x+1)(3x-5)$

   c $(4y-9)(4y+9)$

   d $(5x+2)^2$

3 a $(x+6)(x+10)$

   b $x(3x+5)$

   c $(2a-7b)^2$

   d $3a(b-5a)$

4 a $4(2-5x)$

   b $8a(2-3a)$

   c $(y+2z)^2$

   d $(6y-z)(6y+5z)$

5 a $(4a+3)(3a-11)$

   b $(x+11)(9-x)$

   c $(4a+1)^2$

   d $(5a-7)^2$

6 a $(2x+5)(1-10x)$

   b $5a(2a-b)$

   c $(6z-13y)^2$

   d $3p(3p-4q)$

7 a $4x(x-4)+2(3x-2)$

   b $5x(7-x)-5(2x-1)$

   c $6(3-9x)$

   d $7p(2q-3p)-3p(2q+4p)$

8 a $3p(2q-5p)$

   b $3x(1-4x)-x(2x-5)$

   c $x(4x-3)$

   d $5p(3-2p)+2p(p+2)$

9 a $5(3x-7)-4x$

   b $-3p(5-2p)-p(2p-5)$

   c $-4p(2p+q)+5p(2p+3)$

   d $(5x+3y)(2z+3)$

10 a $3(2-a)$

   b $4a(2b+c)$

   c $(a+4)(a-5)$

   d $(3x+1)(2x+3)$

11 a $(5a+2b)(2c+5d)$

   b $3x(5x+7)-5x(5-6x)$

   c $(5x-2)(5x+2)$

   d $5p(4p-q)$

12 a $(x-7)(x-12)$

   b $-4x(3-2x)+5x(2x-6)$

   c $(3x-7)^2$

   d $8b^2-5b(1-4b)$

13 a $(a+7)(a+9)$

   b $5a(2a-4)-3a(4-3a)$

   c $(5x+2y)(5x-2y)$

   d $(7a-3b)(4-6c)$

14 a $(3x+5y)(3w-4z)$

   b $(z-9)(z+3)$

   c $(2a-3b)(2a+b)$

   d $(2a+5)^2$

**PRACTICAL
WORK**

In this chapter we have shown algebraically that

$$(x + a)^2 = x^2 + 2ax + a^2$$

and $(x + a)(x - a) = x^2 - a^2$

These expansions can be proved geometrically as you will find if you follow these instructions.

1 To show geometrically that $(x + a)^2 = x^2 + 2ax + a^2$

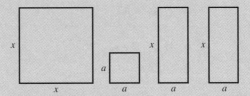

a Draw a square of side x cm and another square of side a cm. Choose any values you wish for x and a. Using the same values of x and a, draw two rectangles each x cm long and a cm wide.

b Write down the area of each of the four shapes in terms of x and/or a. Find their total area in terms of x and a expressing this area as simply as possible.

c Cut out the four shapes and rearrange them to form a large square. What is the length of a side of this square in terms of x and a? Write down the area of this square as the square of the length of its edge.

d Compare your answers to parts **b** and **c**. This shows geometrically that $(x + a)^2 = x^2 + 2ax + a^2$

2 Draw a square of side x cm and then cut a square of side a cm from one corner.

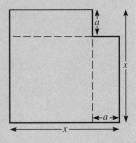

Write down an expression for the area of the remaining shape. Cut the shape into three pieces and rearrange them to form a rectangle. Write down an expression for the area of this rectangle. Explain how your two expressions show that

$$(x + a)(x - a) = x^2 - a^2$$

FORMULAS

A newspaper headline reports that a skull has been found in a peat bog. From this single part of the skeleton it is possible to draw several conclusions about the person to whom the skull belonged. For instance the scientists say that it belonged to a man who was between 1.78 m and 1.80 m tall. Have you ever wondered how they do this? They draw on experience which shows that an adult's height is just over three times the distance round their head measured immediately above the eyebrows.

- This is an example of a simple relationship between two quantities and it can be expressed as a formula.

  The formula might be written: height = 3 × circumference of head

  or, in letters: $H = 3C$ where H cm is the height and C cm is the circumferences of the head just above the eyebrows.

Experiments can confirm whether or not this formula is true. Perhaps the formula should be $H = 3.2C$ for a particular group of people, or H should be somewhere between $3.1C$ and $3.2C$. The important thing is that there is a relationship which can be used to deduce useful information when only a limited amount of information is available.

- When a definite relationship between two quantities has been established we can find one when we are given the other. In this case we can find the height if we know the circumference of the skull.

The relationship between the above quantities is not exact but in other cases it may be, e.g. if grapefruit cost 33 p each, the formula $C = 33n$ enables us to find the exact cost, C pence, of n grapefruit.

In this chapter we revise some of the work we studied in Book 9B, Chapter 5, and then look at some formulas that are more complicated than the ones we studied in previous books.

EXERCISE 9A

Discuss with members of a group whether or not each of the following statements is true. If you come to the conclusion that a particular statement is true, list examples to support your conclusion.

1 There are many examples to show that two quantities can be connected by an exact relation.

2 Sometimes two quantities are related, but not in an exact way. (If you can, list some quantities that are very closely related and others that are related but not strongly.)

3 In some cases one quantity can be related to several different quantities at the same time.

4 There are cases where two quantities are not related in any way.

CONSTRUCTING FORMULAS

Electricity bills are presented every quarter. They are made up of a fixed charge, called a standing charge, plus the cost of the number of units used in the quarter.

By using letters for the unknown quantities, we can construct a formula for a quarterly electricity bill.

If £C is the total bill, £R the standing charge, x pence the cost of one unit and N units are used, then

the cost of the units is $N \times x$ pence, i.e. Nx pence or $£\dfrac{Nx}{100}$

therefore $\qquad C = R + \dfrac{Nx}{100}$

Notice that the cost of the units was converted from pence to pounds so that we added pounds to pounds, not pounds to pence.

It is important that the units in a formula are consistent.
For example, a formula giving speed in miles per hour must have the distance in miles and the time in hours.

EXERCISE 9B

> A number p is equal to the sum of a number q and twice a number r. Write down a formula for p in terms of q and r.
>
> $p = q + 2r$

1 Write down a formula connecting the given letters.

   a A number a is equal to the sum of two numbers b and c.

   b A number m is equal to twice the sum of two numbers n and p.

   c A number z is equal to the product of two numbers x and y.

   d A number d is equal to the difference of two numbers e and f, where e is greater than f.

   e A number n is equal to the sum of a number p and its square.

   f A number v is equal to the sum of a number u and the product of the numbers a and t.

2 Cloth is sold at £p per metre. The cost of N metres is £R. Find a formula for R in terms of N and p.

3 The amount of lace edging wound on a card is P metres. Nerys buys n pieces of edging, each x centimetres long. If the length of edging left on the card is Q metres, find a formula for Q in terms of P, n and x.

4 A shop sells two brands of baked beans. It has N tins of baked beans altogether, y of them are one brand and z of them are the other brand. Find a formula for N in terms of y and z.

5 Fertiliser is applied at the rate of a grams per square metre. It takes b kilograms to cover a field of area c square metres. Find a formula for b in terms of a and c.

6 A bag contains x ten-pence coins and y twenty-pence coins. The total value of the coins is £R. Find a formula for R in terms of x and y.

7 A rule for estimating the cost, £C, of my quarterly electricity bill is to divide by 10 the number, n, of units used and then add 25. Write this rule as a formula for C in terms of n.

8 The purchase price of goods and services, including value added tax, is £C. When VAT is levied at the rate of $17\frac{1}{2}\%$ the amount of VAT, £T, can be found by multiplying the purchase price by 7 and dividing the result by 47. Find a formula for T in terms of C.

9 The surface area, A cm^2, of a sphere can be found by squaring its radius, r cm, and multiplying the result by π and by 4. Give this instruction as a formula for A in terms of r.

SUBSTITUTING NUMBERS INTO FORMULAS

There are many situations where a given formula has to be used. For example, at the scene of a murder, a forensic scientist can work out, approximately, the time of death by taking the temperature of the body and using a formula. The formula is $y = 10(\frac{1}{2})^t$ where y is the difference between the body temperature and the surrounding temperature, and t is the time in hours since death.

EXERCISE 9C

Do not use a calculator for this exercise.

If $z = xy$ find z when

a $x = 3$ and $y = -4$ **b** $x = -2$ and $y = -6$

$$z = xy$$

Remember that xy means $x \times y$.

a When $x = 3$ and $y = -4$

$$z = (3) \times (-4)$$
$$= -12$$

Notice that we have put each number in brackets; this is particularly important in the case of negative numbers. Remember that unlike signs multiplied together give a $-$ sign.

b When $x = -2$ and $y = -6$

$$z = (-2) \times (-6)$$
$$= 12$$

Like signs multiplied together give a $+$ sign.

---

1 If $A = 2b + c$ find A when $b = 5$ and $c = 2$

2 If $P = qr$ find P when

    a $q = 2.5$ and $r = 9.6$ **b** $q = \frac{3}{4}$ and $r = 1\frac{1}{3}$

3 Given that $P = 2(a + b)$ find P when

    a $a = 15$ and $b = 9.6$ **b** $a = \frac{2}{3}$ and $b = \frac{1}{6}$

4 $Q = rs + t$. Find Q when $r = 0.8$, $s = 3.4$ and $t = 2.9$

5 If $I = \dfrac{PRT}{100}$, find I when $P = 5000$, $R = 4.28$ and $T = 3$

6 Given that $C = 2a + 3b$, find C when $a = \frac{2}{5}$ and $b = \frac{3}{4}$

7 $P = 2qr - s$. Find P when $q = 2.5$, $r = 2.8$ and $s = 5.4$

8 Given that $A = \dfrac{1}{a} + \dfrac{1}{b}$, find A when $a = \frac{3}{5}$ and $b = \frac{6}{7}$

9 If $A = bc$, find A when

    a $b = -4$ and $c = 5$ **b** $b = -6$ and $c = 1.5$

10 If $Q = RT$, find Q when

    a $R = 3$ and $T = -4.5$ **b** $R = -2.4$ and $T = -3\frac{1}{2}$

11 If $P = R - S$ find P when

    a $R = 10$ and $S = -4$ **b** $R = -3$ and $S = -7$

12 If $z = \dfrac{y}{x}$, find z when

    a $x = 3$ and $y = -12$ **b** $x = -2$ and $y = -24$

13 Given that $H = abc$, find H when $a = 4$, $b = -5$ and $c = -3$

14 If $z = x - 2y$, find z when

    a $x = 5\frac{1}{2}$ and $y = \frac{3}{4}$ **b** $x = \frac{7}{8}$ and $y = -1\frac{1}{2}$

15 Given that $C = 10a - b$, find C when

    a $a = 0.35$ and $b = -6$ **b** $a = 0.734$ and $b = 8.23$

16 Copy and complete the table where $y = 5x - 4$

x	-4	-2	0	2	4
y					

17 Given that $v = \dfrac{u - t}{3}$, find v when

    a $u = 9$ and $t = 3$ **b** $u = 4$ and $t = -2$

18 Given that $z = \dfrac{1}{x} + \dfrac{1}{y}$, find z when

    a $x = 2$ and $y = 4$ **b** $x = \frac{1}{2}$ and $y = \frac{1}{3}$

19 If $P = \dfrac{q - r}{s}$, find P when $q = -4$, $r = -8$ and $s = 2$

20 If $P = 2Q + 5RT$, find P when $Q = 8$, $R = -2$ and $T = -\frac{1}{2}$

21 If $a = (b - c)(c - d)$, find a when $b = 2$, $c = 4$ and $d = 7$

22 Given that $y = 2x^2 - 1$ copy and complete the table to find the corresponding values of y for the given values of x.

x	1	2	3	4	5	6	7
y							

23 Given that $y = x^3 + x^2$, find the value of y when $x = -3$

EXERCISE 9D   You will need a calculator for this exercise.

If $s = ut - \frac{1}{2}gt^2$, find s when $u = 7.5$, $t = 6$ and $g = -9.8$

$$s = ut - \frac{1}{2}gt^2$$

When $u = 7.5$, $t = 6$ and $g = -9.8$

$$s = (7.5)(6) - \frac{1}{2}(-9.8)(6)^2$$

$$= 45 - (-4.9)(36)$$

$$= 45 - (-176.4)$$

$$= 45 + 176.4$$

i.e. $s = 221.4$

> Remember to put each number in brackets. The intermediate steps do not have to be written down; the calculation can be done in one step on a calculator:
>
> `7.5 × 6 – 0.5 × (–)9.8 × 6x² =`

Give answers that are not exact correct to 3 significant figures.

1 If $H = \dfrac{2a+b}{c}$ find H when $a = 7.35$, $b = 4.02$ and $c = 3.6$

2 If $P = \dfrac{ab}{2c}$ find P when $a = 3.7$, $b = 4.2$ and $c = 7.5$

3 If $p = x + x^2$, find p when

    a $x = 2$ **b** $x = 3.4$ **c** $x = 0.79$ **d** $x = -3$

4 Given that $s = \frac{1}{2}(a + b + c)$, find s when

    a $a = 6$, $b = 9$ and $c = 5$

    b $a = 5.04$, $b = 7.35$ and $c = 4.83$

5 If $a = (b + c)^2$, find a when

    a $b = 8$ and $c = -5$ **b** $b = 4.1$ and $c = 7.8$

6 If $a = b(c - d)$, find a when $b = 5.4$, $c = -8.2$ and $d = -2.7$

7 Given that $V = \frac{1}{2}(X - Y)^2$, find V when

    a $X = 3$ and $Y = -5$ **b** $X = 3.4$ and $Y = -5.2$

8 Find the value of $\sqrt{R^2 - r^2}$ when $R = 3.76$ and $r = 1.56$, writing down the complete display on your calculator. Now give this value correct to 2 decimal places.

9 Use the formula $N = 2.5 \times (1.05)^t$ to find N when $t = 25$.

10 Given that $y = x^2 - 2x$, find y when $x = -3.42$

11 Use the formula $T = 2.6 \times (2)^{-n}$ to find T when $n = 8.4$

12 The displacement $D\,\text{cm}^3$ of an engine is given by the formula

$$D = \pi n \times \left(\frac{b}{2}\right)^2 \times s$$

where n is the number of cylinders, b is the bore of each cylinder in centimetres and s is the length of the stroke in centimetres.
Find the displacement of a 4-cylinder petrol engine that has a bore of 78 mm and a stroke of 84 mm.

13 The surface area of a cylindrical can is given by the formula
$A = 2\pi r(r + h)$ where r is the radius of the can and h its height.

a Without using a calculator estimate the value of A when
$r = 0.52$ cm and $h = 0.88$ cm.
(Assume that π is approximately 3.)

b Use your calculator to find the value of A correct to 3 significant figures.

14 John uses the formula $s = \frac{1}{2}(u + v)t$ to find the value of s when
$u = 16.42$, $v = 38.64$ and $t = 18.5$. John first estimates the value of s without using a calculator.

a Write down numbers that John could use in the formula to estimate the value of s.

b Using these values work out an estimate for s.

c Use your calculator to work out the value of s correct to the nearest whole number.

15 The diagram shows a seven-sided polygon with all its diagonals.
If you count the diagonals you should find that there are 14.

The formula $2d = n^2 - 3n$ gives the
number of diagonals d in a polygon
with n sides. Use this formula to

a check the number of diagonals in
the seven-sided figure shown

b find the number of diagonals in a
polygon with

i 6 sides   **ii** 10 sides.

16 A person's mean blood pressure, P millimetres of mercury, is calculated using the formula

$$P = D + \frac{(S - D)}{3}$$

where D is the diastolic pressure and S is the systolic pressure, both measured in millimetres of mercury (mm/Hg). Use this formula to find Greg's mean blood pressure if his diastolic pressure is 82 mm/Hg and his systolic pressure is 146 mm/Hg.

17 The gross yield of a Government stock, as a percentage, is given

by the formula Gross yield $= \frac{I}{P} \times 100$ where I is the annual

percentage rate of interest and £P is the price of £100 of the stock. Find the gross yield on

a $11\frac{3}{4}\%$ stock priced at £121 **b** 4% stock priced at £94.

18 A litter bin is in the form of a cylinder.
The formula to find the total outside surface area of the bin is $A = \pi r(r + 2h)$ where r is the radius of the bin and h is its height.
Paul uses this formula to find the surface area of a bin that has a radius of 0.38 m and a height of 0.76 m.

a Without using a calculator estimate the value of A.
 (Assume that π is approximately 3.)

b Use your calculator to find the value of A.

19 If $z = y^2 + y^5$, find the value of z when y is **a** 0.8 **b** 2.7

20 Two numbers x_1 and x_2 are given by the formulas

$$x_1 = \frac{-b + \sqrt{b^2 - 4ac}}{2a} \quad \text{and} \quad x_2 = \frac{-b - \sqrt{b^2 - 4ac}}{2a}$$

a Find x_1 and x_2 when $a = 2$, $b = -5$ and $c = -12$.
b Find the value of **i** $x_1 + x_2$ **ii** $x_1 x_2$.
  How are these values related to the values of a, b and c?
c Explain why it is not possible to find values for x_1 and x_2
  when $a = 2$, $b = -5$ and $c = 8$.

21 The formula $y = 10(\frac{1}{2})^t$, connects the difference, y degrees Celsius, between the temperature of a dead body and the surrounding temperature t hours after death.

a A person has been dead for 1 hour. What is the difference between the temperature of the body and the surrounding temperature ?

b Repeat part **a** for a person who has been dead for $3\frac{1}{2}$ hours.

**FURTHER
SUBSTITUTIONS**

Sometimes the letter whose value we need to find is not isolated on one side of a formula. For example, to use the formula $v = u + at$ when $v = 20$, $u = 8$ and $t = 2$ we substitute the values for v, u and t. This gives the equation $20 = 8 + 2a$ which can then be solved to find a.

EXERCISE 9E

> Given that $p = q - 5r$ find
>
> **a** the value of q when $p = 5$ and $r = 2$
> **b** the value of r when $p = 4$ and $q = 24$.
>
> **a** $$p = q - 5r$$
> Replacing p by 5 and r by 2, gives $5 = q - 10$ ⎰ Add 10 to both sides.
> $$15 = q$$
>
> **b** $$p = q - 5r$$
> When $p = 4$ and $q = 24$, $4 = 24 - 5r$ ⎰ Add $5r$ to both sides.
> $$5r + 4 = 24$$ Subtract 4 from each side.
> $$5r = 20$$ Divide both sides by 5.
> $$r = 4$$

1 If $a = b + 2c$ find

    a b when $a = 10$ and $c = 2$ **b** c when $a = 13$ and $b = 5$.

2 Given that $x = y - z$ find

    a y when $x = 9$ and $z = 4$ **b** z when $x = 5$ and $y = 98$.

3 For $p = qr$ find

    a q when $p = 36$ and $r = 9$ **b** r when $p = 24$ and $q = 8$.

4 Given that $v = u + 8t$ find

    a u when $v = 45$ and $t = 3.5$
    b t when $v = 64$ and $u = 0$.

5 Use the formula $s = \frac{1}{2}(a + b + c)$ to find

    a a when $s = 5.8$, $b = 4.5$ and $c = 3.4$
    b c when $s = 4.7$, $a = 2.7$ and $b = 3.8$.

6 a For $v = u + at$ find a when $v = 38$, $u = 8$ and $t = 3$.
   b If $v^2 = u^2 + 2as$ find s when $v = 7$, $u = -4$ and $a = 6$.

7 a Given that $P = qr - s$ find s when $P = 4.5$, $q = 2.2$ and $r = 3.4$.

b Given that $I = \dfrac{2ab}{c}$ find c when $I = 6$, $a = -3$ and $b = 5$.

8 The formula to convert a temperature of C degrees Celsius into F degrees Fahrenheit is

$$F = \frac{9C}{5} + 32$$

What temperature, in degrees Fahrenheit, corresponds to a temperature of

a 25 degrees Celsius

b 0 degrees Celsius

c 100 degrees Celsius?

9 Use the formula $C = \frac{5}{9}(F - 32)$ to find

a C when $F = 95$ **b** F when $C = 95$.

10 Given that a number y is one more than the square of a number x find

a the value of y when x is   **i** 4   **ii** 7

b the positive value of x when y is 26

c the negative value of x when y is 37.

11 At an athletics meeting a points system operates for the long jump event. The number of points scored P is calculated using the formula

$$P = a \times (L - b)^2$$

where L is the distance jumped in metres, measured correct to the nearest centimetre, and a and b are non-zero constants.

a The points score for a jump of 6 metres is 0. Which constant does this information enable you to find? What is the value of this constant?

b A jump of 8 metres gives a score of 400 points. Find the value of the other constant.

c What is the shortest jump that will score points?

d How many points are scored for a jump that measures

   i 6.5 m   **ii** 7.34 m?

12 Assuming that no three chords of a circle all pass through the same point, n chords will divide a circle into $\frac{1}{2}(n^2 + n + 2)$ regions.

a How many regions will result if the number of chords drawn is

i 9   **ii** 12?

b Find, by trial and improvement, how many chords must be drawn in a circle to give 56 regions.

MIXED EXERCISES

EXERCISE 9F   **Do not use a calculator for this exercise.**

1 If $s = \frac{1}{2}(a + b + c)$ find s when $a = 3.4$, $b = 2.7$ and $c = 4.9$.

2 If $v = u + at$ find u when $v = \frac{3}{5}$, $a = \frac{1}{10}$ and $t = 4$.

3 Given that $M = np + q$ find M when $n = 3$, $p = 4$ and $q = 20$.

4 Given that $H = \dfrac{3x + y}{4}$ find H when $x = 3.5$ and $y = 2.5$.

5 If $P = qr - s$ find P when $q = \frac{2}{3}$, $r = 0.2$ and $s = \frac{3}{8}$.

6 Copy and complete the table for values of y when $y = 4x - 1$.

x	-3	-1	0	2	5
y					

7 A number N is equal to the square of a number a added to the product of the numbers b and c. Write down a formula for N in terms of a, b and c.

8 If $p = r(2t - s)$, find r when $p = \frac{1}{2}$, $t = 3$ and $s = -2$.

9 If $r = \dfrac{2}{s + t}$, find r when $s = \frac{1}{2}$ and $t = \frac{1}{4}$.

10 Copy and complete the table given that $y = 5 - 3x$.

x	-3	-1	0	2	4
y					

EXERCISE 9G

1 If $E = Ri^2$ find E when $R = 3.5$ and $i = 0.7$.

2 Given that $s = ut + \frac{1}{2}at^2$ find s when $u = 5.4$, $t = 1.5$ and $a = 4$.

3 If $W = x(2y - z)$ find the value of W when $x = -3.2$, $y = 4.7$ and $z = -1.2$.

4 If $A = 2a + b - c$ find b when $A = \frac{31}{60}$, $a = \frac{1}{3}$ and $c = \frac{3}{4}$.

5 Given that $v = u - gt$, find u when

   a $v = 16$, $g = -10$ and $t = 4$

   b $v = 13.2$, $g = 9.8$ and $t = 3.5$.

6 Given that $y = x^3 - 4x + 2$ find the value of y when

   a $x = 3$ **b** $x = 0$ **c** $x = -4$

7 Given that $z = 2x - 3y$, find z when $x = 4.37$ and $y = 2.76$.

8 Find, correct to 3 significant figures, the value of Q when $p = 1.29$ given that $Q = 3p^4 - 2p^3$.

9 If $E = a(b^2 - c^2)$ find, correct to 2 decimal places, the value of E when $a = 4.6$, $b = 2.7$ and $c = \frac{5}{8}$.

10 Before being used, weedkiller needs to be diluted with water at the rate of 15 ml of weedkiller for each litre of water. Find a formula for k in terms of L where k ml is the quantity of weedkiller to be added to L litres of water. Find L when $k = 45$.

PRACTICAL WORK

At the beginning of the chapter we stated that there was a formula connecting a person's height and the circumference of their skull. Investigate the truth of the statement for the students in your group. Is the factor by which the circumference of the skull is multiplied to get the height the same for young boys as it is for young girls? What is the formula for a group of men or a group of women?

LENGTH, AREA
AND VOLUME

Kate works for a company that designs and makes packaging.
She is given this design for the outer box to hold a glass perfume bottle.

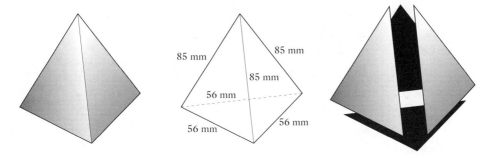

It is to be made from foil-covered card weighing 1200 grams per square
metre. It has to be assembled from individual triangles to give a box with
the dimensions shown, all correct to the nearest millimetre.

Kate's job is to cost this design and to order enough material to make
50 000 of these boxes.

- To do this, Kate needs to know how to find the surface area of the
  box. This involves knowing and using the correct formula for finding
  the area of a triangle. It also involves being able to work out the
  heights of the triangles from the information given.
- Kate also needs to know how efficiently the individual shapes can be
  cut from a rectangular sheet; do they tessellate (this will affect the
  quantity of wasted card)? There is some leeway for the
  measurements given in the design; for example, the sides of the base
  triangle can be from 55.5 mm up to 56.5 mm and still fit the
  specification. If the boxes are made so that the measurements are as
  low as possible, will the number of boxes that can be cut from one
  sheet be greater or not?
- When Kate has calculated the number of boxes that can be cut from
  one sheet of card, she can find the number of sheets needed to make
  the 50 000 boxes. The storage area can hold a maximum weight of
  1 tonne, so she must find the weight of these sheets; this will
  determine whether they can be bought in one batch or will have to be
  ordered in several batches.

EXERCISE 10A

1 Kate could not remember whether the area of a triangle was given by

$$\tfrac{1}{2}(\text{length of base}) \times (\text{perpendicular height})$$

or by $\tfrac{1}{2}(\text{length of base})^2 \times (\text{perpendicular height})$

One of these expressions cannot give an area. Discuss how you can tell which one this is.

2 Kate has to find the surface area of the box. The sides of the box are triangles but their heights are not given.
This is the triangle that forms the base of the box.
Discuss

a how the height of this triangle can be found

b how accurate the result needs to be

c what are the advantages and disadvantages of different ways of finding the height.

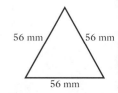

3 Discuss how you can find the largest number of these bases that can be cut in just one row across the width of a sheet of card that is 850 mm wide. Does the way they are arranged matter? Would it make any difference if the triangles were cut so that the sides were each **55.5** mm long?

4 Discuss what you need to know about the sheets of card so that you can find the weight of **500** of these sheets. If the specification is changed to a different card, what else do you need to know?

THE DIMENSIONS OF A FORMULA

Kate could not remember whether the area of a triangle was given by

$$A = \tfrac{1}{2}b \times h \quad \text{or} \quad A = \tfrac{1}{2}b^2 \times h$$

It is possible to check whether either or both of these formulas gives an area but it is not possible to tell whether it is the correct expression.

Formulas for finding lengths, areas and volumes all contain letters, each of which represents a number of units of length or area or volume.

An expression that has only one 'length unit' letter (or the *sum* of two or more such letters) is *one-dimensional* and represents a length as a number of miles, centimetres, kilometres, etc.

When an expression contains the *product* of two length symbols it is *two-dimensional* and represents an area as a number of (length unit)^2 such as cm^2, m^2, etc.

An expression with three length symbols multiplied together (or an area symbol multiplied by a length symbol) is *three-dimensional*. It represents a volume as a number of (length unit)^3, e.g. m^3, mm^3, etc.

Sometimes in a formula there is also a number, or a symbol that stands for a number such as π. This does not represent a number of units of length, area or volume and so does not affect the dimensions of an expression.

Suppose, for example, that d is a number of length units, then

$2d$ is one-dimensional
$4d^2$ is two-dimensional
πd^3 is three-dimensional.

Checking units and dimensions can help us to decide whether a given quantity represents length, area or volume.
For example, if a sentence refers to 'z cm^3', then z must be a number of volume units.

Similarly, if a sentence contains 'a cm', 'b cm' and '$X = ab$' then ab must be (a number of cm) $\times$ (a number of cm), which is a number of cm^2. Therefore X represents a number of area units.

On the other hand, suppose we are told that the formula for the volume, V cubic units, of a container is $V = 3\pi ab$ where a and b are numbers of length units. V is three-dimensional but $3\pi ab$ is two-dimensional. So the formula must be incorrect.

EXERCISE 10B

1 State whether each of the following quantities is a length, an area or a volume.

a 10 cm   **c** 85 cm^2 **e** 630 mm

b 21 cm^3 **d** 4 m^3 **f** 93 km^2

2 State whether each of the following quantities should be measured in length or area or volume units.

a Diameter of a circle   **d** Perimeter of a pentagon

b Amount of air in a room   **e** Region inside a square

c Space inside a sphere   **f** Surface of a sphere

3 a, b and c represent numbers of centimetres. Give a suitable unit (e.g. cm^2) for X.

a $X = a + b$ **c** $X = 4\pi a^2$ **e** $X = \pi c$

b $X = 4ab$ **d** $X = abc$ **f** $X = \frac{4}{3}\pi a^3$

In questions **4** and **5**, a, b and c represent numbers of length units, A, B and C represent numbers of area units and V represents a number of volume units.

4 State whether each of the letters P to Y used in the following formulas represents numbers of length or area or volume units.

a $P = \pi bc$ **d** $Q = A + B$ **g** $R = \dfrac{ab}{c}$

b $S = \pi a^2 b$ **e** $T = 4bA$ **h** $U = \dfrac{2A}{c}$

c $W = 2a + 3b$ **f** $X = a^2 + b^2$ **i** $Y = \dfrac{V}{a}$

5 Some of the following formulas are wrongly constructed. State which formulas are incorrect and justify your statement.

a $B = ac$ **c** $C = a^2 + b^3$ **e** $V = ab + c$

b $C = \pi a^2$ **d** $V = 6a^2 b$ **f** $A = a(b + c)$

6 Peter had to find the area of a circle whose diameter was $18\,cm$. He wrote down

$$
\begin{aligned}
\text{Area} &= 2\pi r\,cm^2 \\
&= 2 \times \pi \times 9\,cm^2 \\
&= 56.5\,cm^2
\end{aligned}
$$

Louise knew nothing about circle formulas but was able to tell Peter that he was wrong. How did she know?

7 Jane copied a formula that she was supposed to use to find the volume of a solid but she found that she could not read the index number. All she had was $V = \pi x^? y$. She knew that x and y were numbers of length units.
What is the index number?

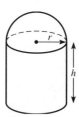

This bollard is a cylinder with a hemisphere (half a sphere) on top.
From the list given below, pick out the formula for

a the overall height of the bollard

b the surface area of the bollard

c the volume of the bollard.

$$P = 3\pi r^2 + 2\pi rh \qquad Q = \pi r^2 + h \qquad H = r + h$$

$$S = \pi r^2 h + \tfrac{2}{3}\pi r^3 \qquad T = \pi rh + \tfrac{4}{3}\pi r^3$$

a Height is one-dimensional so the formula must have single letter terms only.

The overall height is given by $H = r + h$.

b Area is two-dimensional so each term in the formula must have a product of two letter terms.

The surface area is given by $P = 3\pi r^2 + 2\pi rh$.

c Volume is three-dimensional so each term in the formula must have a product of three letter terms.

The volume is given by $S = \pi r^2 h + \tfrac{2}{3}\pi r^3$.

8

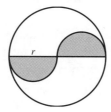

From the list of expressions given below, choose the correct one for

a the perimeter of the shaded region

b the area of the unshaded region.

A $2r + \pi r^2$ **B** $2r + \pi r$ **C** $\pi r^2 - \tfrac{1}{4}\pi r^2$ **D** $\pi r^2 - 2\pi r$

9 Which of these formulas could give the volume of this cone?

A $V = \pi r h$ **C** $V = \pi r^2 + \frac{1}{3} h$

B $V = \frac{1}{3} \pi r^2 h$ **D** $V = \pi r \sqrt{r^2 + h^2}$

Give reasons for your answer.

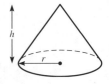

10 The mathematical name for this ring-doughnut shape is a torus.

Which of the following expressions could give

a its surface area
b its volume?

A $\frac{1}{4} \pi^2 (R + r)(R - r)^2$

B $\pi^2 (R^3 - r^2)$

C $\frac{3}{4}(\pi^2 R^2 - 3\pi Rr + R^3)$

D $\pi^2 (R^2 - r^2)$

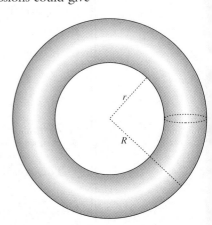

11 Alice wasn't sure of the formula for the surface area of a closed cylinder of radius r and height h. Her elder brother thought that the formula was $A = 2\pi r^2 (r + h)$ while her younger brother thought it was $A = \pi(2r + h)$. Her father suggested $A = 2\pi r(r + h)$.
One of these formulas is correct. Which one is it? Justify your choice.

12 In each of the following expressions, a and b are numbers of centimetres. Write down the value of n that makes each expression represent an area.

a $a^n b$ **b** $2(a^n + ab)$ **c** $4a(a^n + b^n)$

13 Which of the expressions below give the area of this oval?

A $\pi a^2 b^2$ **B** πab **C** $\pi(a + b)$

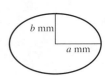

Kate has to find the area of this triangle.
To use the formula

$$\text{area} = \tfrac{1}{2}\,\text{base} \times \text{height}$$

she needs to find the value of h.

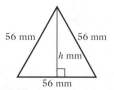

An accurate value for h can be found by using Pythagoras' Theorem.

Pythagoras' Theorem states that, in any
right-angled triangle, the square of the
hypotenuse is equal to the sum of the
squares of the other two sides,

i.e. in $\triangle ABC$,
$$AC^2 = AB^2 + BC^2$$

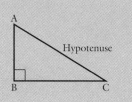

For extra practice working with this theorem, use Revision Exercise 1.4
at the front of this book.

This triangle is equilateral and the height divides it into two equal right-
angled triangles.

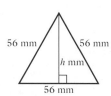 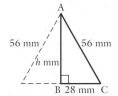

Using Pythagoras' theorem on $\triangle ABC$

gives $\quad AC^2 = AB^2 + BC^2$

i.e. $\quad 56^2 = h^2 + 28^2$

$\Rightarrow \quad\quad h^2 = 2352$

i.e. $\quad\quad h = 48.49\ldots$ (We do not need the negative square root
because h must be a positive number.)

So the height of this triangle is **48.5** mm corrected to 3 significant figures.
Now we can find the area;

$$\text{Area } \triangle = \tfrac{1}{2} \times 56 \times 48.49\ldots\,\text{mm}^2$$

$$= 1357.9\ldots\,\text{mm}^2$$

$$= 1400\,\text{mm}^2 \quad (\text{ correct to 2 s.f. })$$

EXERCISE 10C

For the problems in this exercise, you will need to find a right-angled triangle so that you can use Pythagoras' Theorem. In most cases this will involve adding a line to the diagram to form this triangle.

You will also need to know how to find the areas of squares, rectangles, parallelograms and trapeziums. The formulas for these areas are given on page 12, Summary 1.

The cross-section of a railway embankment is the isosceles trapezium shown. Find the height of the embankment.

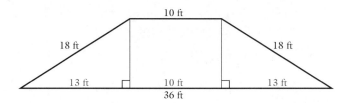

We must first find a right-angled triangle: we can form two such triangles by dropping perpendicular lines from the top of the trapezium to the base as shown in the diagram. As the trapezium is isosceles, these two triangles are identical. Using the symmetry of the shape, we can see that the triangles are 10 ft apart so the sum of their bases is 26 ft. This means that the base of each triangle is 13 ft.

It is easier to see what we need to do, and to describe what we are doing if we make a separate drawing of one of these triangles and label it.

Using Pythagoras' Theorem in △ABC gives

$$AC^2 = AB^2 + BC^2$$

i.e. $18^2 = 13^2 + BC^2$

$324 = 169 + BC^2$ Subtract 169 from both sides.

$155 = BC^2$

∴ $BC = \sqrt{155} = 12.44\ldots$

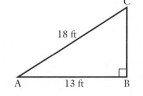

The height of the embankment is **12.4 ft** correct to **3 significant figures.**

---

1 The diagram shows the cross-section through an embankment.

   a How far apart are the vertical walls?

   b Find the area of the cross-section.

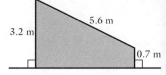

2 This is one of the sides of the packaging box described at the start of this chapter.

   Find

   a the height of the triangle

   b the surface area of the triangle.

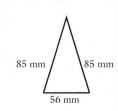

3 Find **i** the height **ii** the area of each triangle.
(You can turn a diagram round if necessary.)

a
5 cm   5 cm
5 cm

b 220 mm
450 mm 450 mm

c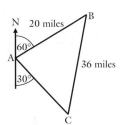
3.8 m   2.1 m
2.1 m

4 The course for a speedboat race is
shown in the diagram.
Find

a angle BAC

b the length of AC

c the length of the course.

N   20 miles   B
60°
A
30°   36 miles
C

5
A   20 cm   B

37 cm

C

The diagram shows a shelf bracket
which has to be screwed to a wall at A
and at C.
How far below the hole for the screw
at A does the hole for the screw at C
need to be drilled?

6 Lengths of fencing are
made by bolting equilateral
triangular frames together
as shown.

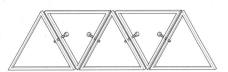

The sides of the frames are each 110 cm long.
How high is the fence?

7
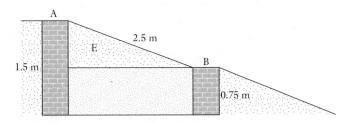

A
2.5 m
E
1.5 m
B
0.75 m

The diagram shows how some sloping ground is terraced.
A wall 1.5 m deep is built at A and another wall 0.75 m deep is built
at B, a distance of 2.5 m down the slope. The triangular cross-
section of earth, E, is then dug out and placed below the wall at B.
Find the area of the cross-section E.

8 A bannister for a flight of
stairs is a parallelogram.
The bannister is 1 m high
and 5 m long.
The vertical edge is at 60°
to the slope of the stairs.

Find the shortest distance
between the sloping edges
of the bannister.
(*Hint* You will need to find
half an equilateral triangle.)
Hence find the area of
the bannister.

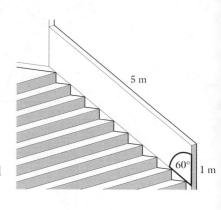

9 An aeroplane flies 200 km due
north from Southampton, S, to
a point R where it refuels. It
then changes course and flies
to a field F in France where it
is 270 km due east of S.
How far is the aeroplane now
from its refuelling stop ?

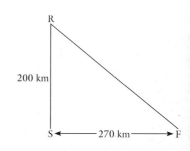

10 The cross-section of a rubbish
skip is an isosceles trapezium.
How deep is the skip ?

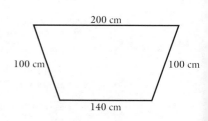

11 The cross-section of this bar
of chocolate is an isosceles
trapezium.

The top is 18 mm wide, the base is 24 mm wide and the sloping
edges of the cross-section are each 12 mm long.

a Find the area of the cross-section.

The bar is 40 mm long.

b Find the volume of chocolate in the bar.

12 The cross-section of this polythene plant protector is part of a circle.

The radius of the circle is 30 cm and the distance across the base of the cross-section is 50 cm. Find the height of the plant protector.

13 The diagram shows design for a square paved area.
The stone in the centre is a square of side 30 cm and it is surrounded by 4 isosceles triangles to form a larger square.

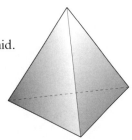

a Find the length of the sides of this larger square.

Four identical isosceles trapeziums form the outer ring of stones.
The distance between the parallel sides of each of these trapeziums is 30 cm.

b Find the length of a side of the paved area.

PYRAMIDS

The shape of the packing at the start of this chapter is a pyramid. Any solid with a flat base whose sides come up to a point is called a pyramid. The shape of the base is often used to describe the pyramid. The base of the packing box is a triangle; it is an example of a triangular-based pyramid. Triangular pyramids are also called *tetrahedrons*.

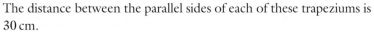

When the top point (the vertex) is above the centre of the base, the pyramid is called a *right pyramid*.

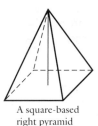
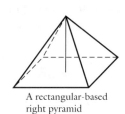

A square-based right pyramid

A rectangular-based right pyramid

A triangular-based pyramid. This one is not a right pyramid.

SURFACE AREA

Kate needs to find the surface area of this pyramid.
We can see that this solid has 4 faces: the base which is an equilateral triangle and the 3 sides, each of which is an isosceles triangle.

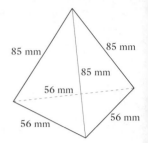

A sketch of a net for this pyramid shows the shapes of the triangles clearly.

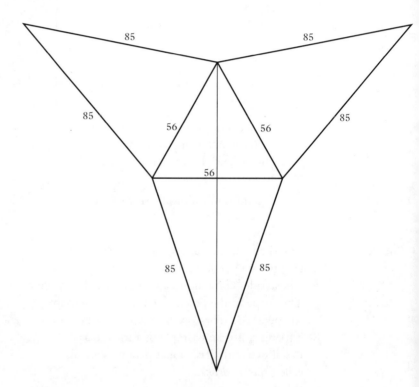

Now we can see that the surface area is equal to
(the area of the base) + (3 × area of one of the sides)

On page 179 we found that the area of the base is $1357.9 \ldots$ mm^2 and, from question **2 Exercise 10C**, the area of a side triangle is $2247.1 \ldots$ mm^2

Therefore the surface area of this prism is

$$1357.9 \ldots + 3 \times 2247.1 \ldots \text{ mm}^2 = 8099.3 \text{ mm}^2$$
$$= 8100 \text{ mm}^2 \text{ (correct to 2 s.f.)}$$

EXERCISE 10D

1 Cuboids made of metal are
enamelled and linked together
to make necklaces.

Each cuboid has a square cross-section
of edge 2 mm and is 3 mm long.
One of these cuboids is drawn on
an isometric grid.

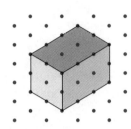

a Use squared paper
to copy and complete
this net for the
cuboid.

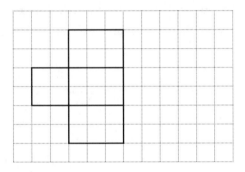

b Find the area of enamel on one cuboid.

c It costs 1.5 pence to enamel one cuboid. Twenty cuboids are
used to make a necklace. What is the cost of enamelling these
twenty cuboids?

2 A presentation medal is packed in a box which is an open tray with a
sleeve. The tray has a square base of side 3 cm and is 1 cm deep.
The sleeve, which is open at both ends, fits exactly over the tray.
The two parts of the box are drawn on isometric paper.

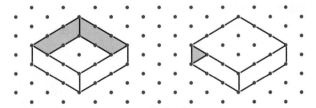

a The tray is made from plastic sheet material. On squared paper,
draw a net for the tray. Hence find the area of plastic used to
make the tray.

b The sleeve is made from a single layer of card except for one of
the narrow sides which is a double layer stuck together.
Draw a net for the card used to make one sleeve and find its
surface area.

3 A chocolate bar is packed in a box whose cross-section is an equilateral triangle of side 2 cm. The box is 7 cm long.

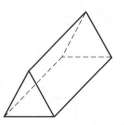

a Copy and complete this sketch to give a net for the box. It does not need to be drawn accurately, but mark in the lengths known.

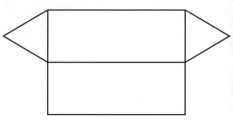

b Find the surface area of this box.

c Find the volume that this box will hold.

4 The roof on a house is a right square-based pyramid.

a Copy and complete this sketch which gives a net for the roof.

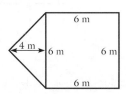

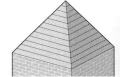

b The roof is lined with a single layer of insulating material on all faces including the base. Find the area of the insulating material used.

5 The diagram shows part of a sketch of the net for a right pyramid on a triangular base.

a Copy and complete the net.

b Sketch the pyramid.

c Find the total surface area of the pyramid.

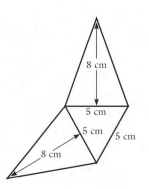

6 The roof of a house is a prism whose cross-section is an isosceles triangle. The diagram is a sketch of part of a net for this prism.

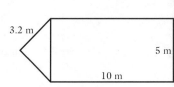

a Copy and complete this sketch.

b Sketch the prism.

c The sloping rectangular sides of the roof are covered with roofing felt. Find the area of this felt.

7 The diagram shows part of
   the net of a pyramid drawn
   accurately on squared paper.

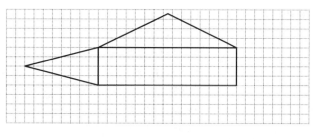

   a Copy and complete the net.

   b Use measurements from
      your net to calculate the
      total surface area of the
      pyramid.

   c Sketch the pyramid.

8 The diagram shows a sketch of a wooden door wedge.

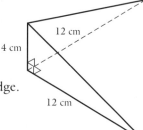

   The base is an isosceles right-angled triangle whose
   equal sides are 12 cm long. The vertical edge of the
   wedge is 4 cm.

   a On 5 mm squared paper, draw an accurate net for this wedge.

   b Find the total surface area of this wedge.

9 Chocolate medallions are packed in boxes
   whose shape is a prism with a hexagonal
   cross-section as shown in the diagram. The
   sides of the hexagon are 3 cm long and the box
   is 17 cm long.

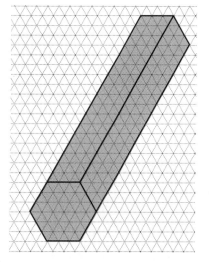

   a Use measurements from the drawing to find
      the area of the hexagon.

   b Find the volume of the box.

   c Sketch a net for the box and use it to help you
      to find the total surface area of the box.

10 A model house, made from card, is a closed prism.
   The cross-section is shown in the diagram and the
   model is 200 mm long.

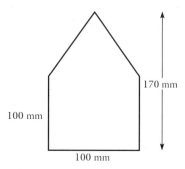

   a Draw a net for this prism.

   b Calculate the total surface area of the prism,
      giving your answer correct to 3 significant
      figures.

DENSITY

Returning to the packing boxes that Kate is concerned with, we can find the mass of one of the boxes because we have information about the mass per unit area of the material they are to be made from.

We know the surface area of one box; on page 184 we found this to be 8099 mm² to the nearest square millimetre.
We also know that the boxes are to be made from card weighing 1200 grams per square metre.

Now if   1 m² has a mass of 1200 g
     1 mm² has a mass of $1200 \div 1000^2$ g
          = 0.0012 g

> 1 mm = 1000 mm,
> so 1 m² = 1000² mm²

Therefore 8099 mm² has a mass of $8099 \times 0.0012 \text{ g} = 9.718\ldots$ g
i.e.   the card used to make one box weighs 9.72 g correct to 3 s.f.

The 'weight' of a sheet material, such as card, is described by giving the mass per unit of area; this is because the thickness is constant.

For materials that do not come in sheet form, such as wood, lead, and so on, we need to know the mass of one unit of volume.
This is called the *density* of the material.

For example, the density of silver is 10.5 g/cm³.
This means that 1 cm³ of silver has a mass of 10.5 g.

We can use the density of a material to find the mass of a known volume of that material. This is particularly useful in situations where we cannot weigh an object; at the design stage for example.

If we know the volume and mass of an object, we can work out the density of the material it is made from.

For example,
a piece of rock has a volume of
250 cm³ and weighs 505 grams.
To find the density we want the
mass of 1 cm³.

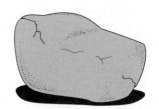

As   250 cm³ has a mass of 505 grams,

     1 cm³ has a mass of $\dfrac{505}{250}$ grams $= 2.02$ grams,

i.e.   the density of the rock is 2.02 g/cm³

This illustrates that $$\text{density} = \frac{\text{mass}}{\text{volume}}$$

EXERCISE 10E

A gold ingot is a cuboid measuring $4\,\text{cm} \times 4\,\text{cm} \times 2\,\text{cm}$.
Given that the density of gold is $19.3\,\text{g/cm}^3$, find the mass of the ingot.

Volume of ingot $= 4 \times 4 \times 2\,\text{cm}^3$

$$= 32\,\text{cm}^3$$

Mass $= 32 \times 19.3\,\text{g} = 617.6\,\text{g}$

> Density $= 19.3\,\text{g per cm}^3$
> so $32\,\text{cm}^3$ has a mass of $32 \times 19.3\,\text{g}$.

$$= 618\,\text{g} \ (\text{correct to 3 s.f.})$$

> For a material as valuable as gold, the mass would probably be found more accurately, but to do this we need to know the density more accurately than to 3 significant figures as given.

Give all answers correct to 3 significant figures.

1 The density of oak is $0.8\,\text{g/cm}^3$. Find the mass of a piece of oak that has a volume of $120\,\text{cm}^3$.

2 The density of copper is $8.9\,\text{g/cm}^3$. Find the mass of a length of copper pipe if $260\,\text{cm}^3$ of copper has been used to make it.

3 A block of brass has a volume of $14.3\,\text{cm}^3$. Given that the density of brass is $8.5\,\text{g/cm}^3$, find the mass of the block.

4 Find the mass of 1 litre of milk given that the density of milk is $0.98\,\text{g/cm}^3$.

5 A rectangular block of wood measures 6 cm by 8 cm by 24 cm. The density of the wood is $0.85\,\text{g/cm}^3$. Find the mass of the block.

6 The diagram shows a block of paraffin wax cast into the shape of a triangular prism. The density of the wax is $0.9\,\text{g/cm}^3$. Find the mass of the block.

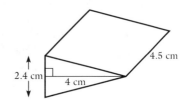

7 The volume of a block of wood is $500\,\text{cm}^3$ and the mass of the block is $460\,\text{g}$. Find the density of the wood.

8 The diagram shows the cross-section of a water trough, 1.5 m long, which is full of ice.

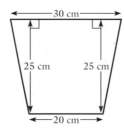

Using the measurements given on the diagram find

a the area of cross-section in cm²

b the mass of the ice in the trough given that the density of ice is 0.917 g/cm³.

9 This candle holder is made of brass.
Its volume is 750 cm³ and its mass is 5090 g.
Find the density of the brass.

10 The volume of a rubber ball is 407 cm³ and its mass is 356 g.
Find the density of the rubber it is made from.

11 A solid polystyrene cylinder has a diameter of 21 cm and it is 40 cm high. The mass of the cylinder is 3000 g.
Find the density of the material it is made from.

12 A hollow cylinder has an internal diameter of 1.2 cm and is 3 cm deep. It is filled with mercury which has a density of 13.6 g/cm³.
Find the mass of the mercury in the cylinder.

13 This is the cross-section of a channel for cables (conduit) showing the internal and external measurements.

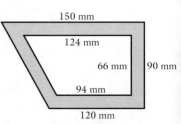

a Find the area of material in the cross-section.

b Find the volume of material needed to make a length of 2.5 metres of this conduit.

c The material used to make this conduit has a density of 0.75 g/cm³. Find the mass of the 2.5 metre length.

14 The diagram shows the cross-section through a coping-stone which is used on the top of a wall. Each stone is 50 cm long. Find

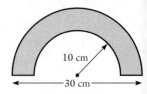

a the area of the cross-section

b the mass of the stone if the density of the material it is made from is 3.5 g/cm³.

RANGE OF VALUES FOR A CORRECTED NUMBER

Suppose we are told that, correct to the nearest ten, 250 people boarded a particular train. People are counted in whole numbers only. In this case, 245 is the lowest whole number that gives 250 when corrected to the nearest 10 and 254 is the highest whole number that can be corrected to 250. We can therefore say that the actual number of people who boarded the train is any whole number from 245 to 254.

Returning again to the problem at the beginning of this chapter, Kate is given the measurements of a box correct to the nearest millimetre; the triangle that forms the base of the box has sides that are 56 mm long correct to the nearest millimetre.

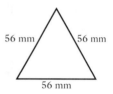

Look at this magnified section of a measuring gauge:

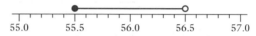

The lowest number that can be rounded up to 56 is **55.5**. The highest number that can be rounded down to 56 is not so easy to determine. All we can say is that any number up to, but not including, **56.5** can be rounded down to 56.

The length of a side is therefore in the range from **55.5** mm up to, but not including, **56.5** mm.

If l mm is the length of a side, we can write

$$55.5 \leqslant l < 56.5$$

To illustrate this on the diagram we use a solid circle to show that **55.5** is included in the range and an open circle to show that **56.5** is not included in the range.

55.5 is called the *lower bound* of l and **56.5** is called the *upper bound* of l.

EXERCISE 10F

> Illustrate on a number line the range of values of x given by $0.1 < x \leqslant 0.8$
>
>

1 Illustrate the range of values on x on a number line like this.

−5	0	5	10	15	20

a $5 \leqslant x \leqslant 10$ **c** $-2 \leqslant x \leqslant 6$ **e** $0 \leqslant x < 10$

b $0 < x \leqslant 15$ **d** $5 \leqslant x < 15$ **f** $-5 < x \leqslant 5$

2 Illustrate the range of values of x on a number line like this.

a $0 < x < 0.1$ **c** $0.05 < x < 0.15$ **e** $0.02 < x < 0.08$

b $0.1 < x < 0.2$ **d** $0.08 < x < 0.16$ **f** $0.03 < x < 0.13$

A number is given as **3.15** correct to 2 decimal places. Illustrate on a number line the range in which this number lies.

3.15 is between 3.14 and 3.16 so we will use just that part of the number line.

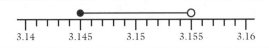

---

3 Illustrate on a number line the range of possible values for each of the following numbers which are correct to 1 decimal place.

a 1.5   **b** 0.6   **c** 0.2   **d** 1.3   **e** 0.1   **f** 6.2

4 Illustrate on a number line the range of possible values for each of the following numbers which are correct to 2 decimal places.

a 0.25   **b** 0.52   **c** 1.15   **d** 6.89   **e** 12.26   **f** 0.05

It is stated that a packet of pins contains 500 pins to the nearest 10. Find the range in which the actual number of pins lies.

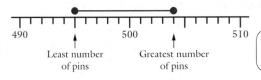

Least number of pins   Greatest number of pins

There must be a whole number of pins in the packet.

If n is the number of pins in the packet then n is a whole number such that $495 \leqslant n \leqslant 504$

A copper tube is sold as having an internal bore (diameter) of 10 mm to the nearest millimetre. Find the range in which the actual bore lies.

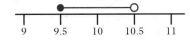

If d mm is the diameter of the tube then $9.5 \leqslant d < 10.5$

In some of the following questions you are asked to find a range of values for a quantity that can only have whole number values. When this is the case, it must be clearly stated in your answer:

5 The weight, w kg, of a bag of sand is given as 5.6 kg correct to 1 decimal place. Find the range of values in which w lies.

6 A shop is said to make a profit of £2500 a month. If this figure is given correct to the nearest £100, find the range in which the actual monthly figure, £x, lies.

7 On a certain model of bicycle, to work efficiently the brake pads have to be 12.5 mm thick. If the brake pads are x mm thick, find the range in which x lies, correct to 1 decimal place.

8 Referring to a football match, a newspaper headline proclaimed '75 000 watch England win'. Assuming that this figure for the number of spectators is correct to the nearest 1000, find the range in which x, the number of people who actually attended the match, lies. If, in fact, 75 000 was a guess, what can you say about x?

9 One of the component parts of a metal hinge is a pin. In order to work properly this pin must have a diameter of 1.25 mm correct to 2 decimal places.
If d mm is the diameter, find the range in which d must lie.

10 Alan measured the width of a space between two kitchen units in metres correct to 1 decimal place, and wrote down 1.6 m.

   a Find the range within which the width of the space lies.

   b The cupboard bought to go into the space is 1.62 m wide correct to 2 decimal places. Will it fit the space?

11 One hundred people were asked if they ate cornflakes for breakfast that morning. To the nearest 10, 40 people said they did. Of the 100 people interviewed, what is the largest possible number who did not eat cornflakes?

12 The length of a car is given as 455 cm. If this figure is correct to the nearest 5 cm, find the range in which the actual length lies.

13 A cube of side 34 mm, correct to the nearest millimetre, is to be packed in a cubical box whose internal sides are 34.2 mm correct to 3 significant figures. Explain why the cube may not fit in the box.

WORKING WITH CORRECTED NUMBERS

These pieces of card need to be stamped out of a sheet to make packing boxes. We need one 'base' triangle and three identical 'side' triangles for each box.

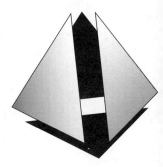

Triangles tessellate, so one way to cut these from a sheet is to have one row of 'bases' and three rows of 'sides' across the width and repeat this down the sheet.

The number of triangles that can be fitted into one row obviously depends on the width of the sheet, but it also may depend on the precise measurements of the sides of the triangles.

The horizontal edges must be 56 mm to the nearest millimetre, so the length, l mm, of one edge could be anywhere in the range $55.5 \text{ mm} \leqslant l < 56.5 \text{ mm}$. The least possible length of one edge is 55.5 mm. The greatest possible length is 56.4999... mm which, when corrected to any number of decimal places, becomes 56.5 mm.

So for practical purposes, the greatest possible value of this length is 56.5 mm.

Suppose that we place 10 of these triangles in a row as shown.

Length of row

The least possible length of this row is 10 times the least possible length of a side of a triangle, i.e. $10 \times 55.5 \text{ mm} = 555 \text{ mm}$

The greatest possible length of this row is 10 times the greatest possible length of a side of a triangle, i.e. $10 \times 56.5 \text{ mm} = 565 \text{ mm}$

The difference between the greatest and least possible length of the row is 10 mm. If we had a row of 100 triangles, the difference would be 100 mm. This means that if the card they are to be stamped from is wide enough to have 100 triangles in a row when the sides are 56.5 mm long, one more triangle could be stamped from the row when the sides are only 55.5 mm long.

EXERCISE 10G

1 The weight of a wall tile is given as 40 g to the nearest gram. A DIY store sells these tiles in polythene-wrapped packs of ten. Ignoring the weight of the wrapping, find the range in which the weight of one of these packs lies.

2 The length of a side of a square carpet tile is 29.9 cm correct to 1 decimal place. One hundred of these carpet tiles are laid end to end on the floor of a shop. Find the range in which the length of this line of tiles lies. Hence give the difference between the length of the longest possible line of 100 tiles and the shortest possible line of 100 tiles.

3 In a manufacturing process a rectangular sheet of stainless steel, measuring 35 mm by 23 mm correct to the nearest millimetre, has to be edged with wire.

    a What length of wire is needed to make sure that there is enough to edge one of these sheets?

    b The wire costs £18.20 per metre. What is the cost of enough wire to ensure that 500 000 of these sheets can be edged? (Assume that there is no waste.)

4 A pair of digital scales gives weights correct to the nearest gram. When one nail is weighed on these scales, the reading is 8 grams. When 100 identical nails are weighed, the reading is 775 grams.

    a Explain the apparent contradiction in the readings.

    b Give a more accurate weight for one nail than the scales are capable of showing when only one nail is weighed.

A sheet of card is 58 cm long. A strip of length 20 cm is cut from it. Both measurements are correct to the nearest centimetre. What is the greatest possible value of the length that is left?

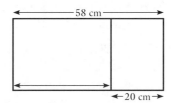

> The length remaining when the strip is cut off is shown in purple on the diagram. This is greatest when the sheet it is cut from is as long as possible, i.e. 58.5 cm, and the piece removed is as short as possible, i.e. 19.5 cm.

The greatest possible length remaining is 58.5 cm − 19.5 cm
$$= 39\,\text{cm}$$

The worked example illustrates a general fact.

> $a - b$ has its greatest value when a is as large as possible and when b is as small as possible.
>
> Similarly $a - b$ has its least value when a is as small as possible and when b is as large as possible.

5 A wooden pole is 450 mm long and a 200 mm length is cut from it. Both of these measurements are correct to the nearest millimetre. What can you say about the length of the remaining section of the pole?

6 When asked about their ages John and Debbie both said that they were 15. What is the greatest possible difference in their ages?

7 A roll of carpet has 25 metres on it. A length of 3 metres is cut from the roll. Each measurement is correct to the nearest metre. What is the least length of carpet left on the roll?

8

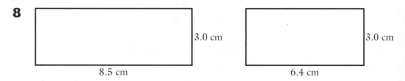

8.5 cm 3.0 cm 6.4 cm 3.0 cm

All the measurements on these two rectangular pieces of card are correct to 1 decimal place.

a The two pieces are placed edge to edge as shown.

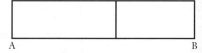

A   B

Find   **i** the largest possible value of the length AB
       ii the smallest possible value of the length AB.

b The two pieces are rearranged to form a symmetrical letter T.

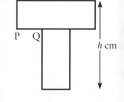

P   Q h cm

  i What is the smallest possible value for the length PQ?

  ii Find the upper bound for the height, h cm, of this T-shape.

9 A one-penny coin has a diameter of 0.8 inches correct to 1 decimal place.
In a charity event, 10 000 of these coins are laid end to end in a line. Josh says 'That line must be at least 1 mile long.'
Is he right? Justify your answer. (1 mile = 63 360 inches)

10 Four identical rectangular cards are arranged to form a square, with a square hole in the centre as shown.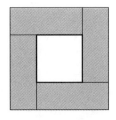

Each card is 33 mm long and 12 mm wide where both measurements are correct to the nearest millimetre.

   a Find the greatest possible length of a side of the outer square.

   b Find the least possible length of a side of the square hole.

   c Find the least possible area of the hole.

11 This triangle forms the base of a packing box. The lengths of the sides are correct to the nearest centimetre. Find the difference between the largest possible area and the smallest possible area of this triangle.

20 cm

12 cm

MIXED EXERCISES

EXERCISE 10H   **Do not use a calculator for this exercise.**

1 Which of the following formulas gives the volume of this pyramid?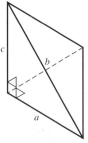

   A $\frac{1}{2}a^2bc$ **C** $\frac{1}{6}abc$

   B $\frac{1}{4}a(b+c)$ **D** $\pi(a^2+b^2+c^2)$

2 This is an isosceles triangle.

   Find **a** its height   **b** its area.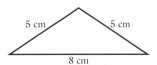

5 cm   5 cm

8 cm

3 The diagram shows part of a sketch of the net for a pyramid on a rectangular base. The diagram is not drawn to scale.

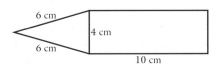

6 cm

4 cm

6 cm

10 cm

   a Copy and complete the diagram, marking in all the measurements that are known.

   b Sketch the pyramid.

4 A lump of solid copper has a volume of 500 cm^3 and its mass is 4450 grams. Find the density of the copper.

5 The diagram shows a packing insert for cases holding microwave ovens. It is a prism whose cross-section is a right-angled triangle and it is made from polystyrene whose density is 0.2 g/cm^2.

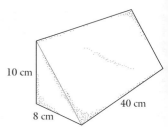

Find, in tonnes, the weight of 10 000 of these inserts.

6 Rectangular paving stones are 50 cm long by 30 cm wide, both measurements being correct to the nearest centimetre.

a

Three of these paving stones are laid end to end. Find the greatest possible length of this line of stones.

b Two of these paving stones are placed at right angles as shown.

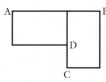

Find **i** the greatest possible length of AB
      ii the least possible length of DC.

EXERCISE 10I

1 The cross-section of a skip is an isosceles trapezium. The internal measurements are given in the diagram.

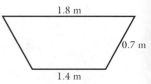

a Find the depth of the skip.

b The internal width of skip is 1.3 m. Find the capacity of the skip.

c The skip is filled level to the top with clay whose density is 850 kg/m^3. Find the weight of clay in the skip.

2 This rubber ball has a radius of 2.7 cm. Find the volume of this ball by using the correct expression from those given below.

A $\frac{1}{2}\pi r^2$ **B** $\frac{4}{3}\pi r^3$ **C** $\frac{1}{4}\pi r(r^2 + r)$

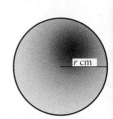

3 The diagram shows a right pyramid on a square base.

    a Sketch a net for this pyramid.

    b Find the total surface area of the pyramid.

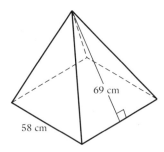

69 cm

58 cm

4 A statue is carved from stone. The volume of the statue is $480 \, \text{cm}^3$ and it weighs 5 kg.

    a Find the density of the stone it is made from.

    b A statue whose volume is $2500 \, \text{cm}^3$ is carved from the same stone. How much does it weigh?

PRACTICAL WORK

This is a design for a plastic lid for a butter dish.

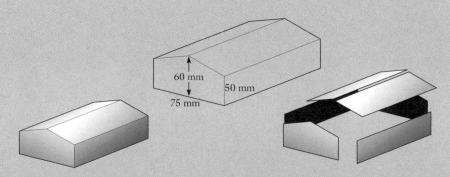

60 mm

50 mm

75 mm

The lid is open at the base and it is made by stamping out the shapes from a sheet of plastic that weighs 1 kg per square metre.
The measurements are correct to the nearest millimetre.

    a Find the range in which the mass of one lid may lie.

    b Investigate the most efficient way of stamping these shapes from a rectangular sheet of plastic measuring 1 metre by 2 metres.

    c A number of sheets of plastic have to be ordered, sufficient for 5000 of these lids to be cut from them. How many sheets are needed?

    d There is enough storage for 40 kg of plastic sheet in the cutting room. How many batches of sheets are needed and how many sheets should there be in each batch?

ENLARGEMENT

Terry wants to use this design as a logo for his business. He needs a different size of this tree for each use.

He can use graphic software on a computer to do this.

These are copies of the picture. Each is a differently scaled version of the original.

Larger overall   Smaller overall   Stretched sideways   Stretched upwards

In this chapter we look at ways of drawing, by hand, versions of a design that are larger overall or smaller overall than the original.

We use the word *transformation* to cover any change made to the position and/or shape of an object. We use *enlargement* to cover making an object both larger overall and smaller overall.

You will be able to tell which is which when you have worked through this chapter.

EXERCISE 11A

1 Joy wants to photocopy a newspaper article. The copier can be set to scale the original document from 25% to 250%. Discuss what size the copy will be if Joy sets the scale to

a 125%   **b** 75%

2 Measure the width of this square.
If this page is copied on a photocopier
with the scale set to 50% discuss which
of the following statements will be true
of the copy of this square.

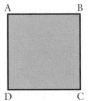

a AB will be twice as long as the original length.

b AD will be half as long as the original length.

c The area of the square will be half the area of the original.

ENLARGEMENT

We looked at enlargements in Book 9B. A summary of what we found
there is given below. The diagram shows a square ABCD and an
enlargement, A'B'C'D', of that square.

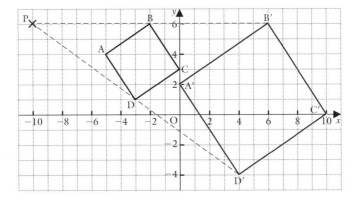

The black square is the *object* (i.e. the original) and the purple square is
the *image*.

The *scale factor* of the enlargement gives the length of the sides of the
image compared with the length of the sides of the object.
In this case, the scale factor is 2 because A'B' = 2 × AB.

The broken lines that join corresponding corners of the object and the
image are *guidelines* and the point P where they meet is the *centre of the
enlargement*. The guidelines are used

either to find the centre of enlargement when the image is given (by
joining corresponding points on the image and object and finding
where they meet)

or to draw the image when the centre of enlargement and the scale factor
are given. (In this diagram, we would draw PB and then extend it to B' so
that PB' = 2 × PB, and so on for the other three corners of the square.)

If the position of an enlargement does not matter, the image can be
drawn anywhere. All we need is the scale factor.

EXERCISE 11B

1 Copy the diagram onto 5 mm squared paper using 1 cm for 1 unit on both axes.

Find the scale factor and draw guidelines to find the centre of enlargement used to produce the purple image.

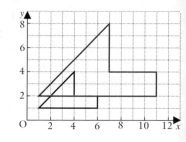

2 Find the scale factor and the coordinates of the centre of the enlargement which produces the purple image from the black object.

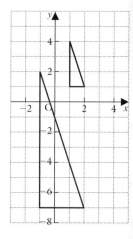

3 Find the scale factor used to produce each image in this diagram.

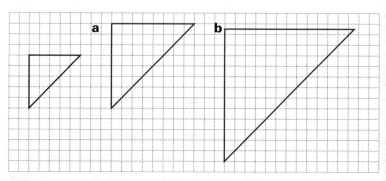

4 Find the scale factor and the centre of enlargement used to produce the image.

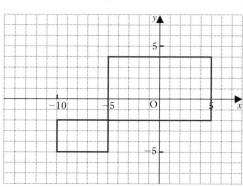

5 Find the scale factor and the centre of enlargement used to produce the image.

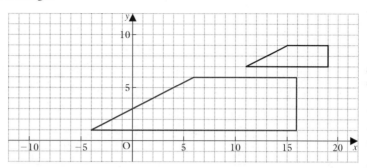

In questions **6** and **7**, draw the copy near the left-hand edge of the paper.

6 a Copy this shape onto squared paper. Draw an enlargement, scale factor 4, of this shape.

  b Copy this shape onto graph paper, using a 1 cm square for each square on the diagram, and then draw an enlargement, scale factor 1.8, of this shape.

7 Copy the diagram and enlarge the shaded shape by a scale factor of 1.5, centre P.

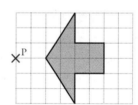

**FRACTIONAL
SCALE FACTORS**

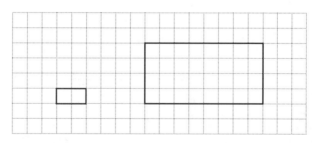

In this diagram the image is smaller than the object.
The lengths of the sides of the image are one-quarter of the lengths of the corresponding sides of the object so the scale factor is $\frac{1}{4}$.

> When the scale factor is larger than 1, the image is larger than the object.
> When the scale factor is smaller than 1, the image is smaller than the object.

EXERCISE 11C

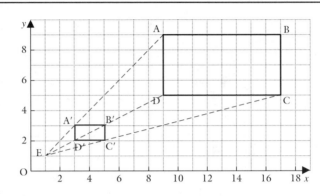

A′B′C′D′ is the image of the rectangle ABCD.

a Find the scale factor.

b Write down the coordinates of the centre of enlargement.

a A′B′ = $\frac{1}{4}$ AB so the scale factor is $\frac{1}{4}$.

b **The centre of enlargement is the point (1, 1).**

> Drawing the guidelines, we see that they meet at the point we have marked E. This is the centre of the enlargement.

1 In this question the square, A′B′C′D′ is the image of the square ABCD. Find the coordinates of the centre of enlargement and the scale factor.

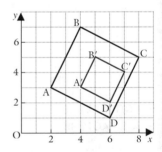

2 Find the scale factor and write down the coordinates of the centre of enlargement.

a

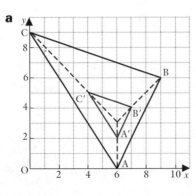

b

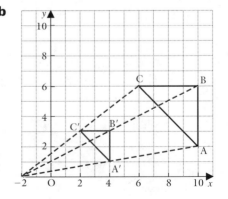

3 Describe fully the transformation that maps the object to the purple image.

a

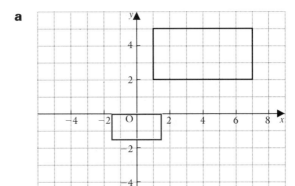

b

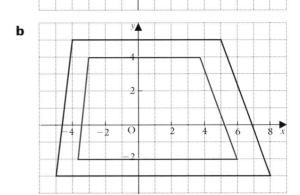

4 Copy this shape onto squared paper and then draw an enlargement, scale factor $\frac{1}{2}$, of the shape.

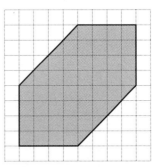

5 Copy the shape onto squared paper and draw an enlargement of the shaded shape using a scale factor of $\frac{1}{4}$.

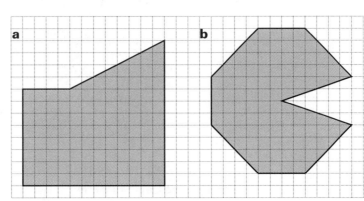

6 a Copy the diagram and draw an enlargement of triangle ABC, scale factor $\frac{1}{2}$, centre P. Label the image A′B′C′.

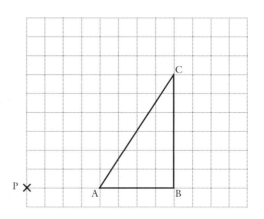

b On the same copy, draw the enlargement of triangle ABC, scale factor $1\frac{1}{2}$, centre P. Label the image A″B″C″.

c What is the scale factor that enlarges triangle A′B′C′ to triangle A″B″C″?

7 The square labelled **B** is an enlargement of the square labelled **A**.

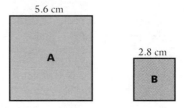

What is the scale factor of the enlargement?

8 The triangle PQR is an enlargement of the triangle ABC.

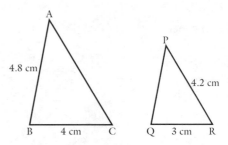

a Write down the scale factor used.

b Find the length of **i** PQ **ii** AC.

9 Copy the diagram onto 1 cm squared paper. Use a pair of compasses to draw the circle.

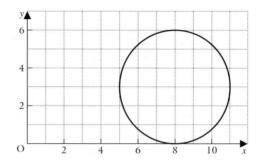

Use only two guidelines to draw an enlargement of the circle scale factor $\frac{1}{2}$ and centre of enlargement O.

10

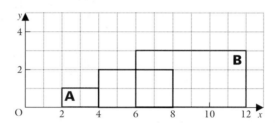

Both purple rectangles are enlargements, centre O, of the black rectangle.

a Give the scale factor of the enlargement that produces rectangle A.

b Give the scale factor of the enlargement that produces rectangle B.

c What is the scale factor that enlarges rectangle A to rectangle B? Describe the position of this centre of enlargement.

d Describe fully the transformation that enlarges B to A.

11 This tree is enlarged to give the images shown.

A   B

Find, approximately, the scale factor used to produce

a the image A   **b** the image B   **c** the image B from A.

COMPOUND
TRANS-
FORMATIONS

As we saw in Book 9B, we can perform one transformation on an object and then perform another transformation on its image. The shape that we then get is the result of a compound transformation.

In this diagram the object is first reflected in the x-axis, then the image is enlarged by a scale factor 2, centre P, to produce shape A.

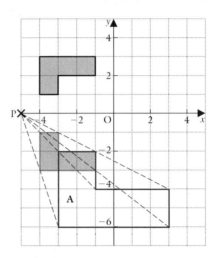

EXERCISE 11D   In these questions, copy the diagram and carry out the given compound transformation. Label the final image X.

1 An enlargement, scale factor 3, centre (4, 6) followed by a reflection in the y-axis.

2 A reflection in the x-axis followed by an enlargement, centre (2, 3), scale factor 2, followed by a translation of 4 units parallel to the x-axis to the right.

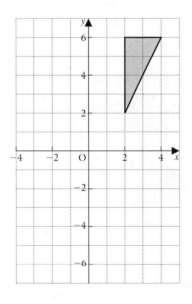

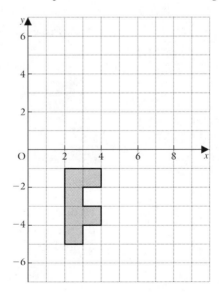

3 An enlargement with scale factor 2, centre (4, 5) followed by a rotation of 90° clockwise about O.

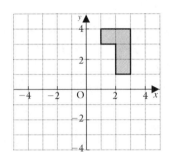

5 A rotation of 90° clockwise about O followed by an enlargement, scale factor $\frac{1}{2}$, centre (0, −4).

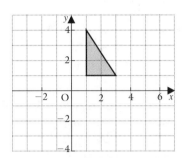

4 A reflection in the *y*-axis followed by an enlargement with scale factor $\frac{1}{2}$, centre (3, 3).

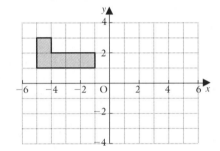

6 A translation of 7 units horizontally to the right followed by an enlargement, centre (−3, −1) scale factor $\frac{1}{2}$.

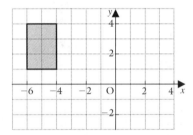

INVESTIGATION

The diagram shows an enlargement of a rectangle by a scale factor of 2.
The scale factor 2 is the number by which we multiply lengths on the object to give corresponding lengths on the image; we call this the *linear scale factor*. We call

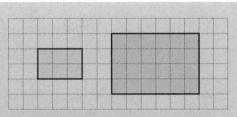

the number by which we multiply the area of the grey rectangle to give the area of the purple rectangle, the *area scale factor*.

a What is the area scale factor for the enlargement shown?

b Investigate the relationships between the linear scale factor and the area scale factor when the linear scale factor is   **i** 3   **ii** 4   **iii** $\frac{1}{2}$.

c Continue the investigation for other shapes and other scale factors.

d Find a general relationship between the linear and area scale factors of an enlargement.

SUMMARY 3

When two quantities are related so that when one of them trebles, say, the other also trebles, the quantities are *directly proportional* (that is, they are always in the same ratio).

When two quantities are related so that when one of them trebles, say, the other becomes a third of its original size, the quantities are *inversely proportional* and their product is constant.

ALGEBRA

The **coefficient** of a letter means the number the letter is multiplied by. In the expression $3x - 4y$, for example, the coefficient of x is 3 and the coefficient of y is -4.

Product of two brackets

$(a + b)(c + d)$ means $a \times (c + d) + b \times (c + d) = ac + ad + bc + bd$, i.e. each term in the second bracket is multiplied by each term in the first bracket. The order in which the terms are multiplied does not matter, but it is sensible to stick to the same order each time, e.g.

$$(2x - 3)(4x + 5) = (2x)(4x) + (2x)(5) + (-3)(4x) + (-3)(5)$$
$$= 8x^2 + 10x - 12x - 15$$
$$= 8x^2 - 2x - 15$$

In particular,
$$(x + a)^2 = (x + a)(x + a) = x^2 + 2ax + a^2$$
$$(x - a)^2 = (x - a)(x - a) = x^2 - 2ax + a^2$$
$$(x + a)(x - a) = x^2 - a^2$$

A **formula** gives the relationship between different quantities.
For example, the formula $A = lb$ gives the relationship between the area, A square units, of a rectangle and its length, l units, and width, b units. When two of these quantities are known, the other can be found by substituting the values for the letters and then solving the resulting equation.

Dimensions of a formula

A formula gives a length (which is one-dimensional) when it contains only one letter or the sum of letters that represent lengths,

e.g. $P = 4d$

A formula gives an area (which is two-dimensional) when it contains only the product of two letters that represent lengths, or the sum of such products, e.g. $A = lb + l^2$

A formula gives a volume (which is three-dimensional) when it contains only the product of three letters that represent lengths, or the sum of such products, e.g. $V = a^2b + \pi r^2h$ (remember, π is a number, not a length).

PYRAMIDS

A pyramid is a solid on a flat base whose sides come up to a point.
A *right pyramid* has the vertex (the top point) above the centre of the base.

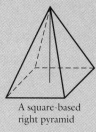 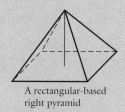 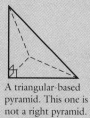

A square-based   A rectangular-based   A triangular-based
right pyramid   right pyramid   pyramid. This one is
                                                    not a right pyramid.

DENSITY

The *density* of a material is the mass of one unit of volume of the material. For example, the density of silver is 10.5 g/cm^3, i.e. 1 cm^3 of silver weighs 10.5 g.

$$\text{Density} = \frac{\text{Mass}}{\text{Volume}}$$

ROUNDED NUMBERS

When a number has been rounded, its true value lies within a range that can be shown on a number line.
For example, if a nail is 23.5 mm long correct to 1 decimal place, then the length is from 23.45 mm up to, but not including 23.55 mm as shown on this number line.

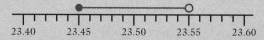

23.45 mm is the *lower bound* and 24.55 mm is the *upper bound*.

When a and b are corrected numbers,

$a + b$ has its greatest value when a and b are as large as possible, and has its least value when a and b are as small as possible.

$a - b$ has its greatest value when a is as large as possible and when b is as small as possible,
and has its least value when a is as small as possible and when b is as large as possible.

ENLARGEMENT

When an object is enlarged by a scale factor 2, each line on the image is twice the length of the corresponding line on the object.

The diagram shows an enlargement of a triangle, with centre of enlargement X and scale factor 2. The dashed lines are guidelines. XA$'$ = 2XA

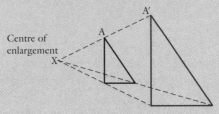

When the scale factor is less than one, the image is smaller than the object.

This diagram shows an enlargement with scale factor $\frac{1}{4}$ and centre of enlargement O. OA$'$ = $\frac{1}{4}$OA

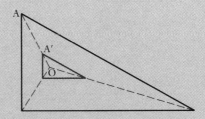

COMPOUND TRANSFORMATIONS

A compound transformation is the result of applying one transformation followed by another, for example, the result of reflecting an object in the *y*-axis and then rotating the image obtained by 90° about the origin.

REVISION EXERCISE 3.1

(Chapters 7 to 9)

1 It costs £288 to cover a floor of area 8 m^2 with a particular carpet.

  a How much would it cost to cover a floor area of 11 m^2 with the same carpet?

  b What floor area would be covered by carpet costing £378?

2 When the average speed of an aircraft is 390 mph the flying time for a journey is 5 hours.

  a Find the average speed of the aircraft when the total flying time for the same journey is 6 hours.

  b Find the total flying time if the average speed is reduced to 300 mph.

3 a Two varying quantities p and q are directly proportional. Copy and complete the table.

p	1	3	5	8	10
q		15			

b Two varying quantities x and y are inversely proportional. Copy and complete the table.

x	0.5	1	2	4	10
y				3	

4 Expand

   a $3(2-x)$ **b** $(a+b)(a+3b)$ **c** $(x-4)(x-2)$

5 Expand

   a $(x+7)(x-4)$ **b** $(x-5)(3x+5)$ **c** $(3x-2)(5x+1)$

6 Expand

   a $(x+5)^2$ **c** $(2x+3y)(2x-3y)$
   b $(x+1)(x+2)+x(x+4)$ **d** $(4-x)(4+x)$

7 Write down a formula connecting the given letters.

   a A number x is equal to three times the sum of two numbers p and q.

   b A number z is twice the product of two numbers x and y.

   c A number w is the sum of x and y minus their product.

8 Given that $a = b^2 + c$ find a when

   a $b = 2$ and $c = 3$ **b** $b = -1$ and $c = 4$
   c $b = -3$ and $c = -2$

9 Given that $R = 3at^2$ find R when

   a $a = -9.8$ and $t = 1.5$ **b** $a = 9\frac{1}{2}$ and $t = \frac{1}{2}$

10 Grapefruit are sold at x pence each. The cost of n grapefruit is C pence. Find a formula for C in terms of x and n.

11 Multiply out and simplify **i** $3(2x-y)-2y$ **ii** $(x-3)(2x-1)$
                                                                        (SEG)

12 A swimming pool holds 15 000 litres of water. It takes 24 minutes to fill the pool.

a The pool is increased in size so that it now holds 18 500 litres. How long will it now take to fill this pool?

b Water usually enters the pool through 5 pipes of equal size. One pipe is blocked so only 4 pipes are in use.
How long will it now take to put 15 000 litres into the pool?

(NEAB)

13 The length of a man's forearm (f cm) and his height (h cm) are approximately related by the formula

$$h = 3f + 90.$$

a Part of the skeleton of a man is found and the forearm is 20 cm long. Use the formula to estimate the man's height.

b A man's height is 162 cm. Use the formula to estimate the length of his forearm.

c George is 1 year old and he is 70 cm tall.
Find the value the formula gives for the length of his forearm and state why this value is impossible.

(MEG)

REVISION EXERCISE 3.2
(Chapters 10 and 11)

1 a a, b and c represent numbers of millimetres. Give a suitable unit (e.g. mm^3) for X.

i $X = 3bc$ **iii** $X = 10a + b + c$ **v** $X = 2ab + 3bc$
ii $X = \pi a^2$ **iv** $X = \pi c^3$ **vi** $X = a^2 b$

b If a and b represent numbers of length units, A represents a number of area units and V represents a number of volume units, state whether each of the letters P, Q and R below represent numbers of length or area or volume units.

i $P = \dfrac{A}{a}$ **ii** $Q = \dfrac{V}{\pi b^2}$ **iii** $R = \dfrac{3V}{2A}$

2

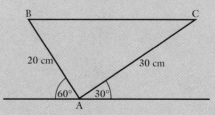

The diagram shows the triangular cross-section, ABC, of a feeding trough for cattle which is 3 metres long. Find

a angle BAC

b the width, BC, of the trough at the top

c the area of the cross-section.

3 a A gold ingot is a cuboid measuring 5 cm by 5 cm by 3 cm. Given that the density of gold is $19.3 \, \text{g/cm}^3$, find the mass of the ingot.

b A rectangular wooden block is 6 cm long, 5 cm wide and x cm thick. The block has a mass of 91.8 g and is made from wood of density $0.9 \, \text{g/cm}^3$. Find

   i the volume of the block   **ii** its thickness.

4 The base of a pyramid is a horizontal square ABCD. The vertex of the pyramid, E, is vertically above A. AB = 6 cm and AE = 6 cm.

a Draw a sketch of a net for this pyramid.

b Find, giving answers correct to 3 significant figures,

   i AC **ii** EB **iii** EC

   iv the total surface area of the pyramid.

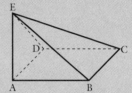

5 a Illustrate on a number line the range of possible values for each of the following corrected numbers.

   i 0.4 correct to 1 d.p.   **ii** 5.45 correct to 2 d.p.

b The length of a rectangular carpet is 3.2 m, correct to 1 decimal place. Find the length, x m, within which the actual length of the carpet lies.

c A box contains 150 screws, correct to the nearest 10. Find the largest number of screws that could be in the box.

6

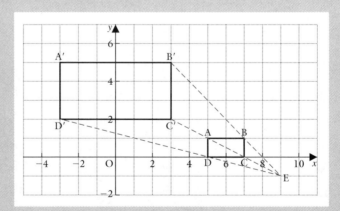

A′B′C′D′ is the image of rectangle ABCD, and E is the centre of enlargement.

a Write down the coordinates of the centre of enlargement.

b Find the scale factor.

7 Copy the diagram onto squared paper. Draw AA′, BB′, CC′ and DD′ and extend the lines until they meet. Write down the coordinates of the centre of enlargement and find the scale factor.

8 Copy the diagram, then carry out this compound transformation: a reflection in the x-axis followed by an enlargement with scale factor $\frac{1}{2}$, centre $(5, 1)$. Label the final image P.

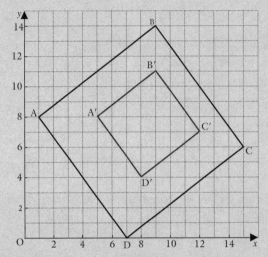

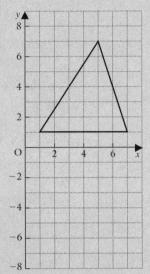

9 Draw axes for x and y from 0 to 15 using 1 cm as 1 unit. Draw △ABC with A$(2, 0)$, B$(4, 2)$ and C$(4, 6)$. With the origin as the centre of enlargement and scale factor $2\frac{1}{2}$, draw the image of △ABC and mark it A′B′C′.
Write down the coordinates of A′, B′ and C′.

10

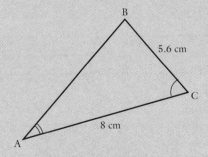

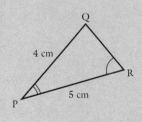

△PQR is an enlargement of △ABC.

a Write down the scale factor used.

b Find the length of **i** AB   **ii** QR.

11 The diagram shows two transformations of the shaded rectangle PQRS.

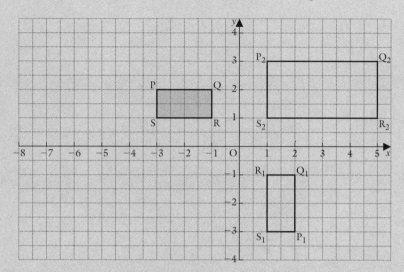

Describe fully the single transformation which maps

a PQRS onto $P_1Q_1R_1S_1$ **b** PQRS onto $P_2Q_2R_2S_2$.   (SEG)

12 The diagram, which is drawn accurately, is part
of a net of a pyramid with a rectangular base.

a Copy the diagram and complete the net.

b Sketch the pyramid.

c Using the dimensions shown on the diagram,
calculate the total surface area of the pyramid.

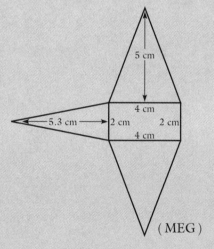

(MEG)

13 Natalie measured the distance between two points on a map.
The distance she measured was 5 cm correct to the nearest centimetre.

a Write down the

i upper bound of the measurement
ii lower bound of the measurement.

The scale of the map is 1 to 20 000.

b Work out the actual distance in real life between the upper and lower bounds. Give
your answer in kilometres.   (London)

1 A car uses 12 litres of petrol for a journey of 84 miles. At the same rate,

   a how far could it go on 20 litres

   b how many litres would it use for a journey of 126 miles?

2 Which of the following quantities are directly proportional, which are inversely proportional and which are neither?

   a The number of litres of petrol I buy each week at 90p a litre and my weekly petrol bill.

   b The number of people travelling on a bus and the total number of parcels they are carrying.

   c The number of tickets I can buy for £100 and the price of each ticket assuming that all the tickets are the same price.

   d The number of dogs I keep and the weight of food they eat.

3 Expand

   a $5(2 - 3a)$ **c** $(p - 3)(p - 8)$

   b $(3x + 2y)(1 - 2z)$ **d** $(3x + 4)(3 - x)$

4 Expand and simplify

   a $(3x - 1)^2$ **b** $(x + 2)(x + 3) + 4(x + 4)$

5 If $R = (p + 2q)^2$ find R when

   a $p = 10$ and $q = -3$ **b** $p = 2.1$ and $q = 3.7$

   c $p = -3.4$ and $q = -2.7$

6 If $V = 2xy^2 + \dfrac{y^4}{x}$ find the value of V when $x = \frac{1}{4}$ and $y = 2$.

7 A right pyramid VABCD has a square base of side 8.4 cm. E is the midpoint of DC and VE = 10.2 cm.

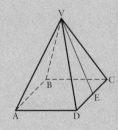

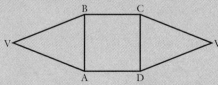

The faces VDC and VAB are opened out as shown in the sketch. If each dimension is correct to 1 decimal place find the maximum distance from V to V.

8 The diagram shows the section through a cylindrical bottle top which is 1.5 mm thick. Its external diameter is 16 mm.

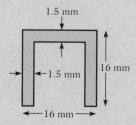

Find

a the volume of material used to make the bottle top

b the mass of the bottle top, in grams, if the density of the material from which it is made is 2.5 g/cm^3.

9 Copy the diagram onto squared paper using 1 cm as 1 unit. Draw AA′, BB′ and CC′ and extend the lines until they meet. Give the coordinates of the centre of enlargement and the scale factor.

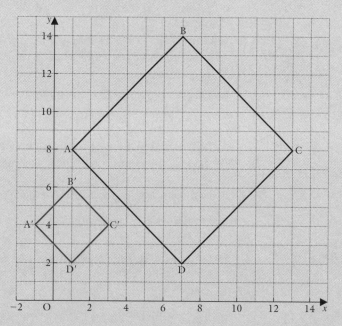

10 Draw axes for x and y from 0 to 16 using 1 cm as 2 units on both axes. Draw $\triangle$ABC with A(1, 14), B(13, 8) and C(7, 2). Taking the point (1, 2) as the centre of enlargement and a scale factor of $\frac{1}{3}$, draw the image of $\triangle$ABC. Mark the image A′B′C′ and write down the coordinates of the vertices of the image triangle.

Do not use a calculator for this exercise.

1 a Which is the larger? **i** 10^3 or 10^5 **ii** 10^{-3} or 10^{-4}

  b Find

  i $\frac{3}{4} \div \frac{1}{2}$ **ii** $7 \div \frac{4}{7}$ **iii** $3 \div \frac{2}{5}$ **iv** $2\frac{1}{3} \div 4$

2 Estimate the value of

  a 18.74×9.8 **c** $\dfrac{39.48 \times 87.39}{14.86}$ **e** $\sqrt{15..88}$

  b $53.72 \div 11.47$ **d** 0.7654^2 **f** $\dfrac{8.042^2}{32.63}$

3 a Write the following numbers in standard form.

  i $490\,000\,000$ **ii** $0.000\,000\,08$ **iii** 0.38 **iv** 934

  b Write as ordinary numbers

  i 7.8×10^4 **ii** 6.5×10^{-5}

4 A black dice and a white dice are rolled. What is the probability of getting

  a a 2 or a 3 on the black dice   **c** a 6 on both dice

  b a 3 or a 4 on the white dice   **d** an odd number on both dice?

5 a One of the terms in the sequence 7, 12, 17, 23, 27, 32, 37, ...
    has been changed. Find which term has been changed and give
    its correct value.

  b This is a sequence of pairs of numbers

$$(1, 1), (2, 4), (3, 9), (4, 16), \ldots$$

  i Write down the next pair in the sequence.
  ii Find an expression, in terms of n, for the nth pair.

6 A book with 400 pages is 20 mm thick.

  a How thick is a book with 500 pages which uses the same type of
    paper?

  b How many pages would a book 17.5 mm thick have?

7 Expand

  a $5a(2b + 5c)$ **c** $(7x + 4)(x + 1)$
  b $(1 - a)(a + 4b)$ **d** $(x - 4y)^2$

8 My electricity bill for a quarter, $£C$, is calculated by finding the cost
  of the number, n, of units of electricity I use at 7 pence per unit and
  adding this amount to a fixed charge of £20.
  Find a formula for C in terms of n.

9 In this question the parallelogram $A'B'C'D'$ is the image of the parallelogram ABCD. Find the coordinates of the centre of enlargement and the scale factor.

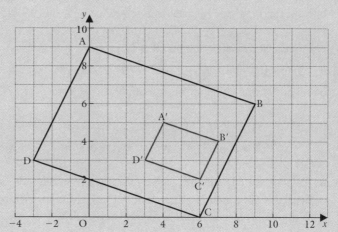

10 a Simplify, where possible **i** $\dfrac{4}{8a}$ **ii** $\dfrac{3a^2b}{9ab}$ **iii** $\dfrac{a+b}{3a}$

b Solve these equations.

i $\dfrac{x}{4} - \dfrac{1}{3} = \dfrac{x}{5}$ **ii** $\dfrac{x}{5} - \dfrac{3}{4} = 0$ **iii** $\dfrac{2x+5}{3} = \dfrac{x}{4}$

REVISION EXERCISE 3.5 (Chapters 1 to 11)

1 a Given that $1350 = 2^x \times 3^y \times 5^z$ find the values of x, y and z.

b Simplify

i $x^2 \times x^3$ **ii** $a^5 \div a^7$ **iii** $b^2 \times b^4 \times b^5$ **iv** $(x^6 \div x^4) \times x^3$

c Find the value of

i 6.7×10^{-3} **ii** 5^{-2} **iii** 15^{-1} **iv** 3.6×10^3

2 a Find, correct to 3 s.f. **i** 5.382×6.293 **ii** $19.54^2 - 14.83^2$

b Find, correct to 3 s.f., the value of $\frac{4}{3}\pi r^3$ when $r = 3.74$.

3 In this question first estimate the answer and then give the answer correct to 3 significant figures.

a $16.4 \times 2.09 \times 10^3$ **c** $198 \times 1.03 \times 10^{-3}$

b $16.4 \div (2.09 \times 10^3)$ **d** $0.62 \times 1.34 \times 10^{-2}$

4 Vic is asked to choose a date at random from the year 1998. Calculate the probability that the day is

a a day in April **c** a day in November

b a Sunday in February **d** a day in April or November

Would any answers be different if the chosen year was 2004 instead of 1998? Explain your answer.

5 a The rule for giving a sequence is 'Subtract 1 from the previous number, then multiply by 3'. The second number in a sequence is 9. Find the first and third numbers in this sequence.

b Find the next two terms in the sequence 4, 7, 12, 19, 28, ...

6 The mass of $0.8\,\text{cm}^3$ of a metal is $12\,\text{g}$.

a What is the mass of   **i** $1\,\text{cm}^3$ **ii** $2.4\,\text{cm}^3$?

b What volume of metal has a mass of   **i** $18\,\text{g}$ **ii** $7.5\,\text{g}$?

7 Expand   **a** $3x(5y - 2z)$ **c** $(5x + 3y)(z + 4)$

b $(a + 4)(a + 6)$ **d** $(a + 3b)^2$

8 a An approximate rule to change temperature in degrees Celsius, C, into temperature in degrees Fahrenheit, F, is to double the Celsius temperature and then add 30. Write this rule as a formula for F in terms of C.

b $Q = 3b + \dfrac{8a}{b}$.   Find the value of Q when $a = 3.5$ and $b = 1\frac{1}{2}$.

9 Draw the image of the square ABCD using the point $(-2, 2)$ as the centre of enlargement and a scale factor of $\frac{1}{3}$. Mark the image square $A'B'C'D'$ and write down the coordinates of the vertices of this square.

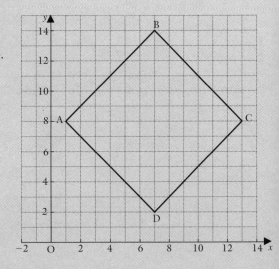

10

A yoghurt container is a prism with a cross-section in the form of an isosceles trapezium whose dimensions are given on the diagram.

a How deep is the container?

b The container has a capacity of $\frac{1}{4}$ litre. Calculate the width of the container, marked x cm on the diagram.

c Find   **i** the total external surface area of the open container

ii the area of foil needed to cover the top of the container if an extra $10\,\text{cm}^2$ must be included to allow for overlap and sealing.

STRAIGHT LINE GRAPHS

12

This chapter continues the work on straight lines started in Books 8B and 9B. On page 16 of Summary 1 you can look up the facts about the equations of straight lines covered in those books.

Kevin repairs domestic equipment. He charges a call-out fee together with an hourly charge. Customers often ask for an estimate before the work is begun and he uses this graph to help him get an idea of likely charges.

- Some information can be read directly from this graph, for example a repair taking 2 hours will cost about £48.
- Some information cannot be read: the cost of a repair taking 6 hours, for example. We can estimate the cost by trying to judge where the line would be if we mentally extended both axes. This is likely to give a very rough estimate.
- A much better estimate can be obtained by using the information on the graph to work out the equation of the line and then use the equation to calculate the cost of a repair taking 6 hours.

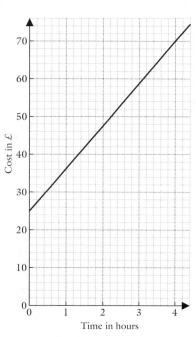

EXERCISE 12A

1 What does Kevin charge his customers for a repair that takes $2\frac{1}{2}$ hours?

2 What is Kevin's call-out fee?

3 Discuss with a group how you can find an equation for this line.

**CONVERSION
GRAPHS**

Straight line graphs are useful in a variety of practical applications where the coordinates of points represent real quantities.

For example, if you go to Spain on holiday, it is useful to be able to convert prices given in pesetas quickly to the equivalent price in sterling and vice-versa.

When the exchange rate is 210 pesetas (pta) to £1,
if y pta is equivalent to £x, we see that $y = 210x$,
Comparing this formula with $\qquad y = mx$
shows that plotting values of y against values of x will give a straight line through the origin.

To draw the graph we need points giving corresponding values of pounds and pesetas. We can get these direct from the exchange rate, e.g. £1 = 210 pta, £10 = 2100 pta, and so on. We also know that £0 = 0 pta.
Putting these values in a table we have

£ Sterling	0	10	100
Pesetas	0	2100	21 000

Plotting the points in the table gives this graph.

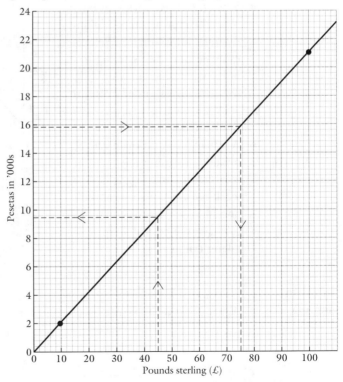

From the graph we can see immediately that £45 ≈ 9500 pesetas
and that 15 800 pesetas ≈ £75

EXERCISE 12B

1 Use the conversion graph on page 224 for this question.

  a Why do you think this graph is drawn on graph paper rather than 5 mm squared paper?

  b The scales on the axes are not equal. Why do you think that 1 cm for 10 units is *not* used for both scales?

  c We could choose different scales, 1 cm for 2100 pta on the vertical axis, for example. Why is this not a good scale to use?

  d We did not use the point given by £1 = 210 pta, i.e. (1, 210), to plot the line. Why not?

  e Can you find the cost in pounds sterling of a mountain bike priced at 100 000 pta from this graph?

  f To what values would the axes need to be extended for this graph to be used to convert prices up to £500 into pesetas?

2 This graph can be used to convert values up to £100 into Norwegian kroner. Use the graph to find

  a the cost in pounds sterling of a pair of shoes priced at 760 kroner

  b how many kroner are equivalent to £46

  c the exchange rate on which this graph is based.

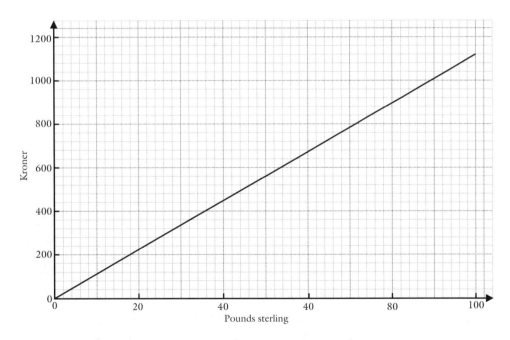

3 There are electronic gadgets that will convert from one currency into any other currency. The calculations can also be done using an ordinary calculator. Discuss the advantages and disadvantages that conversion graphs have over electronic aids.

Use 2 mm graph paper for the remaining questions in this exercise.

4 The table shows the conversion from US dollars to pounds sterling for various amounts of money.

US dollars ($)	50	100	200
Pounds (£)	35	70	140

Plot these points on a graph and draw a straight line to pass through them. Let 4 cm represent 50 units on both axes.
Use your graph to convert

a i 160 dollars into pounds (£)   **ii** 96 dollars into pounds (£)

b i £122 into dollars   **ii** £76 into dollars

c What is the exchange rate between pounds (£) and dollars ($) that this graph is based on ?

5 The table shows the conversion of various sums of money from Deutschmarks to French francs.

Deutschmarks (DM)	100	270	350
French francs (f)	310	837	1085

Plot these points on a graph and draw a straight line to pass through them. Take 2 cm to represent 50 units on the Deutschmarks axis and 100 units on the francs axis.
Use your graph to convert

a 16 DM into francs   **c** 440 f into Deutschmarks

b 330 DM into francs   **d** 980 f into Deutschmarks

6 The table shows the distance a girl walks in a given time.

Time walking in hours	0	1	$2\frac{1}{2}$	4	5
Distance walked in km	0	6	15	24	30

Choose your own scales and draw a graph using these values.

a How far has she walked in   **i** 2 hours   **ii** $3\frac{1}{2}$ hours ?

b How many hours does she take to walk   **i** 10 km   **ii** 21 km ?

c At what speed does the girl walk ?

d Find the gradient of the line.

e What is the connection between your answers to parts **c** and **d** ?

7 The table shows the distance an aircraft has travelled at various times on a particular journey. Draw a graph using these results. Take 2 cm to represent 1 hour on the horizontal axis and 500 km on the vertical axis. What can you conclude about the speed of the aircraft?

Time after departure (hours)	0	1	$3\frac{1}{2}$	6
Distance travelled from take-off (km)	0	550	1925	3300

  a How far does the aircraft fly in **i** $1\frac{1}{2}$ hours **ii** $4\frac{1}{2}$ hours?

  b What time does it take the aircraft to fly **i** 1000 km **ii** 2500 km?

  c Find the gradient of your line.

  d What is the connection between the answer to part **c** and the speed of the aircraft?

8 These graphs can be used to convert between £ and US$ when £1 = $1.70.

  a Use each graph to find **i** £18 in dollars **ii** $74 in pounds.

  b State, with reasons, which of these four graphs is the easiest to use.

  c Assume that you have a whole sheet of graph paper and have to draw a graph to convert between dollars and £ for amounts up to £100. What scales would you use for the axes? Give reasons for your choice.

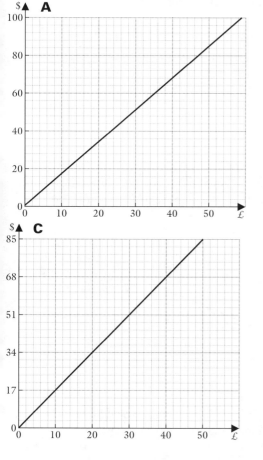

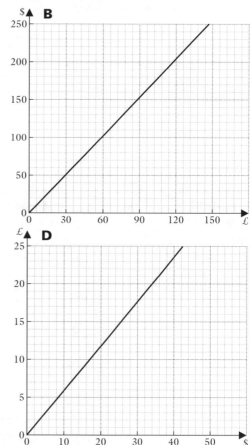

9 Marks in an examination range from 0 to 65. Choose your own scales and draw a graph which enables you to express the marks in percentages from 0 to 100. Note that a mark of 0 is 0% while a mark of 65 is 100%.
Use your graph

  a to express marks of 35 and 50 as percentages

  b to find the original mark for percentages of 50% and 80%.

10 The table gives temperatures in degrees Fahrenheit (°F) and the equivalent values in degrees Celsius (°C).

Temperature in °F	57	126	158	194
Temperature in °C	14	52	70	90

Choose your own scales and plot these points on a graph for Celsius values from 0 to 100 and Fahrenheit values from 0 to 220.
Use your graph to convert

  a 97 °F into °C   **b** 172 °F into °C   **c** 25 °C into °F   **d** 80 °C into °F

  e Explain why this graph does not pass through the origin.

11 a Given that 20 mph = 32 km/h, find in km/h **i** 40 mph   **ii** 60 mph

  b Use the values found in part **a** to draw a graph to convert between speeds in mph and speeds in km/h.

12 Given that 1 gallon is equivalent to **4.546** litres, draw a graph to convert from 0 to 100 litres into gallons.
Give an example of a situation where this conversion chart would be useful.

FINDING THE EQUATION OF A LINE FROM A GRAPH

This graph shows the relationship between quarterly domestic electricity bills from a supply company and the number of units consumed.

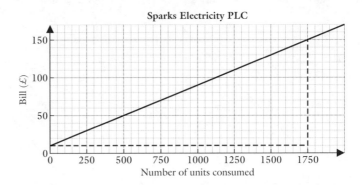

To find the equation of this line we need an *x*-axis and a *y*-axis; let *x* be the number of units consumed and let £*y* be the quarterly bill.

To find the equation of any line, we start with the fact that the equation of any straight line is of the form $y = mx + c$ where m is the gradient of the line and c is the intercept on the y-axis.

Reading from the graph, $c = 10$ and $m = \dfrac{140}{1750} = 0.08$

> Remember, we find the gradient of a line by calculating
>
> $$\frac{\text{increase in } y \, (\text{or equivalent})}{\text{increase in } x \, (\text{or equivalent})}$$
>
> when moving from any one point on the line to any other point on the line.

Therefore the equation of this line is $y = 0.08x + 10$

It is important to realise that $y = 0.08x + 10$ is *not* an exact relationship between y and x. This is because we have read values from a graph and these cannot be exact.

As the gradient of a line is given by $\dfrac{\text{increase in } y \, (\text{or equivalent})}{\text{increase in } x \, (\text{or equivalent})}$

it follows that

> the gradient of a line tells us how much y (or equivalent)
> increases when x (or equivalent) increases by 1 unit.

Therefore the gradient of this line gives the increase in the bill for an increase of 1 unit consumed, so the gradient represents the cost of 1 unit of electricity.

EXERCISE 12C

1 a Use the graph on page 228 to find
   i the fixed charge payable per quarter irrespective of the number of units used
   ii the bill for a quarter in which 900 units are used
   iii the cost of 1 unit of electricity.

b How are the answers to parts **i** and **iii** above related to the equation of the line?

c Any two points on a line can be used to calculate the gradient of that line. Discuss why we chose to take the points as far apart as practical.

d Use the equation $y = 0.08x + 10$ to find
   i the value of y when $x = 2500$
   ii the value of x when $y = 450$

e Ari shares a house with 8 other people. He tells his house-mates that the next quarter's electricity bill must be less than £500. What is the maximum number of units that can be used by the household?

2 Use information from the graph to find the equation of the line.

a
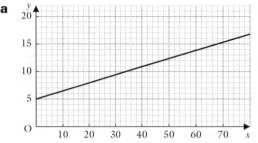

c
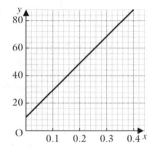

b
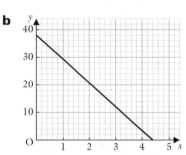

d
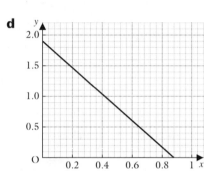

3 For each graph give the value of the gradient and what the gradient means in the context of the graph.

a
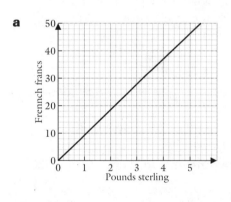

c
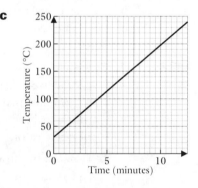

b
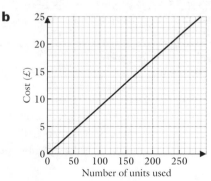

d
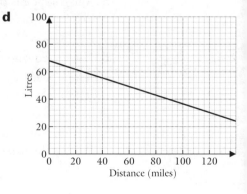

4 This graph shows how the quantity of water in a reservoir varies with time. When full it contains 2 000 000 gallons.

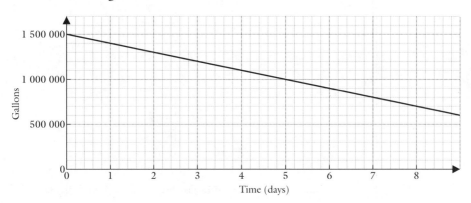

a Use the graph to find **i** the volume of water in the reservoir after three days

ii after how many days the reservoir is half empty.

b What is the gradient of the graph and what does it represent?

c What is the value of the intercept on the vertical axis and what does it represent?

d What do you think the weather was like during the period referred to?

5 Use Kevin's graph on page 223 to find the equation of the line.
Hence find   **a** the cost of a job that takes 6 hours

b how long Kevin has to spend on a repair to earn £100

c Kevin's hourly charge rate.

PARALLEL LINES

The gradient of a line measures the slope of the line. So

when two lines are parallel, they have the same gradient.

INTERSECTION

The point where two lines (or curves) cross is called their *point of intersection*. At this point, the value of x and the value of y are the *same* for both lines.

In the diagram, the lines $y = 3$ and $y = 5 - 2x$ intersect at the point P. Therefore the y-coordinate of P is 3 because P is on the line $y = 3$.

Since P is also on the line $y = 5 - 2x$,
the x-coordinate of P is where $3 = 5 - 2x$,
i.e.   where $2x = 5 - 3 \Rightarrow 2x = 2 \Rightarrow x = 1$.
Hence P is the point (1, 3).

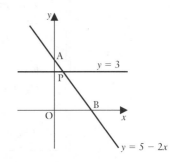

EXERCISE 12D

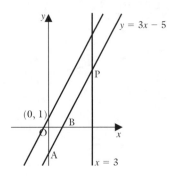

a The line $y = 3x - 5$ crosses the y-axis at A and crosses the x-axis at B.
Find the coordinates of the point
i A   **ii** B

b The line $y = 3x - 5$ crosses the line $x = 3$ at P.
Find the coordinates of P.

c Find the equation of the line that passes through the point $(0, 1)$ and is parallel to the line $y = 3x - 5$.

a **i** | In the equation $y = mx + c$, c is the value of y where the line crosses the y-axis.
$y = 3x - 5$ crosses the y-axis where $y = -5$ and $x = 0$.

A is the point $(0, -5)$

ii | The line crosses the x-axis where $y = 0$. We can use this fact to form an equation which we can solve to find x.

When $y = 0$, $3x - 5 = 0$

$$3x = 5 \Rightarrow x = \tfrac{5}{3}$$

B is the point $(\tfrac{5}{3}, 0)$

b P is on the line $y = 3x - 5$ and at P, $x = 3$
so $y = 3(3) - 5 = 4$
P is the point $(3, 4)$

c | The line we need is parallel to $y = 3x - 5$ so it has the same gradient, i.e. 3.
The line passes through $(0, 1)$, i.e. it crosses the y-axis where $y = 1$.
Any line has equation $y = mx + c$, and we now know $m = 3$ and $c = 1$.

The equation of the line is $y = 3x + 1$

In questions **1** to **6**, use the information in the diagrams to find the coordinates of the points A, B and C.

1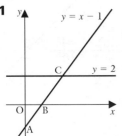

3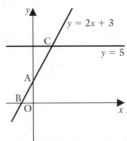

5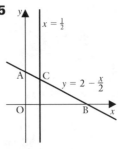

2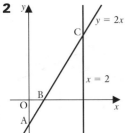

4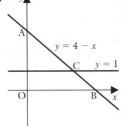

6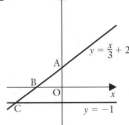

7 Find the equation of the line that passes through $(0, 4)$ and is parallel to the line $y = x - 1$.

8 Find the equation of the line that passes through $(0, -2)$ and is parallel to the line $y = 3x + 1$.

9 Find the equation of the line that passes through $(0, 6)$ and is parallel to the line $y = 3 - 2x$.

10 Find the equation of the line that passes through $(0, -3)$ and is parallel to the line $y = 7 - 4x$.

11 a Copy the diagram which shows a sketch of the line $y = 2x + 3$.

   b Add to your sketch the lines

   i $y = 2x + 6$ **ii** $y = 2x - 2$

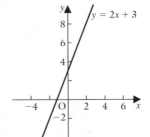

12 Copy the diagram which shows
a sketch of the line $y = 4 - x$.
Add to your sketch the lines

a $y = 6 - x$ **b** $y = 4 - 2x$

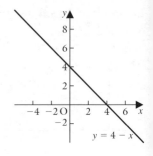

13 a Copy the diagram which shows a
sketch of the line $2y = 2 - x$.

b Add to your sketch the line which
is parallel to $2y = 2 - x$ and which
crosses the y-axis where $y = 5$.
Write down the equation of this line.

c Add the line $y = 3$ to your sketch
and find the coordinates of the
points where the line $y = 3$ crosses
the other two lines.

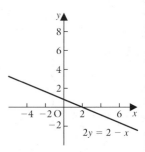

USING GRADIENT   The gradient gives the increase in y (or equivalent) for each unit increase
in x (or equivalent). Therefore the rate at which y increases determines
the gradient of the line, that is, if y increases rapidly, the gradient is large
and the line slopes steeply uphill. If y decreases, the line has a negative
gradient, that is, the line slopes downhill.

The diagram shows the cross-section through a garden pond. The pond
is filled from a hose that delivers water at a constant rate.

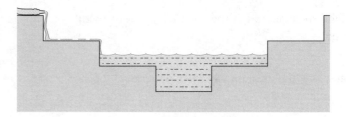

To get an idea of how the depth of water changes as the pond is filled,
we can use what we know about gradients of lines to sketch a graph
showing how the depth changes as the time increases while the hose is
on.

The depth will increase quite quickly in the narrow bottom section so this part of the line will be fairly steep. The depth will increase more slowly in the next section because the water has to spread over a larger surface area, so the line will be less steep. The depth will increase even more slowly in the top section, giving an even flatter line.

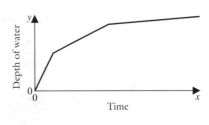

EXERCISE 12E

1 Liquid is poured into this glass at a constant rate.
Which of the graphs below show the depth of liquid in the container as it is being filled?

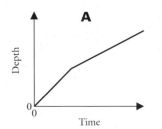 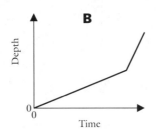 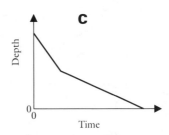

2 Which of the graphs shown in question **1** shows the depth of liquid in this glass as it is filled at a constant rate?

3 Oil is poured into this tank at a constant rate.

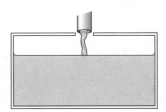

Which of these graphs shows the depth of oil as the tank is being filled?

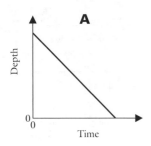 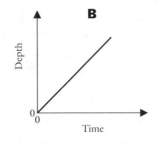 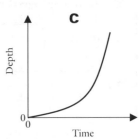

4 When the tank in question **3** is full, oil is pumped out of it at a constant rate. Which of the graphs given in question **3** shows the depth as the oil is removed from the tank?

5 Grain is taken out of each of these silos at a constant rate.

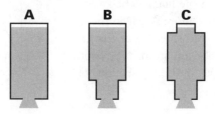

Each graph shows the depth of grain in one of these silos as the grain is taken out. Write down the letter of the silo that the graph refers to.

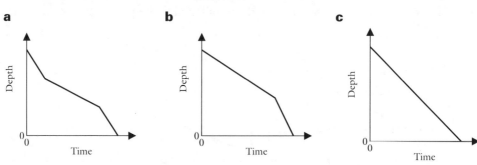

The sketch represents the journeys of two trains between Atherton and Boxbourne.

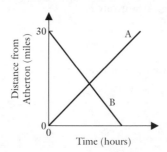

a Which line shows the journey of the train from Atherton to Boxbourne?

b Which train travels faster?

a Line A

> The line A slopes uphill showing that, for this line, the distance from Atherton is increasing.

b

> Speed is the rate at which distance changes. The slope of a line represents change in miles from Atherton each hour, i.e. miles per hour which is speed.
> The slope of line B is greater than the slope of line A so the speed of the train it represents is greater than the speed of the other train. Line B slopes downhill so the distance from Atherton is decreasing, i.e. the train is travelling towards Atherton.

The train travelling from Boxbourne to Atherton.

6 A car travels from London to Rugby, stopping at a motorway service station on the way. The average speed of the car is greater for the second part of its journey than the first. Which of these graphs represents this journey?

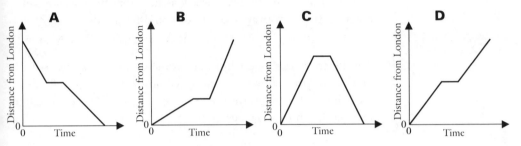

7 The sketch represents the journey of an aeroplane from Birmingham to Cape Town with a stopover at Brussels.

For which section of the journey was the average speed of the aircraft greatest?

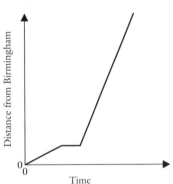

8 The sketch shows the journeys of two cyclists, Tom and Fran, between the villages Driden and Endford. Tom and Fran both cycled as fast as they could, but one of them had a puncture on the way and had to stop to mend it.

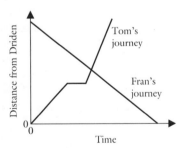

  a In which direction did Tom cycle?

  b In which direction did Fran cycle?

  c Who had the puncture?

  d One of the villages is at the bottom of a steep hill and the other village is at the top of the hill. Which village do you think is at the bottom of the hill? Give a reason for your answer.

9 A coach travels from Glasgow to Oxford. The first part of the journey is on motorways. The coach then stops at a service station and continues the journey on non-motorway roads. Draw a sketch of a graph to illustrate this journey; assume that the coach travels faster on the motorways than it does on other roads.

10 Ann Peters travels by car from her home to the supermarket at the maximum speed allowed by the speed limit. She stops to do her shopping and then returns home at a speed less than the speed limit. Draw a sketch to show her journey.

11 Draw a sketch of a graph showing the depth of liquid in each container as liquid is poured in at a constant rate.

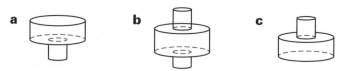

12 Draw a sketch of a graph showing the depth of water in each pool as water is pumped out at a constant rate.

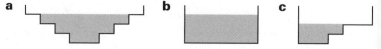

13 Each graph shows the depth of liquid in a container as liquid is poured in at a constant rate. Sketch a shape for the cross-section of a container that could give the graph.

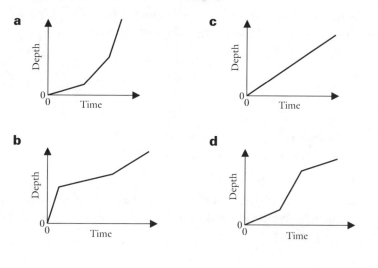

MIXED EXERCISE

EXERCISE 12F   **Do not use a calculator for this exercise.**

1 This graph can be used to estimate the quarterly charge for using gas.

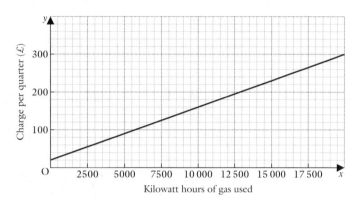

Use the graph to estimate

a the charge for using 11 000 kilowatt hours of gas

b the number of kilowatt hours used when the charge is £80

c the value of y where the line meets the y-axis and say what this value means

d the gradient of the line and say what it means.

2 Find the equation of the line shown on the graph.

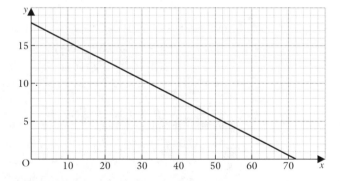

3 Liquid is poured into this pool at a constant rate.
Sketch a graph showing how the depth of liquid in the pool varies with time.

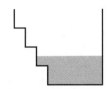

4 **a** Copy the diagram which shows a sketch of the line $y = 3 - 2x$.

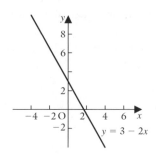

b Write down the equation of the line that goes through the point $(0, 5)$ and is parallel to $y = 3 - 2x$ and add this line to your sketch.

c Add the line $x = -1$ to your sketch.

d Give the coordinates of the points where $x = -1$ intersects the other two lines.

PRACTICAL WORK

An electricity supply company offers three tariffs.

Tariff A: A fixed charge of £5 a quarter plus a charge of 10 pence per unit used.

Tariff B: A fixed charge of £20 a quarter plus a charge of 5 pence per unit used.

Tariff C: A prepayment meter at a charge of 15 pence per unit.

a On the same set of axes, draw a graph for each tariff to show the charges for using from 0 to 500 units of electricity.

b Use your graph to find the range of units that need to be used

   i for Tariff A to be the cheapest option

  ii for Tariff B to be the cheapest option

 iii for Tariff C to be the cheapest option.

c The Black family looks at the number of units they used in each quarter for the previous 12 months. The figures are 250, 370, 480, 190.

They have to use one tariff for the whole of the next 12 months. Write a short report advising them which tariff they should use.

SIMILAR FIGURES

13

In Chapter 11 we studied ways of enlarging one shape to produce
another. In the diagram below,
rectangle **A** is enlarged by a scale factor 2 to give rectangle **B**,
rectangle **A** is also enlarged by a scale factor of $\frac{1}{3}$ to give rectangle **C**.
(Remember the word enlargement is used to describe both an image
that is larger and an image that is smaller than the object.)

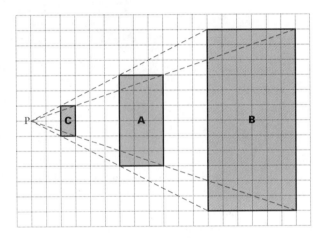

Enlargement changes the size of a figure but does not change its shape.
The three rectangles **A**, **B** and **C** are different in size but they are all
exactly the same shape.

When we say that two figures are the same shape, we mean that

- the angles in one figure are the same as the corresponding angles in
  the other figure (the corners of rectangles **A**, **B** and **C** are all right-
  angles),
- corresponding sides remain in the same proportion (in each of the
  rectangles, the long side is twice the length of the short side).

When one figure is an enlargement of another, the two figures are
similar. Even when the position of one figure is changed, the figures are
still similar; if rectangle **B** is rotated to a different position for example, it
is still similar to rectangles **A** and **C**.

Two figures are similar when they are the same shape but different in size.

In the diagram below, any one of the figures is similar to all the others.

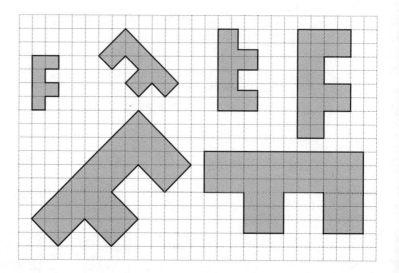

Notice that the mathematical use of the word similar is very precise; it is used only to describe figures where one shape is an enlargement of the other.

The definition of similar figures applies equally well to solid figures. These three cubes are similar because they are all the same shape but different in size.

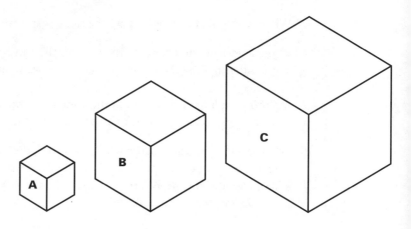

EXERCISE 13A

1 State whether the pairs of figures are similar.

a

e

b

f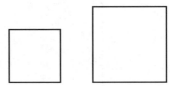

c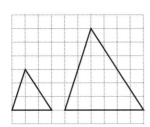

g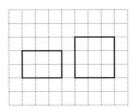

d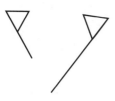

h

2 Which two rectangles are similar?

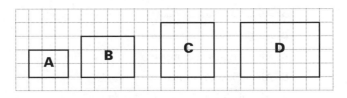

3 Which of the other five triangles are similar to triangle **X**?

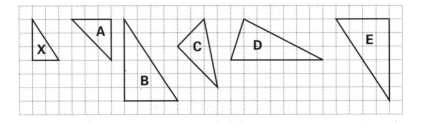

4   Which of the other five rectangles are similar to rectangle **X**?

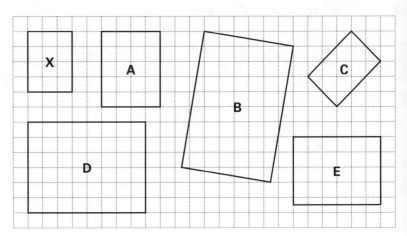

5   Which of these kites are similar to kite **X**?

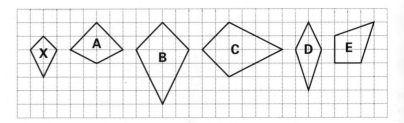

6   Some of the following statements are true and the others are false. Write T if a statement is true. If a statement is false, draw a sketch showing two of the figures that are not similar.

a All squares are similar.

b All rectangles are similar.

c All triangles are similar.

d All circles are similar.

e All cubes are similar.

f All cuboids are similar.

g All equilateral triangles are similar.

h All parallelograms are similar.

i All regular hexagons are similar.

j All isosceles triangles are similar.

k All spheres are similar.

l All square-based pyramids are similar.

FINDING
UNKNOWN
LENGTHS

When we know the scale factor that enlarges one figure to a similar figure, we can find unknown lengths.

EXERCISE 13B   *Note*   In this exercise diagrams are not drawn to scale.

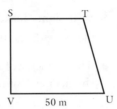

ABCD is a scale drawing of a plot of land STUV. The scale used is $1:200$.

Find   **a**   the length of DC on the scale drawing

b   the length of SV on the ground

c   the angle TUV on the ground.

> Any scale drawing is similar to the object it represents. In this problem, the scale used is $1:200$. This means that each length on the scale drawing is $\frac{1}{200}$ th of the length on the ground it corresponds to.
> We can therefore treat the scale drawing as an enlargement of the plot by a scale factor of $\frac{1}{200}$.

a $DC = \frac{1}{200} \times VU$

i.e. $DC = \frac{1}{200} \times 50\,m = 0.25\,m = 25\,cm$

b   > The plot is an enlargement of the scale drawing by a scale factor of 200.

$SV = 200 \times AD = 200 \times 8\,cm$

i.e. $SV = 1600\,cm = 16\,m$

c $T\hat{U}V = 75°$ > Angles are not changed by an enlargement.

1 $\triangle XYZ$ is an enlargement of $\triangle ABC$ by a scale factor of 2.
Find   **a**   XY
b   XZ
c   BC

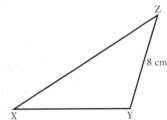

2

A car designer makes a model of his design for a new car. The model is $\frac{1}{10}$ th the length of the proposed car.

a The diameter of the wheels on the model is 6 cm. What will be the diameter of the wheels on the actual car?

b The length of the model is 52 cm. How long will the actual car be?

c The windscreen of the model slopes at $45°$ to the vertical. At what angle to the vertical will the actual windscreen slope?

d The model has six windows. How many windows will the actual car have?

3 $\triangle ABC$ is an enlargement of $\triangle ADE$, scale factor 3.
Find **a** AB
     b AC
     c DE

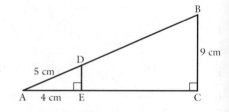

4

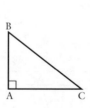
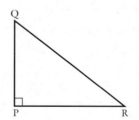

$\triangle ABC$ and $\triangle PQR$ are similar and the scale factor for enlarging $\triangle ABC$ to $\triangle PQR$ is 2.

a $AB = 5$ cm, find PQ.

b $PR = 12$ cm, find AC.

c Calculate the area of **i** $\triangle ABC$ **ii** $\triangle PQR$.

d By what factor has the area increased under this enlargement?

5

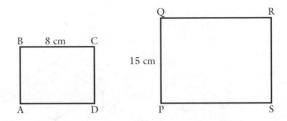

Rectangles ABCD and PQRS are similar, and the scale factor for enlarging ABCD to PQRS is $2\frac{1}{2}$.

a Find **i** QR **ii** CD.

b Find the area of ABCD and the area of PQRS.

c By what factor is the area of ABCD increased by the enlargement?

6 Parallelograms PQRS and WXYZ are similar and the scale factor for enlarging PQRS to WXYZ is $1\frac{1}{4}$. PQ = 8 cm and the perpendicular height of PQRS is 12 cm.

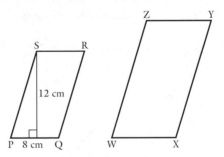

Find **a** WX

b the perpendicular height of WXYZ

c the area of WXYZ.

7 The diagram is a scale drawing.
AC is 10 cm long and represents a tree.
B is a point on level ground some distance from the base of the tree.

a Find $A\widehat{C}B$.

b Describe △ABC and write down the length of AB.

c The scale used for the diagram is 1 : 100. Find the height of the tree.

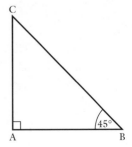

8

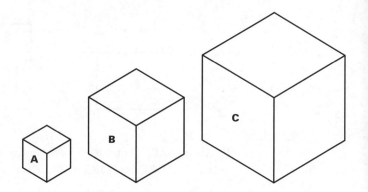

A, **B** and **C** are cubes. Each edge of **A** is 2 cm long. The scale factor for enlarging **A** to **B** is 2 and the scale factor for enlarging **A** to **C** is 3.

a Find the lengths of the edges of **B**.

b Find the lengths of the edges of **C**.

c Find the volumes of **A**, **B** and **C**.

d A fourth cube **D**, not shown, is such that the scale factor for enlarging **A** to **D** is 6. Find the lengths of the edges of **D**.

9

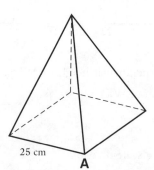

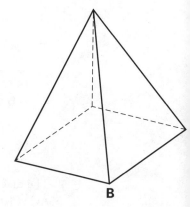

A and **B** are similar square-based pyramids. The scale factor for enlarging **A** to **B** is 1.6.

a The edges of the base of pyramid **A** are 25 cm. Find the length of the edges of the base of **B**.

b The perpendicular height of **A** is 34 cm. Find the perpendicular height of **B**.

10 This sheet of paper, which measures
210 mm by 148 mm, is to be photocopied
to make an enlarged copy.
The scaling is set to 140% (i.e. the edges
of the copy are 140% of the original
lengths).
Find the measurements of the copy.

USING CORRESPONDING LINES TO FIND THE SCALE FACTOR

In the last exercise we were given the scale factor. However we can work out the scale factor when we know that two figures are similar provided that we also know the lengths of a pair of corresponding sides.

The trapeziums ABCD and PQRS are similar so we can think of ABCD as an enlargement of the trapezium PQRS.

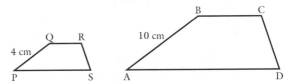

The side AB in ABCD comes from enlarging the side PQ in PQRS, so AB and PQ are *corresponding sides*.

Now $\dfrac{AB}{PQ} = \dfrac{10}{4} = 2.5$

Multiplying both sides by PQ gives $AB = 2.5 \times PQ$

Therefore scale factor of this enlargement is **2.5**.

$\dfrac{AB}{PQ}$ is called the *ratio of a pair of corresponding sides* and its value is the scale factor.

This is true of any pair of corresponding lengths,

i.e. $\dfrac{AB}{PQ} = \dfrac{BC}{QR} = \dfrac{CD}{RS} = \dfrac{AD}{PS}$ ($= 2.5$)

and it remains true when the positions of the trapeziums are changed.

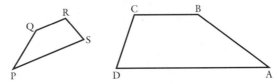

This demonstrates a general fact.

> When two figures are similar,
> their corresponding sides are in the same ratio.
> The value of this ratio is the scale factor.

EXERCISE 13C

These two rectangles are similar. Find the length of SP.

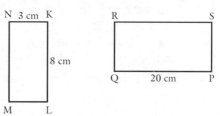

$$\frac{QP}{LK} = \frac{20}{8} = \frac{5}{2},$$

> QP and LK are corresponding sides.

The scale factor that enlarges KLMN to PQRS is $\frac{5}{2} = 2.5$

> SP is an enlargement of NK.

$$SP = 2.5 \times NK$$
$$= 2.5 \times 3\,cm$$
$$= 7.5\,cm$$

The length of SP is 7.5 cm.

1 The figures, which are not drawn to scale, are similar. Find the scale factor that enlarges the black shape to the purple shape.

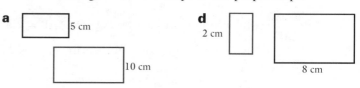

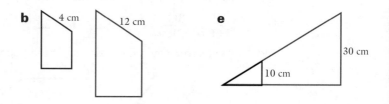

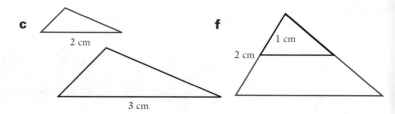

These two figures are similar.
Find the length of the side marked

a x cm   **b** y cm

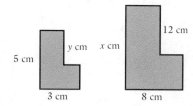

a The sides marked 8 cm and 3 cm correspond; the scale factor that enlarges the smaller L-shape to the larger one is $\frac{8}{3}$.

The scale factor that enlarges **5 cm to x cm is $\frac{8}{3}$.**

$x = \frac{8}{3} \times 5 = \frac{40}{3}$ so x cm $= 13\frac{1}{3}$ cm

b y cm is a side on the smaller shape; we want the scale factor that enlarges the larger to the smaller; this is $\frac{3}{8}$.

$y = \frac{3}{8} \times 12 = \frac{9}{2}$ so y cm $= 4\frac{1}{2}$ cm

2 The two figures are similar. Find the length of each side marked with a letter.

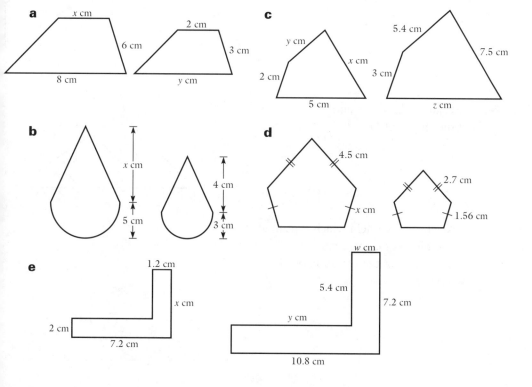

3

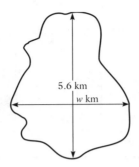

The sketches show the length and width of a lake on a map and the corresponding length of the actual lake. What is the width of the lake at this widest point?

4

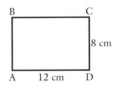
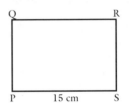

ABCD and PQRS are similar rectangles. Find the length of PQ.

5 The diagram shows a pair of similar cuboids. Find the height of the larger cuboid.

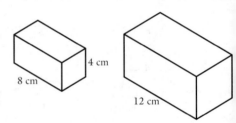

6 △ABC and △ADE are similar. Find the length of DE.

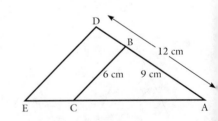

7 The sketch shows a field which is planted with two different cereal crops. Find the length of the common border between the two crops.

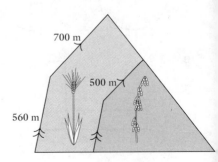

8

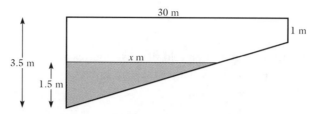

The diagram shows the cross-section of a swimming pool which is 3.5 m deep at one end and 1 m deep at the other. The pool is 30 m long and 10 m wide. Water flows into the pool to a depth of 1.5 m at the deep end. What are the dimensions of the surface of the water?

9

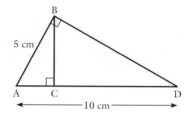

△ABC is similar to △ADB.

a Which side of △ABD corresponds to AB in △ABC?

b Draw △ABD and △ABC separately so that they are both the same way round, with the right angles at the top and the shortest sides on the left.

c On the diagrams drawn for part **b**, mark the lengths of as many sides as are given above.

d Find the length of AC.

10

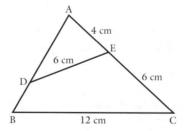

△ABC is similar to △AED.

a Which angle of △AED corresponds to angle ABC in △ABC?

b Draw △ABC and △ADE separately so that they are the same way round, with the angles A at the top and the shortest sides on the left.

c On the diagrams drawn for part **b**, mark the lengths of as many sides as you can.

d Find any remaining lengths.

SIMILAR TRIANGLES

In most cases we need to be told that two figures are similar. However in the case of triangles, it is easy to see whether they are similar.

The angles in these two triangles are the same so the triangles must be the same shape; i.e. they are similar.

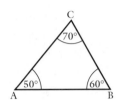

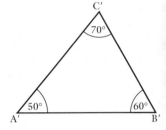

We can say that two triangles are similar if we can show that they have the same angles.

EXERCISE 13D

State whether the two triangles are similar. If they are, find AB.

Mark AB as x cm.

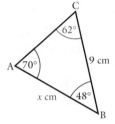

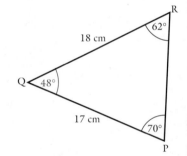

We can use the fact that the sum of the three angles in any triangle is $180°$ to find the third angle in each triangle.

$\hat{C} = 180° - (70° + 48°) = 62°$ and $\hat{Q} = 180° - (70° + 62°) = 48°$

Therefore the angles in the triangles are the same so the triangles are similar.

CB and QR are both opposite the 70° angles so they are corresponding sides.

The scale factor that enlarges $\triangle$PQR to $\triangle$ABC is $\dfrac{BC}{QR} = \dfrac{9}{18} = \dfrac{1}{2}$

The side corresponding to AB is QP. (They are both opposite the 62° angles.)

Therefore $AB = \frac{1}{2} \times QP$ i.e. $x = \frac{1}{2} \times 17 = 8.5$

$AB = 8.5$ cm

In questions **1** to **5**, state whether the triangles are similar. If they are, find the required side.

1 Find PR.

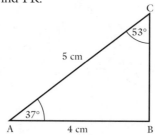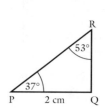

2 Find QR.

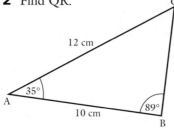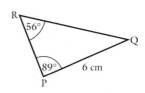

3 Find BC.

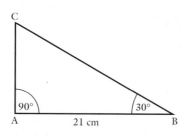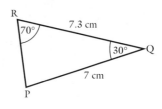

4 Find PR.

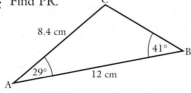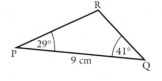

5 Find QR.

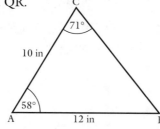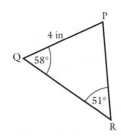

AB and DE are parallel.

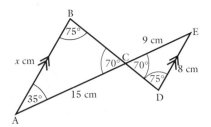

Find **a** $C\widehat{D}E$ **b** $E\widehat{C}D$ **c** the length of AB.

a $C\widehat{D}E = 75°$ ($\widehat{B}$ and $\widehat{D}$ are alternate angles)

b $B\widehat{C}A = 70°$ (sum of angles of $\triangle ABC$)
$E\widehat{C}D = B\widehat{C}A$ (vertically opposite angles)
$\therefore$ $E\widehat{C}D = 70°$

c $\triangle ABC$ and $\triangle CED$ are similar (the angles are the same).

> AC and CE are corresponding sides so we can find the scale factor from them.
> AB and DE are corresponding sides, i.e. DE is enlarged to AB.

The scale factor that enlarges $\triangle CED$ to $\triangle ABC$ is $\frac{15}{9} = \frac{5}{3}$.

$\therefore$ AB $= \frac{5}{3} \times$ ED,

i.e. $x = \frac{5}{3} \times 8 = \frac{40}{3}$

AB $= 13\frac{1}{3}$ cm

6 Use the information on the diagram to find

a the size of angles BDE and EBD.

b the length of BC.

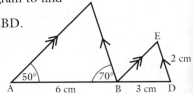

7 Use the information on the diagram to find

a the size of angles ACB and CAB.

b the lengths of CD and DE.

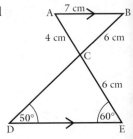

8 a ABCD is a square. EF is drawn at right angles to the diagonal DB.
Explain why △ABD and △DEF are similar.

b Use the information on the diagram to find the length of EF.

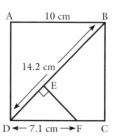

9 In △ABC and △XYZ, $\widehat{A} = \widehat{X}$ and $\widehat{B} = \widehat{Z}$.

a Explain why △ABC and △XYZ are similar.

b AB = 6 cm, BC = 5 cm and XZ = 9 cm.
Find the length of YZ.

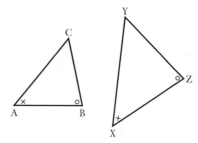

10 a Explain why triangles ABC and ADE are similar.

b Use the information in the diagram to find the length of

i DE **ii** AE **iii** CE.

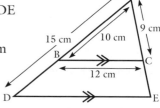

MIXED EXERCISE Do not use a calculator for questions **1** to **5**.

EXERCISE 13E **1** Which of the following shapes are similar to **X**?

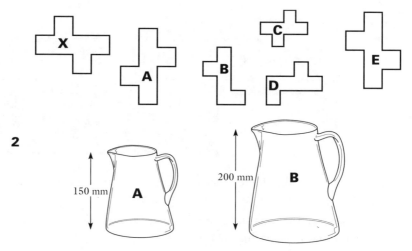

2

These two jugs are similar. Give the scale factor that enlarges **A** to **B**.

3 In one of these pairs of triangles the triangles are similar. State which pair contains the similar triangles and give the scale factor that enlarges △ABC to △DEF.

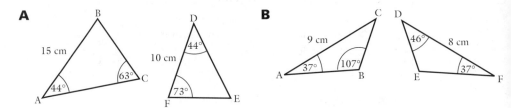

4 The two given shapes are similar. Find the lengths marked with letters.

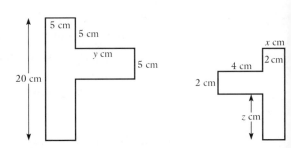

5 Use the information in the diagram to find the length of BC.

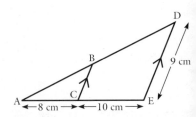

6 This is an exact model of a house made using a scale of 1 : 250.

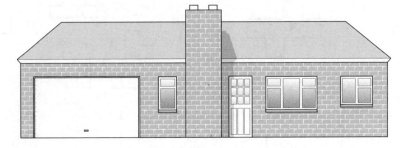

a The height of the chimney stack on the real house is **5.7** metres. How high is the chimney stack on the model?

b The front of the roof on the model slopes at 25° to the horizontal. What is the slope of the real roof?

c The model house is 75 mm long. How long is the real house?

7 These two figures are similar. Find the marked lengths.

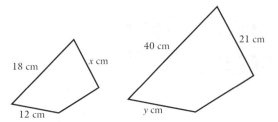

8 a Explain why △ABC is similar to △DEC.

b Use the information in the diagram to find the length of CD.

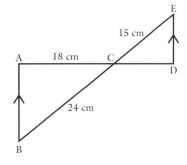

INVESTIGATION

ABCD is a quadrilateral in which the sides are all of different lengths.
P is the midpoint of AB, Q is the midpoint of BC, R is the midpoint of DC and S is the midpoint of AD.

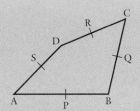

a Make your own copy of the diagram.
Join PQ, QR, RS and SP to form the quadrilateral PQRS.
Are the quadrilaterals ABCD and PQRS similar?

b Investigate whether joining the midpoints of the sides of other quadrilaterals, including the special quadrilaterals, gives a pair of similar quadrilaterals.

c Describe the properties of initial quadrilaterals for which a similar quadrilateral is formed by joining the midpoints of the sides.

d Extend the investigation to triangles.

CHANGING THE SUBJECT OF A FORMULA

The gross yield, G, of a Government stock is given by the formula

$$G = \frac{I}{P} \times 100$$

where I is the annual rate of interest and P the price of the stock.
This formula can be used to find G directly for different values of I and P.

A financial adviser may want to use this formula to find the interest rate
for a gross yield of 10% when the price of the stock is 120.
This can be done by substituting the numbers directly into the formula
to give

$$10 = \frac{I}{120} \times 100$$

and then solving this equation for I. This gives $I = 12$.

The advisor may wish to find the values of I for several different values of
G and P. He can repeat the method used above or he can start by
rearranging the formula so that I is alone on the left-hand side.
We can do this by thinking of $G = \frac{I}{P} \times 100$ as an equation and solving
it for I.

This equation contains the fraction $\frac{I}{P}$ so we start by getting rid of this
fraction.

We do this by multiplying both sides by P,

i.e. $\qquad P \times G = P \times \dfrac{I}{P} \times 100 \Rightarrow PG = 100I$

Then dividing both sides by 100 gives $\dfrac{GP}{100} = I$

i.e. $\qquad I = \dfrac{GP}{100}$

Now I can be found directly for different values of G and P.

When the formula is in the form $G = \dfrac{I}{P} \times 100$, G is called the *subject* of the formula.

When the formula is written $I = \dfrac{GP}{100}$, I is the subject of the formula.

Rearranging $G = \dfrac{I}{P} \times 100$ as $I = \dfrac{GP}{100}$ is called *changing the subject of the formula*.

When a formula is entered into a spreadsheet, it has to be in the form where the required quantity is the subject of the formula. Most of us, at some time in our lives are likely to need to use spreadsheets. It is therefore important to be able to change the subject of a formula. Since changing the subject of a formula is like solving an equation, we start by solving some equations; first straightforward equations and then some where the letter is in the denominator of a fraction.

EXERCISE 14A

Do not use a calculator for this exercise.

Solve the equation $4x + 7 = 19$

$$4x + 7 = 19$$

Subtract 7 from both sides $\quad 4x = 12$

Divide both sides by 4 $\qquad\qquad x = 3$

> To solve an equation our aim is to get the letter on its own.

Solve the following equations.

1
  a $6x + 3 = 27$ **d** $5z + 11 = 6$ **g** $17 = 3 + 7x$

  b $20 = 10x - 40$ **e** $3a + 17 = 17$ **h** $3x + 4 = 1$

  c $9 + 2a = 18$ **f** $2 + 3b = 10.4$ **i** $2p + 7 = 13$

2
  a $5 = 8 - 3x$ **d** $6 = 3 - 2x$ **g** $13.6 - 2.1x = 4.15$

  b $15 - 4x = 7$ **e** $5 - 2x = 9$ **h** $11 - 5x = 3$

  c $4 - 7x = 1$ **f** $0 = 12 - 4x$ **i** $15.5 = 19.2 - 3.7x$

Solve the equation $\dfrac{3}{x} + 4 = 6$

$$\dfrac{3}{x} + 4 = 6$$

> Multiplying each term by x gets rid of the fraction.

$$\dfrac{3}{{}_{1}x} \times \dfrac{x^{1}}{1} + 4 \times x = 6 \times x$$

$$3 + 4x = 6x$$

> Take $4x$ from both sides.

$$3 = 2x$$

i.e. $\qquad x = \dfrac{3}{2}$

Solve the following equations.

3 a $\dfrac{4}{x} = 5$ 　　　　**d** $\dfrac{2}{3x} = 1$ 　　　　**g** $1 - \dfrac{7}{x} = 9$

　　b $1 + \dfrac{2}{a} = 3$ 　　　**e** $\dfrac{5}{y} = 2$ 　　　　**h** $9 = \dfrac{2}{t}$

　　c $3 - \dfrac{4}{t} = 6$ 　　　**f** $4 + \dfrac{2}{x} = 7$ 　　　**i** $2 + \dfrac{5}{3x} = 7$

4 a $\dfrac{5}{p} = 3$ 　　　　**d** $\dfrac{5}{x} + 7 = 12$ 　　　**g** $\dfrac{9}{4p} + 1 = 3$

　　b $\dfrac{3}{4t} - 2 = 7$ 　　　**e** $1 + \dfrac{3}{A} = 9$ 　　　**h** $\dfrac{9}{5t} + 6 = 18$

　　c $9 - \dfrac{5}{x} = 4$ 　　　**f** $5 - \dfrac{8}{x} = 1$ 　　　**i** $2 = \dfrac{3}{t}$

Solve $\dfrac{3}{x-1} = 4$

$$\dfrac{3}{(x-1)} = 4$$

> Place the two-term denominator in brackets; this ensures that the two terms stay together.

Multiply both sides by $(x-1)$

$$\dfrac{{}^{1}\cancel{(x-1)}}{1} \times \dfrac{3}{\cancel{(x-1)}_{1}} = (x-1) \times 4$$

$$3 = 4(x-1)$$

$$3 = 4x - 4$$

$$7 = 4x$$

$$x = \dfrac{7}{4}$$

Solve the equations

5 a $\dfrac{2}{1+x} = 1$ **c** $\dfrac{4}{3-x} = 3$ **e** $\dfrac{3}{2+t} = 5$

   b $\dfrac{6}{3+x} = 1$ **d** $\dfrac{5}{1+2x} = 4$ **f** $\dfrac{10}{3x+1} = 3$

6 a $\dfrac{15}{1-H} = 3$ **c** $\dfrac{5}{4-x} = 1$ **e** $\dfrac{1}{3A-2} = 2$

   b $\dfrac{5}{2+x} = 2$ **d** $\dfrac{1}{p-4} = \dfrac{1}{2}$ **f** $\dfrac{5}{3-2s} = \dfrac{1}{2}$

CHANGING THE SUBJECT OF A FORMULA

To change the subject of a formula, think of it as an equation in the letter you want to make the subject. Then solve the equation for this letter.

EXERCISE 14B

> Make t the subject of the formula $v = u + t$
>
> > We need to solve for t; so we use the same methods as for solving a linear equation in one unknown.
>
> $$v = u + t$$
>
> Subtracting u from both sides gives $v - u = t$
>
> i.e. $$t = v - u$$
>
> > If you cannot see how to proceed, replace all the letters except t with numbers,
> >
> > e.g.   change $v = u + t$ to $2 = 3 + t$;
> >
> > Now it is clear that we need to take 3 from both sides to find t.
> > As 3 replaced u, we need to take u from both sides in the formula.

Make the letter in brackets the subject of the formula.

1 a $p = s + r$ (s) **d** $X = Y - Z$ (Y)
   b $x = 3 + y$ (y) **e** $r = s + 2t$ (s)
   c $a = b - c$ (b) **f** $k = l + m$ (m)

2 a $u = v - 5$ (v) **d** $N = P - Q$ (P)
   b $z = x + y$ (y) **e** $y = u + 10t$ (u)
   c $M = m + n$ (n) **f** $R = 8s + t$ (t)

Make y the subject of the formula $x = 5y$

$$x = 5y$$

Dividing both sides by 5 $\qquad \dfrac{x}{5} = \dfrac{5y}{5}$

$$\dfrac{x}{5} = y$$

i.e. $\qquad y = \dfrac{x}{5}$

Make the letter in brackets the subject of the formula.

3 **a** $x = 2y$ (y) **d** $a = 3b$ (b)

    b $v = \frac{1}{2}t$ (t) **e** $X = \frac{1}{10}N$ (N)

    c $a = 3.5b$ (b) **f** $v = \frac{1}{5}u$ (u)

4 **a** $t = \dfrac{u}{3}$ (u) **d** $n = \dfrac{p}{4}$ (p)

    b $3 = \dfrac{m}{k}$ (m) **e** $6 = \dfrac{p}{q}$ (p)

    c $A = \dfrac{r}{6}$ (r) **f** $8 = \dfrac{M}{m}$ (M)

Make t the subject of the formula $v = ut$

$$v = ut \qquad \boxed{\text{Remember that } ut \text{ means } u \times t.}$$

Divide both sides by u $\qquad \dfrac{v}{u} = \dfrac{u \times t}{u}$

$$\dfrac{v}{u} = t$$

i.e. $\qquad t = \dfrac{v}{u}$

Make the letter in brackets the subject of the formula.

5 **a** $p = \dfrac{q}{r}$ (q) **d** $v = at$ (a)

    b $a = bc$ (c) **e** $r = st$ (s)

    c $n = \dfrac{p}{q}$ (p) **f** $A = ab$ (a)

6 **a** $z = 3xy$ (y) **e** $z = \dfrac{x}{2y}$ (x)

     b $X = \dfrac{z}{2y}$ (z) **f** $a = \dfrac{V}{b^2}$ (V)

     c $\dfrac{x}{2} = \dfrac{y}{3}$ (y) **g** $\dfrac{p}{4} = \dfrac{q}{5}$ (q)

     d $3a = \dfrac{b}{4}$ (b) **h** $5x = \dfrac{y}{4}$ (y)

One operation only was needed to change the subject of a formula in the last exercise. In the following exercise, more than one operation is needed.

EXERCISE 14C

> Make t the subject of the formula $v = u + 2t$
>
> > Start by isolating the term containing t on one side of the formula; i.e. solve the formula for the term containing t.
>
> $$v = u + 2t$$
> Take u from both sides $v - u = 2t$
> $\therefore$ $2t = v - u$
> Divide both sides by 2 $t = \dfrac{(v - u)}{2}$

> **a** Make y the subject of the formula $z = x - wy$
> **b** Find y when $z = 6$, $x = 12$ and $w = 3$.
>
> **a** $z = x - wy$
>
> Add wy to both sides $wy + z = x$ We want the term containing y to be positive so we add wy to both sides.
>
> Subtract z from both sides $wy = x - z$ To isolate the term in y.
>
> Divide both sides by w $y = \dfrac{x - z}{w}$
>
> **b** When $z = 6$, $x = 12$ and $w = 3$ $y = \dfrac{12 - 6}{3}$
>
> $= \dfrac{6}{3} = 2$

Make the letter in brackets the subject of the formula.

1 a $p = 2s + r$ (s)
  b $v = u - 3t$ (t)
  c $a = b - 4c$ (c)
  d $V = 2v + 3u$ (v)

  e $x = 2w - y$ (w)
  f $m = k + 4t$ (t)
  g $w = x - 6y$ (y)
  h $N = IT - 2s$ (s)

2 a $x = \dfrac{3y}{4}$ (y)
  b $u = v + 5t$ (t)
  c $A = P + \frac{1}{10}I$ (I)
  d $z = x - \dfrac{y}{3}$ (y)

  e $V = \dfrac{2R}{I}$ (R)
  f $p = 2r - w$ (r)
  g $a = b + \frac{1}{2}c$ (c)
  h $p = q - \dfrac{r}{5}$ (r)

3 a Make u the subject of the formula $v = u + at$
  b Find u when $v = 80$, $a = -10$ and $t = 6$.

4 a Make s the subject of the formula $P = rs - t$
  b Find the value of s when $P = 5$, $r = 4$ and $t = -30$.

5 a Change the formula $X = p + qr$ so that q is subject.
  b Find the value of q when $X = 25$, $p = 10$ and $r = -5$.

6 a Change the subject of the formula $V = abc$ from V to c.
  b Find c when $V = 9$, $a = 1.5$ and $b = 2.4$.

7 a Make w the subject of the formula $Z = wx + xy$
  b Find w when $Z = -19.5$, $x = -2.5$ and $y = 4.4$.

8 a Change the subject to a, given that $A + bc = ac$
  b Find the value of a when $A = \frac{5}{24}$, $b = \frac{1}{3}$ and $c = \frac{1}{2}$.

9 a Make c the subject of the formula $a - b = bc$
  b Find c when $a = 9$ and $b = 1.2$.

10 a Given that $z - xy = y$, make x the subject.
  b Find x when $y = 3.6$ and $z = 11.52$.

11 a Make R the subject of the formula $P = Q + \dfrac{R}{S}$

   b Find the value of R when $P = 8$, $Q = 7.2$ and $S = 5$.

12 a Change the subject of the formula $z = \frac{1}{2}x - 3t$ from z to x.

   b Find the value of x when $z = -4$ and $t = -3$.

13 a Make y the subject of the formula $z = x - 5y$

   b Find the value of y when $z = 2$ and $x = 12$.

14 Given the formula $v = u - 8t$,

   a make u the subject

   b find the value of u when $v = 9.5$ and $t = 1.4$.

15 a Make z the subject of the formula $W = xy - yz$

   b Find the value of z when $W = 4$, $x = -3$ and $y = -4$.

16 a Change the subject of the formula $A = \dfrac{C}{100} + B$ from A to B.

   b Find B when $A = 20$ and $C = 250$.

17 A number a is equal to the sum of a number b and twice a number c.

   a Find a formula for a in terms of b and c.

   b Find a when $b = 8$ and $c = -2$.

   c Make b the subject of the formula.

18 The length of a man's forearm f cm and his height h cm are approximately related by the formula $h = 3f + 85$

   a Part of the skeleton of a man is found and the forearm is 25 cm long. Use the formula to estimate the man's height.

   b A man's height is 159 cm. Use the formula to estimate the length of his forearm.

   c James is 18 months old and is 80 cm tall. Find the value the formula gives for the length of his forearm. Why is this value impossible?

   d Use the formula to find an expression for f in terms of h.

19 A number x is equal to the product of a number z and twice a number y.

   a Find a formula for x in terms of y and z.

   b Find x when $z = 3$ and $y = 2$.

   c Make y the subject of the formula.

20 A number d is equal to the square of a number e plus twice a number f.

    a Find a formula for d in terms of e and f.

    b Make f the subject of the formula.

    c Find f when $d = 10$ and $e = 3$.

21 The heat setting on a gas oven is called its Gas Mark. The formula $F = 25G + 250$ will convert a Gas Mark G into a temperature $F°$ Fahrenheit.

    a Sally puts a joint into her gas oven which she has previously set at Gas Mark 6. What is the temperature inside the oven?

    b Make G the subject of the formula.

    c Gary wants to bake some bread. The recommended baking temperature is $450°$ Fahrenheit.
    What Gas Mark should Gary set on the oven?

22

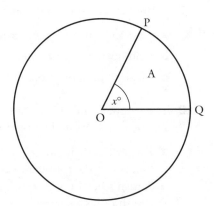

POQ is a sector in a circle, centre O and radius r cm.
The angle POQ at the centre of the circle is $x°$ and the area of the sector POQ is A cm^2. These quantities are related by the formula
$$A = \frac{\pi r^2 x}{360}$$

    a Find the area of the sector POQ when $\widehat{POQ} = 100°$ and the radius of the circle is 7.5 cm.

    b Rewrite the formula with x as the subject.

    c Calculate the size of the angle POQ when the radius is 12 cm and the area of the sector is 40 cm^2.

23 A Gas Mark G may be converted to a temperature of $C°$ Celsius using the formula $C = 14G + 121$.

a Make G the subject of the formula.

b Hence find the Gas Mark that corresponds to a temperature of

i $163\,°C$ **ii** $219\,°C$.

c Use the formula $C = \frac{5}{9}(F - 32)$ together with the formula $C = 14G + 121$ to find a formula for F in terms of G. Give any number that is not a whole number correct to the nearest whole number.

FORMULAS INVOLVING SQUARES AND SQUARE ROOTS

Remember that if $x^2 = 4$ then x has two values, i.e. $x = \pm 2$
Similarly, if $x^2 = a$ then $x = \pm\sqrt{a}$
Remember also that $\sqrt{a}$ means only the positive square root of a.

EXERCISE 14D

Find x if **a** $4x^2 = 9$ **b** $ax^2 = b$

> Isolate x^2 then take the square root of each side.

a $4x^2 = 9$

$x^2 = \frac{9}{4}$

$x = \pm\frac{3}{2}$

b $ax^2 = b$

$x^2 = \dfrac{b}{a}$

$x = \pm\sqrt{\dfrac{b}{a}}$

Find x in terms of the other letters or numbers.

1 a $x^2 = 16$

b $9x^2 = 25$

c $px^2 = q$

d $px^2 = q^2$

2 a $3x^2 + 4 = 9$

b $x^2 = p$

c $x^2 = p + q$

d $\dfrac{ax^2}{b} = c$

Make the letter in brackets the subject of the formula.

3 a $2R^2 = A$ (R)

b $V = ba^2$ (a)

c $P = r^2 + 2c$ (r)

d $5v^2 = as$ (v)

e $a = b + c^2$ (c)

f $R = \dfrac{t^2}{s}$ (t)

Make x the subject of the formula $p = 2(x - a)^2$

First isolate the squared bracket then take the square root of both sides.

$$\frac{p}{2} = (x - a)^2$$

i.e. $\qquad (x - a)^2 = \frac{p}{2}$

$$(x - a) = \pm \sqrt{\frac{p}{2}}, \quad \text{i.e.} \quad x - a = \pm \sqrt{\frac{p}{2}}$$

$\Rightarrow \qquad\qquad x = a \pm \sqrt{\frac{p}{2}}$

4 Find x in terms of the other letters or numbers.

a $(x - 4)^2 = 9$ $\qquad\qquad$ **c** $4 = 9(x - 3)^2$

b $(x - a)^2 = b$ $\qquad\qquad$ **d** $s = t(x - 5)^2$

5 Make the letter in brackets the subject of the formula.

a $3r = (A - 2)^2$ $\quad (A)$ $\qquad$ **c** $2(T - 3)^2 = M$ $\quad (T)$

b $8 = (H - L)^2$ $\quad (H)$ $\qquad$ **d** $a(b - c)^2 = 5$ $\quad (b)$

Make x the subject of the formula

a $a = b\sqrt{x}$ $\qquad$ **b** $a = \sqrt{b + x}$ $\qquad$ **c** $a = b + \sqrt{x}$

First isolate the term containing the square root then square both sides.

a $\quad a = b\sqrt{x}$ $\qquad$ **b** $\qquad a = \sqrt{b + x}$ $\qquad$ **c** $\qquad\qquad a = b + \sqrt{x}$

$\quad \dfrac{a}{b} = \sqrt{x}$ $\qquad\qquad$ Note that $\sqrt{b + x}$ is *not* $\sqrt{b} + \sqrt{x}$. $\qquad\qquad a - b = \sqrt{x}$

$\quad \dfrac{a^2}{b^2} = x$ $\qquad\qquad\qquad a^2 = b + x$ $\qquad\qquad\qquad (a - b)^2 = x$

i.e. $\quad x = \dfrac{a^2}{b^2}$ $\qquad\qquad a^2 - b = x$ $\qquad\qquad$ i.e. $\quad x = (a - b)^2$

$\qquad\qquad\qquad\qquad$ i.e. $\quad x = a^2 - b$

Find x in terms of the other letters or numbers.

6 a $\sqrt{x} = 4$ **c** $p\sqrt{x} = q$ **e** $\sqrt{x} + 3 = 10$

 b $3\sqrt{x} = 2$ **d** $\sqrt{px} = r$ **f** $a = b + \sqrt{x}$

7 a $\sqrt{3x} = 9$ **c** $\sqrt{x} = p\sqrt{q}$ **e** $\sqrt{x-1} + 4 = 7$

 b $\sqrt{x} = a$ **d** $\sqrt{x+a} = 4$ **f** $s = t + \sqrt{x-t}$

8 Make the letter in brackets the subject of the formula.

 a $\sqrt{r} = L$ (r) **c** $5a = 3\sqrt{b}$ (b) **e** $P = \sqrt{T-1}$ (T)

 b $2\sqrt{L} = t$ (L) **d** $r = \sqrt{\dfrac{A}{3}}$ (A) **f** $v = u + \sqrt{s}$ (s)

In questions **9** to **18** make the letter in brackets the subject of the formula.

9 $A = (a - b)^2$ (a) **14** $3a^2 = 2\sqrt{b}$ (b)

10 $Z = k(x + y)^2$ (y) **15** $P = \frac{4}{3}\pi r^2$ (r)

11 $A = \pi r^2$ (r) **16** $a = \sqrt{A}$ (A)

12 $V = 3\sqrt{R}$ (R) **17** $5\sqrt{x} = \dfrac{y^3}{z}$ (x)

13 $a = \dfrac{b - a^2}{2a}$ (b) **18** $3x = \dfrac{x^2 - y}{2x}$ (y)

19 The points system used for the High Jump at an athletics meeting uses the formula $P = k(H - a)^2$ where H cm is the height jumped, P is the number of points scored and k and a are non-zero constants.

 a For a jump of 80 cm no points are scored. What is the value of a?

 b Show that $H = 80 + \sqrt{\dfrac{P}{k}}$

 c Sara jumps 135 cm and scores 121 points. Find the value of k.

 d Using your values for k and a find

   i how many points a jump of 140 cm scores
   ii the height of a jump that scores 289 points.

20 The Body Mass Index, I, for an adult is given by the formula $I = \dfrac{W}{H^2}$ where W is the weight of the person in kilograms and H the height in metres.

 Use this formula to express H in terms of I and W and hence find the height of a person whose Body Mass Index is 23.4 who weighs 94.2 kg. Give your answer correct to 1 decimal place.

**MIXED
EXERCISES**

EXERCISE 14E   **Do not use a calculator for this exercise**

1 Solve the equation

    a $5x - 4 = 21$ **b** $5 - \dfrac{6}{x} = 3$

2 Make b the subject of the formula $A = b + c$

3 If $\dfrac{p}{3} = q$ make p the subject.

4 If $a = 3b + c$, make b the subject of the formula.

5 Make m the subject of the formula $y = mx + c$. Hence find the gradient of a straight line that passes through the point $(1, 2)$ and makes an intercept of -3 on the y-axis.

6 Sid takes a weekly magazine costing x pence, daily newspapers from Monday to Saturday costing y pence each and a Sunday paper costing z pence.

    a Make a formula for the total amount, C pence, he must pay the newsagent for these items for one week.

    b If his Sunday paper costs twice as much as his daily paper find an expression for C in terms of x and y.

    c His total bill for a week's papers is £6.10. If the magazine costs £2.50 find the cost of his Sunday paper.

7 Make y the subject of the formula

    a $2y + x = 7$ **b** $3x = \dfrac{2y}{3} + 2$ **c** $3x = \sqrt{4 - 2y}$

EXERCISE 14F   In this exercise give numerical answers correct to 3 significant figures.

1   **a** Make b the subject of the formula $V = abc$.

    b Find b when $V = 147$, $a = 6.21$ and $c = 4.93$.

2 Make x the subject of the formula $Z = k(x - y)^2$

3   **a** Make q the subject of the formula $4p = \dfrac{p^2 + q}{3p}$

    b Find the value of q when $p = 0.87$.

4 A rocket is fired vertically upwards with a velocity of u metres per second. The velocity of the rocket t seconds later is v metres per second where $v = u - gt$

   a Calculate the value of v when $u = 175$, $t = 15$ and $g = 9.8$.

   b Rearrange the formula to express t in terms of the other letters.

   c Calculate t when $u = 26.5$, $v = 100$ and $g = 9.8$.

PRACTICAL WORK

Periodically a person from the electricity company and/or from the gas company calls at your home to read a meter.

   a Investigate the unit of measurement used on each meter. How does one unit of gas compare with one unit of electricity?

   b Obtain an electricity bill and a gas bill. Is the same unit of heat used on both these bills? If so, what is it?

   c Construct a formula that connects the number, n, of units shown by the gas meter as having been used and the number, N, of units of heat consumed.

   d Repeat part **c** for the information given on the electricity bill.

   e Which fuel provides the cheaper way of buying one unit of heat?

   f Is your answer to part **e** the same if you also take standing charges into account?

FACTORISING

In Chapter 8 we saw that we can expand algebraic expressions involving brackets.

For example, $2x(3x - 5)$ can be multiplied out to give $6x^2 - 10x$.
Later we will meet situations where we need to reverse this process, that is we need to change $6x^2 - 10x$ into $2x(3x - 5)$.
In this chapter we build up the skills necessary to do this.

When we reverse the process of expanding expressions we are finding the factors of an expression. This is called *factorising*.

COMMON FACTORS

In the expression $7a + 14b$ we could write the first term as $7 \times a$ and the second term as $7 \times 2b$, i.e. $7a + 14b = 7 \times a + 7 \times 2b$
The 7 is called a common factor because it is common to $7a$ and $14b$.
However we already know that $7(a + 2b) = 7 \times a + 7 \times 2b$
$\therefore \qquad 7a + 14b = 7 \times a + 7 \times 2b = 7(a + 2b)$

EXERCISE 15A

Factorise $3x - 12$

$$3x - 12 = 3 \times x - 3 \times 4$$
$$= 3(x - 4)$$

Expand your answer to check that it is correct.

Factorise and then expand your answer in your head, to check that it is correct.

1 **a** $4x + 4$ **c** $12x - 3$ **e** $6a + 2$
     b $5a - 10b$ **d** $10a - 5$ **f** $2a + 4b$

2 **a** $3t - 9$ **c** $12a + 4$ **e** $14x - 7$
     b $5x + 15y$ **d** $8b - 16c$ **f** $18a - 12b$

Factorise $x^2 - 7x$

$x^2 - 7x = x \times x - 7 \times x$

$= x(x - 7)$

Remember that $7 \times x = x \times 7$,
so $x \times x + 7 \times x = x \times x + x \times 7$

3 a $x^2 + 2x$ **c** $2x^2 + x$ **e** $x^2 - 4x$

   b $x^2 - 8x$ **d** $4t - t^2$ **f** $b^2 + 4b$

4 a $a^2 + 6a$ **c** $x^2 + 5x$ **e** $4a^2 - a$

   b $p^2 + 3p$ **d** $2x - x^2$ **f** $5y - 2y^2$

Factorise $9ab + 12bc$

$9ab + 12bc = 3b \times 3a + 3b \times 4c$

$= 3b(3a + 4c)$

When there is more than one common factor, we may not 'see' all of them to begin with.
In this case we might have spotted 3 but not b, giving $9ab + 12bc = 3(3ab + 4bc)$.
A check on the terms inside the bracket shows that b is also a common factor so we can
take b outside the bracket giving $3(3ab + 4bc) = 3b(3a + 4c)$.

Factorise and remember to check your answer by expanding it.

5 a $2x^2 - 6x$ **c** $12x^2 + 16x$ **e** $2a^2 - 12a$

   b $2z^2 + 4z$ **d** $5ab - 10bc$ **f** $6p^2 + 2p$

6 a $25a^2 - 5a$ **c** $3y^2 - 27y$ **e** $9y^2 - 6y$

   b $3p^2 + 9p$ **d** $8x - 4x^2$ **f** $2y^2 - 12y$

Factorise $ab + 2bc + bd$

$$ab + 2bc + bd = b(a + 2c + d)$$

Factorise

7 a $2x^2 + 4x + 6$ **b** $3x^2 - 6x + 9$ **c** $10a^2 - 5a + 20$

8 a $4a^2 + 8a - 4$ **b** $ab + 4bc - 3bd$ **c** $5xy + 4xz + 3x$

9 a $8x - 4y + 12z$ **b** $5ab + 10bc + 5bd$ **c** $9ab^2 - 6ac - 3ad$

10 a $2xy - 4yz + 8yw$ **b** $3xy - 9yz + 6xz$ **c** $4a^2 + 12a + 4$

Factorise $8x^3 - 4x^2$

$$8x^3 - 4x^2 = 4x^2(2x - 1)$$

In this case, we may spot that 4 is a common factor and not 'see' the x^2, giving

$$8x^3 - 4x^2 = 4(2x^3 - x^2)$$

A check on the terms inside the bracket shows that there is another common factor, namely x^2

so $\qquad 4(2x^3 - x^2) = 4x^2(2x - 1)$ (remember: $x^3 = x^2 \times x$)

Remember to check that *all* the common factors have been removed from inside the bracket.

Factorise

11 a $x^3 + x^2$ **c** $a^2 + a^3$ **e** $20a^2 - 5a^3$

   b $x^2 - x^3$ **d** $b^3 - b^2$ **f** $12x^3 - 16x^2$

12 a $4x^4 + 12x^2$ **c** $10x^2 - 15x^4$ **e** $4x^3 - 2x^2$

   b $16x^3 - 12x^4$ **d** $9a^4 - 3a^2$ **f** $27a^2 - 18a^3$

13 a $12x + 8$ **c** $x^2 - 8x$ **e** $9x^2 - 6x + 12$

   b $8x^2 + 12x$ **d** $12 + 9y^2$ **f** $5x^3 - 10x$

14 a $8pq^2 + 4qr$ **c** $12abc - 8bcd$ **e** $12xy + 16xz + 8x$

   b $4x^3 + 6x$ **d** $15x^2 - 5x - 10$ **f** $3ab + 9bc + 15ca$

Factorise   **a** $2\pi r^2 + 2\pi rh$ **b** $\frac{1}{2}Mu^2 - \frac{1}{2}mu^2$

a $2\pi r^2 + 2\pi rh = 2\pi r(r + h)$

b $\frac{1}{2}Mu^2 - \frac{1}{2}mu^2 = \frac{1}{2}u^2(M - m)$

Factorise

15 a $\frac{1}{2}ah + \frac{1}{2}bh$ **c** $mg - ma$ **e** $P + \dfrac{PRT}{100}$

   b $\frac{1}{2}mv^2 - \frac{1}{2}mu^2$ **d** $\frac{1}{2}mv^2 - mgh$ **f** $2\pi r^2 + \pi rh$

16 a $\pi R^2 + \pi r^2$ **c** $\frac{1}{2}mu^2 + \frac{1}{2}mv^2$ **e** $\frac{4}{3}\pi r^3 - \frac{1}{3}\pi r^2 h$

   b $2gh_1 - 2gh_2$ **d** $\frac{1}{2}bc - \frac{1}{4}ca$ **f** $3\pi r^2 + 2\pi rh$

17 a $3x^2 + 6xy$ **c** $3pq^2 + 9p^2q$ **e** $16x^2 - 12xy$

     b $\frac{1}{2}Mu^2 + \frac{1}{2}mu^2$ **d** $\frac{1}{6}b^2c - \frac{1}{3}bc^2$ **f** $6a^2b + 15ab^2$

18 a $12ab^2 - 3ab$ **c** $9xy^2z - 6xyz^2$ **e** $\pi r^2h + \pi R^2h$

     b $8x^2y + 16xy^2$ **d** $10x^3y - 15x^2y$ **f** $Mn^2 - M^2n$

FACTORISING QUADRATIC EQUATIONS

The type of expression we are most likely to want to factorise is one such as $x^2 + 7x + 10$.

Expressions like $x^2 + 7x + 10$ are called *quadratic expressions*.

When we expanded $(x + 2)(x + 4)$ we had

$$(x + 2)(x + 4) = x^2 + 6x + 8$$

If we write $x^2 + 6x + 8 = (x + 2)(x + 4)$ we say we have factorised $x^2 + 6x + 8$

i.e. just as 10 is 2×5 so $x^2 + 6x + 8$ is $(x + 2) \times (x + 4)$

So, to factorise such an expression we look for two brackets whose product is the original expression.

To factorise an expression of the form $x^2 + 7x + 10$, which is a quadratic where all the terms are positive, we remind ourselves of the patterns we observed in Chapter 8 and summarised on page 158.

We found when expanding brackets that

- if the sign in each bracket is $+$ then the number term in the expansion is $+$
- the x^2 term comes from $x \times x$
- the number term in the expansion comes from multiplying the numbers in the brackets together
- the middle term, or x term in the expansion, comes from collecting the product of the outside terms in the brackets and the product of the inside terms in the brackets.

Using these ideas in the reverse order

$x^2 + 7x + 10 = (x + \quad)(x + \quad)$ Now we need two numbers whose product is 10 and whose sum is 7.

$= (x + 2)(x + 5)$ (The other pair of numbers whose product is 10 is 1 and 10 but the sum of 1 and 10 is 11 not 7.)

EXERCISE 15B

Factorise $x^2 + 8x + 15$

> The product of 3 and 5 is 15, and their sum is 8.
> The other possible pair is 1 and 15, but $1 + 15 = 16$ not 8.

$$x^2 + 8x + 15 = (x + 3)(x + 5)$$

> Remember that 2×3 is the same as 3×2
> so that $(x + 3)(x + 5)$ is the same as $(x + 5)(x + 3)$
> i.e. the order in which the brackets are written does not matter.

Check: $(x + 3)(x + 5) = x^2 + 3x + 5x + 15$

Factorise and check your answer by expanding it.

1 **a** $x^2 + 3x + 2$ **c** $x^2 + 8x + 7$ **e** $x^2 + 7x + 12$
  b $x^2 + 6x + 5$ **d** $x^2 + 8x + 12$ **f** $x^2 + 4x + 3$

2 **a** $x^2 + 21x + 20$ **c** $x^2 + 12x + 20$ **e** $x^2 + 13x + 12$
  b $x^2 + 8x + 16$ **d** $x^2 + 6x + 9$ **f** $x^2 + 16x + 15$

3 **a** $x^2 + 15x + 36$ **c** $x^2 + 20x + 36$ **e** $x^2 + 22x + 40$
  b $x^2 + 19x + 18$ **d** $x^2 + 9x + 18$ **f** $x^2 + 9x + 8$

4 **a** $x^2 + 10x + 21$ **c** $x^2 + 12x + 35$ **e** $x^2 + 11x + 30$
  b $x^2 + 10x + 9$ **d** $x^2 + 10x + 16$ **f** $x^2 + 14x + 40$

To factorise an expression of the form $x^2 - 6x + 8$ remember the pattern

- the numbers in the brackets must multiply to give $+8$, that is, they must have the same sign.
  Since the middle term in the expression is $-$ they must both be $-$
- the x^2 term comes from $x \times x$
- the middle term, or x term, comes from collecting the product of the outside terms and the product of the inside terms.

Using this pattern in reverse order

$$x^2 - 6x + 8 = (x - \quad)(x - \quad)$$

> We need two numbers whose product is 8 and whose sum is 6.

$$= (x - 2)(x - 4)$$

EXERCISE 15C

Factorise $x^2 - 7x + 12$

> The product of -3 and -4 is $+12$ and their sum is -7.
> Other pairs looked at and discarded are -2 and -6, and -1 and -12.

$x^2 - 7x + 12 = (x - 3)(x - 4)$

Factorise and check your answer by expanding it.

1 **a** $x^2 - 9x + 8$ **c** $x^2 - 8x + 12$ **e** $x^2 - 11x + 28$

   b $x^2 - 5x + 6$ **d** $x^2 - 13x + 30$ **f** $x^2 - 18x + 32$

2 **a** $x^2 - 16x + 15$ **c** $x^2 - 6x + 9$ **e** $x^2 - 13x + 42$

   b $x^2 - 17x + 30$ **d** $x^2 - 6x + 5$ **f** $x^2 - 12x + 20$

3 **a** $x^2 - 16x + 63$ **c** $x^2 - 12x + 35$ **e** $x^2 - 8x + 7$

   b $x^2 - 10x + 9$ **d** $x^2 - 5x + 4$ **f** $x^2 - 6x + 5$

Using the pattern again we know that when the number term in the expansion is negative the signs in the brackets are different.
So to factorise $x^2 + x - 12$ we start with

$$x^2 + x - 12 = (x + \quad)(x - \quad)$$

We want two numbers whose product is 12 and, in this case, whose *difference* is 1; this is because, when we collect the product of the inside terms and the outside terms, one is positive and the other is negative. These numbers are 3 and 4.

As the middle term is $+x$, we want the larger number with the $+$ sign.

$$\therefore \qquad x^2 + x - 12 = (x + 4)(x - 3)$$

EXERCISE 15D

Factorise and check your answer by expanding it.

1 **a** $x^2 - x - 6$ **c** $x^2 + x - 20$ **e** $x^2 + 2x - 15$

   b $x^2 + 3x - 28$ **d** $x^2 + 7x - 30$ **f** $x^2 - x - 12$

2 **a** $x^2 + 6x - 27$ **c** $x^2 - 9x - 22$ **e** $x^2 - 2x - 24$

   b $x^2 - 2x - 35$ **d** $x^2 + x - 30$ **f** $x^2 - 4x - 5$

3 **a** $x^2 - x - 20$ **c** $x^2 - 7x - 18$ **e** $x^2 + x - 42$

   f $x^2 + 3x - 40$ **d** $x^2 - 9x - 10$ **f** $x^2 - 4x - 45$

Most of the values in the previous three exercises have been easy to spot. If you have problems in finding the numbers, set out all possible pairs, as shown below, until you find the pair that gives the original expression when you multiply back.

a Factorise $x^2 - 11x + 24$

> Because the number term is + the two numbers in the brackets must have the same sign. Because the x term is − the signs are both −.

Possible numbers		Sum
−1	−24	−25
−2	−12	−14
−3	−8	−11

$$\therefore\ x^2 - 11x + 24 = (x - 3)(x - 8)$$

b Factorise $x^2 + 5x - 24$

> Because the number term is − the two numbers in the brackets must have different signs. The middle term on the LHS is $+5x$ so the + sign goes with the larger of the two possible numbers.

Possible numbers		Sum
−1	+24	+23
−2	+12	+10
−3	+8	+5

$$x^2 + 5x - 24 = (x - 3)(x + 8)$$

Remember that '+' before the number term means that the signs in the brackets are the same, whereas a '−' before the number term means that they are different.

Factorise $x^2 + 13x + 36$

> The possible pairs of numbers whose product is 36 are 1×36, 2×18, 3×12, 4×9 and 6×6; 4×9 is the only pair that gives a sum of 13.

$$x^2 + 13x + 36 = (x + 4)(x + 9)$$

Factorise

1 a $x^2 + 9x + 14$ **c** $x^2 + 5x - 14$ **e** $x^2 + 9x + 8$

   b $x^2 - 10x + 21$ **d** $x^2 + x - 30$ **f** $x^2 - 10x + 25$

2 a $x^2 + 8x - 9$ **c** $x^2 + x - 56$ **e** $x^2 - 6x - 27$

   b $x^2 - 15x + 26$ **d** $x^2 + 32x + 60$ **f** $x^2 + 16x - 80$

3 a $x^2 + 14x + 13$ **c** $x^2 + 2x - 80$ **e** $x^2 + 8x - 48$

   b $x^2 + 12x - 28$ **d** $x^2 - 11x + 30$ **f** $x^2 + 18x + 72$

4 a $x^2 + 17x + 52$ **c** $x^2 + 11x + 24$ **e** $x^2 - 18x + 32$

  b $x^2 - 12x - 28$ **d** $x^2 - 11x - 42$ **f** $x^2 - 7x - 60$

5 a $x^2 - 9x + 18$ **c** $x^2 + 3x - 28$ **e** $x^2 - 12x - 13$

  b $x^2 + 7x - 18$ **d** $x^2 - 15x + 44$ **f** $x^2 + 4x - 12$

6 a $x^2 + 14x - 15$ **c** $x^2 - 7x - 8$ **e** $x^2 + 16x + 63$

  b $x^2 - x - 42$ **d** $x^2 - 12x + 35$ **f** $x^2 + 4x - 5$

Factorise $6 + x^2 - 5x$

This needs to be rearranged into the familiar form,
i.e. x^2 term first, then the x term and finally the number.

$$6 + x^2 - 5x = x^2 - 5x + 6$$
$$= (x - 2)(x - 3)$$

Possible pairs
1, 6, sum 7, reject
2, 3, sum 5, correct.

---

7 a $8 + x^2 + 9x$ **c** $11x + 28 + x^2$ **e** $9 + x^2 + 6x$

  b $9 + x^2 - 6x$ **d** $x - 20 + x^2$ **f** $8 + x^2 - 9x$

8 a $17x + 30 + x^2$ **c** $x^2 + 22 + 13x$ **e** $7 + x^2 - 8x$

  b $6x - 27 + x^2$ **d** $x^2 - 11x - 26$ **f** $x + x^2 - 42$

9 a $x^2 - 5x - 24$ **c** $28x + 27 + x^2$ **e** $x^2 - 27 - 6x$

  b $14 + x^2 - 9x$ **d** $2x - 63 + x^2$ **f** $48 - 16x + x^2$

Factorise $x^2 + 6x + 9$

If you cannot see the numbers required, write down all the pairs whose product is 9.

$$x^2 + 6x + 9 = (x + 3)(x + 3)$$
$$= (x + 3)^2$$

3, 3 or 1, 9

---

10 a $x^2 + 10x + 25$ **c** $x^2 + 12x + 36$ **e** $x^2 - 4x + 4$

  b $x^2 + 4x + 4$ **d** $x^2 + 18x + 81$ **f** $x^2 + 16x + 64$

11 a $x^2 - 10x + 25$ **c** $x^2 - 12x + 36$ **e** $x^2 + 8x + 16$

  b $x^2 - 14x + 49$ **d** $x^2 - 18x + 81$ **f** $x^2 - 6x + 9$

EXERCISE 15F

> Factorise $6 - 5x - x^2$
>
> > When the x^2 term is negative, the terms should be arranged: number term, then the x term and finally the x^2 term. This means that the x term appears at the end of each bracket but with different signs.
>
> $6 - 5x - x^2 = (6 + x)(1 - x)$
>
> Check: $(6 + x)(1 - x) = 6 + x - 6x - x^2$
>
> > 2, 3 or 1, 6

Factorise

1 **a** $2 - x - x^2$ **c** $4 - 3x - x^2$

    b $6 + x - x^2$ **d** $3 - 2x - x^2$

2 **a** $8 + 2x - x^2$ **c** $2 + x - x^2$

    b $6 - x - x^2$ **d** $8 - 7x - x^2$

3 **a** $8 - 2x - x^2$ **c** $12 + 4x - x^2$

    b $10 - 3x - x^2$ **d** $9 + 8x - x^2$

4 **a** $5 - 4x - x^2$ **c** $6 + 5x - x^2$

    b $14 - 5x - x^2$ **d** $10 + 9x - x^2$

5 **a** $20 - x - x^2$ **c** $12 + x - x^2$

    b $15 - 2x - x^2$ **d** $12 + 11x - x^2$

THE DIFFERENCE BETWEEN TWO SQUARES

In Chapter 8, one of the expansions we listed was

$$(x + a)(x - a) = x^2 - a^2$$

If we reverse this we have

$$x^2 - a^2 = (x - a)(x + a)$$

or $$x^2 - a^2 = (x + a)(x - a)$$

(The order of multiplication of two brackets makes no difference to the result.)

This result is known as *factorising the difference between two squares* and is very important.

When factorising do not confuse $x^2 - 4$ with $x^2 - 4x$.

$$x^2 - 4 = (x + 2)(x - 2)$$

whereas $$x^2 - 4x = x(x - 4)$$

> $4x$ is *not* a square.

EXERCISE 15G

Factorise $x^2 - 9$

$x^2 - 9 = x^2 - 3^2$

$\quad\quad = (x + 3)(x - 3)$ $\quad$ or $(x - 3)(x + 3)$

Factorise

1 a $x^2 - 25$ $\quad$ **b** $x^2 - 1$ $\quad$ **c** $x^2 - 36$ $\quad$ **d** $x^2 - 100$

2 a $x^2 - 4$ $\quad$ **b** $x^2 - 64$ $\quad$ **c** $x^2 - 81$ $\quad$ **d** $x^2 - 16$

3 a $x^2 - 49$ $\quad$ **b** $x^2 - 0.16$ $\quad$ **c** $x^2 - 0.04$ $\quad$ **d** $x^2 - 0.81$

Factorise $4 - x^2$

$4 - x^2 = 2^2 - x^2$

$\quad\quad = (2 + x)(2 - x)$ $\quad$ or $(2 - x)(2 + x)$

Factorise

4 a $9 - x^2$ $\quad$ **b** $a^2 - b^2$ $\quad$ **c** $25 - x^2$ $\quad$ **d** $100 - x^2$

5 a $36 - x^2$ $\quad$ **b** $9y^2 - z^2$ $\quad$ **c** $81 - x^2$ $\quad$ **d** $16 - x^2$

6 a $x^2 - y^2$ $\quad$ **b** $9x^2 - 16$ $\quad$ **c** $4a^2 - 25$ $\quad$ **d** $x^2 - y^2 z^2$

We began this chapter by considering common factors. A little revision
is now necessary followed by factorising expressions such as
$2x^2 - 8x - 10$ where 2 is a common factor.

EXERCISE 15H

Factorise $12x - 6$

$12x - 6 = 6(2x - 1)$

Factorise

1 a $3x + 12$ $\quad$ **b** $14x + 21$ $\quad$ **c** $9x^2 - 18x$ $\quad$ **d** $12x^2 - 8$

2 a $25x^2 + 10x$ $\quad$ **b** $4x^2 + 2$ $\quad$ **c** $20x + 12$ $\quad$ **d** $8x^2 - 4x$

Factorise completely $2x^2 - 8x - 10$

$2x^2 - 8x - 10 = 2(x^2 - 4x - 5)$
$= 2(x - 5)(x + 1)$

Now check to see if the quadratic expression factorises.

Factorise completely

3 a $3x^2 + 12x + 9$ **b** $2x^2 - 18x + 28$ **c** $5x^2 - 15x - 50$

4 a $4x^2 - 24x + 20$ **b** $4x^2 + 8x - 32$ **c** $3x^2 + 18x + 24$

5 a $3x^2 - 12$ **b** $5x^2 - 45$ **c** $3x^2 - 12x - 63$

6 a $6x^2 - 6x - 12$ **b** $18 - 3x - 3x^2$ **c** $2x^2 - 32$

7 a $4x^2 + 4x - 24$ **b** $3x^2 + 6x - 24$ **c** $3x^2 - 3x - 36$

CALCULATIONS

EXERCISE 15I   **Do not use a calculator for this exercise.**

Find $1.7^2 + 0.3 \times 1.7$

$1.7^2 + 0.3 \times 1.7 = 1.7(1.7 + 0.3)$
$= 1.7 \times 2 = 3.4$

$1.7^2 + 0.3 \times 1.7$
$= 1.7 \times 1.7 + 1.7 \times 0.3$

Find

1 a $2.5^2 + 0.5 \times 2.5$ **b** $5.2^2 + 0.8 \times 5.2$ **c** $5.9^2 - 2.9 \times 5.9$

2 a $1.3 \times 3.7 + 3.7^2$ **b** $2.6 \times 3.4 + 3.4^2$ **c** $4.3^2 - 1.3 \times 4.3$

Find $100^2 - 98^2$ $100^2 - 98^2$ is equivalent to $a^2 - b^2$

$100^2 - 98^2 = (100 + 98)(100 - 98)$
$= 198 \times 2 = 396$

3 Find

a $55^2 - 45^2$ **b** $10.2^2 - 9.8^2$ **c** $20.6^2 - 9.4^2$ **d** $13.5^2 - 6.5^2$

4 Find

    a $7.82^2 - 2.82^2$ **c** $8.79^2 - 1.21^2$

    b $2.667^2 - 1.333^2$ **d** $0.763^2 - 0.237^2$

MIXED QUADRATIC EXPRESSIONS

Some quadratic expressions such as $x^2 + 9$ and $x^2 + 3x + 1$ will not factorise. The next exercise includes some expressions that will not factorise.

EXERCISE 15J

Do not use a calculator for this exercise.
Factorise where it is possible; where it is not possible write NP.

1 **a** $x^2 + 13x + 40$ **c** $x^2 - 8x + 12$ **e** $x^2 - 36$
   b $x^2 - 11x + 18$ **d** $x^2 - 11x - 10$ **f** $x^2 + 4$

2 **a** $x^2 - 11x + 24$ **c** $x^2 + 8x + 12$ **e** $x^2 + 6x - 7$
   b $x^2 + 11x + 12$ **d** $x^2 - x - 30$ **f** $x^2 + 13x - 30$

3 **a** $x^2 + 14x - 15$ **c** $x^2 - 49$ **e** $x^2 - 7x - 10$
   b $28 - 12x - x^2$ **d** $x^2 - 7x + 2$ **f** $x^2 + 13x + 42$

4 **a** $x^2 - 9$ **c** $a^2 - 16a + 63$ **e** $x^2 + 13x - 68$
   b $x^2 - 10x + 24$ **d** $28 + 3x - x^2$ **f** $x^2 + 11x - 26$

5 **a** $x^2 + 9x + 7$ **c** $24 - 5x - x^2$ **e** $x^2 + x - 110$
   b $x^2 - 12x + 35$ **d** $x^2 - 10x - 9$ **f** $25 - x^2$

MIXED EXERCISE

Do not use a calculator for this exercise.

EXERCISE 15K

Factorise

1 **a** $10a + 20$ **c** $15p^2 - 10p$ **e** $8z^3 - 4z^2$
   b $4ab - 8bc$ **d** $5b^2 + 15b - 5$ **f** $x^2 - 6x - 27$

2 **a** $a^2 + 9a + 18$ **c** $x^2 - 7x - 8$ **e** $x^2 + 12x + 35$
   b $21 + 10x + x^2$ **d** $10 - 7x + x^2$ **f** $a^2 - 6a - 27$

3 **a** $a^2 - 36$ **c** $16 - x^2$ **e** $7x - 8 + x^2$
   b $12z^2 - 6z$ **d** $8xy - 12yz$ **f** $5xy - 20yz$

4 a $x^2 + 10x + 25$ **c** $x^2 - 2x - 24$ **e** $7a - a^2$

b $a^2 + a - 6$ **d** $x^2 + 7x - 44$ **f** $2a^2 - 6a - 8$

5 a $b^2 - 49$ **c** $16p^2 - p$ **e** $x^2 - 9$

b $30 - 17x + x^2$ **d** $12 - x - x^2$ **f** $a^2 - 14a + 49$

Find

6 a $13.2 \times 6.8 + 13.2^2$ **b** $7.38^2 - 2.38 \times 7.38$

7 a $4.92^2 + 5.08 \times 4.92$ **b** $6.09^2 - 1.09 \times 6.09$

8 a $0.553^2 - 0.447^2$ **b** $997^2 - 797^2$

9 a $10.3^2 - 9.7^2$ **b** $0.643^2 - 0.357^2$

10 a $3.7^2 + 1.3 \times 3.7$ **b** $7.7 \times 2.3 + 2.3^2$

11 a $101^2 - 99^2$ **b** $5.21^2 - 4.79^2$

INVESTIGATION

Using the digits 3 and 6 it is possible to make two two-digit numbers, namely 36 and 63.

The difference between the squares of these two numbers is

$$63^2 - 36^2 = 2673$$
$$= 99 \times 27$$
$$= 99 \times 9 \times 3$$
$$= 99 \times (\text{ the sum of the original digits })$$
$$\times (\text{ the difference between the original digits })$$

Try this on some other pairs of digits. What do you notice?

Now suppose that the two digits you start with are x and y. Write down the two numbers in terms of x and y (They are not xy and yx!)

Write, in terms of x and y, the difference between the squares of the two numbers.

Use the knowledge you have gained from this chapter to prove that this will always give you

$99 \times (\text{ the sum of the original digits })$
$\times (\text{ the difference between the original digits })$

FRACTIONAL AND PERCENTAGE CHANGE

16

Ben Oakham is a buyer in the men's department of a large store. He buys a batch of shirts from a manufacturer for £11.50 each. His normal practice is to add a mark-up of 50%, and then value added tax (VAT) at $17\frac{1}{2}$% has to be added to give the selling price.

$$\text{Cost of shirt} = £11.50$$
$$\text{Mark-up at 50\% is } 0.5 \times £11.50 = £5.75$$

Therefore selling price (excluding VAT) is

$$£11.50 + £5.75 = £17.25$$
$$\text{VAT at } 17\frac{1}{2} \text{ is } 0.175 \times £17.25 = £3.02$$

(to nearest penny)

∴ selling price to the customer is £17.25 + £3.02 = £20.27

He wants to keep the price of the shirt under £20, so decides to sell it at £19.95 including VAT. This means that the amount of VAT to be added has changed.

- Ben needs to work out how much of the £19.95 is VAT, because he will have to pass this amount on to Customs and Excise. He must be able to work backwards to find the amount of value added tax included in the price of £19.95.

To do these calculations he needs to increase his knowledge of percentages.

EXERCISE 16A   Discuss what you need to be able to do to deal with the following situations.

1   It is rumoured that when Sitco & Sons is taken over, the workforce will be cut by $\frac{1}{3}$ during the first year but after that it should expand by $\frac{1}{10}$ each year for the next four years. The local authority would like to know whether the workforce will then be larger or smaller than it is now.

2   The total number of a certain species of bird in the United Kingdom is estimated to be 5000 pairs. It is believed that this number is decreasing at the rate of 5% a year. The RSPB would like to find out how many years it will take before the population drops below 2000 pairs.

Discussion of the above situations shows that, when dealing with a variety of problems involving fractions and percentages, it is very important to have a clear understanding of *what the fraction or percentage is of.*

> A fractional or percentage change is always a fraction or percentage of the original quantity,
> i.e. the quantity *before* any changes are made.

FRACTIONAL CHANGE

First we consider problems involving fractional changes. You will need to be able to work with fractions for this exercise. If you need reminding how to do this, look at Summary 1, page 3 and Revision Exercise 1.2 for practice.

EXERCISE 16B

Do not use a calculator for this exercise.

In an auction a car makes $\frac{2}{5}$ more than its reserve price. If the reserve price is £3400, calculate the selling price of the car.

Selling price of car = reserve price + $\frac{2}{5}$ of the reserve price

$$= \tfrac{7}{5} \text{ of the reserve price} \quad \left(1 + \tfrac{2}{5} = \tfrac{5}{5} + \tfrac{2}{5} = \tfrac{7}{5} \right)$$

But the reserve price is £3400

$$\therefore \quad \text{selling price of the car is } \ \tfrac{7}{5} \times \text{£}3400 = \text{£}\frac{7}{\cancel{5}} \times \frac{\cancel{3400}^{680}}{1}$$

$$= \text{£}7 \times 680$$

$$= \text{£}4760$$

1   Lou got 60 marks in a test. He was told that he needed $\frac{1}{3}$ more than this to reach the pass mark.

a   By how many marks was Lou short of a pass?

b   What was the pass mark?

2 Lyn Perry estimates that it should cost about £750 to repair his roof. The builder tells him that it will cost at least $\frac{1}{4}$ more than this. What does the builder estimate the cost of the repair to be?

3 The stadium at Castrey has 1255 seats. The council decide to improve the capacity by increasing the number of seats by $\frac{3}{5}$. How many seats will there be in the stadium after the improvement?

4 Production at Stepco Industries is expected to increase by $\frac{1}{8}$ over the next year. At present they produce 1840 units a week. What should the weekly production be next year if the target is to be met?

A radio casette recorder cost £45.60 when new. During its first year it loses $\frac{3}{8}$ of its value. Calculate its value when it is one year old.

Value after 1 year = value when new $- \frac{3}{8}$ value when new

$\qquad\qquad = \frac{5}{8}$ value when new $\quad \left(1 - \frac{3}{8} = \frac{5}{8} \right)$

$\qquad\qquad = \frac{5}{8} \times £45.60$

$\qquad\qquad = £\dfrac{5}{\cancel{8}} \times \dfrac{\overset{5.7}{\cancel{45.60}}}{1}$

$\qquad\qquad = £28.50$

---

5 Dave proposes to reduce his electricity bill by $\frac{1}{8}$. His last bill was £328. What does he hope his next bill will be?

6 When a writer has completed a book she finds that it comes to 360 pages. Her publisher tells her that she must cut the length by $\frac{1}{6}$. Find the maximum number of pages acceptable to the publisher.

7 A bicycle costing £144 loses $\frac{1}{4}$ of its value in the first year. How much is it worth when it is one year old?

8 Records show that the average daily number of customers kept waiting for more than 2 minutes at a branch of the Redfern Building Society is 40. They wish to reduce this figure by $\frac{3}{4}$. What number do they aim to get it down to?

9 A farmer has a herd of 65 cattle and a flock of 300 sheep. He proposes to reduce his herd by $\frac{1}{5}$ but to increase his flock by the same fraction. How many cattle and how many sheep will the farmer have if he goes ahead with the proposal? Will the total number of animals change and, if so, by how many?

10 Three-fifths of the selling price of a TV set goes to the manufacturer, $\frac{3}{10}$ to the retailer and the remainder to the distributor. A television set sells for £425.

    a How much does the manufacturer receive?

    b How much goes to the distributor?

    c If the amount the manufacturer receives is reduced by $\frac{1}{10}$, and the money saved is then divided equally between the retailer and the distributor, find

      i the amount the retailer now receives

     ii the fraction by which the distributor's share increases.

The number of units failing to pass a quality test at a factory was reduced from 35 to 25. By what fraction did the number of failures change?

The number of failures reduced from 35 to 25 i.e. it reduced by 10

$$\textbf{Fraction by which the number of failures decreased} = \frac{\textbf{decrease}}{\textbf{original number}}$$

Remember that the fractional decrease is the decrease as a fraction of the original number.

$$= \frac{\overset{2}{\cancel{10}}}{\underset{7}{\cancel{35}}}$$

$$= \tfrac{2}{7}$$

∴   **the number of failures decreased by $\frac{2}{7}$.**

In questions **11** to **15** find the fractional change in the quantities referred to. In each case say whether the change is an increase or a decrease.

11 In 1996 there were 85 serious accidents in Naxborough; while in 1997 there were 65.

12 In the test last week Penny scored 48 marks out of 80, but this week she has scored 64 out of 80.

13 At the last count there were 800 pairs of oyster-catchers on an island. Now there are 1000 pairs.

14 Last year a youth club had 84 members. This year there are 77 members.

15 The census of 1990 showed that the population of Overtown was 2464. The latest count shows that it is 2912.

PERCENTAGE INCREASE AND PERCENTAGE DECREASE

Percentage increase or decrease occurs in many different aspects of life. We may read that certain workers are to receive an increase of 4% in their wages; that value added tax (VAT) on fuel has been reduced from $17\frac{1}{2}$% to 5%; that the lowest rate of income tax is to fall from 20% to 10%; or that all the items in a sale are offered at a discount of 20%.

Changes are always expressed *as a percentage of the quantity before the changes are made*.

If a wage of £100 per week increases by 4%, the increase is 4% of £100 so the new wage is $(100 + 4)$% of £100

i.e. $\quad$ 104% of £100 $= 1.04 \times £100$
$$= £104$$

If an article costs £55 plus VAT at $17\frac{1}{2}$%, then the full cost is $(100 + 17\frac{1}{2})$% of £55

i.e. $\quad 117\frac{1}{2}$% of £55 $= 1.175 \times £55$
$$= £64.63 \ (\text{correct to the nearest penny})$$

If a woman has to pay tax on earnings of £556 at 20% she actually receives $(100 - 20)$% of £556, that is, 80% of £556.

$$80\% \text{ of } £556 = 0.8 \times £556$$
$$= £444.80$$

If a discount of 33% is offered in a sale, a piece of furniture originally marked at £750 will cost

$$(100 - 33)\%, \text{ i.e. } 67\% \text{ of } £750 = 0.67 \times £750$$
$$= £502.50$$

Retailers buy-in goods which are usually sold at an increased price. The increase is often called the *mark-up* and is given as a percentage of the buying-in price. Occasionally goods are sold at a decreased price, that is they are sold at a loss. The loss is also given as a percentage of the buying-in price.

If a store applies a mark-up of 50% to an article it buys for £100, its mark-up is

$$50\% \text{ of } £100 = 0.5 \times £100 = £50$$

and the selling price is 150% of $£100 = 1.5 \times £100 = £150$

You will need to remember how to work with percentages for the following exercises. You can revise this by turning to Summary 1 on page 7 and to Revision Exercise 1.3 on page 24.

EXERCISE 16C

A second-hand car dealer bought a car for £3500 and sold it for £4340. Find his percentage mark-up.

$$\text{Mark-up} = \text{selling price} - \text{buying price}$$
$$= £4340 - £3500 = £840$$

> Remember, percentage mark-up is the mark-up expressed as a percentage of the buying-in price.

$$\% \text{ mark-up} = \frac{\text{mark-up}}{\text{buying-in price}} \times 100$$

$$= \frac{£840}{£3500} \times 100 = 24$$

Therefore the mark-up is 24%.

1 Find the percentage mark-up.

   a Buying-in price £12, mark-up £3

   b Buying-in price £28, mark-up £8.40

   c Buying-in price £16, mark-up £4

A retailer bought a leather chair for £375 and sold it for £285. Find her percentage loss.

$$\text{Loss} = \text{buying-in price} - \text{selling price}$$
$$= £375 - £285 = £90$$

> Percentage loss is the loss as a percentage of the buying-in price.

$$\% \text{ loss} = \frac{\text{loss}}{\text{buying-in price}} \times 100$$

$$= \frac{£90}{£375} \times 100 = 24$$

Therefore the loss is 24%.

2 Find the percentage loss.

   a Buying-in price £20, loss £4

   b Buying-in price £125, loss £25

   c Buying-in price £64, loss £9.60

An article costing £30 is sold at a gain of 25%. Find the selling price.

The selling price is $(100\% + 25\%)$ of £30

$$= 125\% \text{ of } £30$$
$$= 1.25 \times £30 = £37.50$$

Therefore the selling price is £37.50

> Alternatively, we can find the gain, which is 25% of the original cost, and add this to the original cost.
>
> Gain $= 25\%$ of £30 $= 0.25 \times £30 = £7.50$
>
> Selling price $= £30 + £7.50 = £37.50$

3 Find the selling price.

   a Cost £50, gain 12%   **c** Cost £4.96, gain $12\frac{1}{2}\%$ **e** Cost £75, loss 64%

   b Cost £64, gain 122%   **d** Cost £36, loss 50%   **f** Cost £6.40, loss $2\frac{1}{2}\%$

4 Find the weekly cash increase for each of the following employees.

   a Ian Dickenson earning £120 per week receives a rise of 10%.

   b Lyn Wyman earning £270 per week receives a rise of 9%.

   c Joe Bright earning £300 per week receives a rise of 7%.

5 In this question, which is the better cash pay rise, and by how much?

   a 12% on a weekly pay of £100, or 8% on a weekly pay of £250

   b 7% on a weekly pay of £90, or $3\frac{1}{2}\%$ on a weekly pay of £200

In real-life situations the numbers are often more complicated than those we have used so far.

   a Peter earns £287.50 a week and gets a rise of 4.67%. Find his new weekly wage.

   b A table bought by a retailer for £166 is sold at a loss of $16\frac{2}{3}\%$. Find its selling price correct to the nearest pound.

a New wage is 100% of original wage $+ 4.67\%$ of original wage

$$= 104.67\% \text{ of original wage}$$
$$= 1.0467 \times £287.50 = £300.926\ldots$$

i.e. Peter's new wage is £300.93 correct to the nearest penny.

b Selling price is 100% of £166 $- 16\frac{2}{3}\%$ of £166

$$= 83\frac{1}{3}\% \text{ of } £166$$
$$= 83.33\ldots\% \text{ of } £166$$

> Express $83\frac{1}{3}$ as a decimal;
>
> $\frac{1}{3} = 0.33\ldots$ $\therefore$ $83\frac{1}{3} = 83.33\ldots$

$$= 0.8333 \times £166 = £138.33\ldots$$

i.e. selling price of the table is £138 correct to the nearest £.

6 Find the selling price. Give answers as accurately as you think are appropriate.

a Cost £639, loss $33\frac{1}{3}$% **c** Cost £18.65, gain $7\frac{5}{7}$%

b Cost £345.70, gain 8.35% **d** Cost £216, gain $66\frac{2}{3}$%

7 Find the weekly cash increase for each employee.

a Alma Fidler earning £347 per week receives a rise of 4.25%.

b Sue Edgar earning £293 per week receives a rise of 3.47%.

8 Which is the better cash pay rise, and by how much?

a 3.45% on a wage of £240, or 2.84% on a wage of £286

b 2.88% on a wage of £258.90 or 3.37% on a wage of £188.60

9 A t-shirt that was selling for £14.50 is marked down in a sale to £10.99. What percentage reduction is this? Give your answer to the appropriate degree of accuracy.

10 Mr & Mrs Exall bought a house for £96 000 in 1996 and sold it in 1997 at a loss of $12\frac{1}{2}$%.

a How much did they lose on the deal?

b What did they sell the house for?

11 On Monday last week 916 lunches were served at Lumsden Comprehensive School. On Monday of this week 854 lunches were served. Find the percentage decrease. Give your answer to an appropriate degree of accuracy.

12 Gary Clare's event is the discus. In his first competition of the season he throws 50.54 m. He hopes that he can improve this distance by 4% by the end of the season.

a What distance is he aiming at?

b By the end of the season his best throw was 52.31 m. By what percentage had he improved? Did he succeed in reaching his goal?

FINDING THE ORIGINAL QUANTITY

Sometimes we are given an increased or decreased quantity and we want to find the original quantity. For example, if the cost of a chair including VAT at $17\frac{1}{2}$% is £176.25, we might need to find the price of the chair before the VAT was added.

EXERCISE 16D

An article is sold for £252. If this includes a mark-up of 5% find the buying-in price.

> Remember that the mark-up is 5% of the buying-in price.
> We do not know the buying-in price, so we call it £x.

There is a mark-up of 5% so selling price = 105% of the buying-in price

$$= 1.05 \times \text{buying-in price}$$

If the buying-in price is £x then $252 = 1.05 \times x$

> Divide both sides by 1.05.

$$\frac{252}{1.05} = x \quad \text{giving} \quad 240 = x$$

Therefore the buying-in price is £240.

In questions **1** to **3**, selling price is abbreviated to SP. Find the buying-in price.

1 **a** SP £98, mark-up 40%   **c** SP £12, mark-up 100%   **e** SP £1008, mark-up 125%

  b SP £28, mark-up 75%   **d** SP £40, mark-up 25%   **f** SP £84.80, mark-up 112%

A CD is sold for £6.08. This includes a mark-up of $33\frac{1}{3}$%. Find the buying-in price.

The mark-up is $33\frac{1}{3}$%

Selling Price = $133\frac{1}{3}$% of the buying-in price

$\qquad\qquad$ = $133.33\ldots$ % of the buying-in price

> Convert $133\frac{1}{3}$ to a decimal.

$\qquad\qquad$ = $1.3333\ldots$ of the buying-in price

The buying-in price is £x so $6.08 = 1.3333\ldots \times x$

> Divide both sides by 1.3333...

i.e. $\quad \dfrac{6.08}{1.3333\ldots} = x$ which gives $x = 4.56$

∴ the buying-in price of the CD was £4.56.

2 Find the buying-in price.

  a SP £21.50, mark-up $7\frac{1}{2}$%

  b SP £284.40, mark-up $18\frac{1}{2}$%

  c SP £9.60, mark-up $66\frac{2}{3}$%

  d SP £99, mark-up $37\frac{1}{2}$%

  e SP £54, mark-up $12\frac{1}{2}$%

  f SP £816, mark-up $13\frac{1}{3}$%

A book is sold for £6.30 at a loss of 30%. Find the buying-in price.

> The loss of 30% is 30% of the buying-in price, so the selling price is (100% − 30%) i.e. 70% of the buying-in price.

Selling price = 70% of the buying-in price

Then, if the buying-in price is £x, 6.30 = 70% of x

$$6.3 = 0.7 \times x$$

∴ $$6.3 \div 0.7 = x \quad \text{i.e.} \quad x = 9$$

The buying-in price of the book is £9.

3 Find the buying-in price.

   a SP £30, loss 25%   **c** SP £45, loss 10%   **e** SP £1200, loss 40%

   b SP £56, loss 30%   **d** SP £120, loss 25%   **f** SP £128, loss $33\frac{1}{3}$%

After a pay rise of 5% Edna's weekly pay is £126. How much did she earn before the rise ?

> The 5% pay rise is 5% of Edna's original pay, so her new pay will be (100% + 5%), i.e. 105% of her original pay.

If Edna's original pay was £x

then   126 = 105% of x

             126 = 1.05 × x

i.e. $x = \dfrac{126}{1.05} = 120$

Edna's original weekly pay was £120.

4 The following table shows the weekly wage of a number of employees after percentage increases as shown. Find the original weekly wage of each employee.

	Name	% increase in pay	Weekly wage after increase
a	George Black	10%	£132
b	John Rowlands	15%	£299
c	Beryl Lewis	7%	£196.88

> The purchase price of a watch is £70.50. If this includes VAT at $17\frac{1}{2}\%$, find the price before VAT was added.
>
> > VAT is a percentage of the price before VAT has been added so
> > purchase price $= (100\% + 17\frac{1}{2}\%)$ i.e. 117.5% of the price before VAT is added.
>
> **If the price of the watch before VAT is added is £C**
>
> then $\quad 1.175 \times C = 70.5$
>
> i.e. $\quad\quad\quad C = 70.5 \div 1.175$
>
> $\quad\quad\quad\quad = 60$
>
> **The price before VAT was added was £60.**

5 The purchase price of a hairdryer is £13.80. If this includes VAT at 15%, find the price before VAT was added.

6 I paid £763.75 for a dining table and four chairs. If the price includes VAT at $17\frac{1}{2}\%$ find the price before VAT was added.

7 John's income last week was £112 after deductions that totalled 30% of his income. Calculate his income before deductions.

8 Water increases in volume by 4% when frozen. How much water is needed to make $884\,\text{cm}^3$ of ice?

9 The stretched length of an elastic string is 31 cm. If this is 24% more than its unstretched length, find its unstretched length.

10 Jean sold her house for £112 000 which was 40% more than she paid for it. How much did Jean pay for her house?

11 Dave paid £141 for a CD player. This included VAT at $17\frac{1}{2}\%$. What was the price before VAT was added?

12 The returns for the furniture factory where Alex works show that 2599 units were produced in October. This was 8% less than the number of units produced in September. How many units were produced in September?

USING FRACTIONS

Changes are often expressed in fractions rather than percentages.

EXERCISE 16E

Do not use a calculator in this exercise.

The value of an antique plate increased by $\frac{1}{4}$ of the price I paid for it. It is now worth £60. How much did I pay for it?

The increase in price $= \frac{1}{4}$ of original price

$\therefore$ current price $=$ original price $+ \frac{1}{4}$ of the original price

$\qquad\qquad = 1\frac{1}{4}$ of original price

If the price I paid for it is £x

$\qquad 60 = 1\frac{1}{4} \times x$

$\therefore \qquad x = 60 \div 1\frac{1}{4}$ ┌ Turn $1\frac{1}{4}$ into an improper fraction. ┐

$\qquad\quad = 60 \div \frac{5}{4}$

$\qquad\quad = \frac{\overset{12}{\cancel{60}}}{1} \times \frac{4}{\cancel{5}_1}$ ┌ To divide by a fraction turn it upside down and multiply. ┐

$\qquad\quad = 48$

I paid **£48** for the plate.

---

1 The number of people belonging to a youth group has increased by $\frac{1}{8}$ during the last year. At present there are 45 members. How many members were there a year ago?

2 In a sale all the dresses on a rail were marked '$\frac{1}{3}$ off'. I paid £40 for a winter dress. What was the price of the dress before the reduction?

3 Nevets and Co. have a workforce of 117. This is half as many again as the workforce was two years ago. What was the workforce then?

4 The value of my camera has decreased by $\frac{2}{5}$ since I bought it. Its estimated value now is £210. What did I pay for it?

5 John's investments have increased by $\frac{3}{5}$ over the last five years. His investments now are worth £7200. What were they worth five years ago?

6 The number of coaches owned by a coach company has increased by $\frac{3}{4}$ since it was formed three years ago. They have 70 coaches now. How many did they have when they were formed?

7 My motorbike has decreased in value by $\frac{2}{3}$ since I bought it two years ago. It is now worth £600. What did I pay for it?

8 Sally collects old postcards and has 426. This is an increase of one-fifth on the number she had two years ago. How many postcards did Sally have two years ago?

MIXED PROBLEMS INVOLVING INCREASE AND DECREASE

Remember that a percentage increase or decrease is always calculated as a percentage of the quantity before the change. Questions that ask you to find the original quantity, for example question **4** below, can be checked by using your answer to work through the given information.

EXERCISE 16F

1 A house is bought for £68 000 and sold at a profit of 14%. Find the selling price.

2 Carpets that had been bought for £18.50 per square metre were sold at a loss of 26%. Find the selling price per square metre.

3 Potatoes bought at £4.50 per 50 kg bag are sold at 12 p per kg. Find the percentage profit.

4 An art dealer sold a picture for £1980 thereby making $\frac{1}{3}$ profit. What did she pay for it?

5 My present average weekly grocery bill is £40.50, which is 8% more than the same goods cost me, on average, each week last year. What was my average weekly grocery bill last year?

6 Between two elections the size of the electorate in a constituency fell by one eighth. For the second election, 37 191 people were entitled to vote. How many could have voted at the first election?

7 If Terry begins his journey after 9 a.m. he is allowed a discount of 30% on the cost of his rail ticket. He pays £22.75 for a ticket to London, leaving on the 9.15 a.m. train.

   a Express the discounted price as a percentage of the full price.

   b Calculate the cost of the ticket before deducting the discount.

8 A camera bought for £300 loses $\frac{2}{5}$ of its value in the first year.

 a What is it worth when it is one year old?

 b Express its value after one year as a percentage of the amount by which it has depreciated.

9 Andrew Bullen received £955 pay last month. This sum was made up of a fixed basic wage of £245 plus commission at 2% on the value of the goods he had sold in the previous month. Find the value of the sales Andrew made last month.

10 In a sale at a department store the price of a tea set is reduced by $\frac{1}{8}$. The sale price is £61.25. Find

 a the pre-sale price   **b** the discount.

INTEREST

Many organisations, for example banks and building societies, offer savings accounts. If you put money into such an account (this is called investing), the bank uses your money for other purposes and pays you for that use. The amount that the bank pays for the use of the money is called *interest*.

On the other hand the time may come when you wish to use someone else's money to buy an expensive item such as a car or even a house. You will normally have to pay for the use of borrowed money, that is you will have to repay more than you borrow. The extra you pay is called *interest*.
Interest on money borrowed (or lent) is usually a percentage of the sum borrowed (or lent). This percentage is often given as a charge per year (per annum, or p.a.) and it is then called the *interest rate*.
For example, if £100 is put into a bank account with an interest rate of 5% p.a., then after one year, the bank pays interest of

5% of £100, i.e. £5

EXERCISE 16G

1 Pam is given £500 for her 18th birthday. She puts the money into a savings account with an interest rate of 6% p.a. How much is added to her account after one year?

2 Ann Crawshay is given a loan of £650 from the bank which she agrees to repay after one year. How much does she have to repay if the rate of interest is $12\frac{1}{2}$% p.a.?

3 Find the interest payable after one year on each of the following sums of money invested (i.e. put in a savings account) at the given rate of interest. If any answers are not exact give them correct to the nearest penny.

a £500 at 4% p.a.   **c** £352 at 7.5% p.a.   **e** £10 000 at 4.25% p.a.

b £750 at 7% p.a.   **d** £740 at 4.56% p.a.   **f** £2600 at 8.3% p.a.

What annual rate of interest is necessary to give interest of £45.60 after one year on an investment of £760 ?

We do not know the rate of interest so we will call it r%

Then   interest = r% × amount invested

$$= \frac{r}{100} \times \text{amount invested}$$

> To convert a % into a fraction divide the % by 100.

i.e. $45.60 = \frac{r}{100} \times 760$

$$4560 = 760r$$

> Multiply both sides by 100.

$$\frac{4560}{760} = r$$

> Divide both sides by 760.

$$6 = r$$

∴   **the annual rate of interest is 6%.**

---

4 What annual rate of interest is necessary to give interest of

   a £238 after one year on an investment of £2800

   b £31.20 after one year on an investment of £600

5 What is the original size of a loan that costs £45 when repaid after one year when the interest rate is 9% p.a. ?

6 Find the original sum borrowed if £287.50 has to be repaid after one year when the interest rate is 15%.

7 Mr & Mrs Surefoot invest a sum of money in a deposit account with the Highway Bank. The bank quotes a gross rate of 8% but deducts income tax at 20% from the gross interest before adding the net interest to the account. One year after the investment was made to the account net interest of £800 was added. Find

   a the gross interest paid by the bank

   b the amount of money invested.

COMPOUND INCREASE AND DECREASE

There are many occasions when a percentage increase or decrease happens more than once. Suppose that a house is bought for £50 000 and increases in value (appreciates) by 10% of its value each year. After one year, its value will be 110% of its initial value,

i.e.   110% of £50 000 = 1.1 × £50 000 = £55 000

The next year it will increase by 10% of the £55 000 it was worth at the beginning of the year, so its value after two years will be

110% of £55 000 = 1.1 × £55 000 = £60 500

While some things go up in value year after year, many things decrease in value (depreciate) each year. Should you buy a motorcycle or car it will probably depreciate in value more quickly than anything else you buy. If you invest money in a bank or Post Office Savings Account and spend the interest each year as it is paid, the amount in the account will not change and the amount of interest you receive each year will remain the same. This kind of interest is called *simple interest*.

If however, you do not spend the interest but add it to the amount in the account, your money will increase by larger and larger amounts each year if the interest rate stays the same. This kind of interest is called *compound interest*. The sum on which the interest is calculated is called the *principal* and changes each year.

EXERCISE 16H

Find the compound interest on £260.60 invested for 2 years at 8% p.a.

Interest for the first year is 8% of the original principal.
New principal at the end of the first year

= 100% of original principal + 8% of original principal
= 108% of the original principal
= 1.08 × original principal.

∴   **principal at end of first year = 1.08 × £260.60 = £281.448**

> Use all available figures when an intermediate calculation does not work out exactly.

Similarly, new principal at end of second year

= 108% of the principal at the beginning of the second year
= 1.08 × £281.448 = £303.963 . . .

∴   **principal at end of second year = £303.96 correct to the nearest penny.**

i.e. compound interest on £260.60 for 2 years at 8% p.a.

= principal at end of second year − original principal
= £303.96 − £260.60 = £43.36 (correct to the nearest penny)

1 In this question give all answers that are not exact correct to the nearest penny. Find the compound interest on

a £200 for 2 years at 10% p.a.

b £300 for 2 years at 12% p.a.

c £400 for 3 years at 8% p.a.

d £650 for 3 years at 9% p.a.

e £520 for 2 years at 13% p.a.

f £376 for 3 years at 5.4% p.a.

2 A house is bought for £60 000 and appreciates at 8% a year. What will it be worth in 2 years' time?

3 A particular postage stamp increases in value by 15% each year. If it is bought for £50, what will it be worth in 3 years' time?

4 The toll for a car to cross a bridge is £4.50. It is intended to increase this toll by 5% a year, but to round each new amount down to the nearest 5 p. How much will it cost for a car to cross the bridge

a after the second increase

b after the third increase?

5 The number of telephones in Bishton is 4256 now but is likely to increase by 3% a year. Estimate the number of telephones there will be in Bishton in 3 years' time.

A hi-fi system costing £750 decreases in value by 12% a year. Find its value after 3 years. By what percentage does the value of the hi-fi system depreciate over 3 years?

Value of hi-fi system after 1 year

= 100% of the original value − 12% of the original value

= 88% of the original value

∴ value of hi-fi system after 1 year = 0.88 × £750 = £660

after 2 years = 0.88 × £660 = £580.80

after 3 years = 0.88 × £580.80

= £511.10 (to the nearest penny)

Decrease in value over 3 years = £750 − £511.10 = £238.90

Percentage decrease = $\dfrac{\text{decrease}}{\text{original value}} \times 100$

$= \dfrac{£238.90}{£750} \times 100 = 31.85\ldots\ldots$

∴ the hi-fi system decreases in value by 32% (correct to the nearest whole number)

Remember to use all the available figures when an intermediate calculation does not work out exactly.

6 Three years ago David and Charles each invested £30 000. David put his money into shares in a drug company while Charles invested his money in a spectacular car. The value of the car depreciated by 20% a year while shares in the drug company appreciated by 20% a year. Find the value of each investment now.

7 A new car costing £15 000 depreciated in value each year by 18% of its value at the beginning of that year.

a Find its value   **i** after 1 year   **ii** after 4 years.

b Calculate the percentage decrease in the value of the car over 4 years. (Give your answer correct to 1 decimal place.)

8 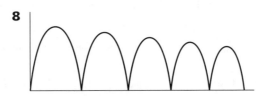 When a ball is dropped, the height of each bounce is 10% less than the height of the previous one.

If the first bounce was to a height of 150 cm, how high did the ball bounce   **a** the second time   **b** the fourth time?

9 The value of a lorry now is £30 000. It is estimated that it will lose 15% of its value in the first year and 10% every year thereafter. Estimate the value of the lorry

a at the end of this year   **b** in three years' time.

10 This September a computer system in a school is valued at £50 000. By next September it is estimated that it will have lost 30% of its value and after that it will then lose 20% of its value from one September to the next. Estimate the value of this computer system

a next September   **b** in September in 4 years' time.

11 In the state of Troika the current amount that a person can earn each year without having to pay income tax is £3500. This amount, rounded up to the nearest £10, is set to increase in line with inflation, the expected rates of which are given in the table.

Number of years from now	1	2	3	4	5
Expected rate of inflation for that year	3%	2.5%	4.5%	6.8%	8.3%

Use these values to find the tax-free amount a single person can earn in   **a** 3 years' time   **b** 5 years' time.

The population of Upton has increased by 4% a year for the last 3 years. If the present population of Upton is 15 000 estimate what the population of Upton was

a 1 year ago   **b** 2 years ago.   (Give your answers correct to the nearest 100.)

a If the population increases by 4% each year
the population this year = 1.04 × the population last year

Hence the population one year ago = the population this year ÷ 1.04

$$= 15\,000 \div 1.04$$

$$= 14\,423.0\ldots \quad \boxed{\text{Leave this number in the display.}}$$

$$= 14\,400\ (\text{to the nearest } 100)$$

b Similarly, population 2 years ago = population 1 year ago ÷ 1.04

$$= 14\,423.0\ldots \div 1.04$$

$$= 13\,868.3\ldots \quad \boxed{\begin{array}{l}\text{Using the value in the display}\\ \text{after finding } 15\,000 \div 1.04\\ \text{and not the corrected value.}\end{array}}$$

$$= 13\,900\ (\text{to the nearest } 100)$$

12 The population of Roxley has increased by 5.5% a year for the last 5 years. The present population of Roxley is 20 000.
Find the population of Roxley   **a** 1 year ago   **b** 2 years ago.

13 The number of hens at Blackwater Poultry Farm has increased by 25% a year for the last four years. At present there are 15 625 hens at the farm.
How many hens did they have   **a** 1 year ago   **b** 3 years ago?

14 The rabbit population of Ditcher's Heath has increased by 20% a year for the last 3 years. The estimated population now is 400 rabbits.

a Estimate, to the nearest 5, how many rabbits were on the heath

i 1 year ago   **ii** 2 years ago   **iii** 3 years ago.

b State whether each of the following statements is true or false ?

A Every year the increase in the number of rabbits is more than the increase was the year before.

B The increase in the number of rabbits is the same every year.

C At the present rate of increase there will be more than twice as many rabbits on the heath within 4 years.

Neil buys a fixed rate bond for £5000 at the start of 1996. Interest is added at the end of each year at 10% of the value of the bond at the start of the year. For how many years will the bond need to be kept before its value is at least £8000?

We need to find the value at the start of each year from 1996 and continue until the value is more than £8000. The working is easier to follow when it is laid out in a table.

Date	Elapsed time (years)	Value
1996	0	£5000
1997	1	110% of £5000 = 1.1 × £5000 = £5500
1998	2	110% of £5500 = 1.1 × £5500 = £6050
1999	3	1.1 × £6050 = £6655
2000	4	1.1 × £6655 = £7320.50
2001	5	1.1 × £7320.50 = £8052.55

Neil will need to keep the bond for 5 years.

15 Mr James grows prize marrows. While growing conditions are ideal, his marrows increase in weight by 10% each day. How many days will it take for a marrow whose weight is now 700 g to increase in weight to at least

    a 800 g   **b** 1000 g   **c** 1400 g

16 A new town of 2000 houses is to be built in the year 2010 and is then planned to increase by 20% each year. At the start of which year will the number of houses be at least doubled?

17 A pest eradication scheme for a railway system aims to reduce the number of rats by 30% a month. At the beginning of July it is estimated that there are 10 000 rats. After how many months will the number of rats be below   **a** 5000   **b** 500?

18 A classic car is bought for £P. Its value appreciates by 8% each year. Find, in terms of P, an expression for the value of the car after

    a 1 year   **b** 2 years   **c** 6 years   **d** n years.

Use the formula you found in part **d** to find the value after 10 years of a classic car bought for £500.

MIXED
EXERCISES

EXERCISE 16I   Do not use a calculator in this exercise.

1 **a** A Building Association plans to build an estate of 256 houses.
After a rethink they decide to increase the number of houses by
three-eighths. How many houses do they now intend to build?

   b The number of students passing a particular examination increased
from 108 to 120 when the time allocated to teaching the course
was increased. By what fraction did the number of successful
students increase?

2 **a** Find the percentage mark-up if an article bought for £12 is sold
for £19.20.

   b Find the percentage loss if a soccer jersey bought for £24 is sold
for £18.

3 **a** Find the buying-in price if, when an article is marked-up by 40% it
sells for £35.

   b Find the buying-in price if, when a pair of shoes is sold at a loss of
30%, the sale price is £21.

4 The population of Oakdale is 300 but is set to increase by 20% a year
for the next 5 years. Find the population of Oakdale in 2 years' time.

5 At what annual rate of interest will £300 increase to £345 when
invested for one year?

6 The number of cars in Foxley has been growing by 10% a year for the
last 3 years. At the latest count the number was 7986. How many
cars were there in Foxley

   a last year   **b** 2 years ago   **c** 3 years ago?

EXERCISE 16J   **1** **a** A book bought for £5.50 is sold at a profit of 75%. What is it sold
for?

   b Some Christmas stock bought for £650 is sold in the January sales
at a loss of 33%. Find the selling price.

2 Which is the better cash rise and by how much?

   a 6.5% on a weekly wage of £212, or

   b 4.75% on a weekly wage of £274

3 **a** Find the purchase price of a kitchen unit marked £65.50 + VAT at $17\frac{1}{2}$%.

b A set of four cast iron saucepans sells for £183.30. The price includes VAT at $17\frac{1}{2}$%. Find

   i the price excluding VAT
   ii the new selling price if value added tax is reduced from $17\frac{1}{2}$% to 15%.

4 £1260 is invested in a deposit account and increases by 4.45% each year. How much will it increase in value

   a in 2 years   **b** in 3 years?

5 The number of recorded cases of a particular disease in the county of Midshire in 1995 was 208. This number has declined by 9% each year since.
How many cases were there   **a** in 1996   **b** in 1997?
Give your answers to an appropriate degree of accuracy.

6 New machinery was installed in a factory and depreciated in value by 15% each year. When it was 2 years old it was worth £50 000.
Estimate its value   **a** when new   **b** in 2 years' time.
Give your answers correct to the nearest £1000.

PUZZLE

Pauline manages an Art Gallery. She buys a picture for £2000 and sells it at a profit of 50%. Six months later she buys it back for 50% less than she sold it for, but soon sells it again at a profit of 50%. This process of buying back at 50% of her selling price, and selling the picture again soon after at a profit of 50%, is repeated on two further occasions. How much profit (or loss) did she make altogether?

SUMMARY 4

STRAIGHT LINES

An equation of the form $y = mx + c$ gives a straight line where m is the gradient of the line and c is the intercept on the y-axis.
The *gradient* gives the increase in y for each unit increase in x.
Two lines that are *parallel* have the same gradient.

SIMILAR FIGURES

Two figures are similar if they are the same shape but different in size, that is, one figure is an enlargement of the other. (One figure may be turned over or round with respect to the other.) It follows that the lengths of corresponding sides are all in the same ratio. The value of this ratio gives the scale factor.

Similar triangles
We can say that two triangles are similar if we can show that the three angles of one triangle are equal to the three angles of the other. (In practice we only need to show that two pairs of angles are equal because, as the sum of the three angles in any triangle is $180°$, the third pair must be equal.)

FORMULAS

The formula $v = u + at$ gives v in terms of u, a and t; v is called the *subject of the formula*.

When the formula is rearranged to give $a = \dfrac{v - u}{t}$, a is the subject.

The process of rearranging $v = u + at$ to $a = \dfrac{v - u}{t}$ is called *changing the subject of the formula*. It is achieved by thinking of $v = u + at$ as an equation which has to be 'solved' to find a.
Start by isolating the term containing a on one side of the formula:
take u from both sides: $v - u = at$

divide both sides by t: $\dfrac{v - u}{t} = a$, i.e. $a = \dfrac{v - u}{t}$

When the letter to be made the subject of a formula is squared, solve the formula for the square and then remember that, if $x^2 = a$, $x = \pm\sqrt{a}$.
For example, to make a the subject of $b = a^2 + c^2$,
first solve for a^2, giving $a^2 = b - c^2$,
then take the square root of both sides, i.e. $a = \pm\sqrt{b - c^2}$

When a formula contains square roots, first isolate the square root and then square both sides.
For example to make m the subject of $h = 3 - \sqrt{m + n}$,
first solve for $\sqrt{m + n}$ giving $\sqrt{m + n} = 3 - h$
then square both sides, i.e. $m + n = (3 - h)^2$, so $m = (3 - h)^2 - n$.

FACTORISING

Factorising is the reverse of the process of expanding (multiplying out) an algebraic expression.

A *common factor* of two or more terms can be seen by inspection and 'taken outside a bracket',

e.g.   the terms $2ab + 4bc$ both have $2b$ as factors,
so $2ab + 4bc = 2b(a + 2c)$. (This can be checked by expanding the result.)

To factorise an expression such as $x^2 + 3x - 10$, we look for two brackets whose product is equal to the original expression.
We start by writing $x^2 + 3x - 10 = (x +)(x -)$.
The sign in each bracket is determined by the signs in the original expression, i.e.

a +ve number term *and* a +ve x term gives a '+' sign in both brackets
a +ve number term *and* a −ve x term gives a '−' sign in both brackets
a −ve number term gives '+' in one bracket and '−' in the other bracket.

The numbers at the ends of the brackets have to satisfy two conditions; their product must equal the number at the end of the original expression, collecting the product of the outside terms and the inside terms in the brackets must give the x term in the original expression.

For $x^2 + 3x - 10$, we need two numbers whose product is 10 (i.e. 10 and 1 or 5 and 2) and whose difference is 3 (i.e. 5 and 2).

∴ $$x^2 + 3x - 10 = (x + 5)(x - 2)$$

If we cannot find two numbers that satisfy the conditions, the expression does not factorise.

PERCENTAGE CHANGE

Changes are expressed in percentage terms as a percentage of the quantity before any changes are made.
If we have the quantity after a change, we can *find the original quantity*.
For example, if the price of a shirt is £25 after a discount of 10%, the discount is 10% of the price before it was reduced,

i.e.   £25 = original price − 10% of original price
            = 90% × original price.
So   £25 = 0.9 × original price
⇒   original price = £$\frac{25}{0.9}$ = £27.78 (to the nearest penny)

Compound percentage change is an accumulating change, e.g. when the value of a house increases by 5% of its value at the start of each year; its value after one year, is 105% of its initial value, after another year, its value is 105% of its value at the start of that year, i.e. 105% of its increased value, and so on.

1 a Use the information in the
diagram to find the coordinates
of the points A, B and C.

b Find the equation of the straight
line that passes through the
point $(0, 5)$ and is parallel to
the line $y = 2 - 3x$.

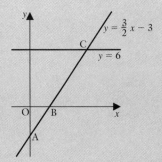

2 Liquid is poured into this glass
container at a constant rate. Which
of the graphs below shows how the
depth of liquid in the container
changes as it is being filled?

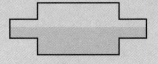

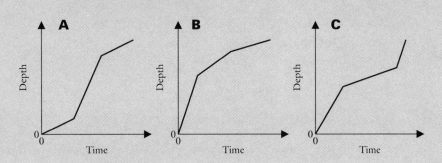

3 State, with reasons, whether or not the following triangles are
similar. If they are, give the ratio of corresponding sides.

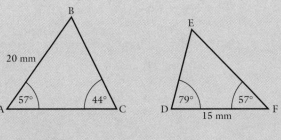

4

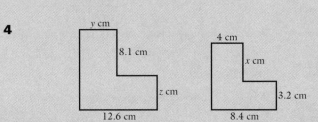

These two figures are similar. Find each length marked with a letter.

5 The graph shows the journey of a car between Amberley and Coldham, via Brickworth.

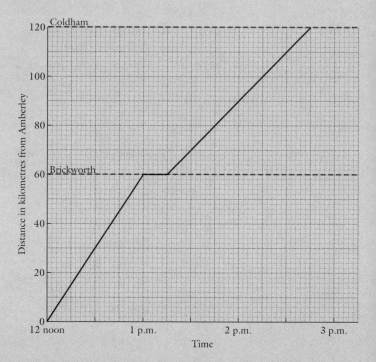

a Was the car moving towards Coldham or away from Coldham?

b On which section of the journey was the speed greatest?

c Where did the car stop and for how long?

6 a Explain why triangles ABC and CDE are similar.

b If $AB = 12$ cm, $BC = 10$ cm, $AC = 9$ cm and $CE = 6$ cm find DE and CD.

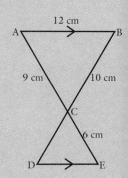

7 Make the letter in brackets the subject of the formula.

   a $a = b - c$ (b) **b** $z = 3x - 2y$ (x) **c** $A = b + \frac{1}{5}c$ (c)

8 Make the letter in brackets the subject of the formula.

   a $v = u + 5t$ (t) **b** $w - x = 4y$ (y) **c** $p = \dfrac{q - p^2}{8p}$ (q)

9 Make the letter in brackets the subject of the formula.

a $a = \dfrac{V}{b^2}$ (b) **c** $p = \sqrt{x+q}$ (x)

b $(x+b)^2 = c$ (x) **d** $ax^2 = \dfrac{b}{c}$ (x)

10 **a** Make k the subject of the formula $V = ka + lb$

    b Find k if $V = 25.2$, $l = 5.4$, $b = 3.5$ and $a = 0.9$.

11 The Fast Foto company use two letter F's as part of their logo.

The letter F's are similar in shape.
The lengths of the large F and the lengths of the small F are in the ratio $3 : 2$.

The height of the large F is 0.9 m.

a Work out the height of the small F.

The width of the small F is 28 cm.

b Work out the width of the large F.   (London)

12 O is the centre of a circle of radius r cm.
AB is the arc of the circle of length x cm and $A\widehat{O}B = y°$.
The length x cm of the arc AB is given by the formula

$$x = \frac{\pi r y}{180}$$

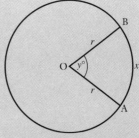

Diagram is not drawn to scale

a Find the length of the arc AB when $A\widehat{O}B = 80°$ and the radius is $4\frac{1}{2}$ cm.

b Rewrite the formula in the form

$$y = \ldots\ldots$$

c Calculate the size of $A\widehat{O}B$ when the radius is 10 cm and the length of AB is 6 cm.   (WJEC)

**REVISION
EXERCISE 4.2**
(Chapters 15
and 16)

1 Factorise **a** $4a + 12$ **b** $x^2 - 5x$ **c** $b^3 - 3b^2$

2 Factorise

 a $x^2 + 11x + 18$ **b** $x^2 - 6x + 8$ **c** $x^2 - 10x + 25$

3 Factorise **a** $x^2 - 2x - 15$ **c** $18 + 9x + x^2$
   b $x^2 + 2x - 8$ **d** $14 + 5x - x^2$

4 a Factorise **i** $a^2 - b^2$ **ii** $p^2 - 4q^2$ **iii** $16x^2 - y^2$
 b Find, without using a calculator
  i $67^2 - 33^2$ **ii** $7.31^2 - 3.69^2$ **iii** $9.83^2 + 9.83 \times 0.17$

5 Factorise **a** $3x^2 - 9$ **c** $9p^2 - p$
   b $2x^2 + 12x + 16$ **d** $3x^2 - 27$

6 a Sam Nolan has an income of £7600 a year. Deductions for
 national insurance, income tax and pension contributions amount
 to 33% of his income. How much remains after the deductions
 have been made ?

 b In a sale, a shirt is marked at £16.50 which includes a reduction
 of 25%. What was the pre-sale price ?

7 a Which is the better cash pay rise, and by how much ?
 A 3.56% on a wage of £250   **B** 2.76% on a wage of £285

 b A car bought for £12 000 depreciates in value by 20% each year.
 Find its value after 3 years.

8 a When a fireside rug is sold for £39 the retailer suffers a loss of
 40%. Find the buying-in price.

 b A dress costing £55 is sold at a loss of 20%. Find the sale price.

9 a Find the interest payable after one year if £8500 is invested at
 5.25% a year.

 b If the original sum, plus the interest, remains invested at the same
 rate, find the total value of the investment at the end of the
 second year.

10 a A particular CD costs a shopkeeper £9.20 from the wholesaler.
 The shopkeeper wants to make a profit of 35% of his costs. What
 price will the CD be in the shop ?

 b Another CD is offered in a sale at a discount of 15%. The sale
 price is £12.41. What was the price of the CD before the sale
 discount ?   (WJEC)

11 Because they are emigrating Mr and Mrs Thomson are anxious to sell their house quickly. They put the house on the market at £100 000 but reduce the price every week by 4% of its price at the beginning of that week. It is sold the first week the price drops below £90 000.

a How many weeks did it take to sell?

b What was the selling price? (Give your answer correct to the nearest £1000.)

12 At the end of 1993 there were 5000 members of a certain rare breed of animal remaining in the world.
It is predicted that their number will decrease by 12% each year.

a How many will be left at the end of 1996?

b By the end of which year will the number be first less than 2500?

(MEG)

13 Factorise completely

a $9a^2b^3 + 15a^3b^2$ **b** $x^2 + 7x - 60$ (London)

REVISION EXERCISE 4.3 (Chapters 12 to 16)

1 a Find the coordinates of the points where the line with equation $y = 4x + 8$ crosses each axis.

b Find the equation of the line that is parallel to the line with equation $y = 4x + 8$ and passes through the point $(0, -4)$.

2 The table shows the conversion from pounds sterling to US dollars for various amounts of money.

Pounds (£)	0	50	100
US dollars ($)	0	78	156

Plot these points on a graph and draw a straight line to pass through them. Let 4 cm represent £50 on the horizontal axis and 1 cm represent $10 on the vertical axis.

a Use your graph to convert

i 46 dollars into pounds **iii** £84 into dollars

ii 132 dollars into pounds **iv** £27 into dollars.

b What is the rate of exchange between pounds and dollars that this graph is based on?

3

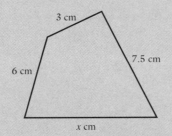 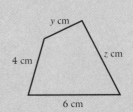

These two quadrilaterals are similar. Find the values of x, y and z.

4

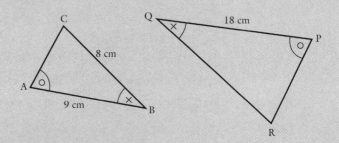

In triangles ABC and PQR, $\hat{A} = \hat{P}$ and $\hat{B} = \hat{Q}$, AB = 9 cm, BC = 8 cm and PQ = 18 cm. Find QR.

5 Make the letter in brackets the subject of the formula.

a $p = 5 + q$ (q)

c $z = \dfrac{x}{y}$ (x)

b $x = \frac{1}{3}t$ (t)

d $(p - x)^2 = q$ (x)

6 a Make c the subject of the formula $a = b - cd$

b Find the value of c when $a = 2$, $b = 10$ and $d = 4$.

7 Factorise

a $15 - 5x$

c $x^2 - 10x + 21$

b $x^2 - 2x - 15$

d $2x^2 + 4x + 8$

8 Factorise

a $12 - 7x + x^2$

c $12 + x - x^2$

b $9 - a^2$

d $x^2 - 6x + 8$

9 a After a pay rise of 3% Sheila's weekly wage is £226.60. How much did she earn before the rise?

b Find the compound interest on £750 invested for 2 years at 4.55%.

10 a Earl wants to cut his car expenses by $\frac{1}{8}$. At the moment his car costs him £28 a week.
What does he hope to get the weekly cost down to?

b Stetford & Co manufacture two types of electric toasters. Last month they made 6720 of the basic model and 3115 of the de-luxe model. As a result of a sales survey they propose to decrease production of the basic model by $\frac{3}{8}$ but increase production of the de-luxe model by $\frac{4}{7}$. How many of each model of toaster do they propose making? Has the total number of electric toasters produced increased or decreased and by how many?

REVISION EXERCISE 4.4 (Chapters 1 to 16)

Do not use a calculator in this exercise.

1 a Express as a power of a whole number

 i $\frac{1}{3^4}$ **ii** $\frac{1}{10^3}$ **iii** $\frac{1}{2^4}$ **iv** $\frac{1}{5^3}$

b Write as an ordinary number
 i 6.2×10^{-3} **ii** 2.9×10^3 **iii** 6.4×10^0

c Write down the reciprocal of
 i 6   **ii** $\frac{9}{4}$ **iii** 3.4   **iv** $1\frac{1}{4}$

2 a Simplify

 i $\frac{12ab^2}{4bc^2}$ **ii** $\frac{15b}{20(a-b)}$ **iii** $\frac{x}{9} \div \frac{1}{3}$ **iv** $\frac{8st}{9t} \times \frac{3t^2}{4s^2}$

b Planet A is 8.44×10^8 km from the Sun and Planet B is 6.56×10^9 km from the Sun.
How far apart are these two planets when the straight line through their positions passes through the Sun and
 i they are on the same side of the Sun
 ii they are on opposite sides of the Sun?
Give your answers in standard form.

3 a Write down the first four terms and the tenth term of the sequence for which the nth term is given by $(n+1)(n+2)$.

b Find, in terms of n, an expression for the nth term of the sequence $0, 5, 10, 15, \ldots$

4 Expand

 a $(a-b)(a-2b)$ **b** $(3x+1)(x+2)$ **c** $(p+q)^2$

5 a Given that $p = q + 2r$ find r when $p = 7.8$ and $q = 3$.

 b If $P = x^2 + 3xy$ find P when $x = 0.5$ and $y = \frac{3}{4}$.

6 The probability that the postman calls before I leave for school in the morning is $\frac{5}{6}$. He never calls at the moment I am leaving. Find the probability that

 a the postman calls after I have left for school

 b next Monday and Tuesday the postman will call before I leave.

7 a Write down the coordinates of the point where the straight line with equation $y = 8 - 2x$ crosses

 i the x-axis **ii** the y-axis.

 b Write down the coordinates of the point where the line $y = 3$ crosses the line $y = 8 - 2x$.

 c Find the equation of the straight line parallel to the line $y = 8 - 2x$ which passes through the point $(0, 2)$.

8 a Make T the subject of the formula $I = \dfrac{PRT}{100}$.

 Find T when $I = 28$, $P = 350$ and $R = 4$.

 b Make **i** s the subject of the formula $v^2 = u^2 + 2as$
 ii x the subject of the formula $p = \sqrt{q + x}$

9 Factorise **a** $x^2 + 6x$ **c** $8 + x^2 - 6x$

 b $x^2 - 10x + 24$ **d** $p^2 - 36$

10 a The selling price of a patio set is £180. This includes VAT at 20%. Find the price excluding VAT.

 b George Sharp buys a greyhound for £360 and sells the dog at a loss of $12\frac{1}{2}$%. How much does he lose?

REVISION EXERCISE 4.5 (Chapters 1 to 16)

1 a Give 34.678 cm correct to the nearest tenth of a centimetre.

 b Solve the following equations

 i $6 = \dfrac{x}{5}$ **iii** $\dfrac{2x}{5} = \dfrac{3}{7}$ **v** $\dfrac{x+3}{5} = \dfrac{x-3}{2}$

 ii $\dfrac{4x}{3} = 24$ **iv** $\dfrac{y}{3} - \dfrac{y}{4} = \dfrac{5}{6}$ **vi** $\dfrac{5}{8} - \dfrac{2}{x} = \dfrac{1}{4}$

2 To transport a plane-load of passengers from the airport to the city centre, eight 42-seater coaches are needed and every seat is occupied. How many 48-seater coaches would be needed to carry the same party of people?

3 Expand

  a $3x(3y - z)$ **c** $(3a + 1)(7 - a)$

  b $(x - 3)(x - 6)$ **d** $(4x - 3)(4x + 3)$

4 **a** If $T = x(y - 3z)$ find T when $x = 3$, $y = 4$ and $z = \frac{3}{4}$.

  b To convert a weight from stones into kilograms an approximate rule is 'multiply by 70 then divide by 11'.

    A boy weighs P stone on one scale and Q kilograms on another. Assuming that both scales measured the boy's weight accurately find a formula to express

    i Q in terms of P **ii** P in terms of Q.

5 Ken has a quantity of rectangular metal blocks, each measuring 12.1 cm by 8.2 cm by 3.4 cm. All dimensions are correct to 1 decimal place.

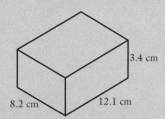

  a Five such blocks are placed end to end in a row.

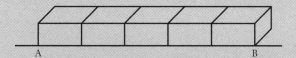

    What is the upper bound of the length AB?

  b The same blocks are placed on end, face to face as shown in the diagram. What is the lower bound of the distance CD?

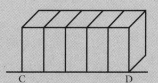

  c One block is placed on another as shown opposite. Find

    i the maximum possible value for the distance EF

    ii the smallest possible value for the distance GH.

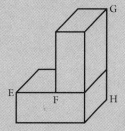

6 A right pyramid stands on a rectangular base measuring 8 cm by 5 cm and is 9 cm high.

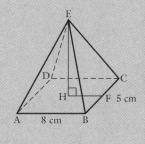

a Sketch a net for this pyramid.

b F is the midpoint of BC. Find, correct to 2 decimal places, the length of EF.

c Find the area of one of the large sloping sides of the pyramid.

d Find, correct to 3 significant figures the total surface area of the pyramid.

7 Copy this shape onto squared paper and then draw an enlargement, scale factor $\frac{1}{2}$, of the shape.

8 Explain whether or not these two triangles are similar. If they are, find the length of DF.

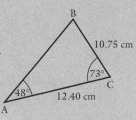

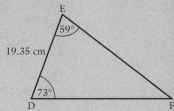

9 a Make the letter in brackets the subject of the formula

i $a = \dfrac{2}{b}$ (b) **iii** $p = \sqrt{x} + q$ (x) **v** $A = 4\pi x^2$ (x)

ii $p = 3qr$ (q) **iv** $A = P + \dfrac{I}{5}$ (I) **vi** $a = \frac{1}{2}b + \frac{1}{3}c$ (c)

b i Change the subject of the formula $Z = ax + by$ from Z to b.
ii Find the value of b when $Z = 6.9$, $a = 3$, $x = 1.8$ and $y = 0.5$.

10 Factorise

a $3t - 6t^2$ **c** $x^2 - 4x - 12$
b $3x^2 + 9x - 12$ **d** $x^2 + 8x + 16$

ORGANISING AND SUMMARISING DATA

The local health authority wants some information about the heights of five-year-old children in its area. The information is obtained from the first school medical examination, when the height of each child is recorded.

- There are 1256 five-year-olds in infant schools in the area covered by the health authority, so the heights have to be organised and summarised before they can give useful information.
- When the health authority has found the information it needs for its own purposes, it may want to compare the distribution of heights in its area with those in other health authority areas.

Data can be organised by grouping it. The data can be summarised by giving the range, and one or more measures of central tendency, that is, the mean, the median or the mode. The Summary at the front of this book can be used to remind you what these measures are.

EXERCISE 17A   Use these questions for discussion.

1   In area A, the height of the shortest child is 92 cm and that of the tallest child is 112 cm; the range of heights is therefore 20 cm. In area B, the range of heights is also 20 cm.

    a Does this mean that the shortest child in area B is 92 cm tall?

    b What can you say about the height of the tallest child in area B?

    c Is the range on its own a good way of describing a set of data?

    d An unusually tall five-year-old joined an infant school in area B. As a consequence, the range of heights in this area increased to 30 cm. Is it reasonable to use the ranges alone to compare the heights in area B with those in area A?

2 The first three children entering a classroom had with them 2 books, 2 books and 8 books respectively.

The next three children carried 3, 4 and 5 books respectively.

a For the first group of children, write down the mean, median and the range of the number of books.

b Repeat part **a** for the second group of children.

c Is the mean number of books, on its own, a satisfactory way of describing either set or is the mean and the range together a better way to describe a set of data?

d Is there any advantage in using the median instead of the mean?

3 The health authority wanted to investigate the possible long-term harm that pupils may suffer by carrying heavy loads to and from school in unsuitable bags. A start was made by gathering information about the weights carried by 800 secondary school pupils.
The data collected made it possible to ask questions such as

What is the range of weights?
What is the mean weight?
What is the median weight?

Discuss how you could go about answering these questions and what problems you might have.

ANALYSING LARGE SETS OF INFORMATION

Discussion arising from the questions in the last exercise should have shown that we need to use either the mean or the median together with the range, to give a reasonable summary of a set of data.
Discussion about question **3** may have produced the conclusion that, without the help of a computer, a large set of data presents problems in carrying out the calculations needed to analyse it.

Consider these figures, collected on behalf of the local health authority.

Heights (rounded down to the nearest centimetre) of 90 five-year-olds from one infant school

99	107	102	98	115	95	106	110	108	105
118	102	114	108	94	104	113	102	105	95
105	110	109	101	106	108	107	107	101	109
108	105	116	109	114	110	97	110	113	116
112	101	92	105	104	115	111	103	110	99
93	104	103	113	107	94	102	117	116	104
99	114	106	114	98	109	107	114	106	107
109	113	112	100	109	113	118	104	94	114
107	96	108	103	112	106	115	111	115	101

These figures were written on record cards in the same order as the children came into the medical examination, so the heights are listed in a random order. Disorganised figures like these are called *raw data*. Some form of summary, such as the mean, the median, the mode and the range, are needed to describe these figures.

- If the mean height of five-year-olds in one school is required, it can be found from the raw figures. For the 90 heights given, the mean can be calculated by adding up the heights and then dividing by 90; this is a tedious job and, even with the help of a calculator, mistakes are likely. With 1256 heights, it is not sensible to use the raw figures unless they have been entered into, say, a spreadsheet that can do the calculations.
- Grouping the data not only helps to give a 'picture' of the distribution of heights, it also reduces the complexity by replacing hundreds of individual figures with a much smaller number of groups of figures; it does, though, reduce the amount of detail given by the individual figures.

First we will organise the data into groups. If we use a number line to represent the heights of these children there is no point on the line which could not represent someone's height, that is heights are continuous measurements. So the grouping we choose must not have any 'gaps' between the values included in consecutive groups.

Taking h cm to represent the height of any child, a suitable grouping is

$$90 \leqslant h < 95,\ 95 \leqslant h < 100,\ 100 \leqslant h < 105,\ 105 \leqslant h < 110,$$
$$110 \leqslant h < 115,\ 115 \leqslant h < 120,$$

and these groups are used to construct the following frequency table.

Height, h cm	Tally	Frequency
$90 \leqslant h < 95$	ⵍⵍⵍ	5
$95 \leqslant h < 100$	ⵍⵍⵍ ////	9
$100 \leqslant h < 105$	ⵍⵍⵍ ⵍⵍⵍ ⵍⵍⵍ //	17
$105 \leqslant h < 110$	ⵍⵍⵍ ⵍⵍⵍ ⵍⵍⵍ ⵍⵍⵍ ⵍⵍⵍ ///	28
$110 \leqslant h < 115$	ⵍⵍⵍ ⵍⵍⵍ ⵍⵍⵍ ⵍⵍⵍ /	21
$115 \leqslant h < 120$	ⵍⵍⵍ ⵍⵍⵍ	10

Total: 90

When you make a frequency table from raw data, work down the columns, making a tally mark in the appropriate row for each value. Do not go through the data looking for values that fit into the first group and the second group and so on.

Now we can see that the modal group (that is the group with the largest number of heights in it) is 105 cm to 110 cm.
We can estimate the range of heights as

(upper bound of last group − lower bound of first group)
$$= (120 - 90)\,\text{cm} = 30\,\text{cm}$$

Next we need a method for finding the mean from grouped data. First we will remind ourselves how to find the mean of an ungrouped frequency distribution.

FINDING THE MEAN OF AN UNGROUPED FREQUENCY DISTRIBUTION

In Book 8B, we found the mean value of a frequency distribution by multiplying each value by its frequency, adding these products and dividing the result by the total number of values, that is the sum of the frequencies.

This example summarises the process.

Test marks

Mark	Frequency	Frequency × mark
0	1	0
1	1	1
2	8	16
3	11	33
4	5	20
5	4	20
	Total: 30	Total: 90

The mean mark is $\dfrac{90}{30} = 3$.

This method can be used to find the mean of any ungrouped frequency distribution, i.e.

the mean value of a frequency distribution is given by

$$\frac{\text{sum of the (frequency} \times \text{value) products}}{\text{sum of frequencies, i.e. total number of values}}$$

FINDING THE MEAN OF A GROUPED FREQUENCY DISTRIBUTION

From the table below we can see that 5 children had heights, h cm, in the range $90 \leqslant h < 95$.

Height, h cm	Frequency
$90 \leqslant h < 95$	5
$95 \leqslant h \leqslant 100$	9
$100 \leqslant h < 105$	17
$105 \leqslant h < 110$	28
$110 \leqslant h < 115$	21
$115 \leqslant h < 120$	10

← If we *estimate* that the mean height of these five children is halfway between 90 cm and 95 cm, i.e. 92.5 cm, then we can find, approximately the total height of the 5 children as 92.5×5 cm $= 462.5$ cm.

The middle value of a group is called the *midclass value*.

Using the midclass value as an estimate for the mean value in each group, we can find (approximately) the total height of the children in each group and hence the total height of all the 90 five-year-olds.

It is easier to keep track of the calculations if we add another two columns to the frequency table.

Height, h cm	Frequency	Midclass value	Frequency $\times$ midclass value
$90 \leqslant h \leqslant 95$	5	92.5	462.5
$95 \leqslant h \leqslant 100$	9	97.5	877.5
$100 \leqslant h < 105$	17	102.5	1742.5
$105 \leqslant h < 100$	28	107.5	3010
$110 \leqslant h < 115$	21	112.5	2362.5
$115 \leqslant h < 120$	10	117.5	1175
Totals:	90		9630

The total height of all 50 children is estimated as 9630 cm,

so the mean height is approximately $\dfrac{9630}{90}$ cm $= 107$ cm.

This process can be used with any grouped frequency distribution, so

the estimated mean value of a grouped frequency distribution is given by

$$\dfrac{\text{sum of the (frequency} \times \text{midclass value) products}}{\text{sum of frequencies, i.e. total number of values}}$$

Remember that this calculation is based on the assumption that the average height in each group is halfway through the group so what we have found is only an estimate for the mean.

EXERCISE 17B

1 The table shows the marks obtained by each of 30 pupils in a maths test.

Find the mean mark.

Mark	Frequency
6	4
7	5
8	10
9	8
10	3

2 Fifty boxes of peaches were examined and the number of bad peaches in each box was recorded, with this result.

Estimate the mean number of bad peaches per box.

No. of bad peaches per box	Frequency
0–4	34
5–9	11
10–14	4
15–19	1

3 Twenty tomato seeds were planted in a seed tray. Four weeks later, the heights of the resulting plants were measured and this frequency table was made.

Estimate the mean height of the seedlings.

Height, h cm	Frequency
$1 \leqslant h < 4$	2
$4 \leqslant h < 7$	5
$7 \leqslant h < 10$	10
$10 \leqslant h < 13$	3

4 The table shows the result of a survey among 100 pupils on the amount of money each of them spent in the school tuck shop on one particular day.

Find an estimate for the mean amount of money spent.

Amount (pence)	Frequency
0–24	26
25–49	15
50–74	38
75–99	21

5 Ishita recorded, in a grouped frequency table, the number of words in each sentence from a passage in the book.

Find the mean number of words.

Number of words	1–10	11–20	21–30	31–40	41–50	51–60
Frequency	7	12	29	31	12	3

6 The bar chart shows the result of an examination of 20 boxes of screws.

Make a frequency table and estimate the mean number of defective screws per box.

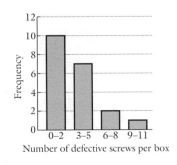

7 A new income-tax form was trialled by asking some people to complete it. The time each person took was recorded and this frequency polygon summarises the results.

a How many people were asked to complete the form?

b Estimate the range of times taken.

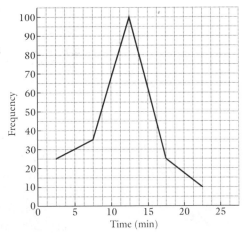

c Copy and complete the table. You may prefer to draw this table vertically, like the tables in questions **1** to **5**.

Midclass value, t minutes	2.5				
Frequency	25				

> Remember that a frequency polygon is constructed by joining the midpoints of the tops of the bars, i.e. the points that are joined represent the midclass values.

d Estimate the mean time taken to complete this form.

8 The weight of tomatoes gathered from each plant grown in 'grow-bags' was measured. The table summarises these weights.

Weight, w grams	Frequency
$0 \leqslant w < 500$	40
$500 \leqslant w < 1000$	200
$1000 \leqslant w < 1200$	452
$1200 \leqslant w < 1400$	185
$1400 \leqslant w < 1600$	103
$1600 \leqslant w < 2000$	60

   a How many plants were involved in this experiment?

   b What do you notice about the width of the groups, and will this cause problems when finding the mean?

   c Find the mean weight.

   d Illustrate this distribution of weights with a frequency polygon.

9 Laura travels to school by bus. She decided to investigate the time it took her to travel to school in the morning. This list gives the time, in minutes, of her journey on each of thirty days.

25	30	24	20	25	21	22	24	25	28
21	24	21	23	29	22	24	25	26	22
27	24	21	20	26	24	21	23	29	22

   a Construct an ungrouped frequency table for these times.

   b Find the mean time.

   c Find the range of the times.

   d Derek lives next door to Laura. He cycles to school. He insists that cycling takes less time and is more reliable than travelling by bus.
   To try to prove that he is right, Derek also keeps a record of his journey times for 30 days and finds that his mean time is 24 minutes and the range of times is 5 minutes.
   Is Derek right? Give reasons for your answers.

10 The speeds of vehicles passing a check-point on an urban road were recorded.
   Between 8 a.m. and 9 a.m. the mean speed was 22 mph and the range of speeds was 8 mph.
   Between 8 p.m. and 9 p.m. the mean speed was 35 mph and the range of speeds was 25 mph.
   Compare the two sets of speeds.

11 The areas of fields used for growing wheat in two different regions of an island are illustrated by these frequency polygons.

Region A is shown in black and Region B in purple.

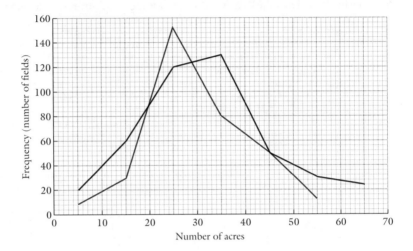

a Without doing any calculation, compare the number of acres in the fields in region A with those in region B.

b Copy and complete this frequency table.

Number of acres in a field	Frequency (number of fields) in region A	Frequency (number of fields) in region B
0–10	20	8
10–20	60	29
20–30	120	
30–40	130	80
40–50		50
50–60	30	
60–70		0

c Find the mean number of acres per field in
   i Region A   **ii** Region B

d Say, with reasons, whether your answers to part **c** make you want to change your answer to part **a**.

THE MEDIAN

We first used the frequency table below to find the mean test mark (see page 324).

We can also use it to find the median test mark.

The median is the middle value, which in this case is the average of the 15th and 16th marks. We can find the 15th and 16th marks by adding a column for the running totals.

Test marks		
Mark	Frequency	Running total
0	1	1 (i.e. the first mark is 0)
1	1	2 (i.e. the second mark is 1)
2	8	10 (i.e. the 3rd to the 10th marks are all 2)
3	11	21 (i.e. the 11th to 21st marks are all 3)
4	5	
5	4	
	Total: 30	

Now we can see that the 15th and 16th marks are both 3; therefore the median mark is 3.

When information is grouped, we do not know individual values so we cannot identify a single value as the median, but we can use running totals to find the group in which the median lies.

Returning to the frequency table for the heights of 90 five-year-old children, the median is the average of the 45th and 46th heights.

Height, h cm	Frequency	Running total
$90 \leqslant h < 95$	5	5
$95 \leqslant h < 100$	9	14 (i.e. 6th to 14th heights are in the group $95 \leqslant h < 100$)
$100 \leqslant h < 105$	17	31 (so the 15th to 31st heights are in this group)
$105 \leqslant h < 110$	28	59 (32nd to 59th heights are in this group, so the median is in this group)
$110 \leqslant h < 115$	21	
$115 \leqslant h < 120$	10	
	Total: 90	

Now we can see that the median height is between 105 cm and 110 cm.

EXERCISE 17C   Find the median value, or the group in which the median value lies.

1

Mark	Frequency
6	4
7	5
8	10
9	8
10	3

3

Amount (pence)	Frequency
0–24	26
25–49	15
50–74	38
75–99	21

2

Number of words	Frequency
1–10	7
11–20	12
21–30	29
31–40	31
41–50	12
51–60	3

4

Height, h cm	Frequency
$145 \leqslant h < 150$	2
$150 \leqslant h < 155$	6
$155 \leqslant h < 160$	43
$160 \leqslant h < 165$	35
$165 \leqslant h < 170$	10
$170 \leqslant h < 175$	4

5   There are 35 questions on the driving theory test and 30 correct answers are needed to pass.

a

Mark	Frequency
8	1
10	1
23	1
27	6
28	7
29	4

These are the marks of 20 people who failed this test at their first attempt.

Find the mean mark and the median mark.

b On their first retake of this test, the mean mark was 31 and the median mark was 32. The range of marks was 15. How many do you think passed this time ? Give a reason for your answer.

MIXED EXERCISE

EXERCISE 17D 1 Every 15 minutes throughout the day, the people queuing at the checkouts in a supermarket were counted. The numbers are recorded in this table.

Number of people queuing	Frequency
1	20
2	55
3	32
4	49
5	27
6	12
7	4
8	4
9	2
10	1

  a Guess the mean and median values.

  b Calculate the mean number queuing.

  c Find the median number queuing.

2 Pupils attending a secondary school were asked how long it took them to travel to school in the morning. The journey times, to the nearest 5 minutes, are recorded in this table.

Time (minutes)	5–15	20–30	35–45	50–60	65–75	80–90
Frequency	98	217	105	63	15	2

Find

  a the mean time

  b the range of times

  c the interval in which the median time lies.

3 For a survey on car use, 40 people were asked how many miles they drove in the last week. The results are summarised in the table. The 25 women in the group drove an average of 11 miles. What was the average number of miles driven by the men?

Miles driven	Number of people
0–10	8
10–40	18
40–100	10
100–500	4

4 A group of Year 10 pupils went on a school outing. The distribution of spending money that the pupils had at the beginning of the trip is shown by two bar charts drawn back to back.

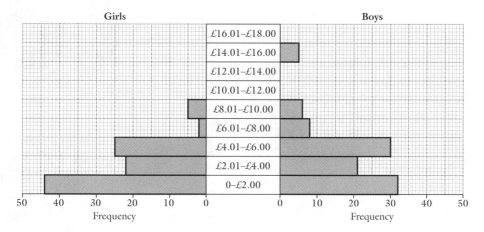

a How many girls went on this trip?

b How many boys went on the trip?

c What fraction of the boys had more than £10 to spend?

d What fraction of the girls had more than £10 to spend?

e Find the mean and range for each set of data.

f Give two ways in which this data shows differences between the girls' and the boys' spending money.

g Find the mean amount of spending money for the whole group.

PRACTICAL WORK

Investigate the weights carried to school by pupils in your year.
Decide on the most appropriate summary of your information.
Decide how you are going to present the information.
If you work in a group, some of you may like to investigate different aspects of the weights, such as

'Are there any differences between the weights carried by boys and by girls?'
'What are the differences between the weights of necessary items and clutter?'
'Do those pupils who bring packed lunches to school carry heavier loads around than those who buy lunch at school?'

CURVED GRAPHS

18

Freda hopes to find a relationship between the time for which a puck is sliding down a slope and the distance it slides in that time.

She collected the following data.

Time, in seconds, after leaving the top of the slope	1	2.7	3.5	4.5	4.9
Distance, in metres, from the top of the slope	0.05	0.4	0.6	1	1.2

To find a relationship between the time and the distance, Freda could

- guess a relationship and see whether the figures in her table fit the guess. This is not likely to give an answer quickly, if ever.
- hope to spot a relationship from the figures in her table. This is not usually possible unless the relationship is a simple one.
- plot the points on graph paper. Freda may then recognise the points as lying on a curve whose equation is of a form she knows.

The ability to recognise the kind of equation that gives a particular shape of curve requires a wide knowledge of different forms of graph. This knowledge is also useful when a graph has to be drawn from its equation because, if we know what shape to expect, mistakes are less likely to be made.

EXERCISE 18A

1 Gail needs to solve all these equations:

$$x^2 - 2x - 4 = 0, \quad x^2 - 2x - 4 = 6 \quad \text{and} \quad 2x^2 - 4x + 1 = 0.$$

Discuss what these equations have in common.

2 Cheryl knows that, for a given voltage, the current flowing in a circuit is inversely proportional to the resistance.
She takes the following readings during an experiment.

Resistance (ohms)	0.5	0.7	1	1.2	1.5	2	2.4
Current (amps)	5.6	4	2.8	2.3	1.9	1.4	1.5

Cheryl then has to plot the values on a graph to confirm the relationship between them. Discuss what knowledge would help her to decide whether the relationship is confirmed and if she has made a mistake in any of her readings.

3 The diagram shows the cross-section of a swimming pool that Peter is designing for a CDT project. He wants to include a sketch showing how the depth of water in the pool increases when it is filled at a constant rate.
Discuss how he could do this and what he needs to know.

Discussion from the last exercise shows that graphs have many uses. In this chapter we look at some of those and extend our knowledge of curves.

STRAIGHT LINES AND PARABOLAS

From Chapter 12 we know that an equation of the form $y = mx + c$ gives a straight line where m is the gradient of the line and c the intercept on the y-axis.
We also know from Book 9B that an equation of the form $y = ax^2 + bx + c$ gives a curve whose shape is called a parabola and looks like this.
When the x^2 term is negative, the curve is 'upside down'.

USING GRAPHS TO SOLVE QUADRATIC EQUATIONS

An equation that contains an x^2 term is called a quadratic equation.
One of the problems discussed in the last exercise concerned solving the quadratic equations

$$x^2 - 2x - 4 = 0, \quad x^2 - 2x - 4 = 6 \quad \text{and} \quad 2(x^2 - 2x) + 1 = 0$$

You may have noticed that, in one form or another, the terms '$x^2 - 2x$' appear in each of these equations. This suggests that we can use one graph to solve all the equations. The worked example in the next exercise shows how this can be done.

EXERCISE 18B

Use the graph of $y = x^2 - 2x - 4$ to solve the equations

a $x^2 - 2x - 4 = 0$ **b** $x^2 - 2x - 10 = 0$ **c** $2x^2 - 4x + 1 = 0$

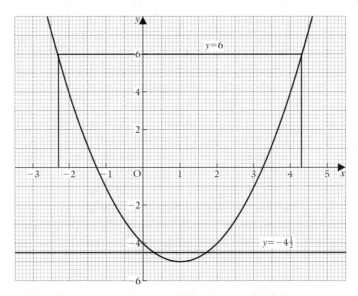

We need to read values from this graph. The accuracy of these values depends partly on how well the graph is drawn and partly on the scales used; aim to read values to the nearest half square.

a $x^2 - 2x - 4 = 0$

When this graph crosses the x-axis, the value of y is 0, i.e. $x^2 - 2x - 4 = 0$
The graph crosses the x-axis where $x = -1.25$ and $x = 3.25$.

$x = -1.25$ or 3.25

b $x^2 - 2x - 10 = 0$

To use the graph of $y = x^2 - 2x - 4$ to solve the equation $x^2 - 2x - 10 = 0$, we must convert the LHS to $x^2 - 2x - 4$. We can do this by adding 6 to both sides.

$x^2 - 2x - 10 + 6 = 6$, i.e. $x^2 - 2x - 4 = 6$

From the equation of the graph of $y = x^2 - 2x - 4$, we see that if $x^2 - 2x - 4 = 6$ then $y = 6$.
Therefore the values of x when $y = 6$ give the solutions to the equation.

$x = -2.3$ or 4.3

c $2x^2 - 4x + 1 = 0$

$x^2 - 2x + \frac{1}{2} = 0$

To use the graph we must convert the LHS to $x^2 - 2x - 4$.
We can do this by dividing both sides by 2, then subtracting $4\frac{1}{2}$ from both sides.

$x^2 - 2x - 4 = -4\frac{1}{2}$

From the graph, when $y = -4\frac{1}{2}$, $x = 0.3$ or 1.7

1   Use the graph of $y = x^2 - 3x - 3$, which is given below, to solve the equations

   a $x^2 - 3x - 3 = 0$ **b** $x^2 - 3x - 3 = 5$ **c** $x^2 - 3x - 7 = 0$ **d** $x^2 - 3x + 1 = 0$

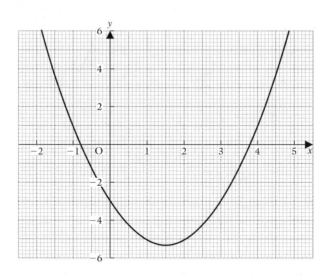

2   The graph of $y = 4 + 4x - x^2$ is given here.

   a Use the graph to solve the equations

   i $4 + 4x - x^2 = 0$
   ii $4 + 4x - x^2 = 5$
   iii $1 + 4x - x^2 = 0$
   iv $1 + 8x - 2x^2 = 0$

   b Use the graph to solve the
   equation $4 + 4x - x^2 = 8$.
   What do you notice?

   c Is it possible to use this graph to
   solve the equation

   $4 + 4x - x^2 = 10$?

   If it is possible, give the solution.
   If it is not possible, explain why.

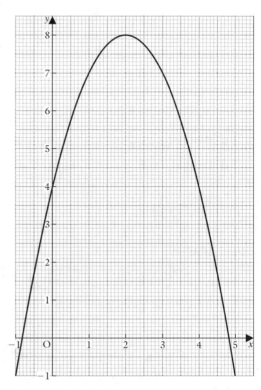

3 **a** Use the graph of $y = x^2 - 5x + 3$, which is shown here, to solve the equations

   i $x^2 - 5x + 3 = 0$
   ii $x^2 - 5x + 3 = 2$
   iii $x^2 - 5x + 5 = 0$

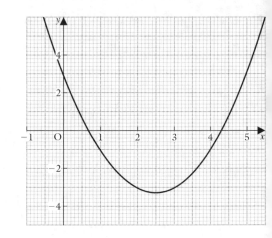

   b Is it possible to use the graph to solve the equation $x^2 - 5x + 3 = -4$? If it is possible, give the solution. If it is not possible, explain why

4 **a** Copy and complete the table which shows the value of $x^2 - 3x - 4$ for values of x from -2 to 5.

x	-2	-1	0	1	2	3	4	5
$x^2 - 3x - 4$		0				-4		

   Hence draw the graph of $y = x^2 - 3x - 4$ using 2 cm as 1 unit on the x-axis and 1 cm as 1 unit on the y-axis.

   b Use your graph to find the lowest value of $x^2 - 3x - 4$ within the given range, and the value of x for which it occurs.

   c Write down the values of x where the graph crosses the x-axis.

   d Draw the line $y = 5$. Estimate the values of x where this line intersects the graph of $y = x^2 - 3x - 4$. What equation is satisfied by these values?

CUBIC GRAPHS

When the equation of a curve contains x^3 (and possibly terms involving x^2, x or a number), the graph is called a *cubic* curve.
These equations all give cubic curves:

$$y = x^3 + 2, \quad y = x^3 - x, \quad y = x^3 - 5x, \quad y = x^3 - 2x^2 + 6$$

We start by plotting the simplest cubic graph, whose equation is $y = x^3$.
The table gives values of x^3 for some values of x from -3 to 3.

x	-3	-2	-1.5	-1	-0.5	0	0.5	1	1.5	2	3
x^3	-27	-8	-3.4	-1	0.1	0	0.1	1	3.4	8	27

Plotting these points and joining them with a smooth curve gives the graph below.

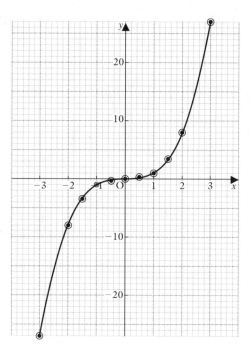

1 Copy and complete the following table which gives values of $2x^3$, for values of x from -3 to 3.

x	-3	-2	-1.5	-1	-0.5	0	0.5	1	1.5	2	3
$2x^3$			-6.8				0.3		6.8		

Hence draw the graph of $y = 2x^3$ for values of x from -3 to 3. Take 2 cm as 1 unit on the x-axis and as 10 units on the y-axis. Use your graph to solve the equations

a $2x^3 = 27$ **b** $2x^3 = -9$

2 Make your own copy of the graph of $y = x^3$.

    a On the same axes draw the line $y = x + 6$.

    b Give the values of x where the curve and straight line intersect.

The graph of $y = x^3 - 4x^2 + 5$ is given below.
Use the graph to find

a the values of x when **i** $y = 4$ **ii** $y = -14$.

b the solutions to the equations

i $x^3 - 4x^2 + 5 = 0$ **ii** $x^3 - 4x^2 + 5 = 13$ **iii** $x^3 - 4x^2 + 8 = 0$

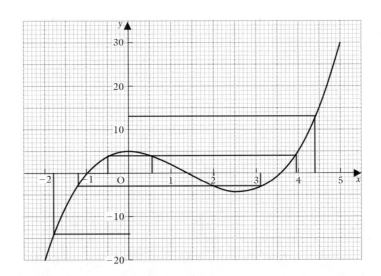

a **i** Drawing the line $y = 4$ we see that there are three values of x when $y = 4$.

$y = 4$ when $x = -0.5$, 0.55 and 3.95

ii The line $y = -14$ cuts the curve once, so there is one value of x when $y = -14$.

$y = -14$ when $x = -1.8$

b **i** $x^3 - 4x^2 + 5 = 0$ when $y = 0$
i.e. where the curve crosses the x-axis, which is when $x = -1$, 1.4 and 3.6

ii $x^3 - 4x^2 + 5 = 13$ where the curve cuts the line $y = 13$,
i.e. when $x = 4.4$

iii $x^3 - 4x^2 + 8 = 0$ can also be written $x^3 - 4x^2 + 5 = -3$ so the solution to
the equation $x^3 - 4x^2 + 8 = 0$ is the x-values where the line $y = -3$ cuts
the graph of $y = x^3 - 4x^2 + 5$
i.e. $x^3 - 4x^2 + 8 = 0$ when $x = -1.25$, 2 and 3.25

3 The graph of $y = x^3 - 10x$ is given. Use the graph to find

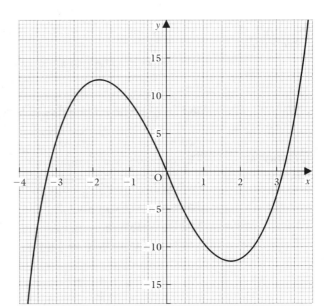

a the values of x when y is
i 5   **ii** -10

b the solution to the equation

   i $x^3 - 10x = 0$
   ii $x^3 - 10x = 5$
   iii $x^3 - 10x + 10 = 0$

c Is it possible to use the graph to solve the equation $x^3 - 10x + 15 = 0$? If it is possible give the solution, if it is not, explain why.

4 The graph of $y = 6x - x^3$ is given below.

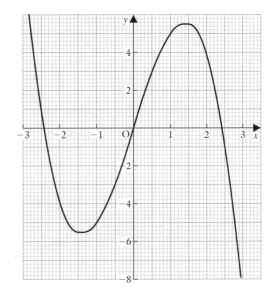

a Use the graph to find the values of y when x is   **i** 2   **ii** -1

b Use the graph to solve the equations

   i $6x - x^3 = 0$
   ii $6x - x^3 = 2$
   iii $7 + 6x - x^3 = 0$

c On a copy of the graph draw the line $y = 4$ and write down the values of x where this line cuts the graph of $y = 6x - x^3$. What equation is satisfied by these values of x?

5 **a** Copy and complete the table which gives values of $x^3 - 5$ for values of x from -3 to 4.

x	-3	-2	-1	0	1	2	3	4
$x^3 - 5$	-32				-4		22	

Draw the graph of $y = x^3 - 5$ for values of x from -3 to 4.
Take 2 cm as 1 unit for x and 2 cm as 10 units for y.

b Use your graph to find the value of **i** y when $x = 1.6$ **ii** x when $y = -1.5$.

c Use your graph to solve the equations
   i $x^3 = 5$ **ii** $x^3 - 5 = 16$ **iii** $x^3 = 47$ **iv** $\frac{1}{2}(x^3 - 5) = 10$

THE SHAPE OF A CUBIC CURVE

From the last exercise we see that a cubic curve looks like

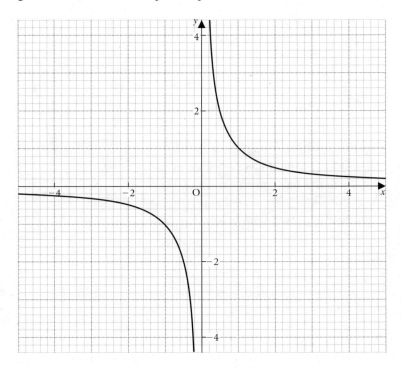

or ⌒⌄ when the x^3 term is positive

and ⌄⌣ or ⌄⌣⌄ when the x^3 is negative.

RECIPROCAL GRAPHS

The equation $y = \dfrac{a}{x}$ where a is a number, is called a reciprocal equation.

The simplest reciprocal equation is $y = \dfrac{1}{x}$.

Making a table showing values of y for some values of x from -4 to -0.25 and from 0.25 to 4 gives

x	-4	-3	-2	-1	-0.5	-0.25	0.25	0.5	1	2	3	4
y	-0.25	-0.33	-0.5	-1	-2	-4	4	2	1	0.5	0.33	0.25

Plotting these points on a graph and joining them with a smooth curve gives this distinctive two-part shape.

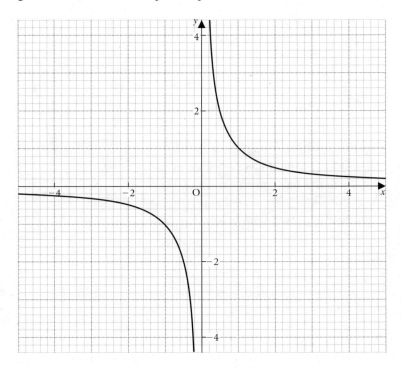

EXERCISE 18D

1 Discuss why the value $x = 0$ was not used in the table to draw the graph of $y = \dfrac{1}{x}$.

2 Use the graph of $y = \dfrac{1}{x}$, drawn opposite, to answer these questions.

    a Give the value of y when $x = 2.5$

    b What is the value of x when $y = 2.5$?

    c What is the value of y when $x = 0.2$?

    d What happens to the value of y when x gets smaller than 0.25?

    e How many forms of symmetry does the graph have and what are they?

3   **a** Copy and complete the table for $y = \dfrac{2}{x}$ for values of x from -4 to -0.5 and from 0.5 to 4 at intervals of half a unit.

x	-4	-3.5	-3	-2.5	-2	-1.5	-1	-0.5	0.5	1	1.5	2	2.5	3	3.5	4
y	-0.5	-0.57		-0.8		-1.3		-4	4	2	1.3		0.8		0.57	

    b Hence draw the graph of $y = \dfrac{2}{x}$ for values of x from -4 to -0.5 and from 0.5 to 4. Use $2\,\text{cm}$ for 1 unit on both axes.

    c Why is there no point on the graph where $x = 0$?

    d Give the values of y when   **i** $x = 2.6$ **ii** $x = -1.8$

4 Draw the graph of $y = \dfrac{12}{x}$ for values of x from 1 to 12 at intervals of 1 unit. Use $1\,\text{cm}$ for 1 unit on both axes.

    a Give the lowest value of y in the given range, and the value of x at which it occurs.

    b If the graph were drawn for values of x from 1 to 100 what would the lowest value of y be?

    c If the graph could be continued for values of x as large as you choose, what would the lowest value of y be then?

5 *Sketch* the graph of $y = \dfrac{1}{x}$ for values of x from -10 to $-\frac{1}{10}$ and from $\frac{1}{10}$ to 10.

    a What happens to the value of y as the value of x increases beyond 10?

    b Is there a value of x for which $y = 0$? Explain your answer.

    c Is there a value of y for which $x = 0$? Explain your answer.

GRAPHS OF RECIPROCAL EQUATIONS

The graph of an equation of the form $y = \dfrac{a}{x}$, where a is a constant (that is, a number), gives a distinctive two-part curve called a *hyperbola*

Notice that there is a break in the graph where $x = 0$. This is because there is no value for y when $x = 0$; we cannot divide by zero.

RECOGNISING GRAPHS

We can now look at the shape of a curve and recognise that its equation could be

- $y = mx + c$
- $y = ax^2 + bx + c$
- $y = ax^3 + bx^2 + cx + d$
- $y = \dfrac{a}{x}$
- none of these.

EXERCISE 18E

For questions **1** to **4**, write down the letter that corresponds to the correct answer.

1 The equation of this curve could be

A $y = x^2$

B $y = \dfrac{1}{x}$

C $y = x^3$

D $y = 4x - x^2$

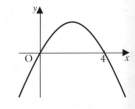

2 The equation of this curve could be

A $y = x^2 + 9$

B $y = x^3 + x^2 + 9$

C $y = \dfrac{9}{x}$

D $y = 9 - 3x$

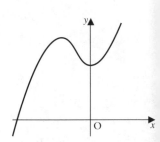

3 The equation of this curve could be

A $y = \dfrac{12}{x}$

B $y = x^2 - 9$

C $y = 9 - x^2$

D $y = x^3$

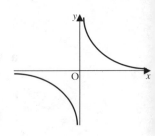

4 The equation of this curve could be

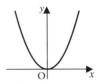

A $y = x^2$ **C** $y = 2x - 6$

B $y = 4 - x^2$ **D** $y = x^3$

For questions **5** to **13**, use squared paper. Draw x- and y-axes but do not scale them. *Sketch* the graph for each of the following equations.

5 $y = 3$ **8** $y = x$ **11** $y = x + 1$

6 $y = x^2$ **9** $y = x^2 + 1$ **12** $y = 1 - x^3$

7 $y = \dfrac{1}{x}$ $(x \neq 0)$ **10** $y = x^3$ **13** $x = 3$

For the remaining questions, write down the letter that corresponds to the correct answer.

14 The graph representing $y = x^2 - 1$ could be

A   **B**   **C**   **D**

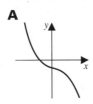

15 The graph representing $y = \dfrac{3}{x}$ could be

A   **B**   **C**   **D**

16 The graph representing $y = 10x^2$ could be

A   **B**   **C**   **D**

17 The graph representing $y = x + 2$ could be

A   **B**   **C**   **D**

18 The graph representing $y = -x^2$ could be

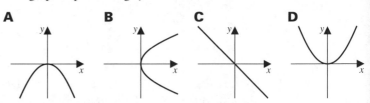

19 The graph representing $y = x^3 + 1$ could be

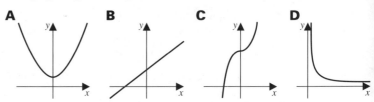

20 The graph representing $y = x^3 - 3x^2 + 2x$ could be

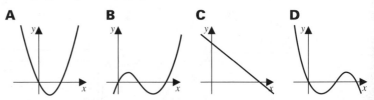

USING GRAPHS

For question **2** in Exercise 18A, Cheryl needed to use the following readings to confirm that the current flowing in a circuit is inversely proportional to the resistance.

Resistance (ohms)	0.5	0.7	1	1.2	1.5	2	2.4
Current (amps)	5.6	4	2.8	2.3	1.9	1.4	1.5

Taking the resistance as R ohms and the current as I amps, Cheryl wants to confirm that I is inversely proportional to R, that is the product of corresponding values of R and I is constant.

This means that the relationship between I and R should be of the form $IR = k$.

Rearranging to make I the subject gives $I = \dfrac{k}{R}$ where k is a constant.

Cheryl also knows that a relationship of the form $y = \dfrac{k}{x}$ gives a curve

whose shape is [graph] when x and y can have positive and

negative values.

If x and y can take positive values only, we get just the right-hand side of this curve, i.e.

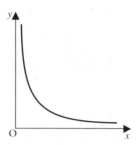

The resistance and the current have positive values only, so this is the shape that Cheryl expects to find when she plots the values of the current I against the values of the resistance R in the table.

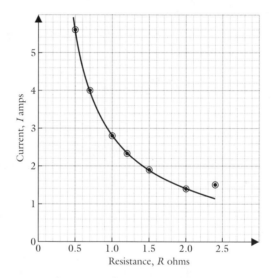

Allowing for slight errors in readings, these points do lie on the curve of the shape expected, except for one. Either a mistake has been made with this point (Cheryl may have made an error with her readings), or it could be that the relationship between R and I no longer applies when $R = 2.4$.

Assuming that $I = \dfrac{k}{R}$, we can substitute a pair of values from the graph to find the value of k,

i.e.   when $R = 2$, $I = 1.4$ so $1.4 = \dfrac{k}{2}$

$$\Rightarrow k = 2 \times 1.4 = 2.8$$

$\therefore$ $I = \dfrac{2.8}{R}$

(We can use another pair of coordinates to check the value found for k.)

INVERSE
PROPORTION

The quantities in the example on page 347 are inversely proportional.

> Any two quantities, x and y, that are inversely
> proportional, are related by the equation $y = \dfrac{k}{x}$ and
> the graph representing them is a hyperbola.

EXERCISE 18F

1 This is a graph relating pressure and
volume. The equation of the graph
is $p = \dfrac{k}{v}$.

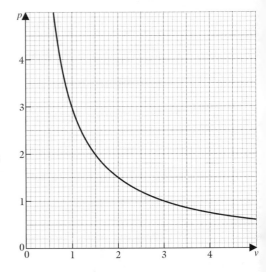

a Use the graph to find

   i the value of p when $v = 1.2$
   ii the value of v when $p = 3.6$

b Use the answer to part **a i** to find the
value of k. Check your answer using
the values found in part **a ii**.

2 Water in a plastic bottle cools down in a fridge. The graph shows how its temperature is
changing.

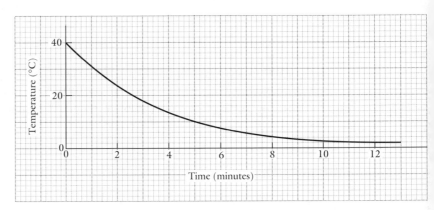

a What is the temperature of the water after   **i** 4 minutes   **ii** 8 minutes?
b How long does it take to cool down to 14 °C?
c Explain why this graph shows that the temperature is not inversely proportional to the
time.

3 This graph shows the height of a cricket ball above the ground at different times during its flight.

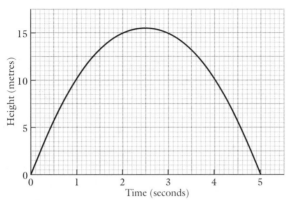

a Use the graph to find

 i the height of the ball above ground 1.5 seconds after it has been hit
 ii the greatest height above the ground reached by the ball
 iii the times at which the ball is 10 m above the ground
 iv the total time of flight.

b Which of the following formulas is likely to be the relationship between h, the height in metres, and t, the time in seconds?

$$\textbf{A } h = \frac{5}{2}(5t - t^2) \qquad \textbf{B } h = 10t + 5 \qquad \textbf{C } h = \frac{10}{t}$$

4 The graph below shows how long a delivery of ration packs for a school camp will last depending on the number of students attending the camp. Each ration pack will feed one student for one day.

a How many students can be catered for if the length of the proposed camp is 8 days?

b How many ration packs were in the delivery?

c If 15 students decide to go to camp what is the maximum number of days they can all remain there before the food runs out?

d Copy the graph and on the same grid draw a graph to show how many days a delivery of 120 ration packs will last.

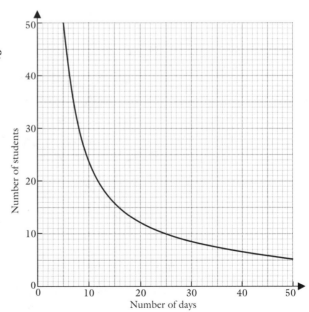

5 The capacity, C litres, and the height, h cm, of each jug in a set of jugs was measured and their values recorded in the following table.

Height, h cm	5	8	10	12	15	20
Capacity, C litres	0.1	0.41	0.80	1.38	2.70	6.40

Which of these graphs could represent the information given in the table?

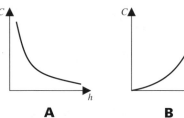
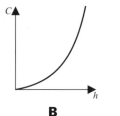
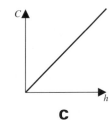

A   **B**   **C**

6 The resistance, R newtons, to the motion of a car and the speed of the car, v km/h, were measured and are recorded in the table.

v (km/h)	10	25	40	60	80	100
R (newtons)	11	70	178	400	712	1110

a Which of these graphs represents the information shown in the table?

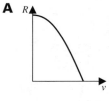
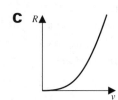
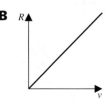
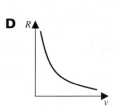

b Which of the following equations describes the information given in the table?   **A** $R = \dfrac{k}{v}$ **B** $R = kv^2$ **C** $R = kv$

GRADIENTS OF CURVES

The gradient of a straight line is the same at any point on the line, that is, the gradient is constant.

The gradient, or slope, of a curve however changes from point to point.

We can give an estimate of the gradient of a curve but it is difficult to calculate because it changes as we move along the curve.

Moving along this curve from left to right, the gradient is zero at A, increases gradually to reach its maximum value at C, and then decreases to zero again at D. The gradient next becomes negative and gets more negative (that is, the downhill slope increases) as we approach B.

EXERCISE 18G

Describe the way in which the gradient changes as we move along each curve from A to B.

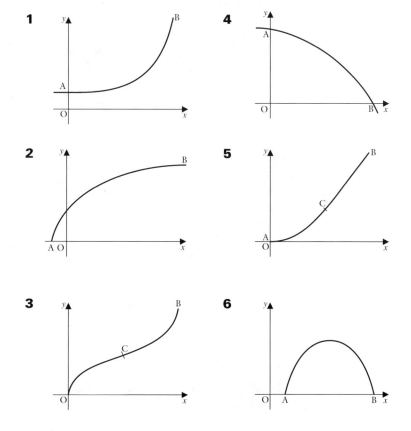

INTERPRETATION OF GRADIENT

The gradient of a graph illustrates how the quantity on the vertical axis is changing as the quantity on the horizontal axis increases.

This graph shows how the temperature of the water in a saucepan changes as time passes.

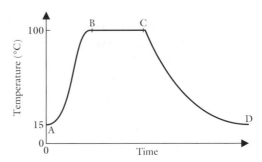

Although there are only two numbers on the axes, we can describe what is happening in general terms.

The water temperature starts at 15 °C at A, increases slowly at first but then more rapidly until it levels off to its maximum value at B. The gradient is positive for the whole of this section of the graph.

From B to C the temperature does not change (the water is boiling and its temperature cannot go above 100 °C). The gradient for this section is zero.

From C to D the temperature is falling, fairly fast to begin with and then more slowly. For this section of the curve the gradient is negative.

> The quantity on the vertical axis is
> increasing when the gradient is positive
> not changing when the gradient is zero
> decreasing when the gradient is negative.

The steepness of the curve tells you how fast the quantity is changing.

EXERCISE 18H

1 The graph shows the temperature of a bowl of soup, from the moment it was served.

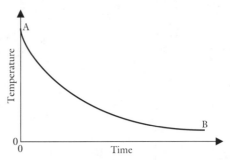

a Describe how the temperature of the soup changes with time.

b Roughly, how is the temperature changing near to B ?

c What roughly, is the temperature of the soup at B ?

2 The graph shows the number of people travelling by air over a period of several years.

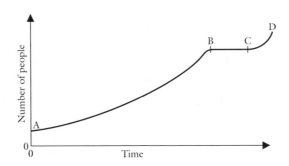

a Does the section of the curve from A to B represent an increase or decrease in the number of people travelling by air?

b Describe how the number of people travelling by air changes for the sections from B to C and from C to D.

3 The graph shows the speed of a car between two sets of traffic lights.

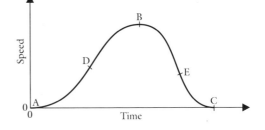

a Which section of the curve indicates
  i increasing speed
  ii decreasing speed?

b What can you say about the speed of the car at the point B?

c What colour is the second set of traffic lights? Justify your answer.

d When is the increase in speed greatest?

e When is the car losing speed most quickly?

4 The graph shows how the surface area changes as a balloon is blown up.

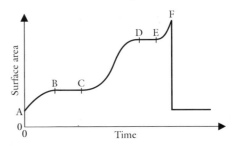

a What do you think happens at F?

b Describe how the surface area changes between
  i A and B   **ii** B and C.

c What do you think is the reason for the gradient of the curve for the sections B to C and D to E?

5 The graph illustrates a 100 metre race between Phyllis and Gita.

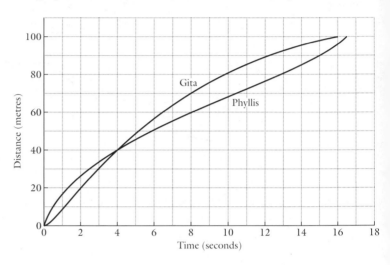

a Who won the race and in what time?

b What was the difference in the times taken to finish the race?

c Who ran faster at the start?

d How far from the start did one competitor overtake the other?

6 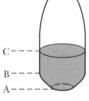 Water is poured into this container at a constant rate.

The graph shows how the depth of water in the container changes with time.

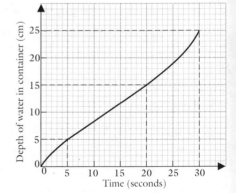

a What is the total depth of the container?

b What is the vertical distance between B and C?

c How long does the water level take to rise from B to D?

7

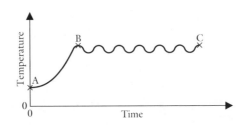

The graph shows the temperature of an oven controlled by a thermostat.

a Why does the curve not start at zero on the vertical axis?

b Describe what is happening for the part of the curve between A and B.

c What do you think can account for the shape of the curve between B and C?

8 Liquid is poured into this container at a constant rate. Which of the following graphs shows the depth of liquid in the container as it is being filled?

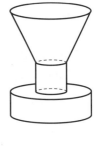

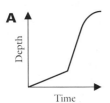
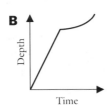
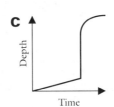

9 Liquid is poured at a constant rate into each of the three containers shown below.

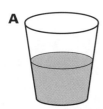
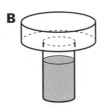
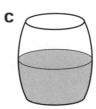

The graphs show the depth of liquid in the containers as they are being filled.

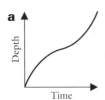
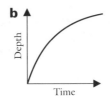
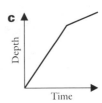

Match each graph with the appropriate container.

10 Liquid is poured at a constant rate into each of the containers whose cross-sections are given below. Sketch a graph showing how the depth of liquid in the container increases with time as the liquid is poured in.

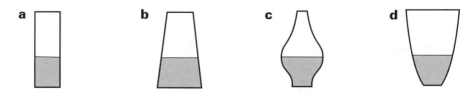

11 In Exercise 18A, you were asked to discuss how Peter could sketch a graph showing how the depth of water in a swimming pool varied with time as the pool was filled at a constant rate.

This is the cross-section of the pool.
Draw the graph for Peter.

12 The diagram shows some grain storage tanks with different shapes. Grain is drawn off at the same constant rate from each tank.

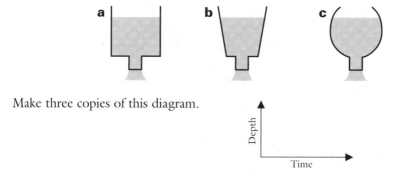

Make three copies of this diagram.

Sketch a graph showing how the depth of grain in each tank varies with time.

13 When an aircraft takes off it accelerates rapidly from zero speed until it reaches half its cruising speed. It then accelerates more and more slowly until it reaches its cruising speed of $400 \, \text{km/h}$. Sketch a graph showing how the speed of the aircraft changes during this time.

14 Derek and Carlos both ran in a marathon (26 miles). Derek started off running fairly fast, covering the first four miles in 30 minutes, but then gradually slowed down to finish the race in 6 hours. Carlos ran at a steady speed throughout the race and finished in $5\frac{1}{2}$ hours.
Sketch, on the same axes, graphs illustrating the two runs. Hence estimate how far Carlos had run when he overtook Derek.

PRACTICAL WORK

Interesting curves can be produced by
joining points that are equally spaced on
straight lines.
This example uses two straight line
drawn at right angles.

The lines create an *envelope*, which in
this case is a curve.

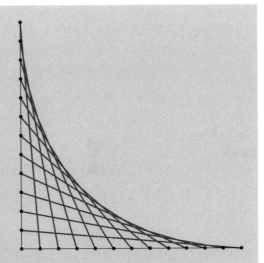

a Draw two lines, approximately 10 cm long, that bisect each other as shown in the
diagram. Mark equally spaced points on the lines about 5 mm apart. Use a ruler, or
compasses which should give a more accurate result if used carefully, to mark the
points. Use a ruler and coloured line to join the points as shown in the diagram, then
continue the pattern to complete the curve. Repeat the pattern on the other half of
the diagram to give two curves.

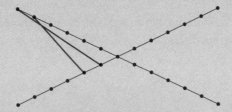

b Experiment with two lines drawn at different angles.

c Now try experimenting with more than two lines.

d This envelope is produced by joining points on
two circles.

See whether you can produce any interesting
curves by experimenting with circles and a
mixture of straight lines and circles.

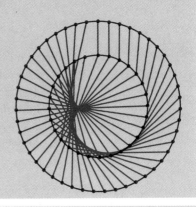

TRIGONOMETRY

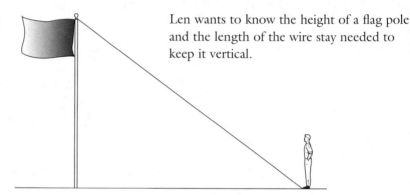

Len wants to know the height of a flag pole
and the length of the wire stay needed to
keep it vertical.

To find the height of the pole and the length of the wire stay he can
measure the distance from the foot of the pole to the point of attachment
of the wire to the ground, and then measure the angle between the wire
and the horizontal ground. The diagram showing this information is this
right-angled triangle.

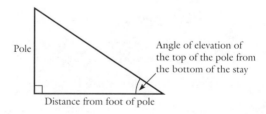

Pole   Angle of elevation of
the top of the pole from
the bottom of the stay

Distance from foot of pole

The diagram can be drawn to scale and the height of the flagpole and the
length of the wire can be measured from the scale drawing.
The disadvantage of this method is that it takes time and precision to get
a reasonably reliable answer. In this chapter we find out how to calculate
such lengths by methods which, with the help of a scientific calculator,
are fast and whose accuracy depends only on the accuracy of the initial
measurements.

We start by investigating the relationship between the size of an angle
and the lengths of two sides in a right-angled triangle.

EXERCISE 19A

1 a Draw the given triangle accurately using a protractor and a ruler.

b Measure $\widehat{A}$.

c Find $\dfrac{BC}{AB}$ as a decimal.

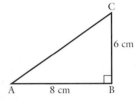

Repeat question **1** for the triangles in questions **2** to **5**.

2

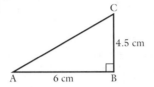

4

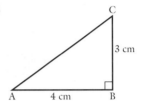

3

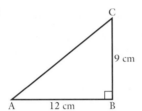

5

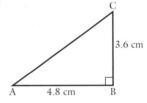

6 Are the triangles in questions **1** to **5** similar?

7 Similar triangles can be drawn so that they overlap, as in this diagram. Copy the diagram below onto squared paper. Choose your own measurements but make sure that the lengths of the horizontal lines are whole numbers of centimetres.

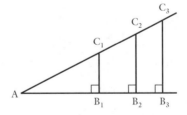

Measure $\widehat{A}$.

Find $\dfrac{B_1C_1}{AB_1}$, $\dfrac{B_2C_2}{AB_2}$ and $\dfrac{B_3C_3}{AB_3}$ as decimals.

How do your values compare?

8 Copy and complete this table using the information from questions **1** to **5**.

$\widehat{A}$	$\dfrac{BC}{AB}$
37°	0.75

9 Measure the length of AC in question **1** and find, as a decimal,

correct to 2 decimal places   **a** $\dfrac{BC}{AC}$ **b** $\dfrac{AB}{AC}$

10 Repeat question **9** using the diagrams given for questions **2** to **5** and gather all your results together in a table.

$\widehat{A}$	$\dfrac{BC}{AC}$	$\dfrac{AB}{AC}$
37°	0.6	0.8

The results for the last two questions of the exercise suggest that, in a right-angled triangle ABC with the right angle at B and a given value for angle A, each of the ratios $\dfrac{BC}{AB}, \dfrac{BC}{AC}, \dfrac{AB}{AC}$ has a fixed value irrespective of the size of the triangle. Next we consider each ratio in detail.

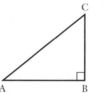 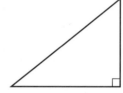

If we consider the set of all triangles that are similar to △ABC then, for every triangle in the set,

the angle corresponding to $\widehat{A}$ is the same

the ratio corresponding to $\dfrac{BC}{AB}$ is the same

where BC is the side *opposite* to $\widehat{A}$
and   AB is the *adjacent* (or neighbouring) side to $\widehat{A}$.

From the last sentence you can see that, in a right-angled triangle the

ratio $\dfrac{\text{opposite side}}{\text{adjacent side}}$ is always the same for a given angle whatever the size of the triangle.

The ratio $\dfrac{\text{opposite side}}{\text{adjacent side}}$ is called the *tangent* of the angle.

$$\text{tangent of the angle} = \dfrac{\text{opposite side}}{\text{adjacent side}}$$

More briefly, $\tan(\text{angle}) = \dfrac{\text{opp}}{\text{adj}}$

This ratio is used so often that we need a complete list of its values for all angles. This list is stored in scientific calculators.

**FINDING
TANGENTS OF
ANGLES**

To find the tangent of 33°, press `tan 3 3 =`. We get a number which fills the display. Write down one more figure than the accuracy required.

e.g. $\tan 33° = 0.649\,40\ldots$
                $= 0.6494$ correct to 4 significant figures.

If you do not get the correct answer, one reason could be that your calculator is not in 'degree mode'. For all trigonometric work at this stage, angles are measured in degrees, so make sure that your calculator is in the correct mode. Calculators also vary in the order in which buttons have to be pressed; if the order given above does not work, try

`3 3 tan` .

EXERCISE 19B

Find the tangent of 56° correct to 3 significant figures.

$\tan 56° = 1.482\ldots$

$= 1.48$ (correct to 3
    significant figures)

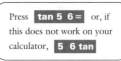
Press `tan 5 6 =` or, if this does not work on your calculator, `5 6 tan`

1 Find the tangents of the following angles correct to 3 significant figures.

   a 20°   **c** 38°   **e** 72°   **g** 53°   **i** 59°
   b 28°   **d** 78°   **f** 33°   **h** 45°   **j** 80°

2 Find the tangents of the angles listed in question **8** in **Exercise 19A**. How do the answers you now have compare with the decimals you worked out? If they are different, give a reason for this.

Find the tangent of 34.2°

$\tan 34.2° = 0.6795\ldots$
         $= 0.689$ (correct to 3 s.f.)

Press `tan 3 4 . 2 =`

3 Find the tangents of the following angles correct to 3 significant figures.

   a 15.5°   **b** 29.6°   **c** 11.4°   **d** 60.1°   **e** 3.8°

THE NAMES OF THE SIDES OF A RIGHT-ANGLED TRIANGLE

Before we can use the tangent for finding sides and angles we need to know which is the side opposite to the given angle and which is the adjacent side.

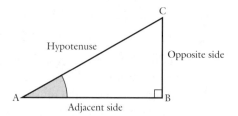

- The longest side, that is the side opposite to the right angle, is called the *hypotenuse*.
- The side which is next to the angle A, but is not the hypotenuse, is called the *adjacent side*. (Adjacent means 'next to')
- The third side is the *opposite side*. It is opposite to the particular angle A that we are concerned with.

Sometimes the triangle is in a position different from the one we have been using.

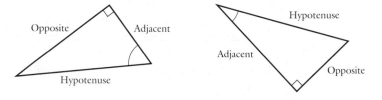

EXERCISE 19C

Sketch the following triangles. The angle we are concerned with is marked with a purple arc like this ◁. Label the sides 'hypotenuse', 'adjacent' and 'opposite'. If necessary, turn the page round so that you can see which side is which.

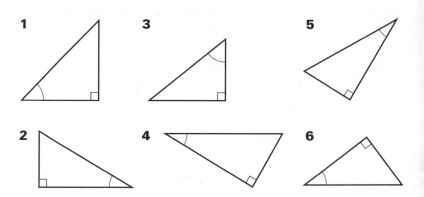

FINDING A SIDE
OF A TRIANGLE
We can now use the tangent of an angle to find the length of the opposite side in a right-angled triangle provided that we know an angle and the length of the adjacent side.

EXERCISE 19D   Use a calculator. Give your answers correct to 3 significant figures.

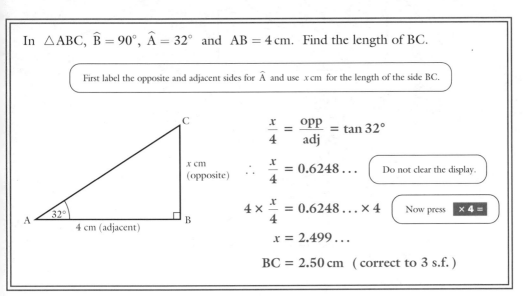

In $\triangle ABC$, $\widehat{B} = 90°$, $\widehat{A} = 32°$ and $AB = 4$ cm. Find the length of BC.

First label the opposite and adjacent sides for $\widehat{A}$ and use x cm for the length of the side BC.

$$\frac{x}{4} = \frac{\text{opp}}{\text{adj}} = \tan 32°$$

$$\therefore \quad \frac{x}{4} = 0.6248\ldots \quad \boxed{\text{Do not clear the display.}}$$

$$4 \times \frac{x}{4} = 0.6248\ldots \times 4 \quad \boxed{\text{Now press } \boxed{\times\ 4\ =}}$$

$$x = 2.499\ldots$$

$$BC = 2.50 \text{ cm} \quad (\text{correct to 3 s.f.})$$

1 Find the length of BC.

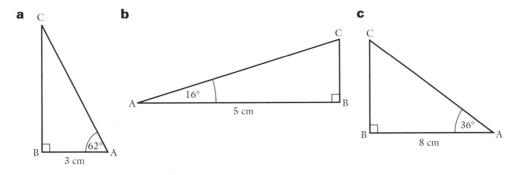

2 Find the length of BC.

a

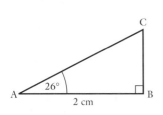

b

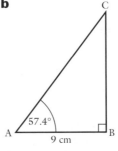

c

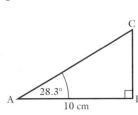

3 In this question different letters are used for the vertices of the triangles. In each case find the side required.

a Find PQ. **b** Find AC. **c** Find YZ.

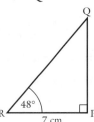
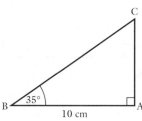
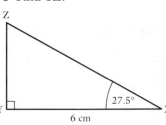

4 Find the length of BC. Turn the page round if necessary to identify the opposite and adjacent sides.

a **b** **c**

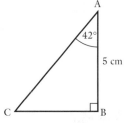
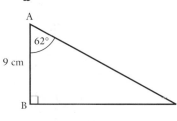
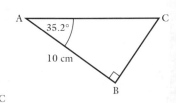

5 Find the length of BC.

a **b** **c**

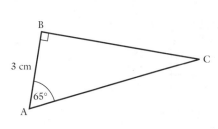
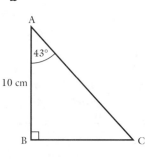
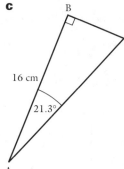

6 **a** Find BC. **b** Find EF.

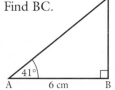
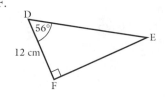

7 **a** Find QR. **b** Find XZ.

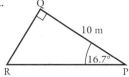
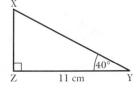

FINDING A SIDE ADJACENT TO A GIVEN ANGLE

Sometimes the side whose length we are asked to find is adjacent to the given angle instead of opposite to it. Using $\dfrac{10}{x}$ instead of $\dfrac{x}{10}$ can lead to an awkward equation so we work out the size of the other angle, which is opposite to x, and use it instead. In this case the other angle is $64°$ and we label the sides 'opposite' and 'adjacent' for this angle.

Using $64°$,

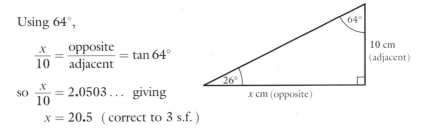

$$\frac{x}{10} = \frac{\text{opposite}}{\text{adjacent}} = \tan 64°$$

so $\dfrac{x}{10} = 2.0503\ldots$ giving

$x = 20.5$ (correct to 3 s.f.)

EXERCISE 19E

Use a calculator. Give your answers correct to 3 significant figures.

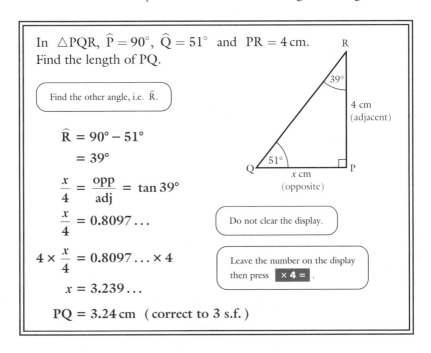

In $\triangle PQR$, $\hat{P} = 90°$, $\hat{Q} = 51°$ and $PR = 4\,\text{cm}$. Find the length of PQ.

Find the other angle, i.e. $\hat{R}$.

$\hat{R} = 90° - 51°$
$\quad = 39°$

$\dfrac{x}{4} = \dfrac{\text{opp}}{\text{adj}} = \tan 39°$

$\dfrac{x}{4} = 0.8097\ldots$

Do not clear the display.

$4 \times \dfrac{x}{4} = 0.8097\ldots \times 4$

Leave the number on the display then press ✕ 4 ＝ .

$x = 3.239\ldots$

$PQ = 3.24\,\text{cm}$ (correct to 3 s.f.)

1 a Find ZY.

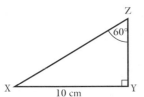

b Find BC.

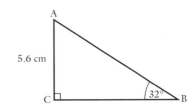

2 a Find QP.

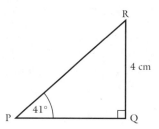

b Find AB.

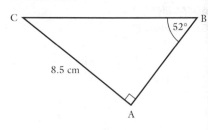

3 a Find XZ.

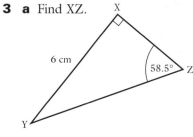

b Find LM.

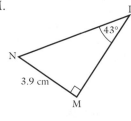

4 a Find FD.

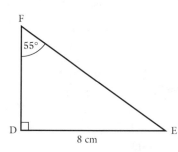

b Find QR.

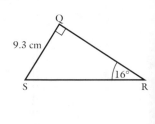

5 a Find RQ.

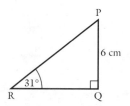

b Find AC.

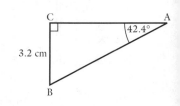

6 a Find YZ.

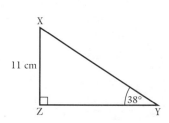

b Find LN.

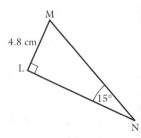

FINDING AN ANGLE GIVEN ITS TANGENT

If we are given the value of the tangent of an angle, we can use a calculator to find that angle.

For example, if the tangent of angle A is 0.732,

i.e.   tan $\widehat{A} = 0.732$,

we find $\widehat{A}$ by using tan^{-1} and then entering ▮ **0.732 =** ▮ in the calculator. This gives the size of the angle in degrees. (tan^{-1} is usually written above the tan key and is accessed by first using the 'shift' key or its equivalent.) Note that tan^{-1} means 'the angle whose tangent is'.

So when tan $\widehat{A} = 0.732$

$$\widehat{A} = 36.20\ldots^\circ = 36.2^\circ \text{ (correct to 1 decimal place)}$$

Check this on your calculator; if it does not give this result, first check that you are using degree mode then, if it is still incorrect, consult your calculator manual.

EXERCISE 19F

1 Find, correct to 1 decimal place, the angles whose tangents are given.

a 2.2   **c** 4.1   **e** 0.6752   **g** 2.0879

b 0.36   **d** 1.4   **f** 0.992 93   **h** 1

Find the angle whose tangent is $\frac{3}{4}$.

tan $\widehat{A} = \frac{3}{4} = 0.75$ (First express $\frac{3}{4}$ as a decimal.)

$\widehat{A} = 36.86\ldots^\circ = 36.9^\circ$ (correct to 1 d.p.)

---

2 Find, correct to 1 decimal place, the angles whose tangents are

a $\frac{3}{5}$ **c** $\frac{1}{2}$ **e** $\frac{3}{20}$ **g** $\frac{3}{8}$ **i** $\frac{3}{25}$

b $\frac{4}{5}$ **d** $\frac{7}{10}$ **f** $\frac{5}{4}$ **h** $2\frac{1}{4}$ **j** $2\frac{2}{5}$

Find the angle whose tangent is $\frac{2}{3}$.

tan $\widehat{A} = \frac{2}{3} = 0.6666\ldots$ (Angle A can be found in one step on the calculator; press **tan^{-1} (2 ÷ 3)=**)

$\widehat{A} = 33.69\ldots^\circ = 33.7^\circ$ (correct to 1 d.p.)

---

3 Find, correct to 1 decimal place, the angles whose tangents are

a $\frac{1}{3}$ **c** $\frac{1}{6}$ **e** $\frac{5}{3}$ **g** $\frac{2}{9}$ **i** $\frac{4}{9}$

b $\frac{1}{7}$ **d** $\frac{5}{6}$ **f** $\frac{3}{7}$ **h** $\frac{7}{3}$ **j** $\frac{4}{3}$

FINDING AN ANGLE IN A RIGHT-ANGLED TRIANGLE

We can now use the tangent of an angle to calculate the size of an angle in a right-angled triangle.

The next worked example shows the method.

EXERCISE 19G Give angles correct to 1 decimal place.

Find angle A in the diagram.

On a copy of the diagram, mark the angle to be found. Then label the opposite and adjacent sides to the angle.

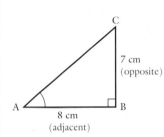

$$\tan \widehat{A} = \frac{\text{opp}}{\text{adj}} = \frac{7}{8}$$

$$= 0.875$$

$$\widehat{A} = 41.18\ldots° = 41.2° \ (\text{correct to 1 d.p.})$$

Find $\widehat{A}$ in questions **1** and **2**.

1 a

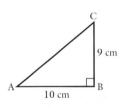

b

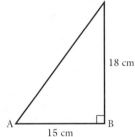

c

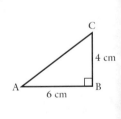

2 a

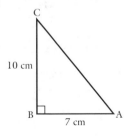

b

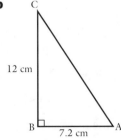

c

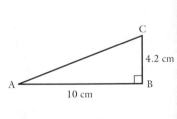

3 a Find $\widehat{P}$.

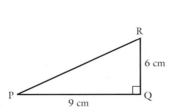

b Find $\widehat{N}$.

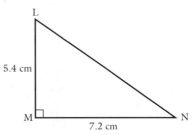

4 a Find $\widehat{B}$.

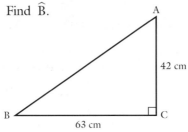

b Find $\widehat{D}$.

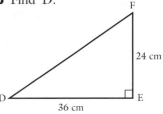

Find $\widehat{A}$ in questions **5** to **7**.

5 a

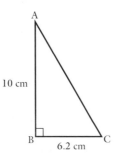

b

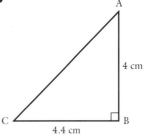

6 a

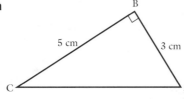

b

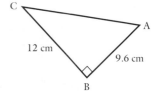

7 a

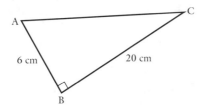

b

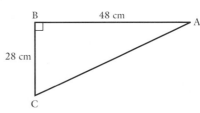

THE SINE OF AN ANGLE

In a right-angled triangle, the ratio formed by the side opposite an angle and the hypotenuse is called the *sine* of the angle.

In this diagram

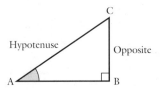

$$\text{sine of angle A} = \frac{\text{opposite}}{\text{hypotenuse}} = \frac{CB}{AC}$$

$$\text{or, briefly,} \quad \sin \widehat{A} = \frac{\text{opp}}{\text{hyp}} = \frac{CB}{AC}$$

All right-angled triangles containing, say, an angle of $40°$ are similar, so the sine ratio, $\dfrac{\text{opp}}{\text{hyp}}$, always has the same value for an angle of $40°$.

The value of the sine ratio of every acute angle is stored in scientific calculators and methods of calculation are similar to those involving tangents.

EXERCISE 19H

> Find, correct to 3 significant figures, the sine of
>
> **a** $72°$ **b** $38.2°$
>
> **a** $\sin 72° = 0.9510\ldots$
> $= 0.951$ (correct to 3 s.f.)
>
> Press
>
> **b** $\sin 38.2° = 0.6184\ldots = 0.618$ (correct to 3 s.f.)

1 Find, correct to 3 significant figures, the sines of the following angles.

    a $26°$ **b** $84°$ **c** $25.4°$ **d** $37.1°$ **e** $78.9°$

> Find, correct to 1 decimal place, the angle whose sine is 0.909
>
> $\sin \widehat{A} = 0.909$
> $\widehat{A} = 65.36\ldots°$
> $= 65.4°$ (correct to 1 d.p.)
>
> Press **shift sin 0 . 9 0 9 =**
> The shift button accesses the $\sin^{-1}$ function which means 'the angle whose sine is'.

2 Find, correct to 1 decimal place, the angles whose sines are

    a 0.834 **c** 0.639 **e** 0.9376 **g** 0.5565

    b 0.413 **d** 0.704 **f** 0.8593 **h** 0.3592

USING THE SINE RATIO

The sine ratio can be used, in the same way as the tangent ratio is used, to find angles and sides in right-angled triangles.

EXERCISE 19I

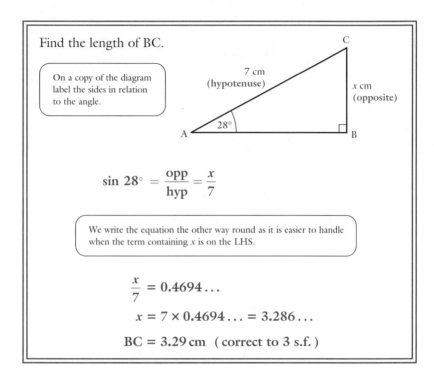

Find the length of BC.

On a copy of the diagram label the sides in relation to the angle.

$$\sin 28° = \frac{\text{opp}}{\text{hyp}} = \frac{x}{7}$$

We write the equation the other way round as it is easier to handle when the term containing x is on the LHS.

$$\frac{x}{7} = 0.4694\ldots$$

$$x = 7 \times 0.4694\ldots = 3.286\ldots$$

$$BC = 3.29 \text{ cm} \quad (\text{correct to 3 s.f.})$$

Give answers correct to 3 significant figures.

1 a Find BC.

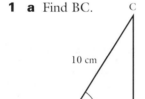

b Find RQ.

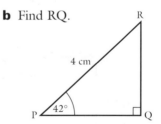

2 a Find BC.

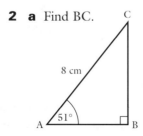

b Find PQ.

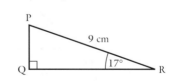

3 a Find AC.

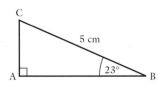

b Find XY.

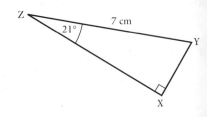

4 a Find BC.

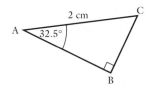

b Find LM.

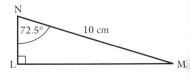

5 a Find QR.

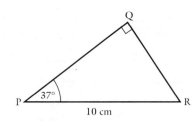

b Find PQ.

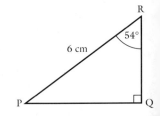

In $\triangle ABC$, $\widehat{B} = 90°$, $AC = 4$ cm and $BC = 3$ cm. Find $\widehat{A}$.

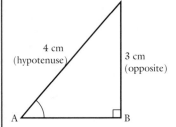

Draw the triangle, then label the sides whose lengths are given in relation to $\widehat{A}$.

$$\sin \widehat{A} = \frac{\text{opp}}{\text{hyp}} = \frac{3}{4}$$

$$= 0.75$$

$$\widehat{A} = 48.59\ldots°$$

$$= 48.6° \ (\textbf{correct to 1 d.p.})$$

Give angles correct to 1 decimal place.

6 a Find $\widehat{A}$.

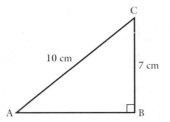

b Find $\widehat{P}$.

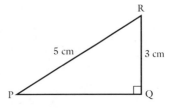

7 a Find $\widehat{A}$.

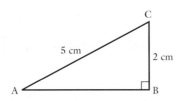

b Find $\widehat{Q}$.

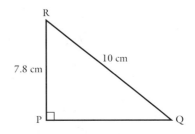

<u>**8**</u> **a** Find $\widehat{Y}$.

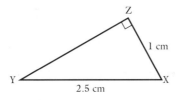

b Find $\widehat{M}$.

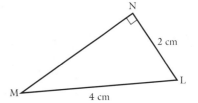

<u>**9**</u> **a** Find $\widehat{P}$.

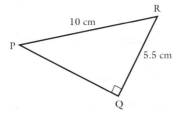

b Find $\widehat{A}$.

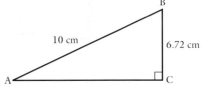

THE COSINE OF
AN ANGLE

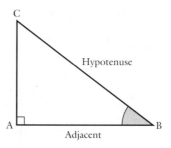

If we are given the adjacent side and the hypotenuse, then we can use a third ratio, $\dfrac{\text{adjacent side}}{\text{hypotenuse}}$.

This is called the *cosine* of the angle (cos for short).

$$\cos \widehat{B} = \frac{\text{adj}}{\text{hyp}} = \frac{AB}{BC}$$

Cosines of acute angles are stored in scientific calculators.

EXERCISE 19J

> Find, correct to 3 significant figures, the cosine of 41°.
>
> cos 41° = 0.7547 ... = 0.755 (correct to 3 s.f.)
>
> > Press   **cos 4 1 =**

1 Find, correct to 3 significant figures, the cosine of

  a 59°   **b** 48°   **c** 4°   **d** 44.9°   **e** 60.1°

> Find, correct to 1 decimal place, the angle whose cosine is 0.493
>
> cos $\widehat{A}$ = 0.493   Press   **SHIFT COS 0 . 4 9 3 =**
>
> $\widehat{A}$ = 60.46 ...° = 60.5° (correct to 1 d.p.)

2 Cos $\widehat{A}$ is given. Find $\widehat{A}$ correct to 1 decimal place.

  a 0.435   **b** 0.943   **c** 0.012   **d** 0.7   **e** 0.24

USING THE
COSINE RATIO

EXERCISE 19K

The cosine ratio can be used, in the same way as we used the sine and tangent ratios, to find angles and sides in right-angled triangles.

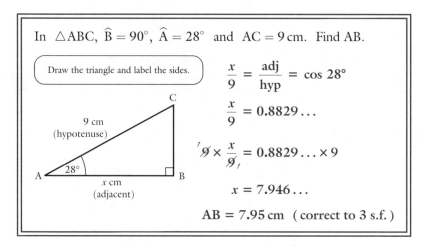

In $\triangle ABC$, $\widehat{B} = 90°$, $\widehat{A} = 28°$ and $AC = 9\,cm$. Find AB.

Draw the triangle and label the sides.

$$\frac{x}{9} = \frac{adj}{hyp} = \cos 28°$$

$$\frac{x}{9} = 0.8829\ldots$$

$$\cancel{9} \times \frac{x}{\cancel{9}} = 0.8829\ldots \times 9$$

$$x = 7.946\ldots$$

$$AB = 7.95\,cm \quad (\text{correct to 3 s.f.})$$

In the following triangles find the required lengths, correct to 3 s.f.

1 a Find AB.

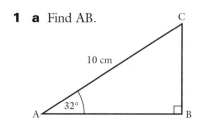

b Find AB.

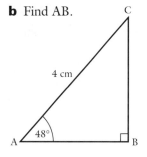

2 a Find PQ.

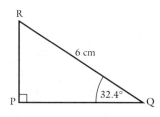

b Find AC.

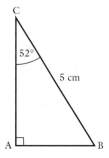

3 a Find PQ.

b Find XZ.

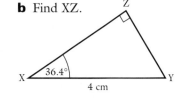

4 a Find PQ. **b** Find PR.

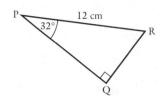
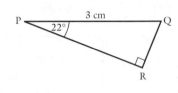

In △ABC, $\widehat{B} = 90°$, AB = 4 cm and AC = 6 cm. Find $\widehat{A}$.

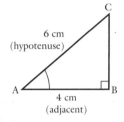

$$\cos \widehat{A} = \frac{\text{adj}}{\text{hyp}} = \frac{4}{6} = 0.6666\ldots$$

$$\widehat{A} = 48.18\ldots°$$

$$= 48.2° \ (\text{correct to 1 d.p.})$$

Give angles correct to 1 decimal place.

5 Find $\widehat{A}$.

a   **b**   **c**

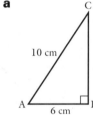
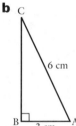
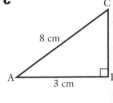

6 a Find $\widehat{Y}$. **b** Find $\widehat{C}$. **c** Find $\widehat{Q}$.

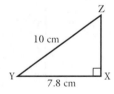
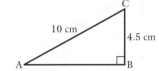
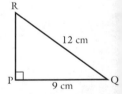

7 a Find $\widehat{C}$. **b** Find $\widehat{R}$.

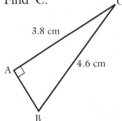
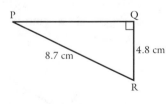

USING ALL
THREE RATIOS

Remember that, in a right-angled triangle,

$$\text{Sin } \hat{A} = \frac{\textbf{O}\text{pposite}}{\textbf{H}\text{ypotenuse}}$$

$$\text{Cos } \hat{A} = \frac{\textbf{A}\text{djacent}}{\textbf{H}\text{ypotenuse}}$$

$$\text{Tan } \hat{A} = \frac{\textbf{O}\text{pposite}}{\textbf{A}\text{djacent}}$$

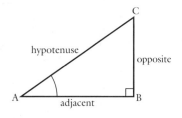

Some people remember these results using the word SOH CAH TOA which comes from the letters in bold above.

EXERCISE 19L

State whether sine, cosine or tangent should be used for the calculation of the marked angle.

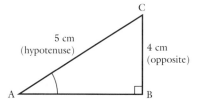

Label the sides whose lengths are given in relation to Â.

The opposite side and the hypotenuse are given so we should use sin Â.

Label the sides whose lengths are known, as 'hypotenuse', 'opposite' or 'adjacent'. Then state whether sine, cosine or tangent should be used to find the marked angle.

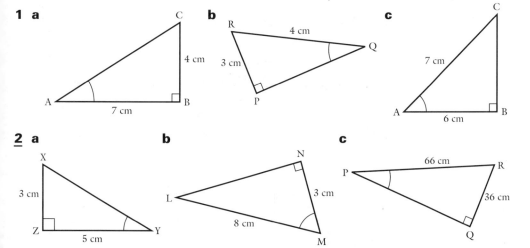

1 a

b

c

2 a

b

c

State whether sine, cosine or tangent should be used for the calculation to find x.

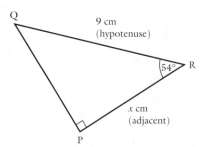

We are given the hypotenuse and want to find the adjacent side so we should use cos $\widehat{R}$.

Use 'opposite', 'adjacent' or 'hypotenuse' to label the side whose length is given and the side whose length is to be found. Then state whether the sine, cosine or tangent should be used to find x.

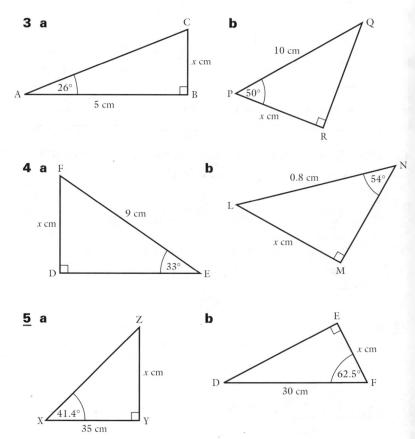

3 a

b

4 a

b

5 a

b

In questions **6** to **8**, find the marked angle correct to 1 decimal place.

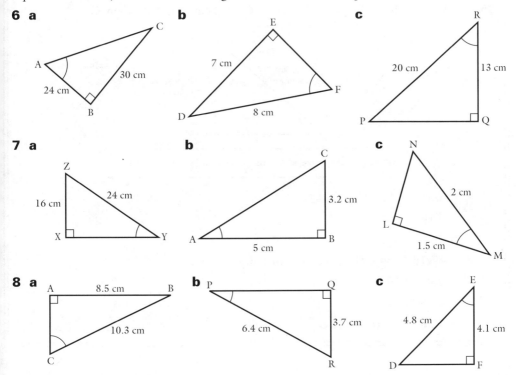

6 a

b

c

7 a

b

c

8 a

b

c

In questions **9** to **11**, find the length of the side marked x cm, giving the answer correct to 3 significant figures.

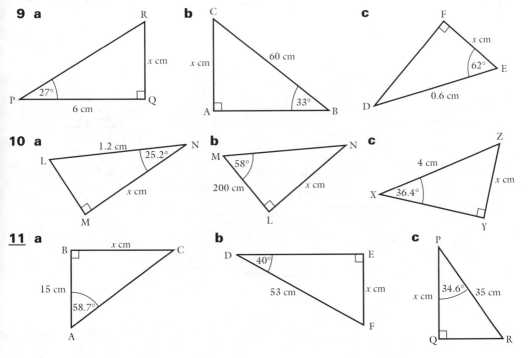

9 a

b

c

10 a

b

c

11 a

b

c

In △ABC, $\widehat{B} = 90°$, AC = 15 cm and BC = 11 cm. Find $\widehat{A}$, then $\widehat{C}$.

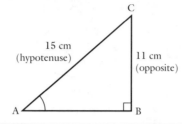

We are given the hypotenuse and the side opposite to $\widehat{A}$ so we use $\sin \widehat{A}$.

$\sin \widehat{A} = \dfrac{\text{opp}}{\text{hyp}} = \dfrac{11}{15}$

$= 0.7333\ldots$

$\widehat{A} = 47.16\ldots = 47.2°$ (correct to 1 d.p.)

$\widehat{C} = 90° - 47.16\ldots°$

$= 42.83\ldots°$

$= 42.8°$ (correct to 1 d.p.)

We know that the 3 angles of the triangle add up to 180°, so we can use this to find $\widehat{C}$.

Give angles correct to 1 decimal place and lengths correct to 3 significant figures.

12 a Find $\widehat{A}$, then $\widehat{C}$.

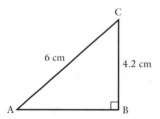

b Find AC.

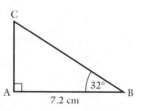

c Find AB.

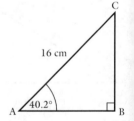

13 a Find PQ.

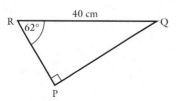

b Find XZ.

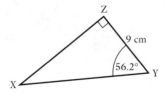

c Find $\widehat{X}$, then $\widehat{Z}$.

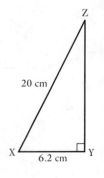

FINDING THE
HYPOTENUSE

So far when finding the length of a side we have been able to form an equation in which the unknown length is on the top of a fraction. This is not possible when the hypotenuse is to be found, and the equation we form takes slightly longer to solve.

EXERCISE 19M

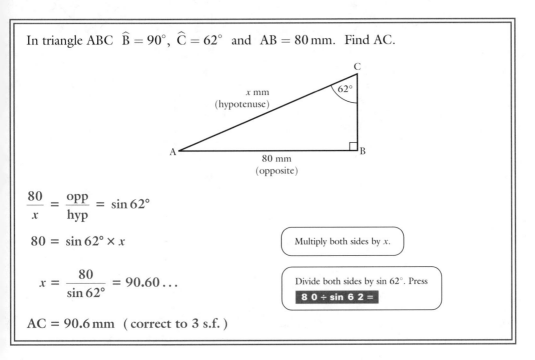

In triangle ABC $\widehat{B} = 90°$, $\widehat{C} = 62°$ and $AB = 80$ mm. Find AC.

$$\frac{80}{x} = \frac{\text{opp}}{\text{hyp}} = \sin 62°$$

$$80 = \sin 62° \times x \qquad \boxed{\text{Multiply both sides by } x.}$$

$$x = \frac{80}{\sin 62°} = 90.60 \ldots \qquad \boxed{\begin{array}{l}\text{Divide both sides by } \sin 62°. \text{ Press} \\ \boxed{8\ 0\ \div\ \sin\ 6\ 2\ =}\end{array}}$$

$AC = 90.6$ mm (correct to 3 s.f.)

In questions **1** and **2**, use the information given in the diagram to find the hypotenuse, correct to 3 significant figures.

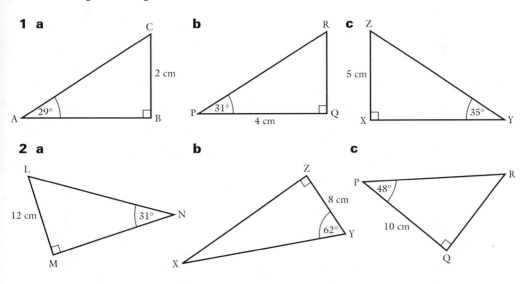

1 a

b

c

2 a

b

c

In questions **3** to **5** use the information given in the diagram to find the hypotenuse, correct to 3 significant figures.

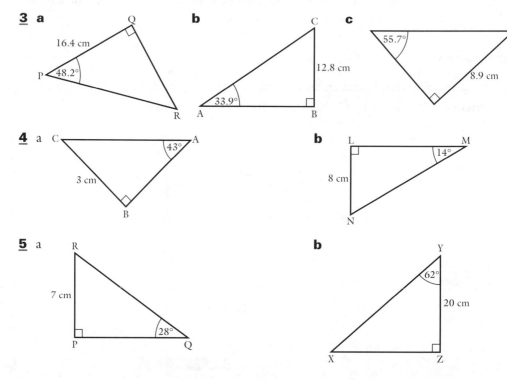

3 a 16.4 cm Q 48.2° P R

b C 12.8 cm 33.9° A B

c 55.7° 8.9 cm

4 a C 43° A 3 cm B

b L 14° M 8 cm N

5 a R 7 cm 28° P Q

b Y 62° 20 cm X Z

For the remaining questions in this exercise find sides correct to 3 significant figures and angles correct to 1 decimal place. Remember that in a right-angled triangle you can use Pythagoras' Theorem to find the length of the third side when you know the lengths of the other two sides.

6 a Find BC and AC.

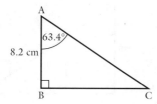

A 63.4° 8.2 cm B C

b Find $\widehat{P}$, PR and QR.

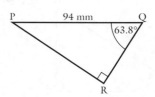

P 94 mm Q 63.8° R

7 a Find $\widehat{Z}$, XY and YZ.

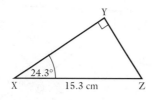

Y 24.3° X 15.3 cm Z

b Find $\widehat{L}$, LN and MN.

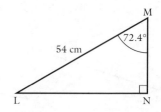

M 72.4° 54 cm L N

8 a Find $\hat{C}$, AC and BC. **b** Find $\hat{D}$, $\hat{F}$ and DF. **c** Find $\hat{X}$, $\hat{Y}$ and XZ.

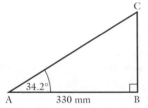 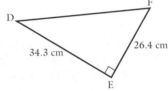 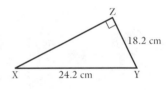

9 a Find $\hat{L}$, $\hat{N}$ and LN. **b** Find $\hat{C}$, AB and BC. **c** Find $\hat{P}$, PR and PQ.

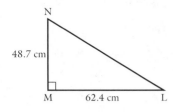 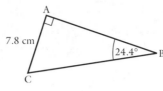 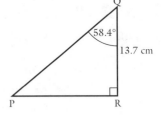

10 a Find $\hat{P}$, RQ and PR. **b** Find $\hat{N}$, $\hat{M}$ and LN. **c** Find $\hat{F}$, $\hat{D}$ and DE.

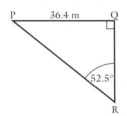 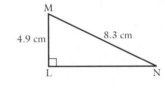 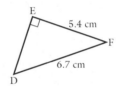

INVESTIGATION

John has a problem. For safety reasons he has to find the inclination of the ladder to the vertical. All he has with him is a scientific calculator and a straight stick. He does not have a ruler or a measuring tape or a protractor and he does not know how long the ladder is. Investigate how John can calculate the angle that the ladder makes with the wall and how accurate an answer he can expect.

SUMMARY 5

STATISTICS

The *mean value* of a frequency distribution is found by multiplying each value by its frequency, adding these products and dividing the result by the total number of values, i.e. the sum of the frequencies.

For *grouped data*, we find an estimate for the mean by multiplying the midclass value by its frequency, adding these products and dividing the result by the total number of values, i.e. the sum of the frequencies.

CURVED GRAPHS

An equation of the form $y = ax^2 + bx + c$ gives a curve whose shape is called a *parabola* and looks like this.
When the x^2 term is negative, the curve is 'upside down'.

When the equation of a curve contains x^3 (and maybe terms involving x^2, x and a number), the curve is called a *cubic* curve. These equations give cubic curves:

$$y = x^3, y = 2x^3 - x + 5, y = x^3 - 2x^2 + 6$$

A cubic curve looks like ⟋ or ⟋⟍ when the x^3 is positive

and ⟍ or ⟍⟋ when the x^3 term is negative.

An equation of the form $y = \dfrac{a}{x}$, where a is a constant (i.e. a number), gives a two-part curve called a *hyperbola*.

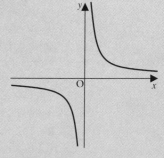

Any two quantities, x and y, that are *inversely proportional*, are related by the equation $y = \dfrac{k}{x}$ and the graph representing them is a hyperbola.

The *gradient*, or slope, of a curve changes from point to point. Gradient shows how the quantity on the vertical axis is changing as the quantity on the horizontal axis increases.

This graph gives the distance covered by an athlete from the start of a 100 m race plotted against time.

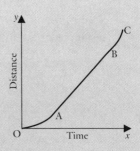

By looking at how the slope of the graph changes we can tell that the distance from the start of the race increases slowly near zero, builds up to a faster rate of increase (O to A) then keeps to a steady increase (the straight line AB) for most of the race, then the rate increases more quickly again towards the end of the race (B to C).

TRIGONOMETRY

In a right-angled triangle

the *tangent of an angle* $= \dfrac{\text{side opposite to the angle}}{\text{side adjacent to the angle}}$

the *sine of an angle* $= \dfrac{\text{side opposite to the angle}}{\text{the hypotenuse}}$

the *cosine of an angle* $= \dfrac{\text{side adjacent to the angle}}{\text{the hypotenuse}}$

or more briefly, in $\triangle ABC$

$\tan \widehat{A} = \dfrac{\text{opp}}{\text{adj}} = \dfrac{BC}{AB}$

$\sin \widehat{A} = \dfrac{\text{opp}}{\text{hyp}} = \dfrac{BC}{AC}$

$\cos \widehat{A} = \dfrac{\text{adj}}{\text{hyp}} = \dfrac{AB}{AC}$

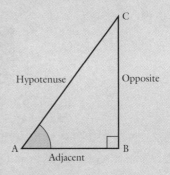

REVISION EXERCISE 5.1 (Chapters 17 to 19)

1 Forty boxes of oranges were examined and the number of bad oranges in each box was noted.

Number of bad oranges	0–5	6–11	12–17	18–23
Frequency	25	8	5	2

a What is the modal group for this distribution?

b Within which group does the median value lie?

c Estimate the mean number of bad oranges per box.

2 The masses of a group of boys were measured and the results recorded in the following table.

Mass, m kg	Frequency
$60 \leqslant m < 65$	3
$65 \leqslant m < 70$	7
$70 \leqslant m < 75$	13
$75 \leqslant m < 80$	15
$80 \leqslant m < 85$	11
$85 \leqslant m < 90$	6

a How many boys were there in the group?

b How many boys had a mass of 79 kg or more?

c Estimate the mean mass of the boys in the group.

d Draw a grouped frequency polygon for this data.

3 The bar chart shows the number of flowers on a new variety of plant grown from the seeds in one packet.

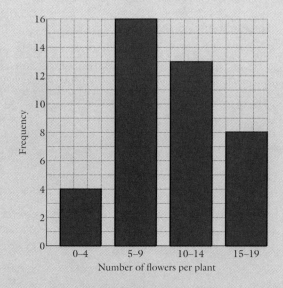

a How many plants were grown from this packet of seeds?

b Make a frequency table and estimate the mean number of flowers per plant.

c Within which group does the median value lie?

4 The graph representing $y = x^2 - x$ could be

A 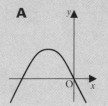 **B** 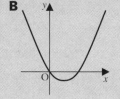 **C** 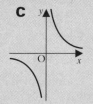 **D**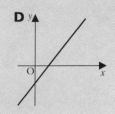

5 The graph of $y = 1 + 5x - x^2$ is given below.

   a Use the graph to solve the equation

      i $1 + 5x - x^2 = 0$ **ii** $1 + 5x - x^2 = 4$ **iii** $5 + 5x - x^2 = 0$

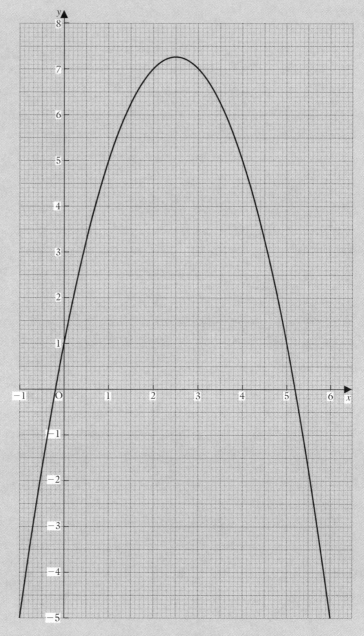

   b Is it possible to use the graph to solve the equation $1 + 5x - x^2 = 8$? If it is possible give the solution. If it is not possible, explain why.

6 The graph shows, over a period of years, the number of spectators at the home games of Combe Porton Football Club.

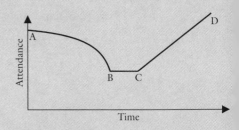

a Does the sector from A to B represent an increase or decrease in the number of spectators attending? Is this change constant?

b Describe the attendance for the section   **i** B to C   **ii** C to D.

7 Find the length of AB.

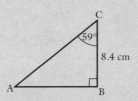

8 a Find $\widehat{P}$.

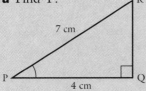

b   Find $\widehat{C}$.

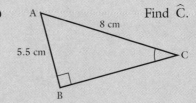

9 Find angle A in each diagram.

a

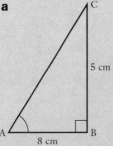

b

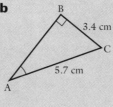

c

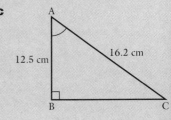

10 a   A   Find AB.

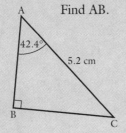

b   C   Find BC.

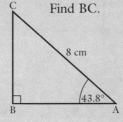

c   A   Find AC.

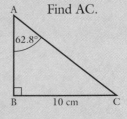

11 Sidney places the foot of his ladder on horizontal ground and the top against a vertical wall. The ladder is 16 feet long.
The foot of the ladder is 4 feet from the base of the wall.

a Work out how high up the wall the ladder reaches.
Give your answer correct to 3 significant figures.

b Work out the angle the ladder makes with the ground.
Give your answer correct to 3 significant figures.

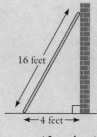

16 feet

←4 feet→

(London)

12 One hundred people, selected at random, are weighed. The results are shown in the table.

Of the people weighed, 40 were females and the mean of their weights is 65.9 kg. Calculate the mean weight of the males.

Weight, w kg	Frequency
$50 \leqslant w < 60$	7
$60 \leqslant w < 70$	49
$70 \leqslant w < 80$	29
$80 \leqslant w < 90$	15

(SEG)

13 Given that $y = x^2 + 1$

a Copy and complete the table below.

x	0	1	2	3	4	5	6	7	8
y				10			37		

b Plot these points on a copy of the grid and hence draw the graph of $y = x^2 + 1$.

c Use your graph to find the value of x when $y = 45$.

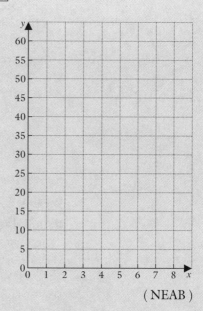

(NEAB)

1 The duration of the telephone calls made from an office on one day were recorded and the frequency polygon summarises the results.

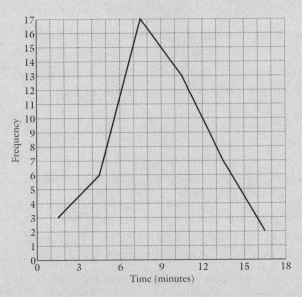

a How many telephone calls were made ?

b Estimate the range of the times taken.

c Copy and complete the table.

Middle value, t minutes	1.5					
Frequency						

d Estimate the mean duration of a telephone call that day. Explain why your answer is an estimate and not the exact value.

2 George decided to keep a record, for one month, of the time in minutes it took him to load his milk float each morning. His times are given below.

20	25	19	15	20	16	17	19	20	23
16	19	16	18	24	17	19	20	21	17
22	19	16	15	21	19	16	18	24	17

a Construct an ungrouped frequency table for these times.

b Find   **i** the mean time   **ii** the range of times.

c Bob also has to load his float every morning with roughly the same amount of milk and other goods. He keeps a record for a month and finds that his mean time is 19 minutes and the range is 5 minutes. Does Bob do the same job faster than George ? Give reasons for your answer.

3 The equation of this graph could be

A $y = \dfrac{12}{x}$

B $y = 3x - 4$

C $y = 4x - x^3$

D $y = x^2 + 4x - 4$

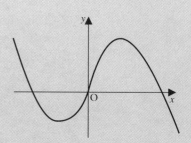

4 Study the statements given below and pair each statement with the graph that best represents it.

a The rate of inflation is increasing but by less each month.

b The rate of inflation is increasing by ever greater amounts each month.

c The rate of inflation is decreasing but more slowly each month.

d The rate of inflation is decreasing at a faster rate each month.

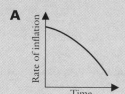
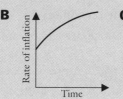
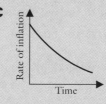

5 Use the information in the diagram to find

a $\widehat{A}$ **b** AC **c** AB

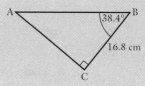

6 The diagram shows the cross-section of a support for a motorway bridge. $BC = 12.4$ m and $\widehat{C} = 42.7°$. Find the length of

a AB **b** AC.

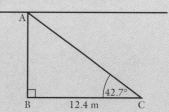

**REVISION
EXERCISE 5.3
(Chapters
1 to 19)**

Do not use a calculator for this exercise.

1 a Write these numbers as ordinary numbers

i 4.73×10^4 **ii** 1.76×10^{-2}

b Correct each number to 1 significant figure and hence give a rough value for $\dfrac{789 \times 0.123}{37.42}$

c Find the value of **i** 2^{-3} **ii** 16^{-1} **iii** 10^0 **iv** $\left(\dfrac{3}{2}\right)^{-2}$

d Simplify **i** $p \times p^3$ **ii** $x^2 \times x^3 \times x^4$ **iii** $p^5 \div p^3$ **iv** $a^{-2} \times a^{-3}$

2 The school bus never leaves early in the morning. The probability that it leaves on time is $\frac{2}{5}$.

   a What is the probability that it leaves late?

   b Copy and complete the following tree diagram by writing the probabilities on the branches.

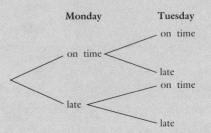

   What is the probability that

   c the bus leaves late on both days

   d the bus is late on one day and on time on the other?

3 **a** Find, in terms of n, an expression for the nth term of the sequence

$$5, 8, 13, 20, \ldots$$

   b Find the first four terms of the sequence in which the nth term is

    i $3n - 2$ **ii** $n^2 + 1$ **iii** $\dfrac{n+1}{n+2}$

4 **a** These two cups are similar.

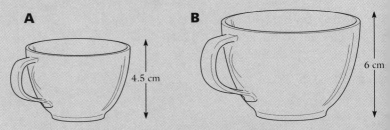

   Give the scale factor that enlarges **A** to **B**.

   b

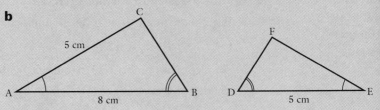

   In triangles ABC and DEF, $\widehat{A} = \widehat{E}$ and $\widehat{B} = \widehat{D}$. AB = 8 cm, DE = 5 cm and AC = 5 cm. Find EF.

5 a A coach journey of 150 miles costs £13.50. At the same rate per mile

   i what would be the cost of travelling 120 miles

   ii how far could you travel for £18?

b The Year 10 pupils in a school were arranged in 8 rows with 15 pupils in each row. If these pupils were rearranged in 10 rows, how many pupils would there be in each row?

6 a i Given that 1 hectare = 2.47 acres, draw a graph to convert from 0 to 100 hectares into acres. State an occupation which would find this graph useful.

   ii Use your graph to convert 150 acres into hectares.

b For each graph find the gradient and give the gradient a meaning within the context of the labels on the graph.

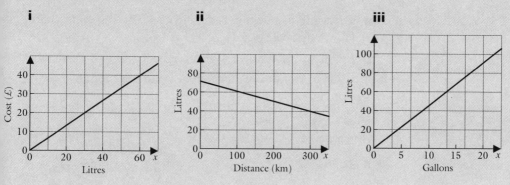

i

ii

iii

7 Copy the diagram, then carry out the compound transformation: a rotation of 90° clockwise about the origin followed by an enlargement, scale factor $\frac{1}{2}$, centre $(-4, -4)$.

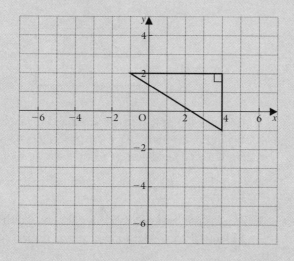

8 a Factorise

   i $a^2 - a^3$ **iii** $x^2 + 10x + 24$
   ii $x^2 - 4x - 21$ **iv** $x^2 - y^2$

   b Find the value of $8.54^2 - 1.46^2$.

   c Simplify

   i $\dfrac{12xy}{8xy^2}$ **ii** $\dfrac{ab}{b(a+b)}$ **iii** $15p \div \dfrac{5p}{4}$ **iv** $\dfrac{3x}{y} \times \dfrac{y}{x} \div \dfrac{3x}{2y}$

**REVISION
EXERCISE 5.4
(Chapters
1 to 19)**

1 Solve the equations.

   a $\dfrac{3x}{5} = \dfrac{1}{4}$ **c** $\dfrac{x}{4} - \dfrac{3}{4} = 3$ **e** $\dfrac{3}{x} + \dfrac{7}{10} = \dfrac{13}{10}$

   b $\dfrac{x}{2} + \dfrac{1}{4} = 2$ **d** $\dfrac{2x}{5} - \dfrac{x}{4} = \dfrac{6}{5}$ **f** $\dfrac{2x}{3} = \dfrac{1}{3} + \dfrac{x}{2}$

2 a The width of a writing desk is 75 cm. This is $\frac{5}{9}$ of its length. How long is the desk?

   b I think of a number x. When $\frac{1}{3}$ is added to $\frac{2}{5}$ of the number the result is $\frac{5}{6}$. Form an equation in x and solve it to find the number.

3 Expand

   a $4a(b - 3c)$ **c** $(4x - 1)(5 + x)$
   b $(x - 6)(x + 2)$ **d** $(5p + 2q)(5p - 2q)$

4

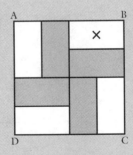

Four identical purple cards are arranged on a white square ABCD as shown in the diagram. Each card measures 65 mm by 32 mm, both measurements being correct to the nearest millimetre.

   a Find the greatest possible length for an edge of the square ABCD.

   b What is the least possible value for the width of one of the 4 identical rectangles, one of which is marked X.

5 **a** Change the subject of each formula to the letter in brackets.

    i $v = \dfrac{u}{4}$ (u) **iii** $c^2 = b^2 - 2at$ (t)

    ii $x = \dfrac{V}{y^2}$ (V) **iv** $a = \frac{1}{2}b - 2c$ (c)

  b **i** Given that $A = \dfrac{B}{C} + D$ change the subject to B.

    ii Find B when $A = \frac{5}{8}$, $C = 1\frac{1}{2}$ and $D = \frac{1}{4}$.

6 **a** A small business made a profit of £8909 this year. This is an increase of 18% on the profit last year. How much profit was made last year?

  b A greengrocer buys a box of 150 Seville oranges for £13.50 and sells them at 14 p each. Find his percentage profit.

7 The heights of Margaret's broad bean plants five weeks after planting are given in the table.

Height, h cm	$0 \leqslant h < 5$	$5 \leqslant h < 10$	$10 \leqslant h < 15$	$15 \leqslant h < 20$
Frequency	3	5	25	13

  a How many broad bean plants did Margaret grow?
  b What was their mean height after five weeks?
  c Illustrate this distribution of heights with a frequency polygon.
  d Find the range for the heights of these plants after five weeks.
  e Within which group does the median value lie?

8 Use the information in the diagram to find
  a $\widehat{P}$ **b** QR   **c** PR

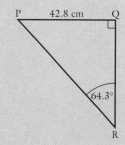

9 A salesman in a large electrical outlet offers a discount of 5% off the list price of any item for cash. The list price of a washing machine is calculated by adding 30% to the buying-in price.

  a How much profit does the salesman make on a washing machine costing him £250 if he sells for cash?
  b Express this profit as a percentage of the buying-in price.

10 a The graph representing $y = 2x - x^2 - x^3$ could be

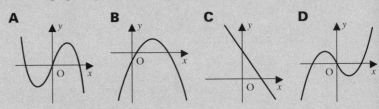

b Three cars were observed approaching a set of traffic lights. The graphs show how the speed of each car changed. Describe the way in which the speed of each car changed.

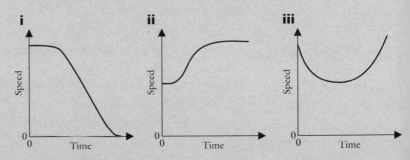

11 Liquid is poured at a constant rate into each of the containers whose cross-sections are shown below. For each shape sketch the graph showing how the depth of liquid in the container increases as the liquid is poured in.

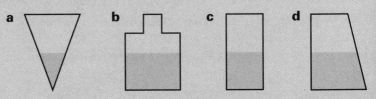

ANSWERS

Answers are given to questions asking for estimates; there is no 'correct' estimate, we have given a likely value. Allow a reasonable margin of error for answers read from graphs. Possible answers are given to questions asking for opinions or reasons or interpretation; any reasonable alternative is also valid.

Diagrams given are intended only to give an indication of shape; no scales are given and axes are not labelled.

Numerical answers are given corrected to three significant figures unless specified otherwise.

The Examination Boards accept no responsibility whatsoever for the accuracy, method or working in the answers given to past examination questions. These answers are the sole responsibility of the authors.

Summary 1

Revision Exercise 1.1 (p. 21)

1. **a** 625   **g** 2584   **m** 192
   b 139   **h** 12 636   **n** 4769
   c 5280   **i** 10 578   **p** 29
   d 24 000   **j** 11 392   **q** 20 r 9
   e 56   **k** 45 105   **r** 17
   f 7   **l** 40 992   **s** 14 r 17

2. **a** **i** 3^4 **ii** 7^6
   b **i** 3^3 **ii** 2^6 **iii** 6^2 **iv** 5^3

3. **a** **i** 9   **iii** 16   **v** 15
      ii 24   **iv** 18   **vi** 24
   b **i** 56   **iii** 54   **v** 18
      ii 36   **iv** 36   **vi** 24

4. **a** 64   **c** 25   **e** 32
   b 243   **d** 81   **f** 125

5. **a** **i** 36   **ii** 64   **iii** 121
   b 37, 41, 43, 47, 53
   c **i** 31, 37, 43
      ii 12, 16, 22, 28, 36, 48
      iii 28, 36   **iv** 9, 16, 36

6. **a** **i** 3.76 **ii** 3.8   **e** **i** 7.00 **ii** 7.0
   b **i** 14.01 **ii** 14   **f** **i** 1.78 **ii** 1.8
   c **i** 45.09 **ii** 45   **g** **i** 0.03 **ii** 0.026
   d **i** 6.08 **ii** 6.1   **h** **i** 0.08 **ii** 0.084

7. **a** **i** 2.785   **f** **i** 0.015   **k** **i** 3.299
      ii 2.78   **ii** 0.0151   **ii** 3.30
   b **i** 0.157   **g** **i** 254.163   **l** **i** 0.001
      ii 0.157   **ii** 254   **ii** 0.000 926
   c **i** 0.073   **h** **i** 7.820   **m** **i** 0.010
      ii 0.0733   **ii** 7.82   **ii** 0.009 64
   d **i** 15.061   **i** **i** 3.333   **n** **i** 0.006
      ii 15.1   **ii** 3.33   **ii** 0.005 84
   e **i** 0.000   **j** **i** 674.826   **p** **i** 36.364
      ii 0.000 378   **ii** 675   **ii** 36.4

8. **a** 29   **c** 39   **e** 13
   b 45   **d** -3 **f** 14

Revision Exercise 1.2 (p. 22)

1. **a** **i** $\frac{17}{7}$ **ii** $\frac{49}{9}$ **iii** $\frac{18}{5}$ **iv** $\frac{39}{4}$
   b **i** $8\frac{2}{5}$ **ii** $4\frac{1}{4}$ **iii** $6\frac{4}{7}$ **iv** $1\frac{9}{17}$

2. **a** $1\frac{5}{8}$ **e** $\frac{7}{10}$ **i** 1   **m** $\frac{71}{126}$
   b $\frac{9}{10}$ **f** $1\frac{7}{10}$ **j** $1\frac{17}{48}$ **n** $1\frac{23}{42}$
   c $\frac{11}{12}$ **g** $2\frac{1}{12}$ **k** $1\frac{3}{4}$ **p** $2\frac{1}{24}$
   d $\frac{2}{3}$ **h** $4\frac{1}{10}$ **l** $2\frac{1}{5}$

3. **a** $\frac{1}{20}$ **d** $\frac{1}{36}$ **g** $1\frac{1}{2}$ **j** $2\frac{11}{12}$
   b $\frac{1}{3}$ **e** $\frac{7}{30}$ **h** $1\frac{3}{4}$ **k** $\frac{1}{8}$
   c $\frac{3}{8}$ **f** $\frac{13}{36}$ **i** $2\frac{3}{4}$ **l** $\frac{31}{40}$

4. **a** $\frac{5}{9}$ **f** 1   **k** $3\frac{1}{2}$ **q** $\frac{3}{22}$
   b $\frac{3}{10}$ **g** $\frac{4}{7}$ **l** $1\frac{1}{6}$ **r** $\frac{10}{21}$
   c $\frac{1}{2}$ **h** $1\frac{4}{5}$ **m** $\frac{14}{81}$ **s** $\frac{3}{14}$
   d 1   **i** 2   **n** $\frac{12}{49}$
   e 2   **j** $1\frac{1}{3}$ **p** $4\frac{1}{2}$

5. **a** $\frac{7}{30}$ **d** $\frac{2}{3}$ **g** $1\frac{5}{7}$ **j** $3\frac{1}{12}$
   b $\frac{13}{21}$ **e** $4\frac{7}{10}$ **h** $\frac{2}{5}$
   c $2\frac{1}{4}$ **f** $2\frac{5}{6}$ **i** $1\frac{1}{2}$

6. **a** 5.01   **e** 4.832   **i** 0.49
   b 19.1   **f** 1.83   **j** 0.361
   c 6.17   **g** 3.2   **k** 0.002 02
   d 8.9   **h** 0.08   **l** 0.0068

7. **a** 0.96   **f** 0.216   **k** 0.02
   b 0.042   **g** 0.360 72   **l** 0.001
   c 0.008   **h** 2.7   **m** 93.8
   d 0.25   **i** 0.08   **n** 5.5
   e 3.355 11   **j** 8560   **p** 12.87

8. **a** 4   **e** 0.703   **i** 0.04
   b 3   **f** 1.3   **j** 0.0364
   c 0.0204   **g** 0.04
   d 0.648   **h** 2.4

9. **a** $\frac{5}{8} < \frac{7}{10}$ **c** $\frac{1}{5} < \frac{4}{15}$
   b $\frac{2}{5} > \frac{1}{3}$ **d** $\frac{4}{7} > \frac{5}{9}$

Revision Exercise 1.3 (p. 24)

1. **a** **i** 0.36   **ii** 0.95   **iii** 0.54   **iv** 0.825
   b **i** $\frac{17}{20}$ **ii** $\frac{21}{50}$ **iii** $\frac{13}{20}$ **iv** $\frac{1}{8}$
   c **i** 44%   **ii** 28%   **iii** 138%   **iv** 92.5%

2. **a** 85, 0.85   **c** $\frac{5}{8}$, 62.5   **e** $1\frac{3}{20}$, 115
   b $\frac{3}{8}$, 0.375   **d** $\frac{23}{400}$, 0.0575   **f** 475, 4.75

3. **a** **i** 18 g   **ii** 19.8 g   **iii** 12.6 m
   b **i** £700.80   **ii** £144   **iii** 234 cm²   **iv** £28.60
   c **i** 17.0 km   **ii** 0.599 m   **iii** 33.1 mm
   d **i** 20%   **ii** $\frac{13}{40}$ **iii** 0.56%   **iv** $\frac{3}{16}$

4. **a** **i** 2 : 3   **iii** 2 : 3   **v** 3 : 5 : 4
      ii 1 : 2 : 3   **iv** 7 : 5   **vi** 18 : 8 : 9
   b **i** 9 : 2   **iii** 17 : 60   **v** 9 : 20
      ii 2 : 5   **iv** 2 : 125   **vi** 50 : 3
   c **i** £20 : £25
      ii 54 m : 42 m
      iii 0.625 kg : 1.25 kg : 3.125 kg
      iv 30 min : $2\frac{1}{2}$ h : 4 h

5. a $1:10\,000$ **b** 4 cm
6. a £24.50 **b i** $\frac{3}{7}$ **ii** £25.68
7. a $\frac{16}{25}$ **b i** 36% **ii** 0.36 **iii** $\frac{9}{25}$
8. 4.85
9. a $\frac{21}{50}$ **b** 0.46 **c** 1485 **d** 12%
10. a i £24 **ii** 25.5 cm **iii** 24 kg
   b 75% of 5 **c** 60% of $\frac{9}{10}$

Revision Exercise 1.4 (p. 26)

1. a $63°$ **b** $e = 70°, f = 40°$
   c $g = 82°, h = 98°, i = 82°$
   d $100°$ **e** $60°$ **f** $70°$
2. a i $24°$ **ii** $18°$
   b i $108°$ **ii** $135°$ **iii** $160°$
   c i 24 **ii** 20
   d i yes, 9 sides **ii** no
   e i yes, 6 sides **ii** yes, 18 sides
   f $50°$
3. a $d = 70°$ **b** $g = 75°$ **c** $j = 57°$
   $e = 110°$ $h = 105°$ $k = 85°$
   $f = 70°$ $i = 75°$ $l = 38°$
4. a $m = 37°$ **b** $q = 54°$ **c** $t = 35°$
   $n = 44°$ $r = 61°$ $u = 70°$
   $p = 99°$ $s = 126°$ $v = 75°$
   $w = 35°$
5. a $20\,\text{cm}^2$ **c** $17\,\text{cm}^2$
   b $10\,\text{cm}^2$ **d** $19.35\,\text{cm}^2$
6. a 4 cm **c** 5 cm **e** 4 cm
   b $4.5\,\text{cm}^2$ **d** 5 m, 25 m²
7. a $60\,\text{cm}^2$ **b** $40\,\text{cm}^2$ **c** $30\,\text{cm}^2$
8. a i 4.804 m **ii** 1015.96 g **iii** 116 inches
   b i 4.5 cm **vii** $6000\,\text{cm}^2$
   ii 560 m **viii** 432 sq inches
   iii 4 ft **ix** $5\,\text{cm}^3$
   iv 39 ft **x** $2000\,\text{cm}^3$
   v $500\,\text{mm}^2$ **xi** $4\,\text{m}^3$
   vi $0.4\,\text{m}^2$ **xii** 720 cubic inches
9. a i 50.3 cm (3 s.f.) **ii** $201\,\text{cm}^2$ (3 s.f.)
   b i 35.7 cm (3 s.f.) **ii** $54.4\,\text{cm}^2$ (3 s.f.)
   c i 65.1 cm (3 s.f.) **ii** $69.3\,\text{cm}^2$ (3 s.f.)
10. a $2025\,\text{cm}^3$ **b** $900\,\text{cm}^3$ **c** $2260\,\text{cm}^3$ (3 s.f.)
11. a $23.94\,\text{cm}^3$ **b** 5 cm
12. a $d = 48°, e = 48°, f = 42°, g = 42°, h = 42°,$
   $i = 96°$
   b $j = 35°, k = 69°, l = 71°$
13. a 2.79 m **c** 25.2 mm
   b 5.24 cm **d** 190 mm

Revision Exercise 1.5 (p. 29)

1. a $3a$ **d** $4a$ **g** $6 - 8a$
   b $2b + 1$ **e** $2b + 9$ **h** $2 + 3x$
   c $5x + 3$ **f** $11 - 7x$ **i** $2 - 2x$
2. a $2xy$ **d** $24t^2$ **g** $10ab$ **j** $3a^3$
   b $12ab$ **e** $2ab$ **h** $24n^2$ **k** $5ab^2$
   c $4ac$ **f** $3x^2$ **i** $8xy$ **l** $12ab^2$
3. a $5x + 21$ **d** $2x - 6$ **g** $4x + 6$
   b $3a - 2$ **e** $6a - 3$ **h** 18
   c $10x + 1$ **f** $a + 20$

4. a i 4 **ii** -14 **iii** -4
   b i $\frac{3}{2}$ **ii** -8 **iii** 18
5. a 5 **e** 3 **i** 7 **m** $\frac{8}{3}$
   b 4 **f** $-5\frac{1}{2}$ **j** 14 **n** $2\frac{1}{2}$
   c 2 **g** 28 **k** 1
   d 2.4 **h** $3\frac{1}{2}$ **l** $\frac{1}{2}$
6. a $x < 10$ **d** $x \leqslant 16$ **g** $x < 2$
   b $5 \geqslant x$ **e** $-6 > x$ **h** $-5 < x$
   c $x > -5$ **f** $x > -4$ **i** $x \geqslant -5$
7. a $x = 3, y = 1$ **f** $x = 2, y = -1$
   b $x = 4, y = 3$ **g** $x = 19, y = -2$
   c $x = 3\frac{2}{3}, y = 5$ **h** $a = 3, b = 1$
   d $x = 2, y = 5$ **i** $x = 5, y = -1$
   e $x = 3, y = -3$
8. a ± 4.80 **b** ± 0.686 **c** ± 2.60

Revision Exercise 1.6 (p. 30)

1. a i $3, 0$ **ii** $2, 6$ **iii** $-\frac{1}{2}, 3$ **iv** $\frac{3}{2}, \frac{5}{2}$
   b i obtuse **iii** acute
   ii obtuse **iv** acute
2. a C **b** D **c** A, E **d** B
3. a 35 miles
   b Molly: 2 hours $22\frac{1}{2}$ min;
   Father: 1 hour 45 min
   c Father, by 5.3 mph
   d at 13.30, 15 miles from Farley
4. C
5. a

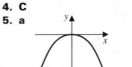

6. a i 105 miles **ii** 5 miles
   b i $1\frac{3}{4}$ hours **ii** 2 h 24 min
   c 12 km/h

Revision Exercise 1.7 (p. 32)

1. a $\frac{19}{40}$ **b** £18 **c** 37.5%
2. a mode 8, median 9, range 6 **b** 9.62
3. a 0.35 **b** 0.7 **c** 0.45
4. a

First dice

	1	2	3	4	5	6
1	2	3	4	5	6	7
2	3	4	5	6	7	8
3	4	5	6	7	8	9
4	5	6	7	8	9	10
5	6	7	8	9	10	11
6	7	8	9	10	11	12

Second dice

b 10 **c** 30
5. a $\frac{1}{4}$ **b** $\frac{2}{3}$ **c** $\frac{1}{2}$
6. a no relationship
   b moderate negative correlation
   c strong positive correlation

7. a i 42 cm **ii** 20 cm

b

Frequency	7	24	8	17	4

c i 29 **ii** 39

d $23 < h \leqslant 28$

e i, ii

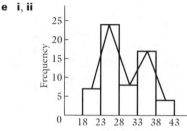

8. a 30 **b**

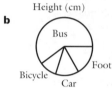

Chapter 1

Exercise 1B (p. 35)

1. a 9 **c** 128 **e** 1.44
 b 125 **d** 10 000 **f** 5
2. a 4 **c** 10 **e** 1.21
 b 1000 **d** 1 000 000 **f** 343
3. a 16 **c** 64 **e** 0.01
 b 64 **d** 400 **f** 0.04
4. a 7200 **d** 3820 **g** 46.3
 b 893 **e** 27.5 **h** 503.2
 c 65 000 **f** 537 000 **i** 709
5. a 12 **d** 540 **g** 100
 b 144 **e** 450 **h** 100
 c 500 **f** 360 **i** 1960
6. a 3^4 **c** 7^1 **e** 5^5 **g** 0.5^3 **i** 4^4 **k** 7^2
 b 8^3 **d** 0.1^2 **f** 12^1 **h** 10^5 **j** 1.5^3 **l** 15^1
7. a $3^2 \times 5$ **d** $3^3 \times 5$
 b $2^2 \times 7^3$ **e** $2 \times 3 \times 13^2$
 c $2^2 \times 3 \times 5^2 \times 7$ **f** $3 \times 5 \times 17^3$
8. a $10x^2$ **e** $8a^3$ **i** $16t^4$
 b t^2 **f** $3y^3$ **j** $80x^3$
 c $2p^2$ **g** $16p^3$ **k** $4s^3$
 d $6s^2$ **h** $27s^3$ **l** $5t^3$
9. a $12b^2$ **e** $10w^3$ **i** $120a^3$
 b $5t^2$ **f** $2a^3$ **j** $125s^3$
 c y^2 **g** $30v^3$ **k** $6x^3$
 d $21x^2$ **h** $8x^3$ **l** $6y^3$
10. a 10^2 **b** 10^3 **c** 10^6 **d** 10^{10}
11. 5 976 000 000 000 000 000 000 000 kg
12. too big **14.** £375
13. a £1100 **b** £1331 **15.** 7.38×10^{19} tonnes

Exercise 1C (p. 38)

1. a $2^2 \times 3^2$ **c** $2 \times 3 \times 13$ **e** $3^2 \times 5 \times 7$
 b $3 \times 5^2 \times 7$ **d** $2^3 \times 3 \times 11$

2. a $2^2 \times 5^2$ **c** $2^2 \times 3 \times 5^2$ **e** 11^2
 b $2^4 \times 3 \times 5$ **d** $2 \times 7 \times 11$
3. a $3^2 \times 7$ **c** 3×37 **e** $3^2 \times 7^2$
 b $2^4 \times 7$ **d** $2^2 \times 11$
4. $2^8 \times 3^2 \times 5^7$ km
5. a 6 **c** 5 **e** 5 **g** 3
 b 2 **d** 3 **f** 15 **h** 30
6. a $3^2 \times 5^2, 15$ **c** $2^8, 16$
 b $5^4, 25$ **d** $2^2 \times 3^2 \times 7^2, 42$

Exercise 1D (p. 40)

1. a 3^7 **b** 2^9 **c** 5^8 **d** 13^5
2. a 7^8 **b** 10^7 **c** 12^9 **d** 4^{16}
3. a 9^{10} **b** 10^{17} **c** 2^{13} **d** 3^6
4. a b^5 **b** r^8 **c** p^{14} **d** v^5
5. a x^3 **b** a^7 **c** t^4 **d** d^6
6. a s^5 **b** x^6 **c** y^5 **d** x^{11}

Exercise 1E (p. 41)

1. a 4^2 **c** 5^1 **e** q^4
 b 7^6 **d** 10^5 **f** 15^4
2. a 6^5 **c** 9^1 **e** 3^4
 b b^2 **d** p^1 **f** 13^3
3. a 3^2 **c** 5^4 **e** 3^1
 b 2^6 **d** p^2 **f** x^4
4. a 11^2 **c** 2^3 **e** 5^6
 b s^1 **d** a^2 **f** x^1
5. a 6^{11} **c** 7^4 **e** a^6
 b 3^3 **d** x^1 **f** 5^4
6. a 2^{15} **c** 2^2 **e** 3^5
 b a^{12} **d** 10^4 **f** p^3
7. a c^3 **c** 3^3 **e** a^6
 b 5^9 **d** b^{13} **f** 10^9

Exercise 1F (p. 42)

1. a $\frac{1}{4}$ **c** $\frac{1}{16}$ **e** $\frac{1}{7}$ **g** $\frac{1}{81}$ **i** $\frac{1}{9}$
 b $\frac{1}{27}$ **d** $\frac{1}{3}$ **f** $\frac{1}{16}$ **h** $\frac{1}{5}$ **j** $\frac{1}{4}$
2. a $\frac{1}{64}$ **c** $\frac{1}{15}$ **e** $\frac{1}{49}$ **g** $\frac{1}{100}$ **i** $\frac{1}{10}$
 b $\frac{1}{36}$ **d** $\frac{1}{6}$ **f** $\frac{1}{125}$ **h** $\frac{1}{8}$ **j** $\frac{1}{64}$
3. a 0.0034 **c** 0.062 **e** 0.000 538
 b 0.26 **d** 0.008 21 **f** 0.74
4. a 0.000 046 7 **c** 0.028 05 **e** 3.004
 b 0.3063 **d** 0.005 173 **f** 0.0826
5. a $\frac{1}{1000}$ **b** $\frac{1}{100 000}$ **c** $\frac{1}{10 000}$ **d** $\frac{1}{10 000 000}$
6. a 0.0001 **c** 0.001
 b 0.01 **d** 0.000 001
7. a 5^{-2} **b** 3^{-3} **c** 6^{-3} **d** 2^2
8. a 10^{-3} **b** b^{-4} **c** 4^5 **d** 2^{a-b}
9. a 5^{-3} **c** 10^{-2} **e** 2^{-5}
 b 2^{-3} **d** 3^{-3} **f** 10^{-4}
10. a 10^{-2} **b** 10^{-3}
11. a 10^{-3} **b** 10^{-8}

Exercise 1G (p. 44)

1. a $\frac{1}{4}$ **c** $\frac{5}{2}$ **e** 8
 b 2 **d** $\frac{1}{10}$ **f** $\frac{11}{3}$

2. **a** $\frac{1}{100}$ **c** $\frac{4}{15}$ **e** $\frac{5}{16}$
   b $\frac{9}{2}$ **d** $\frac{2}{5}$ **f** $\frac{5}{8}$
3. **a** $1\frac{1}{3}$ **c** $\frac{5}{8}$ **e** $\frac{14}{81}$ **g** $\frac{12}{49}$
   b 2 **d** $2\frac{7}{9}$ **f** $\frac{2}{3}$ **h** $4\frac{1}{2}$
4. **a** $\frac{13}{30}$ **b** $\frac{69}{112}$ **c** $\frac{8}{25}$
5. **a** $2\frac{1}{18}$ **b** $5\frac{3}{10}$ **c** $\frac{57}{110}$
6. **a** $4\frac{23}{42}$ **b** $\frac{7}{20}$ **c** $-\frac{1}{2}$
7. **a** $1\frac{2}{3}$ **b** $1\frac{7}{9}$ **c** $\frac{21}{68}$

Exercise 1H (p. 45)

1. **a** 4 **c** 64 **e** 1
   b $\frac{1}{25}$ **d** $\frac{1}{3}$ **f** 125
2. **a** 81 **c** 4 **e** $\frac{1}{1000}$
   b 1 **d** $\frac{1}{36}$ **f** $\frac{1}{8}$
3. **a** 48 **c** 8 **e** 900
   b 45 **d** 300 **f** 243
4. **a** 2 **c** 64 **e** 1
   b $\frac{3}{2}$ **d** 16 **f** 25
5. **a** 2^7 **c** 3^3 **e** a^4
   b 4^3 **d** a^7 **f** 1
6. **a** 5^2 **c** b^0 **e** 5^{-6}
   b 3^0 **d** 4^4 **f** a^{-5}
7. **a** 3^0 **b** 2^{-5} **c** t^{-1} **d** 4^5
8. **a** a^2 **b** x^{-1} **c** k^3 **d** p^{10}
9. **a** 10^5 **b** 10^2 **c** 10^0
10. $10^{-3}, 10^{-2}, 10^0, 10^1, 10^3, 10^4$
11. **a i** 64, 128, 256 **ii** 2^{10} **b** 2^n
12. **a i** $32\frac{1}{3}$ mph **ii** 2.7 mph
    b 4.2 seconds
    c -0.86, no, the vehicle has already stopped

Exercise 1I (p. 46)

1. **a** 64 **b** 0.125 **c** 16 **d** 1
2. **a** 2^5 **b** 2^{-3} 3. **a** $2^4 \times 11$ **b** 11
4. **a** $-4, 10^{-1}, 2^{-2}, 0.3$ **b** $2 \times 3, 2^3, 3^2, 23$
5. $x = 3, y = 2, z = 1$

Chapter 2

Exercise 2A (p. 48)

1 **b, c, d, e, g, i, k** and **l** are wrong.

Exercise 2B (p. 49)

1. **a** too big **d** too small **g** too big
   b too small **e** too big **h** too small
   c too small **f** too small
2. **a** too big **d** too big **g** too small
   b too big **e** too small **h** too big
   c too big **f** too small
3. **a** 1500 **d** 1600 **g** 6000 **j** 14 000
   b 800 **e** 240 **h** 28 000 **k** 120 000
   c 5400 **f** 2400 **i** 18 000 **l** 100 000
4. **a** 1200 **d** 6400 **g** 15 000 **j** 40 000
   b 3500 **e** 630 **h** 18 000 **k** 400 000
   c 4000 **f** 1800 **i** 14 000 **l** 60 000

5. **a** 50 **d** 6 **g** 12.5 **j** 50
   b 30 **e** 2 **h** 40 **k** 8
   c 20 **f** 25 **i** 3 **l** 20
6. **a** 5 **d** 5 **g** 40 **j** 50
   b 45 **e** 9 **h** 70 **k** 70
   c 5 **f** 5 **i** 4 **l** 2
7. **a** 0.08 **d** 0.016 **g** 0.001 **j** 5
   b 0.05 **e** 0.25 **h** 0.05 **k** 0.25
   c 0.12 **f** 0.009 **i** 0.36 **l** 0.044
8. **a** 0.04 **d** 0.004 **g** 0.035 **j** 20
   b 0.04 **e** 0.64 **h** 0.0001 **k** 28
   c 0.15 **f** 0.025 **i** 0.14 **l** 0.006
9. 125 m 11. 9 litres
10. 280 DM 12. £48

Exercise 2C (p. 52)

1. **a** 100 **c** 0.8 **e** 0.1
   b 36 **d** 0.48 **f** 0.003
2. **a** 0.014 **c** 180 000 **e** 0.1
   b 20 **d** 3.6 **f** 4 000 000
3. **a** 600 **c** 30 **e** 0.006
   b 5 **d** 0.003 **f** 0.1
4. **a** 1 **c** 2 **e** 0.8
   b 0.07 **d** 0.9 **f** 0.002
5. **a** 10 **c** 1 **e** 150
   b 0.4 **d** 15 **f** 1000
6. **a** 10 **c** 0.25 **e** 0.3
   b 2 **d** 0.1 **f** 10
7. **a** 8 **b** 8 **c** 90 000 **d** 1
8. 0.1 cm^2 9. 0.05 m
10. **a** £1125
    b less, quantities have been rounded down
11. 14 12. 120 m
13. **a** e.g. 0.4, 0.6556, 0.2556
    b e.g. 0.4, 0.4141, 0.0141
    c e.g. estimate to part **a** can be improved by
       correcting 1.49 to 1.5
14. **a** $\pi \times 6.4^2$
    b $215 \times 418 - 500 \times \pi \times 6.4^2$, 20 000 mm^2
15. **a** e.g. 50 000 **b** an overestimate

Exercise 2D (p. 55)

1. **a** 7.08 **c** 7.02 **e** 7.49
   b 7.55 **d** 7.71 **f** 9.15
2. **a** 8.54 **c** 0.289 **e** 29.9
   b 9.19 **d** 21.1 **f** 0.0438
3. **a** 3.80 **c** 2.94 **e** 17.6
   b 1.50 **d** 0.413 **f** 1.71
4. **a** 1.54 **c** 258 **e** 6.65
   b 1.44 **d** 15.5 **f** 0.319
5. **a** 172 **c** 11.2 **e** 1950
   b 14.7 **d** 36.8 **f** 38.0
6. **a** 1050 **c** 0.536 **e** 14 400
   b 12 600 **d** 1530 **f** 0.000 123
7. **a** 0.174 **c** 204 **e** 10.0
   b 0.223 **d** -0.120 **f** 0.002 68
8. **a** 581 **c** 5.28 **e** 15.8
   b 4.17 **d** 7.76 **f** 0.230

9. **a** 758 **b** 5.56 **c** 6.09 **d** 0.656
10. **a** 24.2 **b** −1.53 **c** 5.91 **d** 0.0110
11. **a** 0.0259 **c** 8.70 **e** 2.04
 b 1.07 **d** 0.339 **f** 1.02
12. **a** 14.7 **c** 0.128 **e** 0.483
 b 0.252 **d** 0.004 95 **f** 0.438
13. **a** 9.52 **d** 11.7 **g** 0.111 **j** 0.499
 b 0.306 **e** 15.2 **h** 11.5 **k** 11.7
 c 1.88 **f** 0.257 **i** 1360 **l** 11 400
14. 190 m^2
15. The answer must be bigger than 2.57 because a number is added to it
16. **a** 3.7101; 1.7101
 b e.g. by correcting each number to 2 s.f.
17. C; $(1.45)^2$ is much nearer 2 than 1.
18. **a** £500 **b** £465

Exercise 2E (p. 59)

1. **a** 13.3 **d** 75.7 **g** 75.4
 b 0.000 399 **e** 22 000 000 **h** 0.123
 c 0.0395 **f** 2090 **i** 0.0156
2. **a** 276 **c** 494 **e** 0.0876
 b 101 000 **d** 0.316 **f** 1.29
3. **a** 2 **b** 1.65
4.

$2x^5$	3.2	11	290	410	1100

Exercise 2F (p. 60)

1. 0.8 is less than 1 so 300 ÷ 0.8 is greater than 300
2. **a** 24 000 **c** 6 **e** 0.4
 b 4900 **d** 5 **f** 0.32
3. **a** 180 **c** 4500 **e** 50
 b 40 **d** 0.4 **f** 0.03

Exercise 2G (p. 60)

1. **a** 166 **c** 4530 **e** 39.2
 b 34.2 **d** 0.368 **f** 0.0338
2. **a** 18.7 **b** 0.0789 **c** 0.885 **d** 3.56
3. 35.8 cells

Chapter 3

Exercise 3B (p. 63)

1. **a** 5500 **g** 4 155 000
 b 13 000 **h** 80 220
 c 7 400 000 **i** 7402
 d 316 000 **j** 577.8
 e 9150 **k** 200 400 000
 f 20 400 000 **l** 310 100 000 000
2. **a** 0.0047 **g** 0.000 310 3
 b 0.000 029 **h** 0.050 08
 c 0.000 51 **i** 0.000 006 027
 d 0.000 013 5 **j** 0.771
 e 0.000 801 **k** 0.000 000 020 52
 f 0.0635 **l** 0.000 000 000 388 9

3. **a** 3780 **f** 4 250 000 000 000
 b 0.001 26 **g** 0.000 477
 c 5 300 000 **h** 0.000 000 908
 d 740 000 000 000 000 **i** 0.000 081 5
 e 0.000 000 064 3
4. **a** 2.5×10^3 **f** 5.3×10^8
 b 6.3×10^2 **g** 2.603×10^4
 c 1.53×10^4 **h** 5.47×10^5
 d 3.907×10^4 **i** 3.06×10^4
 e 4.5×10^6
5. **a** 2.6×10^5 **f** 4.004×10^6
 b 9.9×10^3 **g** 4.06×10^6
 c 2.467×10^5 **h** 7.04×10^2
 d 4×10^4 **i** 3.304×10^5
 e 8×10^{10}
6. **a** 2.6×10^{-2} **f** 7.5×10^{-6}
 b 4.8×10^{-3} **g** 9.07×10^{-1}
 c 5.3×10^{-2} **h** 8.05×10^{-1}
 d 7.9×10^{-1} **i** 8.808×10^{-2}
 e 6.9×10^{-3}
7. **a** 1.8×10^{-5} **f** 5.35×10^{-2}
 b 5.2×10^{-1} **g** 7.044×10^{-4}
 c 1.1×10^{-3} **h** 7.3×10^{-11}
 d 4×10^{-10} **i** 1.005×10^{-3}
 e 6.84×10^{-1}
8. **a** 8.892×10^1 **i** 7.05×10^{-3}
 b 5.06×10^{-5} **j** 3.6×10^1
 c 5.7×10^{-8} **k** 5.09×10^3
 d 5.03×10^8 **l** 2.68×10^5
 e 9.9×10^7 **m** 3.07×10^1
 f 8.4×10^1 **n** 5.05×10^{-3}
 g 3.51×10^2 **p** 8.8×10^{-6}
 h 9×10^{-2}
9. **a** $3.75 \times 10^4, 2.47 \times 10^5, 5.76 \times 10^8,$
 $9.97 \times 10^8, 2 \times 10^{10}$
 b $5.02 \times 10^{-8}, 3.005 \times 10^{-3}, 5.27 \times 10^{-3},$
 $6.0005 \times 10^{-1}, 9.906 \times 10^{-1}$
 c $7.008 09 \times 10^{-3}, 7.05 \times 10^{-2}, 7.08 \times 10^0,$
 $7.93 \times 10^1, 5.608 \times 10^5$
10. **a** 4.8×10^{11}
 b e.g. 4.8E + 11; the calculator is using standard form because the answer is very large. The 11 is the index or power of 10.

Exercise 3C (p. 66)

1. **a** 8.4×10^5 **c** 1.54×10^{-4} **e** 3.2×10^2
 b 1.08×10^{10} **d** 1.15×10^{-5} **f** 7.8×10^{-2}
2. **a** 2×10^3 **c** 3×10^{-2} **e** 3×10^0
 b 7×10^4 **d** 1.4×10^{-5} **f** 1.25×10^8
3. **a** 3.2×10^3 **c** 3.31×10^4 **e** 2.59×10^{-2}
 b 3.2×10^{-2} **d** 4.13×10^{-3} **f** 2.8×10^6
4. **a** 6×10^3 **b** 2.4×10^6 **c** 1.2005×10^5
5. **a** 8.64×10^{-12} **b** 6×10^{-2} **c** 1.128×10^{-5}
6. **a** 1.3×10^3 **c** 2.6005×10^{-3}
 b 5.2×10^7 **d** 2.5995×10^4
7. **a** 2.211×10^6 **c** 2.189×10^6
 b 2×10^2 **d** 2.01×10^2

8. a 3.8×10^{-3} **c** 7.5×10^{0}
   b 3.7×10^{-2} **d** 1.6×10^{-7}
9. a 2×10^{2} **c** $5.000\,12 \times 10^{3}$
   b 1.25×10^{5} **d** 9.996×10^{-1}
10. a 3.8×10^{-2} **c** 1.875×10^{0}
   b -1×10^{-3} **d** 8.5×10^{0}
11. a 9.42×10^{4} **f** 3.31×10^{-5}
   b 6.28×10^{4} **g** 1.38×10^{1}
   c 6.26×10^{-5} **h** 1.55×10^{-6}
   d 3.14×10^{0} **i** 3.58×10^{-4}
   e 8.06×10^{4} **j** 3.53×10^{14}
12. 8.09×10^{-5} seconds
13. 3.00×10^{8} m
14. 1.49×10^{-10}
15. 2.23×10^{-3} g
16. a 6.74×10^{9} **b** 5.16×10^{9}
17. a 9.1×10^{10} km
   b $1 : 0.494$
   c 6×10^{5} seconds ≈ 167 h
18. a $1.26 \times 10^{-6}\,\text{m}^2$ **b** $2.51 \times 10^{-2}\,\text{m}^2$
19. £2.90×10^{8}
20. 3.24×10^{-3}
21. a 4.5×10^{7} **b** 3.37×10^{10} g   **c** 749 g
22. a £6.2×10^{10} b £3875
23. a 15 minutes   **b** 2.12×10^{8}
   c Depends whether they are in line with the sun and whether they are on the same side or on different sides of the sun.
24. a a proton   **b** $1 : 1830$
25. 4.77×10^{-3}

Puzzles

   1. 37.1 years   **3.** googol
   2. 10 billion   **4.** $9^{9^{9}}$

Chapter 4

Exercise 4A (p. 71)

   1. or   **2.** and   **3.** or   **4.** or

Exercise 4B (p. 72)

   1. not both
   2. a not both   **b** both
   3. a both   **b** not both
   4. a not both   **b** both
   5. a not both   **b** both

Exercise 4C (p. 74)

   1. a $\frac{1}{26}$ **2. a** $\frac{1}{6}$ **3. a** $\frac{1}{6}$ **4. a** $\frac{74}{117}$
    b $\frac{1}{26}$ **b** $\frac{1}{3}$ **b** $\frac{1}{6}$ **b** $\frac{43}{117}$
    c $\frac{1}{13}$ **c** $\frac{1}{2}$ **c** $\frac{1}{3}$
   5. a $\frac{4}{7}$ **b** $\frac{11}{14}$
   6. a $\frac{32}{63}$ **b** $\frac{17}{36}$ **c** $\frac{191}{252}$ **d** $\frac{61}{252}$
   7. a $\frac{1}{2}$ **b** $\frac{1}{2}$
    c $\frac{5}{6}$, 2 is both even and prime

Exercise 4D (p. 75)

   1. $\frac{1}{4}$ **3. a** $\frac{1}{4}$ **b** $\frac{3}{4}$ **c** $\frac{9}{16}$
   2. $\frac{1}{36}$ **4. a** $\frac{6}{25}$ **b** $\frac{6}{25}$
   5. a $\frac{1}{2}$ **b** $\frac{1}{4}$ **c** $\frac{1}{4}$
   6. a $\frac{3}{10}$
    b not independent (you cannot eat the same sweet twice)

Exercise 4E (p. 76)

   1. a $\frac{1}{3}$ **b** $\frac{1}{3}$ **c** $\frac{1}{36}$ **d** $\frac{1}{4}$ **6.** 0.4
   2. a $\frac{1}{13}$ **b** $\frac{1}{26}$ **c** $\frac{3}{26}$ **7. a** 0.8   **b** 0.04
   3. a $\frac{2}{5}$ **b** $\frac{8}{15}$ **8.** $\frac{1}{36}$
   4. a $\frac{2}{13}$ **b** $\frac{2}{13}$ **c** $\frac{1}{169}$ **9. a** $\frac{1}{6}$ **b** $\frac{5}{6}$ **c** $\frac{3}{16}$
   5. 0.54

Exercise 4F (p. 80)

The tree diagrams in these answers give only the missing probabilities on the branches.

   1. a $\frac{2}{5}$ **4.** 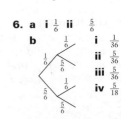 **a** 0.15
    b   **b** 0.35
                                    c 0.35
                                    d 0.15
    c $\frac{7}{20}$ **d** $\frac{3}{40}$
   2. a   **5.**   **a** $\frac{1}{25}$
                                    b $\frac{16}{25}$
                                    c $\frac{8}{25}$
    b $\frac{2}{5}$ **c** $\frac{2}{15}$
   3. a 0.8   **6. a i** $\frac{1}{6}$ **ii** $\frac{5}{6}$
    b   **b**   **i** $\frac{1}{36}$
                                   ii $\frac{5}{36}$
                                  iii $\frac{5}{36}$
                                  iv $\frac{5}{18}$
    c 0.04   **d** 0.64
   7. $\frac{8}{15}$ **8.** $\frac{7}{20}$
   9. a $\frac{5}{8}$ **b** $\frac{1}{3}$
    c $\frac{1}{24}$; 1, because they cover all possibilities
   10. 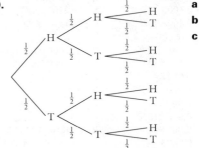   **a** $\frac{1}{8}$
                                   b $\frac{1}{8}$
                                   c $\frac{3}{8}$

11. a Sunday; greater probability as $0.11 > 0.07$

b

    0.11

    0.11

0.93

    0.89

c i 0.008
  ii 0.165

d

    0.3

    0.7

    0.3

    0.7

    0.3

    0.7

    0.3

    0.7

e i 0.579
  ii 0.421

12 b i 0.049   **ii** 0.044

Exercise 4G (p. 84)

1. a $\frac{4}{11}$ **b** $\frac{4}{11}$ **2. a** 0 **b** 1
3. a $\frac{1}{4}$ **b** $\frac{1}{4}$ **c** $\frac{1}{4}$
4. a $\frac{3}{32}$ **b** $\frac{15}{32}$ **c** $\frac{7}{16}$
5. a $\frac{4}{15}$ **b** $\frac{1}{5}$ **c** $\frac{2}{5}$
6. a $\frac{4}{63}$ **b** $\frac{2}{9}$ **c** $\frac{5}{9}$ **d** $\frac{8}{21}$
7. $\frac{4}{5}$ **8. a** 0.7 **b** 0.2 **c** 0.45
9. $\frac{17}{35}$
10. a 20; only a probability not a certainty
  b 0.0294
11. a 0.001   **b** 0.002
  c more blue tickets sold than yellow tickets
12. a 0.111 **b** 0.790 **c** £65.78
13. No, because he does not know the proportion of blue ring pulls for all the cans on sale – he could have been lucky.
14. Each is equally likely to win because the probability of both landing the same way up is the same as one landing head up and the other landing tail up ($= \frac{1}{2}$).

Chapter 5

Exercise 5A (p. 89)

1. 9, 30, 93, 282   **3.** 2, 7, 17, 37, 77
2. 6, 15, 42, 123   **4.** 1, 1, 2, 3, 5, 8, 13
5. 3   **6.** 5   **7.** 7   **8.** 4
9. a 8 **b** 4   **10.** 2, 3, 5
11. a 3, 5, 7, 9 **c** 0, 3, 8, 15 **e** 2, 9, 20, 35
  b 2, 4, 6, 8 **d** 0, 3, 8, 15 **f** $\frac{1}{2}, \frac{2}{3}, \frac{3}{4}, \frac{4}{5}$
12. $\frac{1}{2}, \frac{1}{4}, \frac{1}{8}, \frac{1}{16}, \frac{1}{32}$; forever

Exercise 5B (p. 91)

1. a start with 5 then continue by adding 6 to the previous term

b start with 12 then continue by subtracting 7 from the previous term
c start with 3 then continue by multiplying the previous term by 3
d start with 40 then continue dividing the previous term by 2
2. a 19, 23 **c** 36, 49 **e** $\frac{1}{81}, \frac{1}{243}$
  b 48, −96 **d** 4, −1 **f** 42, 68

Exercise 5C (p. 92)

1. a 15, 17 **c** 22, 27 **e** 42, 56
  b 17, 20 **d** 32, 45 **f** 30, 42
2. a 27, 31 **c** 71, 97 **e** 40, 54
  b 39, 52 **d** 77, 103 **f** 28, 39
3. a 43, 56 **c** 57, 77 **e** 26, 37
  b 49, 70 **d** 99, 135 **f** −10, −10
4. e.g. **a** start with 3, add 4 then double the amount added each time
  b start with 4, add 1 then double the amount added each time
  c start with 3, add 2 then double the amount added each time
  d start with 2, add 3 then double the amount added each time
5. a 39, 55 **b** 37, 60 **c** 37, 48
  d $1 + 3 + 5 + 7 + 9, 1 + 3 + 5 + 7 + 9 + 11$
  e 41, 54 **f** $\frac{6}{5}, \frac{13}{11}$
6. 25 to 24   **7.** 35 to 38
8. a 146 **b** 99 **c** 334
9. a 378 **b** 37 **c** 100
10. a 22, 27, $5n - 3$ **c** 864, 1184
  b 14, 84, 204, 374, 594 **d** 9, 19, 29, 39, 49
11. a 1, 3, 4, 7, 11, 18 **c** 3, 4, 7, 11, 18, 29
  b 2, 3, 5, 8, 13, 21
12. The sequence repeats in the differences after the first or second terms; yes

Exercise 5D (p. 95)

1. a $2n + 3$ **c** $4n + 3$ **e** $9n - 7$
  b $3n - 3$ **d** $7n + 2$ **f** $(n + 2)(n + 4)$
2. a $n(n + 2)$ **c** $4n - 3$ **e** $\frac{1}{n + 2}$
  b $5n - 4$ **d** $\frac{n}{n + 1}$ **f** $2 - 2n$
3. a $(5, 8)$ **b** $(n, n + 3)$
4. a $n^2 + 1$ **c** $(n + 1)^2 - 1$ **e** $n^2 - 1$
  b $n^2 + 6$ **d** $2n^2$ **f** $3n^2 - 3$
5. a

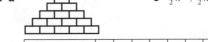

  c $\frac{1}{2}n^2 + \frac{1}{2}n$

b

Number of tiles	1	3	6	10	15	21	28

6. a

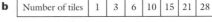

b

Number of tiles	3	8	15	24	35	48	63

  c $n(n + 2)$

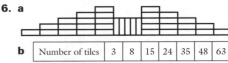

7. a **c** n^2

b

Number of tiles	1	4	9	16	25	36	49

8. a $19\,683,\ 3^{n-1}$ **b** $\frac{1}{1024},\ \frac{1}{n^2}$

   c $1+2+3+4+5+6+7+8+9+10,$
$1+2+3+\ldots+n$

9. a $(n-1)^2$ **b** $2(n+2)$ **c** $3n-1$

10. b 4

   c

Number of pieces	5	9	13	17	21	25

   d multiply 25 by 4 and then add 1 **e** $4n+1$

11. a 6, 11, 16, 21, 26 **c** First 3; 4

   b i $5n+1$ **ii** 151

12. a

1	6	15	20	15	6	1	
1	7	21	35	35	21	7	1
1	8	28	56	70	56	28	8	1

   b 1, 2, 4, 8, 16, 32, 64, 128

   c 256, 2048

   d $2^0, 2^1, 2^2, 2^3, 2^4, 2^5, 2^6;\ 2^{n-1}$

13. a 2, 9, 21, 38, 60 **c** $\frac{1}{2}(5n-1)$

   b $2, 4\frac{1}{2}, 7, 9\frac{1}{2}, 12$ **d** $\frac{1}{2}n(n-1)$

14. $n(n+1)$ **18. a** 1, 3, 6, 10, 15

15. n^2+3n **b** 210

16. $4n^2+2n$ **c** $\frac{1}{2}n(n-1)$

17. a 2 m **19. a** 1, 5, 14, 30, 55

   b 20 m **b** 2870

   c $n(n+1)$ metres **c** $\frac{n(n-1)(2n-1)}{6}$

20. a always odd **c** $2N-1$

   b $\frac{N+1}{2}$ **d** 1 of C1, 4 of each of the other colours

Exercise 5E (p. 101)

1. a 94, 190 **b** 9

2. a 11, 15, 19, 23; 87 **c** 4, 7, 12, 19; 403

   b 1, 6, 11, 16; 96 **d** 12, 20, 30, 42; 506

3. a 38, 51 **b** $\frac{1}{16}, -\frac{1}{32}$ **c** $5\times7, 6\times8$

4. a (5, 12) **b i** (50, 57) **ii** $(n, n+7)$

5. a 17, 20 **b i** 56 **ii** 89 **c** $3n-1$

6. a 28, 33 **b** add 5 **c** $5n-2$

7. a 21 **b** add the 6th and 7th numbers; 55, 89

8. a i 16 **b i** 7 **c i** 8 **d i** b

     ii 25 **ii** 22 **ii** 42 **ii** b

     iii $3n+1$ **iii** $5n+2$ **iii** b

Chapter 6

Exercise 6A (p. 104)

1. a $\frac{x}{4}$ **b** $\frac{a}{2}$ **c** $\frac{p}{q}$ **d** $\frac{x}{y}$ **e** $\frac{1}{2a}$

2. a $\frac{a}{2c}$ **b** $\frac{2}{q}$ **c** $\frac{z}{2}$ **d** $\frac{q}{2}$ **e** $\frac{2}{3y}$

3. a $\frac{pq}{2}$ **b** $\frac{a}{c}$ **c** $\frac{b}{d}$ **d** $\frac{m}{k}$ **e** $\frac{s}{4t}$

Exercise 6B (p. 105)

1. a $\frac{1}{x}$ **b** not possible **c** $p-q$

2. a $\frac{t}{s-t}$ **b** $\frac{x}{2(x-y)}$ **c** $\frac{1}{4-a}$

3. a not possible **b** $\frac{a-b}{2ab}$ **c** not possible

4. a $\frac{1}{v}$ **b** $\frac{2a}{3(a-b)}$ **c** $u-v$

5. a $\frac{1}{2}$ **b** not possible **c** $\frac{1}{s-6}$

Exercise 6C (p. 105)

1. a $\frac{ac}{bd}$ **b** $\frac{ad}{bc}$ **c** $\frac{ac}{b}$ **d** $\frac{3(a-b)}{4(a+b)}$

2. a $\frac{5(x-y)}{2x}$ **c** $\frac{(x+3)(x-2)}{3}$

   b $\frac{x(x-y)}{10}$ **d** $\frac{(x-2)}{3(x+3)}$

3. a $\frac{a}{bc}$ **b** $\frac{pr}{q}$ **c** $\frac{3x}{2y}$ **d** $\frac{3x}{4y}$

4. a $\frac{x}{2}$ **b** $2x$ **c** $\frac{5x}{8}$ **d** $\frac{3x}{10}$

5. a $\frac{x}{6}$ **b** $\frac{3x}{10}$ **c** $\frac{x}{18}$ **d** $\frac{2x}{3}$

6. a $\frac{3x}{2}$ **b** $\frac{3x}{2}$ **c** $2x$ **d** $9x$

7. a $\frac{2x}{3}$ **b** $6x$ **c** $\frac{x}{2}$ **d** $9x$

8. a $\frac{4x}{5}$ **b** $\frac{x}{3}$ **c** $\frac{4x}{5}$ **d** $\frac{2x}{5}$

9. a $\frac{x^2}{6}$ **d** $8b^2$ **g** 2

   b $\frac{3x^2}{8}$ **e** $15x^2$ **h** 15

   c $\frac{a^2}{14}$ **f** $\frac{3}{2}$ **i** 12

10. a $\frac{6b}{a}$ **c** $\frac{12y}{x}$ **e** $\frac{1}{2b}$

   b $\frac{q}{2p}$ **d** $\frac{x}{2y}$ **f** $\frac{2}{3p}$

11. a $\frac{2b^2}{5}$ **c** $\frac{p}{2}$ **e** $\frac{a^3}{b^3}$

   b $\frac{pq}{6}$ **d** $\frac{a}{4b}$ **f** $\frac{y}{2x}$

12. a $\frac{3}{y}$ **c** $\frac{2b}{3}$ **e** $4s$

   b $\frac{2q^2}{p^2}$ **d** $\frac{y^3}{2x}$ **f** $\frac{10q^2}{27p}$

Exercise 6D (p. 108)

1. a pq **c** 30 **e** $wxyz$ **g** uvw

   b rst **d** abc **f** ad **h** pqr

2. a xy **c** $3pq$ **e** abc **g** $5ab$

   b $2x^2$ **d** $2x^2y$ **f** $3p^2$ **h** $3pq^2$

3. a $6x$ **c** $18a$ **e** a^2b **g** $15y$

   b $8x$ **d** 60 **f** $30x$ **h** $12x$

Exercise 6E (p. 109)

1. a $\dfrac{x+y}{xy}$ 2. a $\dfrac{5}{4y}$ 3. a $\dfrac{3y-2x}{xy}$

 b $\dfrac{3q+2p}{pq}$ b $\dfrac{1}{8p}$ b $\dfrac{21a+20b}{28ab}$

 c $\dfrac{2y-3x}{xy}$ c $\dfrac{2t-s}{st}$ c $\dfrac{13}{8a}$

 d $\dfrac{6p+4q}{3pq}$ d $\dfrac{a+6b}{2ab}$ d $\dfrac{4}{21x}$

4. a $\dfrac{5y-6x}{15xy}$ c $\dfrac{5}{6x}$

 b $\dfrac{5a+2b}{2ab}$ d $\dfrac{1}{35x}$

5. a $\dfrac{3a+2b}{4ab}$ c $\dfrac{2s+s^2t}{2t^2}$ e $\dfrac{10y-3}{14xy}$

 b $\dfrac{ab-2a^2}{2b^2}$ d $\dfrac{15b+4}{6ab}$ f $\dfrac{18b-3a}{2a^2b}$

6. a $\dfrac{3y-4}{xy}$ c $\dfrac{3+2x}{3x^2}$ e $\dfrac{3x^2-3y^2}{2xy}$

 b $\dfrac{4-3p}{2p^2}$ d $\dfrac{4y^2-9x^2}{6xy}$ f $\dfrac{14q-15p}{18pq}$

7. a $\dfrac{9a^2+2b^2}{12ab}$ c $\dfrac{5x+4y}{8xy}$ e $\dfrac{5a^2+4ab}{5b^2}$

 b $\dfrac{10q-3p}{4pq}$ d $\dfrac{pq+3p^2}{3q^2}$ f $\dfrac{21+8p}{15pq}$

8. a $\dfrac{9x+3}{20}$ b $\dfrac{5-x}{12}$ c $\dfrac{1-2x}{35}$

9. a $\dfrac{13x+1}{15}$ b $\dfrac{4x+13}{12}$ c $\dfrac{3x+9}{35}$

10. a $\dfrac{5-22x}{21}$ 11. a $\dfrac{22-13x}{6}$ 12. a $\dfrac{20-17x}{24}$

 b $\dfrac{7x+9}{12}$ b $\dfrac{11-7x}{12}$ b $\dfrac{4x+9}{6}$

 c $\dfrac{22-7x}{20}$ c $\dfrac{31x-6}{24}$ c $\dfrac{2-11x}{18}$

 d $\dfrac{10-5x}{6}$ d $\dfrac{11-7x}{10}$ d $\dfrac{1-7x}{12}$

13. a $\dfrac{26x+34}{15}$ c $\dfrac{27x+3}{14}$

 b $\dfrac{17x-1}{12}$ d $\dfrac{19x-73}{9}$

14. a $\dfrac{5x-19}{21}$ c $\dfrac{26x-18}{15}$

 b $\dfrac{42x-49}{10}$ d $\dfrac{104-17x}{30}$

15. a $\dfrac{3a+6}{a(a+3)}$ b $\dfrac{6x+4}{x(x+2)}$ c $\dfrac{7x-4}{x(x-1)}$

16. a $\dfrac{7x-4}{2x(x-4)}$ b $\dfrac{2x-3}{4x(2x+1)}$ c $\dfrac{11x+1}{3x(2x+1)}$

Exercise 6F (p. 112)

1. a $\dfrac{2c-ab}{ac}$ b $\dfrac{r^2q}{p}$ c $\dfrac{8}{pq}$ d $\dfrac{1}{2y}$

2. a $\dfrac{7x-14}{12}$ c $\dfrac{12-2x}{3x^2}$

 b $\dfrac{b^3}{3a}$ d $\dfrac{M-2}{6}$

3. a $\dfrac{1}{12x}$ b $\dfrac{8}{15}$ c $\dfrac{ab}{c}$ d $\dfrac{3}{2}$

4. a $\dfrac{23}{20x}$ c $\dfrac{19x-1}{3x(x-1)}$

 b $\dfrac{3}{10x^2}$ d $\dfrac{2}{x(x-1)}$

5. a $\dfrac{4x+7}{10}$ c $\dfrac{-a-3}{2a^2-2a}=\dfrac{a+3}{2a-2a^2}$

 b $\dfrac{2x^2+7x-4}{50}$

6. a $\dfrac{25}{12x}$ b $\dfrac{25}{24x^2}$ c $\dfrac{3}{y}$

Exercise 6G (p. 113)

1. identity 4. equation 7. equation
2. equation 5. identity 8. identity
3. identity 6. equation 9. identity

Exercise 6H (p. 114)

1. a 15 b 72 c 18
2. a 8 b 63 c 16
3. a 48 b 56 c 96
4. a 12 c $1\frac{2}{5}$ e 21
 b 15 d 32 f $22\frac{1}{2}$
5. a $\frac{1}{6}$ d $1\frac{1}{5}$ g $1\frac{1}{20}$
 b $\frac{3}{20}$ e $\frac{5}{9}$ h $\frac{14}{15}$
 c $1\frac{1}{2}$ f $1\frac{1}{3}$ i $\frac{3}{8}$
6. £300 9. $\frac{2}{3}$ gallon
7. 21.6 m 10. $\frac{7}{8}w=\frac{5}{8}, \frac{5}{7}$ inches
8. $1\frac{1}{4}$ feet 11. 560 mm

Exercise 6I (p. 117)

1. a 20 b 13 c 6
2. a $2\frac{1}{4}$ b $13\frac{3}{4}$ c $12\frac{2}{3}$
3. a $7\frac{1}{2}$ b 20 c −30
4. a $\frac{1}{3}x+\frac{1}{2}x$ b $\frac{1}{3}x+\frac{1}{2}x=10,\ x=12$
5. $\frac{3x}{4}-\frac{3}{7}=1,\ x=1\frac{19}{21}$ 6. £1000
7. a $\frac{3}{4}$ b 2 c $\frac{23}{27}$ d 1
8. a 8 b $\frac{18}{23}$ c 2 d $1\frac{1}{7}$
9. $1\frac{6}{49}$ inches
10. a $1\frac{1}{6}$ b $4\frac{2}{3}$ c 7 d $2\frac{17}{26}$
11. a 6 b $1\frac{1}{3}$ c $7\frac{1}{2}$ d $3\frac{3}{8}$
12. a 8 b −5 c 5 d $9\frac{3}{5}$
13. a 6 b $1\frac{1}{3}$ c $5\frac{1}{4}$ d −1
14. a 1 b 17 c 11 d $3\frac{1}{4}$
15. a 2 b −18 c $-2\frac{1}{2}$
16. a 3 b −1 c 2
17. a 21 b $\frac{4}{9}$ c 1
18. a 1 b 9 c $2\frac{3}{8}$

Exercise 6J (p. 120)

1. a $\dfrac{2x}{y}$ **b** $\dfrac{x-y}{2x}$ **c** $\dfrac{3}{x+y}$

2. a $\dfrac{1}{6p}$ **b** 5 **c** $\dfrac{3y}{2x}$

3. a $6\frac{2}{3}$ **b** $\frac{3}{10}$ **c** $\frac{8}{9}$ **d** $5\frac{3}{5}$ **e** $\frac{2}{5}$ **f** $-\frac{1}{6}$

4. a $\dfrac{7x-6}{12}$ **b** $\frac{13}{2}$ **5. a** $\dfrac{3x-1}{4}$ **b** -5

Summary 2

Revision Exercise 2.1 (p. 123)

1. a i 472 **ii** 64 **iii** 1.44
   b i 2^8 **ii** 10^{17} **iii** 2^2
2. a $\frac{1}{9}$ **c** 0.059 **e** $\frac{1}{16}$
   b $\frac{1}{12}$ **d** $72\,300$ **f** $\frac{1}{125}$
3. a i 10^6 **ii** 10^{-2} **iii** 10^0
   b i 2140 **ii** 0.0521
4. a 2.44 **b** 504 **c** 5.35 **d** 5.02
5. a too small **c** too small
   b too big **d** too small
6. 2.254×10^{-6}
7. a i 9.26×10^{-3} **ii** 7.3×10^5
   b i $0.000\,024\,7$ **ii** 624 **iii** 0.0347
8. a $8.7 \times 10^3, 9.9 \times 10^4, 3.24 \times 10^5, 1.27 \times 10^6$
   b 8.43×10^{-2} by 4.87×10^{-2}
9. a 5.75×10^7 **c** 1.5×10^{-1}
   b 3.75×10^{14} **d** 1.25×10^8
10. 9.46×10^{15} metres
11. a i 4 **ii** 6 **b** 1.3227×10^9 km
12. 2.32×10^6
13. a $0.702\,235\,54$ **b i** $\dfrac{6 \times 10^2}{600 + 200}$ **ii** 0.75

Revision Exercise 2.2 (p. 125)

1. a $\frac{1}{26}$ **b** $\frac{1}{26}$ **c** $\frac{1}{676}$ **4.** $\frac{7}{10}$
2. a $\frac{1}{8}$ **b** $\frac{21}{32}$ **c** $\frac{1}{32}$ **5. a** $\frac{13}{30}$ **b** $\frac{1}{30}$ **c** $\frac{11}{30}$
3. b $\frac{15}{49}$ **c** $\frac{26}{49}$
6. a add twice the difference between the
   2 previous terms to the previous term
   b $17, 20$ **c i** $4, 14, 34, 74$ **ii** $2, 10$
7. a $2, 6, 12, 20; 930$ **b** $n^2 - n$
8. a i 4 **ii** 10 **iii** 18 **iv** 28
   b i 40 **ii** $n^2 + 3n$
9. a i $\dfrac{x}{2}$ **iii** $\dfrac{12x}{5}$ **v** $\dfrac{r}{p}$
   ii $10x$ **iv** $\dfrac{p}{4}$ **vi** $\dfrac{1}{p-4}$
   b i $\dfrac{5a-5b}{3a}$ **ii** $\dfrac{3b^2}{4}$ **iii** $\dfrac{2}{p}$ **iv** $\dfrac{x}{y}$
10. a 20 **c** $1\frac{1}{14}$ **e** 15
   b 18 **d** 6 **f** 5
11. a $17, 20$ **b** 35 **c** $3n-1$
12. a 0.3
   b 0.01
   c Sarah because probability she wins is 0.54
   which is greater than 0.5
13. 9

Revision Exercise 2.3 (p. 128)

1. a i 5970 **ii** $100\,000$ **iii** $\frac{1}{16}$ **iv** 1
   b i 2^8 **ii** 5^9 **iii** a^7 **iv** b^2
2. a $5^2 \times 7^2; 35$ **b i** 5^5 **ii** 4^{-7} **c** 7
3. a i $3^2 \times 7^3$ **ii** $2^3 \times 5^3$
   b i $340\,000$ **ii** 0.086
   c i 10^5 **ii** 10^{-4} **iii** 10^{-2} **iv** 10^{-5}
4. a i 4.7×10^4 **ii** 8.2×10^{-6}
   b i $55\,000$ **ii** $0.000\,724$ **iii** 3.72
   c 0.3
5. a 2×10^{-2} **c** 1×10^{-2}
   b 7.5×10^{-5} **d** 3×10^0
6. a $\frac{7}{9}$ **b** $\frac{2}{9}$
7. a

   b i $\frac{4}{15}$ **ii** $\frac{23}{45}$

8. a i $43, 57$ **ii** $93, 129$
   b i 218 **ii** 60 **iii** 101
9. a add 8 to the previous number **b** $8n-3$
10. a i $6b^2$ **ii** 6 **iii** $a+b$
   b i 28 **ii** $3\frac{1}{3}$ **iii** 3

Revision Exercise 2.4 (p. 130)

1. a $-9, 10^{-1}, 3^{-2}, 0.3$
   b i 3^6 **ii** 5^3 **iii** a^{11} **iv** b^0
2. a 0.302 **b** 1.94 **c** 2.49 **d** 45.5
3. a i 67.0 **ii** 67
   b i 153 **ii** 31.0 **iii** 0.0527 **iv** 2.11
4. a i 0.0074 **ii** 0.01
   b i $\frac{1}{18}$ **ii** $7\frac{1}{2}$ **iii** $1\frac{3}{32}$
   c i 0.371 **ii** 98.9
5. a i 1.91 **ii** 1.91 **iii** 2
   b i 10.6 **ii** 0.684 **iii** 0.0254
6. a i 4.23×10^{-6} **ii** 8.79×10^6
   b i $0.007\,92$ **iii** $820\,000$
   ii 5960 **iv** 0.0002
   c 1.26×10^{-8}
7. a 2.957×10^4 **c** 4.31×10^0
   b 1.3368×10^8 **d** 3.21×10^{12}
8. a 0.1 **b** 0.3 **c** 0.6
9. b i $\frac{16}{75}$ **ii** $\frac{38}{75}$
10. a $4n+7$ **b** $\dfrac{1}{2n}$ **c** $(2n+1)(2n+3)$

Chapter 7

Exercise 7A (p. 133)

1. direct **8.** neither **15.** inverse
2. neither **9.** neither **16.** inverse
3. neither **10.** neither **17.** neither
4. direct **11.** neither **18.** direct
5. inverse **12.** inverse **19.** direct
6. inverse **13.** direct
7. neither **14.** neither

Exercise 7B (p. 134)

1. a £2.70   **b** £10.80   **6.** 15.5 km
2. a 6 units   **b** $\frac{3}{4}$ unit   **7.** £9.80
3. a 72 km   **b** 118.8 km   **8.** £8.30
4. a £1.65   **b** £7.92   **9.** 1.5 p
5. £1.20   **10.** 5.5 cm²

Exercise 7C (p. 136)

1. 3.2 litres   **12. a** 2.25×10^7
2. 3 hours   **b** 8.1×10^6
3. 12.5 units   **c** 1.35×10^5
4. 3.6 hours   **13.** 15 Volts
5. a £70   **14.** 24.7 Joules
　　b 225 miles   **15.** 0.15 kg
6. 700 bottles   **16.** 62.5 mm
7. £5.28   **17.** 70 km/h
8. 20.25 cm   **18.** y: 10, 20, 30, 40
9. £336   **19.** S: 21.3, 42.6, 56.2, 92.9
10. 480 pesos   **20.** 82.6 p, 83 p
11. 65.6 km

Exercise 7D (p. 140)

1. $5\frac{1}{2}$ hours   **5.** 25 cm   **9.** 49 machines
2. 12 sweets   **6.** 20 boxes   **10.** $4\frac{1}{2}$ hours
3. 203 lines   **7.** 16 cm   **11.** $12\frac{1}{2}$ days
4. 8 days   **8.** 48 rooms   **12.** 28.8 hours
13. q: 0.5, 2, 20, 1000   **14.** f: 1.07; w: 25, 7500

Exercise 7E (p. 141)

1. £145.35   **2.** $3\frac{1}{2}$ hours
3. a 17 742 lira   **b** 3.04 F
4. not directly proportional
5. 4.46 cm   **7.** 24   **9.** 1.44 m
6. 49   **8.** 34   **10.** 6 weeks
11. not directly proportional
12. 1.5 amps   **15.** inverse   **18.** neither
13. direct   **16.** direct
14. neither   **17.** inverse

Exercise 7F (p. 143)

1. 320 km   **6. a** £4.28 **b** 16 days
2. 6 hours 40 minutes   **7.** 10 days
3. £60   **8.** 16 rows
4. 3 minutes   **9.** £6
5. 5.6 cm   **10. a** £252 **b** 8 m²

Exercise 7G (p. 144)

1. 217 cups   **6.** 5.78 seconds
2. 204 books   **7.** 5.95 V
3. 428 pages   **8.** 3.32×10^5
4. a £31 000 **b** £56 250   **9.** $30\frac{1}{3}$ inches
5. 2 hours 51 minutes   **10.** 8.68 tonnes

Chapter 8

Exercise 8A (p. 147)

1. a $4x + 4$ **d** $6 + 8x$ **g** $15 - 9x$
　　b $15x - 6$ **e** $10 + 12a$ **h** $7x - 7$
　　c $5x + 20$ **f** $16 - 40b$ **i** $15 - 5x$
2. a $-5x + 15$ **d** $-14 + 21x$ **g** $-10 - 4x$
　　b $-6a - 10$ **e** $-6x + 15$ **h** $-4 + 3x$
　　c $-3x + 11$ **f** $-12b - 8$ **i** $-21x + 6$
3. a $8x + 5$ **c** $10x + 27$ **e** $5x - 12$
　　b $6x + 14$ **d** $3x + 11$ **f** $21x - 12$
4. a $5x - 3$ **c** $6a - 7$ **e** $1 - 6x$
　　b $-5 - 3x$ **d** $4x - 5$ **f** $-2b - 4$
5. a $12 - 4x$ **e** $-2b + 4$
　　b $3ab - 3a^2$ **f** $27 - 6y$
　　c $10 - 6x$ **g** $-15 - 9x$
　　d $-21 + 14x$ **h** $30x - 12$
6. a $3x^2 + 5x$ **e** $-2p^2 - 2pq$
　　b $-15a - 20$ **f** $-4ab + 8a^2$
　　c $10y^2 - 4y$ **g** $-20a^2 + 12a$
　　d $2a^2 - 3ab$ **h** $-4x^2 + x$
7. a $x + 15$ **c** $-6a + 28$
　　b $-7x + 8$ **d** $-10a + 27$
8. a $9x - 3$ **c** $28 - 25b$
　　b $-10x + 15$ **d** $-2c + 2$
9. a $p - 7q$ **c** $23a - 12$
　　b $3 - 2x$ **d** $-3x - 14y$
10. a $-3x^2 + 2x$ **d** $16a^2 - 9a$
　　b $10x^2 - 3xy$ **e** $13a^2 - 12a$
　　c $4p^2 - 3pq + 3q^2$ **f** $3x^2 - 2xy + 6y^2$
11. a $3x^2 - 18x$ **d** $14a - 4a^2$
　　b $25a^2 - 20a$ **e** $2x^2 + 4x$
　　c $-17a^2 + 7a$ **f** $15x^2 - 10x$
12. a $7x - 16$ **d** $6x - 12$
　　b $10x + 6$ **e** $10x + 27$
　　c $23 - 4x$ **f** $x - 20$
13. a $-5x - 14$ **d** $1 - 18x$
　　b $3x^2 - 14x$ **e** $7x^2$
　　c $12x^2 - 7x + 7$ **f** $18x^2 - 9x - 12$
14. a $3x^2 + x$ **d** $28x^2 - 14x$
　　b $x^2 - 17x$ **e** $11x^2 - 3x$
　　c $2x^2 + 7x$ **f** $11x^2 - 24x$

Exercise 8B (p. 150)

1. a $ac + ad + bc + bd$
　　b $ac + ad - bc - bd$
　　c $ps + pt + qs + qt$
2. a $xy + yz + y^2 + yz$
　　b $2ac + 4ad + bc + 2bd$
　　c $6ac + 2ad + 3bc + bd$
3. a $5xz + 15x + 2yz + 6y$
　　b $5xz + 10x + 4yz + 8y$
　　c $xz - 4x + yz - 4y$
4. a $15x - 3xz - 10y + 2yz$
　　b $2ps - 3pt + 2qs - 3qt$
　　c $12pr - 9ps - 4qr + 3qs$

5. a $ac - ad - 2bc + 2bd$
 b $9ac + 12ad - 12bc - 16bd$
 c $6uw - 30ur - 5vw - 25vr$
6. a $21x - 14zx - 6y + 4yz$
 b $6ac - 9ad + 8bc - 12bd$
 c $10ac - 4a + 5bc - 2b$

Exercise 8C (p. 151)

1. a $x^2 + 7x + 12$ **b** $a^2 + 9a + 20$
2. a $x^2 + 6x + 8$ **b** $b^2 + 9b + 14$
3. a $x^2 + 7x + 6$ **b** $c^2 + 10c + 24$
4. a $x^2 + 7x + 10$ **b** $p^2 + 15p + 36$
5. a $x^2 + 11x + 24$ **b** $q^2 + 17q + 70$
6. a $x^2 - 5x + 6$ **b** $x^2 - 7x + 12$
7. a $x^2 - 12x + 35$ **b** $x^2 - 12x + 32$
8. a $a^2 - 10a + 16$ **b** $b^2 - 6b + 8$
9. a $x^2 - 13x + 30$ **b** $a^2 - 8a + 16$
10. a $b^2 - 10b + 25$ **b** $p^2 - 15p + 56$
11. a $x^2 + x - 6$ **b** $x^2 + 5x - 14$
12. a $x^2 + x - 20$ **b** $x^2 + x - 30$
13. a $x^2 - 3x - 28$ **b** $x^2 + 9x - 10$
14. a $a^2 - 7a - 30$ **b** $b^2 - b - 56$

Exercise 8D (p. 152)

1. a $x^2 + 9x + 20$ **b** $x^2 + 14x + 48$
2. a $a^2 + 7a + 10$ **b** $a^2 + 17a + 70$
3. a $x^2 - 9x + 20$ **b** $x^2 - 14x + 48$
4. a $a^2 - 7a + 10$ **b** $a^2 - 17a + 70$
5. a $a^2 - 3a - 10$ **b** $a^2 - 3a - 70$
6. a $y^2 - 3y - 18$ **b** $y^2 + 8y - 20$
7. a $z^2 - 6z - 40$ **b** $z^2 - 11z - 12$
8. a $p^2 - 3p - 40$ **b** $p^2 - 11p - 26$
9. a $p^2 + 13p + 42$ **b** $z^2 + z - 12$
10. a $x^2 + 4x - 21$ **b** $p^2 - 12p + 32$

Exercise 8E (p. 153)

1. a $2x^2 + 3x + 1$ **b** $3x^2 + 5x + 2$
2. a $5x^2 + 12x + 4$ **b** $3x^2 + 11x + 6$
3. a $5x^2 + 17x + 6$ **b** $4x^2 + 7x + 3$
4. a $3x^2 + 19x + 20$ **b** $7x^2 + 23x + 6$
5. a $6x^2 + 13x + 6$ **b** $10x^2 + 31x + 15$
6. a $12x^2 - 25x + 12$ **b** $21x^2 - 20x + 4$
7. a $10x^2 - 3x - 18$ **b** $12x^2 - 5x - 2$
8. a $21a^2 - 58a + 21$ **b** $6b^2 - 5b - 25$
9. a $4a^2 - 9$ **b** $16x^2 - 9$
10. a $9b^2 - 49$ **b** $25y^2 - 4$
11. a $49y^2 - 25$ **b** $9x^2 - 1$
12. a $20a^2 + a - 12$ **b** $16x^2 - 8x - 35$
13. a $8 - 2x - x^2$ **c** $8 + 2x - 3x^2$
 b $21 - 4x - x^2$
14. a $2 + 7x - 4x^2$ **c** $5x - 6 - x^2$
 b $2x - 1 - x^2$
15. a $20 + y - y^2$ **c** $4 - 4x - 3x^2$
 b $20 - 2p - 4p^2$
16. a $6x^2 + 5x + 1$ **c** $4 + 8x - 5x^2$
 b $15x^2 + 26x + 8$

17. a $12 + 13x - 14x^2$ **c** $27x - 9 - 20x^2$
 b $19x - 3 - 6x^2$
18. a $29a - 6 - 35a^2$ **c** $8 + 10x - 3x^2$
 b $12 - p - p^2$

Exercise 8F (p. 155)

1. a $x^2 + 2x + 1$ **5. a** $x^2 + 24x + 144$
 b $b^2 + 8b + 16$ **b** $p^2 + 2pq + q^2$
 c $c^2 + 2cd + d^2$ **c** $u^2 + 2uv + v^2$
2. a $x^2 + 4x + 4$ **6. a** $x^2 + 16x + 64$
 b $x^2 + 2xz + z^2$ **b** $a^2 + 2ab + b^2$
 c $m^2 + 2mn + n^2$ **c** $M^2 + 2Mm + m^2$
3. a $a^2 + 6a + 9$ **7. a** $4x^2 + 4x + 1$
 b $y^2 + 2xy + x^2$ **b** $36c^2 + 12c + 1$
 c $a^2 + 18a + 81$ **c** $9a^2 + 24a + 16$
4. a $t^2 + 20t + 100$ **8. a** $16b^2 + 8b + 1$
 b $p^2 + 14p + 49$ **b** $9a^2 + 6a + 1$
 c $e^2 + 2ef + f^2$ **c** $16y^2 + 24y + 9$
9. a $25x^2 + 20x + 4$ **c** $9W^2 + 12W + 4$
 b $4x^2 + 20x + 25$
10. a $x^2 + 4xy + 4y^2$ **c** $49x^2 + 28xy + 4y^2$
 b $9a^2 + 12ab + 4b^2$ **d** $9x^2 + 6xy + y^2$
11. a $9a^2 + 6ab + b^2$ **c** $4x^2 + 20xy + 25y^2$
 b $9s^2 + 24st + 16t^2$ **d** $9s^2 + 6st + t^2$
12. a $x^2 - 4x + 4$ **c** $x^2 - 2x + 1$
 b $x^2 - 6x + 9$ **d** $x^2 - 12x + 36$
13. a $x^2 - 14x + 49$ **c** $a^2 - 20a + 100$
 b $x^2 - 8x + 16$ **d** $a^a - 2ab + b^2$
14. a $M^2 - 2Mn - n^2$ **c** $u^2 - 2uv + v^2$
 b $x^2 - 2xy + y^2$ **d** $s^2 - 2st + t^2$
15. a $9x^2 - 6x + 1$ **c** $36x^2 - 12x + 1$
 b $4a^2 - 4a + 1$ **d** $16x^2 - 24x + 9$
16. a $25z^2 - 10z + 1$ **c** $4x^2 - 12x + 9$
 b $16y^2 - 8y + 1$ **d** $25x^2 - 30x + 9$
17. a $100y^2 - 180y + 81$ **c** $9p^2 - 24p + 16$
 b $49b^2 - 28b + 4$ **d** $36M^2 - 60M + 25$
18. a $4y^2 - 4xy + x^2$ **c** $9x^2 - 12xy + 4y^2$
 b $a^2 - 6ab + 9b^2$ **d** $49x^2 - 42xy + 9y^2$
19. a $25x^2 - 10xy + y^2$ **c** $A^2 - 4Ab + 4b^2$
 b $m^2 - 16mn + 64n^2$ **d** $9p^2 - 30pq + 25q^2$
20. a $9m^2 - 12mn + 4n^2$ **c** $16x^2 - 24xy + 9y^2$
 b $25a^2 - 20ab + 4b^2$ **d** $4M^2 - 20Mn + 25m^2$

Exercise 8G (p. 157)

1. a $x^2 - 16$ **b** $x^2 - 25$
2. a $b^2 - 36$ **b** $a^2 - 49$
3. a $c^2 - 9$ **b** $q^2 - 100$
4. a $x^2 - 144$ **b** $R^2 - r^2$
5. a $4x^2 - 1$ **b** $25x^2 - 1$
6. a $9x^2 - 1$ **b** $4a^2 - 9$
7. a $49a^2 - 4$ **b** $100m^2 - 1$
8. a $25a^2 - 16$ **b** $36a^2 - 25$
9. a $9x^2 - 16y^2$ **b** $100a^2 - 81b^2$
10. a $4a^2 - 25b^2$ **b** $R^2 - 4r^2$
11. a $1 - 4a^2$ **b** $1 - 9x^2$
12. a $49y^2 - 9z^2$ **b** $9 - 25x^2$

Exercise 8H (p. 159)

1. a $5x + 10$ **c** $x^2 - 20x + 96$
   b $24pq - 16pr$ **d** $16y^2 - 16y - 21$
2. a $6a^2 - 13ab - 5b^2$ **c** $16y^2 - 81$
   b $12x^2 - 17x - 5$ **d** $25x^2 + 20x + 4$
3. a $x^2 + 16x + 60$ **c** $4a^2 - 28ab + 49b^2$
   b $3x^2 + 5x$ **d** $3ab - 15a^2$
4. a $8 - 20x$ **c** $y^2 + 4yz + 4z^2$
   b $16a - 24a^2$ **d** $36y^2 + 24yz - 5z^2$
5. a $12a^2 - 35a - 33$ **c** $16a^2 + 8a + 1$
   b $99 - 2x - x^2$ **d** $25a^2 - 70a + 49$
6. a $5 - 48x - 20x^2$ **c** $169y^2 - 156yz + 36z^2$
   b $10a^2 - 5ab$ **d** $9p^2 - 12pq$
7. a $4x^2 - 10x - 4$ **c** $18 - 54x$
   b $5 + 25x - 5x^2$ **d** $8pq - 33p^2$
8. a $6pq - 15p^2$ **c** $4x^2 - 3x$
   b $8x - 14x^2$ **d** $19p - 8p^2$
9. a $11x - 35$ **c** $2p^2 - 4pq + 15p$
   b $4p^2 - 10p$ **d** $10xz + 15x + 6yz + 9y$
10. a $6 - 3a$ **c** $a^2 - a - 20$
   b $8ab + 4ac$ **d** $6x^2 + 11x + 3$
11. a $10ac + 25ad + 4bc + 4bd$ **c** $25x^2 - 4$
   b $45x^2 - 4x$ **d** $20p^2 - 5pq$
12. a $x^2 - 19x + 84$ **c** $9x^2 - 42x + 49$
   b $18x^2 - 42x$ **d** $28b^2 - 5b$
13. a $a^2 + 16a + 63$
   b $19a^2 - 32a$
   c $25x^2 - 4y^2$
   d $28a - 42ac - 12b + 18bc$
14. a $9wx - 12xz + 15yw - 20yz$
   b $z^2 - 6z - 27$
   c $4a^2 - 4ab - 3b^2$
   d $4a^2 + 20a + 25$

Chapter 9

Exercise 9B (p. 162)

1. a $a = b + c$ **d** $d = e - f$
   b $m = 2(n + p)$ **e** $n = p + p^2$
   c $z = xy$ **f** $v = u + at$
2. $R = Np$ **6.** $R = \dfrac{x}{10} + \dfrac{y}{5}$
3. $Q = P - \dfrac{nx}{100}$ **7.** $C = \dfrac{n}{10} + 25$
4. $N = y + z$ **8.** $T = \dfrac{7C}{47}$
5. $b = \dfrac{ac}{1000}$ **9.** $A = 4\pi r^2$

Exercise 9C (p. 164)

1. 12   **8.** $2\frac{5}{6}$
2. a 24   **b** 1   **9. a** -20 **b** -9
3. a 49.2 **b** $1\frac{2}{3}$ **10. a** -13.5 **b** 8.4
4. 5.62   **11. a** 14   **b** 4
5. 642   **12. a** -4 **b** 12
6. $3\frac{1}{20}$ **13.** 60
7. 8.6   **14. a** 4   **b** $3\frac{7}{8}$

15. a 9.5   **b** -0.89
16. y: $-24, -14, -4, 6, 16$
17. a 2   **b** 2   **19.** 2
18. a $\frac{3}{4}$ **b** 5   **20.** 21
21. 6
22. y: $1, 7, 17, 31, 49, 71, 97$
23. -18

Exercise 9D (p. 166)

1. 5.2   **2.** 1.04
3. a 6   **b** 15.0   **c** 1.41   **d** 6
4. a 10   **b** 8.61
5. a 9   **b** 142
6. -29.7
7. a 32   **b** 37.0
8. 3.421 110 931, 3.42
9. 8.47   **11.** 0.007 70
10. 18.5   **12.** 1610 cm^3
13. a 4 cm^2 **b** 4.57 cm
14. a $u = 16$, $v = 40$, $t = 20$
   b 560   **c** 509
15. b **i** 9   **ii** 35
16. 103 mm/Hg
17. a 9.71% **b** 4.26%
18. a 2 m^2 **b** 2.27 m^2
19. a 0.968 **b** 151
20. a $x_1 = 4$, $x_2 = -1\frac{1}{2}$ **b** **i** $2\frac{1}{2}$ **ii** -6
   c $b^2 - 4ac$ is -ve and you cannot find the square
   root of a -ve number.
21. a 5 °C   **b** 0.884 °C

Exercise 9E (p. 169)

1. a 6   **b** 4   **4. a** 17   **b** 8
2. a 13   **b** 93   **5. a** 3.7   **b** 2.9
3. a 4   **b** 3   **6. a** 10   **b** 2.75
7. a 2.98   **b** -5
8. a 77 °F   **b** 32 °F   **c** 212 °F
9. a 35 °F   **b** 203 °F
10. a **i** 17   **ii** 50   **b** 5   **c** -6
11. a $b = 6$ **c** over 6 m
   b 100   **d** **i** 25 **ii** 180
12. a **i** 46   **ii** 79   **b** 10

Exercise 9F (p. 171)

1. 5.5   **6.** y: $-13, -5, -1, 7, 19$
2. 0.2   **7.** $N = a^2 + bc$
3. 32   **8.** $\frac{1}{16}$
4. 3.25   **9.** $2\frac{2}{3}$
5. $-\frac{29}{120}$ **10.** y: $14, 8, 5, -1, -7$

Exercise 9G (p. 172)

1. 1.72   **3.** -33.9
2. 12.6   **4.** $\frac{3}{5}$
5. a -24 **b** 47.5
6. a 17   **b** 2   **c** -46
7. 0.46   **9.** 31.7
8. 4.01   **10.** $k = 15L$, $L = 3$

Chapter 10

Exercise 10B (p. 175)

1. a length   **c** area   **e** length
   b volume   **d** volume   **f** area
2. a length   **c** volume   **e** area
   b volume   **d** length   **f** area
3. a cm   **c** cm^2 **e** cm
   b cm^2 **d** cm^3 **f** cm^3
4. a area   **d** area   **g** length
   b volume   **e** volume   **h** length
   c length   **f** area   **i** area
5. c is a sum of area and volume; e is the sum of area and length
6. only one length in the formula
7. 2   **11.** $2\pi r(r + h)$
8. a B   **b** C   **12. a** 1   **b** 2   **c** 1
9. B   **13.** B
10. a D   **b** A

Exercise 10C (p. 180)

1. a 5.01 m   **b** $9.77\,m^2$
2. a 80.3 mm   **b** $2250\,mm^2$
3. a i 4.33 cm   **ii** $10.8\,cm^2$
   b i 436 mm   **ii** $48\,000\,mm^2$
   c i 0.894 m   **ii** $1.70\,m^2$
4. a 90°   **b** 31.2 miles   **c** 85.2 miles
5. 31.1 cm   **8.** $0.866\,m$, $4.33\,m^2$
6. 95.3 cm   **9.** 336 km
7. $0.894\,m^2$ **10.** 95.4 cm
11. a $244\,mm^2$ **b** $9760\,mm^3$
12. 13.4 cm
13. a 42.4 cm   **b** 102 cm

Exercise 10D (p. 185)

1. a

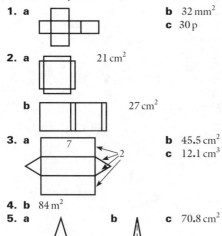

   b $32\,mm^2$
   c 30 p
2. a $21\,cm^2$
   b $27\,cm^2$
3. a   7   2   **b** $45.5\,cm^2$
   c $12.1\,cm^3$
4. b $84\,m^2$
5. a   **b**   **c** $70.8\,cm^2$

6. a 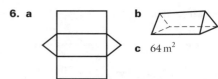 **b**   **c** $64\,m^2$

7. b 145 square units   **c**

8. a 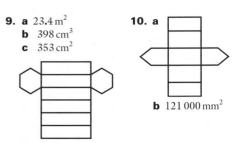   **b** $200\,cm^2$

9. a $23.4\,m^2$
   b $398\,cm^3$
   c $353\,cm^2$

10. a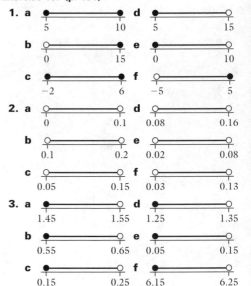
   b $121\,000\,mm^2$

Exercise 10E (p. 189)

1. 96 g   **7.** 0.92 g
2. 2310 g   **8. a** $625\,cm^2$ **b** 860 kg
3. 122 g   **9.** $6.79\,g/cm^3$
4. 980 g   **10.** $0.875\,g/cm^3$
5. 979 g   **11.** $0.217\,g/cm^3$
6. 19.4 g   **12.** 46.1 g
13. a $4956\,mm^2$ **b** $12\,390\,cm^3$ **c** 9.29 kg
14. a $393\,cm^3$ **b** 68.7 kg

Exercise 10F (p. 191)

1. a 5 — 10   **d** 5 — 15
   b 0 — 15   **e** 0 — 10
   c −2 — 6   **f** −5 — 5
2. a 0 — 0.1   **d** 0.08 — 0.16
   b 0.1 — 0.2   **e** 0.02 — 0.08
   c 0.05 — 0.15   **f** 0.03 — 0.13
3. a 1.45 — 1.55   **d** 1.25 — 1.35
   b 0.55 — 0.65   **e** 0.05 — 0.15
   c 0.15 — 0.25   **f** 6.15 — 6.25

4. a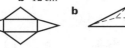

0.245   0.255 6.885   6.895

b

0.515   0.525 12.255   12.265

c

1.145   1.155 0.045   0.055

5. $5.55 \leqslant w < 5.65$

6. $£2450 < £x < £2550$

7. $12.45 \leqslant x < 12.55$

8. $74500 \leqslant x < 75499$, nothing

9. $1.245 \leqslant d < 1.255$

10. a $1.55 \leqslant s < 1.65$

   b no

11. 65

12. $452.5 \leqslant x < 457.5$

13. The edge of the cube may be up to 34.5 mm and this is bigger than the longest possible edge of the box (up to 34.25 mm).

Exercise 10G (p. 195)

1. $395\,g \leqslant w\,g < 405\,g$

2. $2985\,cm \leqslant$ length $< 2995\,cm$, 10 cm

3. a 118 mm

   b £1 073 800

4. a scales show 1 nail has a weight between 7.5 g and 8.5 g

   b 7.75 g

5. between 249 mm and 251 mm

6. 364 days

7. 21 m

8. a i 15 cm   **ii** 14.8 cm

   b i 1.65 cm   **ii** 11.6 cm

9. no, $0.75 \times 10\,000 < 63\,360$

10. a 46 mm

   b 20 mm

   c $400\,mm^2$

11. $16\,m^2$

Exercise 10H (p. 197)

1. C

2. a 3 cm   **b** $12\,cm^2$

3. a   **b**

4. $8.9\,g/cm^2$

5. 3.2 tonnes

6. a 151.5 cm   **b i** 81 cm   **ii** 19 cm

Exercise 10I (p. 198)

1. a 0.67 m   **b** $1.40\,m^3$ **c** 1190 kg (3 s.f.)

2. $82.4\,cm^3$

3. b $11\,368\,cm^3$

4. a $0.0104\,kg/cm^3$ **b** 26 kg

Chapter 11

Exercise 11B (p. 202)

1. $2, (1, 0)$ **4.** $2, (-15, -8)$

2. $3, (2, 5)$ **5.** $2.5; (21, 11)$

3. a 1.6   **b** 2.5

6. a

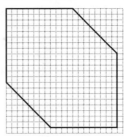

   b Same shape. Bottom edge is 5.4 cm long.

7.

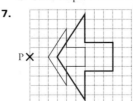

Exercise 11C (p. 204)

1. $(6, 3), \frac{1}{2}$

2. a enlargement scale factor $\frac{1}{3}$, centre $(6, 3)$

   b enlargement scale factor $\frac{1}{2}$, centre $(-2, 0)$

3. a enlargement scale factor $\frac{1}{2}$, centre $(-4, -5)$

   b enlargement scale factor $\frac{3}{4}$, centre $(0, 1)$

4.   **5. a**   **b**

6. a, b

   c 3

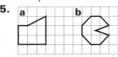

7. $\frac{1}{2}$

8. a $\frac{3}{4}$ **b i** 3.6 cm   **ii** 5.6 cm

9.

10. a $\frac{1}{2}$ **b** $1\frac{1}{2}$ **c** $3, (0, 0)$

   d enlargement scale factor $\frac{1}{3}$, centre $(0, 0)$

11. a $1\frac{1}{2}$ **b** $\frac{2}{3}$ **c** $\frac{4}{9}$

Exercise 11D (p. 208)

1.

4.

2.

5.

3.

6.

Summary 3

Revision Exercise 3.1 (p. 212)

1. a £396 **b** $10.5\,\text{cm}^2$
2. a 325 mph **b** 6.5 hours
3. a

q	5	15	25	40	50

b

y	24	12	6	3	1.2

4. a $6 - 3x$ **6. a** $x^2 + 10x + 25$
  b $a^2 + 4ab + 3b^2$ **b** $2x^2 + 7x + 2$
  c $x^2 - 6x + 8$ **c** $4x^2 - 9y^2$
      d $16 - x^2$
5. a $x^2 + 3x - 28$ **7. a** $x = 3(p + q)$
  b $3x^2 - 10x - 25$ **b** $z = 2xy$
  c $15x^2 - 7x - 2$ **c** $w = x + y - xy$
8. a 7 **b** 5 **c** 7
9. a -66.15 **b** 7.125
10. $C = nx$ **11. i** $6x - 5y$ **ii** $2x^2 - 7x + 3$
12. a 29.6 minutes **b** 30 minutes
13. a 150 cm **b** 24 cm
  c -6.67 cm, a forearm cannot have a negative length

Revision Exercise 3.2 (p. 214)

1. a i mm^2 **iii** mm **v** mm^2
  ii mm^2 **iv** mm^3 **vi** mm^3
  b i length **ii** length **iii** length
2. a 90° **b** 36.1 cm **c** $300\,\text{cm}^2$
3. a 1447.5 g **b i** $102\,\text{cm}^3$ **ii** 3.4 cm
4. a

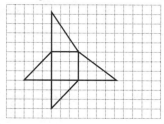

b i 8.49 cm **iii** 10.4 cm
  ii 8.49 cm **iv** $123\,\text{cm}^2$
5. a i

0.35   0.45

  ii

5.445   5.455

  b $3.15 \leqslant x < 3.25$ **c** 154
6. a $(9, -1)$ **b** 3 **7.** $(9, 8), \frac{1}{2}$
8. **9.** $A'(5, 0),$
   $B'(10, 5),$
   $C'(10, 15)$
10. a $\frac{5}{8}$ **b i** 6.4 cm **ii** 3.5 cm
11. a reflection in the line $y = x$
  b enlargement, scale factor 2, centre $(-7, 1)$
12. b **c** $38.6\,\text{cm}^2$

13. a i 5.5 cm **ii** 4.5 cm **b** 200 m

Revision Exercise 3.3 (p. 218)

1. a 140 miles **b** 18 litres
2. a direct **b** neither **c** inverse **d** neither
3. a $10 - 15a$ **c** $p^2 - 11p + 24$
  b $3x - 6xz + 2y - 4yz$ **d** $12 + 5x - 3x^2$
4. a $9x^2 - 6x + 1$ **b** $x^2 + 9x + 22$
5. a 16 **b** 90.25 **c** 77.44
6. 66
7. 28.95 cm
8. a $1290\,\text{mm}^3$ **b** 3.23 g **9.** $(-2, 2), \frac{1}{3}$
10. $A'(1, 6),\quad B'(5, 5),\quad C'(3, 2)$

Revision Exercise 3.4 (p. 220)

1. a i 10^5 **ii** 10^{-3}
  b i $1\frac{1}{2}$ **ii** $12\frac{1}{4}$ **iii** $7\frac{1}{2}$ **iv** $\frac{7}{12}$
2. a 200 **c** 240 **e** 4
  b 5 **d** 0.64 **f** 2
3. a i 4.9×10^8 **iii** 3.8×10^{-1}
  ii 8×10^{-8} **iv** 9.34×10^2
  b i 78 000 **ii** 0.000 065
4. a $\frac{1}{3}$ **b** $\frac{1}{3}$ **c** $\frac{1}{36}$ **d** $\frac{1}{4}$
5. a 23, 22 **b i** (5, 25) **ii** (n, n^2)
6. a 25 mm **b** 350 pages
7. a $10ab + 25ac$ **c** $7x^2 + 11x + 4$
  b $a - a^2 + 4b - 4ab$ **d** $x^2 - 8xy + 16y^2$
8. $C = 0.07n + 20$ **9.** $(6, 3), \frac{1}{3}$
10. a i $\dfrac{1}{2a}$ **ii** $\dfrac{a}{3}$ **iii** not possible
  b i $6\frac{2}{3}$ **ii** $3\frac{3}{4}$ **iii** -4

Revision Exercise 3.5 (p. 221)

1. a $x = 1, y = 3, z = 2$
  b i x^5 **ii** a^{-2} **iii** b^{11} **iv** x^5
  c i 0.0067 **ii** $\frac{1}{25}$ **iii** $\frac{1}{15}$ **iv** 3600

2. a i 33.9 **ii** 162 **b** 219
3. a 34 300 **c** 0.204
 b 0.007 85 **d** 0.008 31
4. a $\frac{6}{73}$ **b** $\frac{4}{365}$ **c** $\frac{6}{73}$ **d** $\frac{12}{73}$
 yes: 2004 is a leap year with 366 days, 1998 is
 not a leap year, it has 365 days
5. a 4, 24 **b** 39, 52
6. a i 15 g **ii** 36 g
 b i 1.2 cm³ **ii** 0.5 cm³
7. a $15xy - 6xz$
 b $a^2 + 10a + 24$
 c $5xz + 20x + 3yz + 12y$
 d $a^2 + 6ab + 9b^2$
8. a $F = 2C + 30$ **b** $23\frac{1}{6}$
9. A′(−1, 4), B′(1, 6), C′(3, 4), D′(1, 2)
10. a 4.58 cm **b** 7.79 cm
 c i 181 cm² **ii** 80.1 cm²

Chapter 12

Exercise 12A (p. 223)

1. £53 **2.** £25

Exercise 12B (p. 225)

1. a more accurate
 b The vertical axis would be much too high.
 c It would make reading values off the graph
 difficult.
 d Difficult to plot.
 e Not directly, but it can be found by converting
 10 000 pesetas into pounds sterling and
 multiplying the answer by 10.
 f £-axis: £500, peseta–axis: 105 (thousands)
2. a £68 **c** £1 = 11.2 kroner
 b 520 kroner
4. a i £112 **ii** £67 **c** $1 = £0.7 or £1 = $1.43
 b i $174 **ii** $109
5. a 50 f **c** 142 DM
 b 1023 f **d** 316 DM
6. a i 12 km **ii** 21 km **d** 6
 b i 1 h 40 min **ii** 3.5 h **e** same value
 c 6 km/h
7. speed is constant
 a i 825 km **ii** 2475 km
 b i 1 h 50 min **ii** 4 h 33 min
 c 550 **d** same value
8. a A **i** £31 **ii** $44 B **i** £30 **ii** $44
 C **i** £30 **ii** $44 D **i** £32 **ii** $42
 b A
 c scales that maximise the lengths of the axes
 and are easy to use e.g. 1 cm ≡ £5 and $5
9. a 54%, 77% **b** 32.5, 52
10. a 36 °C **b** 78 °C **c** 77 °C **d** 176 °C
 e because 0 °C does not equal 0 °F
11. a i 64 km/h **ii** 96 km/h
12. useful for drivers who think in gallons

Exercise 12C (p. 229)

1. a i £10 **ii** £80 **iii** 8 p
 b i gives y-intercept **iii** equals gradient
 d i 210 **ii** 5500
 e 6124 units
2. a $y = 0.15x + 5$ **c** $y = 200x + 10$
 b $y = 38 - 9x$ **d** $y = 1.9 - 2.2x$
3. a 9.2, French francs per £1
 b 0.09, cost/unit in £
 c 17, temperature rise/min
 d −0.3, litres used per mile
4. a i 1 200 000 gallons **ii** 5 days
 b −100 000, water loss per day
 c 1 500 000, level of water when measurement
 started
 d dry
5. $y = 25 + 11.25x$
 a £92.50 **b** 6 h, 40 min **c** £11.25 per hour

Exercise 12D (p. 232)

1. A(0, −1) **3.** A(0, 3) **5.** A(0, 2)
 B(1, 0) B(−$\frac{3}{2}$, 0) B(4, 0)
 C(3, 2) C(1, 5) C($\frac{1}{2}$, 1$\frac{3}{4}$)
2. A(0, −1) **4.** A(0, 4) **6.** A(0, 2)
 B($\frac{1}{2}$, 0) B(4, 0) B(−6, 0)
 C(2, 3) C(3, 1) C(−9, −1)
7. $y = x + 4$ **11.**
8. $y = 3x - 2$
9. $y = 6 - 2x$
10. $y = -4x - 3$

12.  **13.**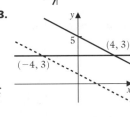

Exercise 12E (p. 235)

1. A **2.** B **3.** B **4.** A
5. a C **b** B **c** A **6.** B
7. Brussels to Cape Town
8. a Driden to Endford
 b Endford to Driden
 c Tom
 d Endford, as Fran took much longer to do the
 same distance
9. **10.**

11. a **b** **c**

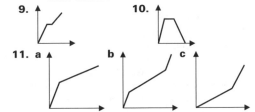

12. a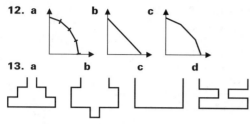

13. a b c d

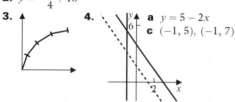

Exercise 12F (p. 239)

1. a £175
   b 4250 kW hours
   c $y = 20$, the basic charge, in £s for using gas
   d 0.014, cost, £s, per kW hour

2. $y = -\frac{x}{4} + 18$

3. **4.** **a** $y = 5 - 2x$
   c $(-1, 5), (-1, 7)$

Chapter 13

Exercise 13A (p. 243)

1. a yes   **c** yes   **e** yes   **g** no
   b no   **d** no   **f** yes   **h** no
2. A, D
3. B, C, E
4. D, E
5. B, C, E
6. a, d, e, g, i and **k** are true

Exercise 13B (p. 245)

1. a 6 cm   **b** 12 cm   **c** 4 cm
2. a 60 cm   **b** 520 cm   **c** 45°   **d** 6
3. a 15 cm   **b** 12 cm   **c** 3 cm
4. a 10 cm   **c i** 15 cm² **ii** 60 cm²
   b 6 cm   **d** 4
5. a i 20 cm   **ii** 6 cm
   b 48 cm² and 300 cm²
   c 6.25
6. a 10 cm   **b** 15 cm   **c** 150 cm²
7. a 45°   **c** 10 m
   b isosceles, 10 cm
8. a 4 cm   **c** 8 cm³, 64 cm³, 216 cm³
   b 6 cm   **d** 12 cm
9. a 40 cm   **b** 54.4 cm
10. 294 mm × 207.2 mm

Exercise 13C (p. 250)

1. a 2   **b** 3   **c** $\frac{2}{3}$ **d** $\frac{1}{4}$ **e** 3   **f** 2
2. a $x = 4$ cm, $y = 4$ cm
   b $x = 6\frac{2}{3}$ cm
   c $x = 5$ cm, $y = 3.6$ cm, $z = 7.5$ cm
   d $x = 2.6$ cm
   e $x = 4.8$ cm, $y = 9$ cm, $w = 1.8$ cm

3. 2.56 km   **6.** 8 cm
4. 10 cm   **7.** 900 m
5. 6 cm   **8.** 18 m by 10 m
9. a AD   **d** 2.5 cm
10. a angle E   **d** AB is 8 cm, AD is 5 cm

Exercise 13D (p. 254)

1. similar, 2.5 cm
2. similar, 7.2 cm
3. not similar
4. similar, 6.3 cm
5. similar, 4.8 in
6. a $\widehat{D} = 70°, \widehat{B} = 50°$ **b** 4 cm
7. a $\widehat{C} = 70°, \widehat{A} = 60°$
   b CD = 9 cm, DE = 10.5 cm
8. a both triangles are isosceles, with the two equal angles being 45°
   b 5 cm
9. a All angles in △ABC are also in △XYZ.
   b YZ = 7.5 cm
10. a BC and DE are parallel, therefore angles B and D and C and E are equal.
   b i 18 cm   **ii** 13.5 cm   **iii** 4.5 cm

Exercise 13E (p. 257)

1. A, C, E
2. $\frac{4}{3}$
3. pair A, $\frac{2}{3}$
4. $x = 2$ cm, $y = 10$ cm, $z = 4$ cm,
5. BC = 4 cm
6. a 2.28 cm   **b** 25°   **c** 18.75 cm
7. $x = 9.45$, $y = 26.7$
8. a $\widehat{A} = \widehat{D}$ and $\widehat{B} = \widehat{E}$ **b** 11.25 cm

Chapter 14

Exercise 14A (p. 261)

1. a $x = 4$ **d** $z = -1$ **g** $x = 2$
   b $x = 6$ **e** $a = 0$ **h** $x = -1$
   c $a = 4\frac{1}{2}$ **f** $b = 2.8$ **i** $p = 3$
2. a $x = 1$ **d** $x = -1.5$ **g** $x = 4.5$
   b $x = 2$ **e** $x = -2$ **h** $x = \frac{8}{5}$
   c $x = \frac{3}{7}$ **f** $x = 3$ **i** $x = 1$
3. a $x = \frac{4}{5}$ **d** $x = \frac{2}{3}$ **g** $x = -\frac{7}{8}$
   b $a = 1$ **e** $v = \frac{5}{2}$ **h** $t = \frac{2}{9}$
   c $t = -\frac{4}{3}$ **f** $x = \frac{2}{3}$ **i** $x = \frac{1}{3}$
4. a $p = \frac{5}{3}$ **d** $x = 1$ **g** $p = \frac{9}{8}$
   b $t = \frac{1}{12}$ **e** $A = \frac{3}{8}$ **h** $t = \frac{3}{2}$
   c $x = 1$ **f** $x = 2$ **i** $t = \frac{3}{2}$
5. a $x = 1$ **c** $x = \frac{5}{3}$ **e** $t = -\frac{7}{5}$
   b $x = 3$ **d** $x = \frac{1}{8}$ **f** $x = \frac{7}{9}$
6. a $H = -4$ **c** $x = -1$ **e** $A = \frac{5}{6}$
   b $x = \frac{1}{2}$ **d** $p = 6$ **f** $s = -\frac{7}{2}$

Exercise 14B (p. 263)

1. a $s = p - r$ **c** $b = a + c$ **e** $s = r - 2t$
   b $y = x - 3$ **d** $Y = X + Z$ **f** $m = k - l$

2. a $v = u + 5$ **c** $n = M - m$ **e** $u = y - 10t$
   b $y = z - x$ **d** $P = N + Q$ **f** $t = R - 8s$

3. a $y = \dfrac{x}{2}$ **c** $b = \dfrac{2a}{7}$ **e** $N = 10X$
   b $t = 2v$ **d** $b = \dfrac{a}{3}$ **f** $u = 5v$

4. a $u = 3t$ **c** $r = 6A$ **e** $p = 6q$
   b $m = 3k$ **d** $p = 4n$ **f** $M = 8m$

5. a $q = pr$ **c** $p = nq$ **e** $s = \dfrac{r}{t}$
   b $c = \dfrac{a}{b}$ **d** $a = \dfrac{v}{t}$ **f** $a = \dfrac{A}{b}$

6. a $y = \dfrac{z}{3x}$ **d** $b = 12a$ **g** $q = \dfrac{5p}{4}$
   b $z = 2Xy$ **e** $x = 2yz$ **h** $y = 20x$
   c $y = \dfrac{3x}{2}$ **f** $v = ab^2$

Exercise 14C (p. 265)

1. a $s = \dfrac{(p-r)}{2}$ **e** $w = \dfrac{(x+y)}{2}$
   b $t = \dfrac{(u-v)}{3}$ **f** $t = \dfrac{(m-k)}{4}$
   c $c = \dfrac{(b-a)}{4}$ **g** $y = \dfrac{(x-w)}{6}$
   d $v = \dfrac{(V-3u)}{2}$ **h** $s = \dfrac{(IT-N)}{2}$

2. a $y = \dfrac{4x}{3}$ **e** $R = \dfrac{VI}{2}$
   b $t = \dfrac{u-v}{5}$ **f** $r = \dfrac{p+w}{2}$
   c $I = 10(A - P)$ **g** $c = 2(a - b)$
   d $y = 3(x - z)$ **h** $r = 5(q - p)$

3. a $u = v - at$ **b** 140

4. a $s = \dfrac{P+t}{r}$ **b** $-6\frac{1}{4}$

5. a $q = \dfrac{X-p}{r}$ **b** -3

6. a $c = \dfrac{V}{ab}$ **b** 2.5

7. a $w = \dfrac{Z-xy}{x}$ **b** 3.4

8. a $a = \dfrac{A+bc}{c}$ **b** $\frac{3}{4}$

9. a $c = \dfrac{a-b}{b}$ **b** 6.5

10. a $x = \dfrac{z-y}{y}$ **b** 2.2

11. a $R = PS - QS$ **b** 4

12. a $x = 2z + 6t$ **b** -26

13. a $y = \dfrac{x-z}{5}$ **b** 2

14. a $u = v + 8t$ **b** 20.7

15. a $z = \dfrac{xy-W}{y}$ **b** -2

16. a $B = A - \dfrac{C}{100}$ **b** 17.5

17. a $a = b + 2c$ **b** 4 **c** $b = a - 2c$

18. a $160\,$cm   **c** $-\frac{5}{3}$ cm, f must be $+ve$
   b $24.7\,$cm   **d** $f = \dfrac{h-85}{3}$

19. a $x = 2yz$ **b** 12 **c** $y = \dfrac{x}{2z}$

20. a $d = e^2 + 2f$ **b** $f = \dfrac{d-e^2}{2}$ **c** $f = \frac{1}{2}$

21. a $400\,°$F   **b** $G = \dfrac{F}{25} - 10$ **c** 8

22. a $49.1\,$cm^2 **b** $x = \dfrac{360A}{\pi r^2}$ **c** $31.8\,°$

23. a $G = \dfrac{C-121}{14}$ **c** $F = 25G + 50$
   b i 3 **ii** 7

Exercise 14D (p. 269)

1. a $x = \pm 4$ **c** $x = \pm\sqrt{\dfrac{q}{p}}$
   b $x = \pm\frac{5}{3}$ **d** $x = \pm\dfrac{q}{\sqrt{p}}$

2. a $x = \pm\sqrt{\frac{5}{3}}$ **c** $x = \pm\sqrt{p+q}$
   b $x = \pm\sqrt{p}$ **d** $x = \pm\sqrt{\dfrac{bc}{a}}$

3. a $R = \pm\sqrt{\dfrac{A}{2}}$ **d** $x = \pm\sqrt{\dfrac{as}{5}}$
   b $a = \pm\sqrt{\dfrac{V}{b}}$ **e** $c = \pm\sqrt{a-b}$
   c $x = \pm\sqrt{P-2c}$ **f** $t = \pm\sqrt{Rs}$

4. a $x = 4 \pm 3$ **c** $x = 3 \pm \frac{2}{3}$
   b $x = a \pm \sqrt{b}$ **d** $x = 5 \pm \sqrt{\dfrac{s}{t}}$

5. a $A = 2 \pm \sqrt{3r}$ **c** $T = 3 \pm \sqrt{\dfrac{M}{2}}$
   b $H = L \pm \sqrt{8}$ **d** $b = c \pm \sqrt{\dfrac{5}{a}}$

6. a $x = 16$ **d** $x = \dfrac{r^2}{p}$
   b $x = \frac{4}{9}$ **e** $x = 49$
   c $x = \dfrac{q^2}{p^2}$ **f** $x = (a-b)^2$

7. a $x = 27$ **d** $x = 16 - a$
   b $x = a^2$ **e** $x = 10$
   c $x = p^2q$ **f** $x = (s-t)^2 + t$

8. a $r = L^2$ **d** $A = 3r^2$
   b $L = \dfrac{t^2}{4}$ **e** $T = P^2 + 1$
   c $b = \dfrac{25a^2}{9}$ **f** $s = (v-u)^2$

9. $a = b \pm \sqrt{A}$ **14.** $b = \dfrac{9a^4}{4}$

10. $y = \pm\sqrt{\dfrac{Z}{k} - x}$ **15.** $r = \sqrt{\dfrac{3P}{4\pi}}$

11. $r = \pm\sqrt{\dfrac{A}{\pi}}$ **16.** $A = a^2$

12. $R = \dfrac{v^2}{9}$ **17.** $x = \dfrac{y^6}{25z^2}$

13. $b = 3a^2$ **18.** $y = -5x^2$

19. a 80 **c** $k = \frac{1}{25}$ **d i** 144 **ii** $165\,\text{cm}$

20. $H = \sqrt{\dfrac{W}{I}}$, $2.0\,\text{m}$

Exercise 14E (p. 272)

1. a $x = 5$
   b $x = 3$
2. $b = A - c$
3. $p = 3q$
4. $b = \dfrac{a - c}{3}$
5. $m = \dfrac{y - c}{x}$, 5

6. a $C = x + 6y + z$
   b $C = x + 8y$
   c $90\,\text{p}$
7. a $y = \dfrac{7 - x}{2}$
   b $y = \dfrac{9x - 6}{2}$
   c $= \dfrac{4 - 9x^2}{2}$

Exercise 14F (p. 272)

1. a $b + \dfrac{V}{ac}$ **b** 4.80
2. $x = y \pm \sqrt{\dfrac{Z}{k}}$
3. a $q = 11p^2$ **b** 8.33
4. a 28 **b** $t = \dfrac{u - v}{g}$ **c** -7.5

Chapter 15

Exercise 15A (p. 274)

1. a $4(x + 1)$ **c** $3(4x - 1)$ **e** $2(3a + 1)$
   b $5(a - 2b)$ **d** $5(2a - 1)$ **f** $2(a + 2b)$
2. a $3(t - 3)$ **c** $4(3a + 1)$ **e** $7(2x - 1)$
   b $5(x + 3y)$ **d** $8(b - 2c)$ **f** $6(3a - 2b)$
3. a $x(x + 2)$ **c** $x(2x + 1)$ **e** $x(x - 4)$
   b $x(x - 8)$ **d** $t(4 - t)$ **f** $b(b + 4)$
4. a $a(a + 6)$ **c** $x(x + 5)$ **e** $a(4a - 1)$
   b $p(p + 3)$ **d** $x(2 - x)$ **f** $y(5 - 2y)$
5. a $2x(x - 3)$ **c** $4x(3x + 4)$ **e** $2a(a - 6)$
   b $2z(z + 2)$ **d** $5b(a - 2c)$ **f** $2p(3p + 1)$
6. a $5a(5a - 1)$ **c** $3y(y - 9)$ **e** $3y(3y - 2)$
   b $3p(p + 3)$ **d** $4x(2 - x)$ **f** $2y(y - 6)$
7. a $2(x^2 + 2x + 3)$ **c** $5(2a^2 - a + 4)$
   b $3(x^2 - 2x + 3)$
8. a $4(a^2 + 2a - 1)$ **c** $x(5y + 4z + 3)$
   b $b(a + 4c - 3d)$
9. a $4(2x - y + 3z)$ **c** $3a(3b^2 - 2c - d)$
   b $5b(a + 2c + d)$
10. a $2y(x - 2z + 4w)$ **c** $4(a^2 + 3a + 1)$
   b $3(xy - 3yz + 2xz)$
11. a $x^2(x + 1)$ **c** $a^2(1 + a)$ **e** $5a^2(4 - a)$
   b $x^2(1 - x)$ **d** $b^2(b - 1)$ **f** $4x^2(3x - 4)$
12. a $4x^2(x^2 + 3)$ **d** $3a^2(3a^2 - 1)$
   b $4x^3(4 - 3x)$ **e** $2x^2(2x - 1)$
   c $5x^2(2 - 3x^2)$ **f** $9a^2(3 - 2a)$
13. a $4(3x + 2)$ **d** $3(4 + 3y^2)$
   b $4x(2x + 3)$ **e** $3(3x^2 - 2x + 4)$
   c $x(x - 8)$ **f** $5x(x^2 - 2)$.

14. a $4q(2pq + r)$ **d** $5(3x^2 - x - 2)$
   b $2x(2x^2 + 3)$ **e** $4x(3y + 4z + 2)$
   c $4bc(3a - 2d)$ **f** $3(ab + 3bc + 5ac)$
15. a $\frac{1}{2}h(a + b)$ **d** $m(\frac{1}{2}v^2 - gh)$
   b $\frac{1}{2}m(v^2 - u^2)$ **e** $P\left(1 + \dfrac{RT}{100}\right)$
   c $m(g - a)$ **f** $\pi r(2r + h)$
16. a $\pi(R^2 + r^2)$ **d** $m(\frac{1}{2}v^2 - gh)$
   b $2g(h_1 - h_2)$ **e** $\frac{1}{3}\pi r^2(4r - h)$
   c $\frac{1}{2}m(u^2 + v^2)$ **f** $\pi r(3r + 2h)$
17. a $3x(x + 2y)$ **d** $\frac{1}{6}bc(b - 2c)$
   b $\frac{1}{2}u^2(M + m)$ **e** $4x(4x - 3y)$
   c $3pq(q + 3p)$ **f** $3ab(2a + 5b)$
18. a $3ab(4b - 1)$ **d** $5x^2y(2x - 3)$
   b $8xy(x + 2y)$ **e** $\pi h(r^2 + R^2)$
   c $3xyz(3y - 2z)$ **f** $Mn(n - M)$

Exercise 15B (p. 278)

1. a $(x + 1)(x + 2)$ **d** $(x + 2)(x + 6)$
   b $(x + 1)(x + 5)$ **e** $(x + 3)(x + 4)$
   c $(x + 1)(x + 7)$ **f** $(x + 1)(x + 3)$
2. a $(x + 1)(x + 20)$ **d** $(x + 3)(x + 3)$
   b $(x + 4)(x + 4)$ **e** $(x + 1)(x + 12)$
   c $(x + 2)(x + 10)$ **f** $(x + 1)(x + 15)$
3. a $(x + 3)(x + 12)$ **d** $(x + 3)(x + 6)$
   b $(x + 1)(x + 18)$ **e** $(x + 2)(x + 20)$
   c $(x + 2)(x + 18)$ **f** $(x + 1)(x + 8)$
4. a $(x + 3)(x + 7)$ **d** $(x + 2)(x + 8)$
   b $(x + 1)(x + 9)$ **e** $(x + 5)(x + 6)$
   c $(x + 5)(x + 7)$ **f** $(x + 4)(x + 10)$

Exercise 15C (p. 279)

1. a $(x - 1)(x - 8)$ **d** $(x - 3)(x - 10)$
   b $(x - 2)(x - 3)$ **e** $(x - 4)(x - 7)$
   c $(x - 2)(x - 6)$ **f** $(x - 2)(x - 16)$
2. a $(x - 1)(x - 15)$ **d** $(x - 1)(x - 5)$
   b $(x - 2)(x - 15)$ **e** $(x - 6)(x - 7)$
   c $(x - 3)(x - 3)$ **f** $(x - 2)(x - 10)$
3. a $(x - 7)(x - 9)$ **d** $(x - 1)(x - 4)$
   b $(x - 1)(x - 9)$ **e** $(x - 1)(x - 7)$
   c $(x - 5)(x - 7)$ **f** $(x - 1)(x - 5)$

Exercise 15D (p. 279)

1. a $(x - 3)(x + 2)$ **d** $(x + 10)(x - 3)$
   b $(x - 4)(x + 7)$ **e** $(x + 5)(x - 3)$
   c $(x + 5)(x - 4)$ **f** $(x - 4)(x + 3)$
2. a $(x + 9)(x - 3)$ **d** $(x - 5)(x + 6)$
   b $(x - 7)(x + 5)$ **e** $(x - 6)(x + 4)$
   c $(x - 11)(x + 2)$ **f** $(x - 5)(x + 1)$
3. a $(x - 5)(x + 4)$ **d** $(x - 10)(x + 1)$
   b $(x + 8)(x - 5)$ **e** $(x + 7)(x - 6)$
   c $(x - 9)(x + 2)$ **f** $(x - 9)(x + 5)$

Exercise 15E (p. 280)

1. a $(x+2)(x+7)$ **d** $(x+6)(x-5)$
  b $(x-3)(x-7)$ **e** $(x+1)(x+8)$
  c $(x-2)(x+7)$ **f** $(x-5)(x-5)$
2. a $(x+9)(x-1)$ **d** $(x+2)(x+30)$
  b $(x-13)(x-2)$ **e** $(x-9)(x+3)$
  c $(x+8)(x-7)$ **f** $(x+20)(x-4)$
3. a $(x+1)(x+13)$ **d** $(x-5)(x-6)$
  b $(x+14)(x-2)$ **e** $(x+12)(x-4)$
  c $(x+10)(x-8)$ **f** $(x+6)(x+12)$
4. a $(x+4)(x+13)$ **d** $(x-14)(x+3)$
  b $(x-14)(x+2)$ **e** $(x-2)(x-16)$
  c $(x+3)(x+8)$ **f** $(x-12)(x+5)$
5. a $(x-3)(x-6)$ **d** $(x-4)(x-11)$
  b $(x+9)(x-2)$ **e** $(x-13)(x+1)$
  c $(x+7)(x-4)$ **f** $(x+6)(x-2)$
6. a $(x+15)(x-1)$ **d** $(x-5)(x-7)$
  b $(x-7)(x+6)$ **e** $(x+7)(x+9)$
  c $(x-8)(x+1)$ **f** $(x+5)(x-1)$
7. a $(x+1)(x+8)$ **d** $(x+5)(x-4)$
  b $(x-3)(x-3)$ **e** $(x+3)(x+3)$
  c $(x+4)(x+7)$ **f** $(x-1)(x-8)$
8. a $(x+2)(x+15)$ **d** $(x-13)(x+2)$
  b $(x+9)(x-3)$ **e** $(x-1)(x-7)$
  c $(x+2)(x+11)$ **f** $(x+7)(x-6)$
9. a $(x-8)(x+3)$ **d** $(x+9)(x-7)$
  b $(x-2)(x-7)$ **e** $(x-9)(x+3)$
  c $(x+1)(x+27)$ **f** $(x-4)(x-12)$
10. a $(x+5)^2$ **c** $(x+6)^2$ **e** $(x-2)^2$
  b $(x+2)^2$ **d** $(x+9)^2$ **f** $(x+8)^2$
11. a $(x-5)^2$ **c** $(x-6)^2$ **e** $(x+4)^2$
  b $(x-7)^2$ **d** $(x-9)^2$ **f** $(x-3)^2$

Exercise 15F (p. 282)

1. a $(2+x)(1-x)$ **c** $(4+x)(1-x)$
  b $(3-x)(2+x)$ **d** $(3+x)(1-x)$
2. a $(4-x)(2+x)$ **c** $(2-x)(1+x)$
  b $(3+x)(2-x)$ **d** $(8+x)(1-x)$
3. a $(4+x)(2-x)$ **c** $(6-x)(2+x)$
  b $(5+x)(2-x)$ **d** $(9-x)(1+x)$
4. a $(5+x)(1-x)$ **c** $(1+x)(6-x)$
  b $(7+x)(2-x)$ **d** $(10-x)(1+x)$
5. a $(5+x)(4-x)$ **c** $(4-x)(3+x)$
  b $(5+x)(3-x)$ **d** $(12-x)(1+x)$

Exercise 15G (p. 283)

1. a $(x+5)(x-5)$ **c** $(x+6)(x-6)$
  b $(x+1)(x-1)$ **d** $(x+10)(x-10)$
2. a $(x+2)(x-2)$ **c** $(x+9)(x-9)$
  b $(x+8)(x-8)$ **d** $(x+4)(x-4)$
3. a $(x+7)(x-7)$ **c** $(x+0.2)(x-0.2)$
  b $(x+0.4)(x-0.4)$ **d** $(x+0.9)(x-0.9)$
4. a $(3+x)(3-x)$ **c** $(5+x)(5-x)$
  b $(a+b)(a-b)$ **d** $(10+x)(10-x)$
5. a $(6+x)(6-x)$ **c** $(9+x)(9-x)$
  b $(3y+z)(3y-z)$ **d** $(4+x)(4-x)$

Exercise 15H (p. 283)

1. a $3(x+4)$ **c** $9x(x-2)$
  b $7(2x+3)$ **d** $4(3x^2-2)$
2. a $5x(5x+2)$ **c** $4(5x+3)$
  b $2(2x^2+1)$ **d** $4x(2x-1)$
3. a $3(x+1)(x+3)$ **5. a** $3(x+2)(x-2)$
  b $2(x-2)(x-7)$ **b** $5(x+3)(x-3)$
  c $5(x-5)(x+2)$ **c** $3(x-7)(x+3)$
4. a $4(x-1)(x-5)$ **6. a** $6(x-2)(x+1)$
  b $4(x+4)(x-2)$ **b** $3(3+x)(2-x)$
  c $3(x+2)(x+4)$ **c** $2(x+4)(x-4)$
7. a $4(x+3)(x-2)$ **c** $3(x+3)(x-4)$
  b $3(x+4)(x-2)$

Exercise 15I (p. 284)

1. a 7.5 **b** 31.2 **c** 17.7
2. a 18.5 **b** 20.4 **c** 12.9
3. a 1000 **b** 8 **c** 336 **d** 140
4. a 53.2 **b** 5.336 **c** 75.8 **d** 0.526

Exercise 15J (p. 285)

1. a $(x+5)(x+8)$ **d** NP
  b $(x-2)(x-9)$ **e** $(x+6)(x-6)$
  c $(x-6)(x-2)$ **f** NP
2. a $(x-3)(x-8)$ **d** $(x-6)(x+5)$
  b NP   **e** $(x+7)(x-1)$
  c $(x+2)(x+6)$ **f** $(x+15)(x-2)$
3. a $(x+15)(x-1)$ **d** NP
  b $(14+x)(2-x)$ **e** NP
  c $(x+7)(x-7)$ **f** $(x+6)(x+7)$
4. a $(x+3)(x-3)$ **d** $(4+x)(7-x)$
  b $(x-6)(x-4)$ **e** $(x+17)(x-4)$
  c $(a-7)(a-9)$ **f** $(x+13)(x-2)$
5. a NP   **d** NP
  b $(x-5)(x-7)$ **e** $(x+11)(x-10)$
  c $(8+x)(3-x)$ **f** $(5+x)(5-x)$

Exercise 15K (p. 285)

1. a $10(a+2)$ **d** $5(b^2+3b-1)$
  b $4b(a-2c)$ **e** $4z^2(2z-1)$
  c $5p(3p-2)$ **f** $(x-9)(x+3)$
2. a $(a+3)(a+6)$ **d** $(5-x)(2-x)$
  b $(7+x)(3+x)$ **e** $(x+5)(x+7)$
  c $(x-8)(x+1)$ **f** $(a-9)(a+3)$
3. a $(a+6)(a-6)$ **d** $4y(2x-3z)$
  b $6z(2z-1)$ **e** $(x+8)(x-1)$
  c $(4+x)(4-x)$ **f** $5y(x-4z)$
4. a $(x+5)^2$ **d** $(x+11)(x-4)$
  b $(a+3)(a-2)$ **e** $a(7-a)$
  c $(x-6)(x+4)$ **f** $2(a-4)(a+1)$
5. a $(b+7)(b-7)$ **d** $(4+x)(3-x)$
  b $(15-x)(2-x)$ **e** $(x+3)(x-3)$
  c $p(16p-1)$ **f** $(a-7)^2$

6. a $(x+y)(x-y)$ **c** $(2a+5)(2a-5)$
  b $(3x+4)(3x-4)$ **d** $(x+yz)(x-yz)$

6. a 264 **b** 36.9
7. a 49.2 **b** 30.45
8. a 0.106 **b** 358 800

9. a 12 **b** 0.286
10. a 18.5 **b** 23
11. a 400 **b** 4.2

Chapter 16

Exercise 16B (p. 288)

1. a 20 **b** 80
2. £937.50
3. 2008
4. 2070
9. 52 cattle, 360 sheep; yes, an increase by 47
10. a £255 **b** £42.50
      c i £140.25 **ii** $\frac{3}{10}$
11. $\frac{4}{17}$ decrease
12. $\frac{1}{3}$ increase
13. $\frac{1}{4}$ increase

5. £287
6. 300
7. £108
8. 10

14. $\frac{1}{12}$ decrease
15. $\frac{2}{11}$ increase

Exercise 16C (p. 292)

1. a 25% **b** 30% **c** 25%
2. a 20% **b** 20% **c** 15%
3. a £56 **c** £5.58 **e** £27
      b £142.08 **d** £18 **f** £6.24
4. a £12 **b** £24.30 **c** £21
5. a 8% on £250 by £8 **b** $3\frac{1}{2}$% on £200 by 70 p
6. a £426 **b** £374.57 **c** £20.09 **d** £360
7. a £14.75 **b** £10.17
8. a 3.45% on £240 by 16 p
      b 2.88% on £258.90 by £1.10
9. 24% **10. a** £12 000 **b** £84 000
11. 6.8% **12. a** 52.56 m **b** 3.5%; no

Exercise 16D (p. 295)

1. a £70 **c** £6 **e** £448
      b £16 **d** £32 **f** £40
2. a £20 **c** £5.76 **e** £48
      b £240 **d** £72 **f** £720
3. a £40 **c** £50 **e** £2000
      b £80 **d** £160 **f** £192
4. a £120 **b** £260 **c** £184
5. £12 **8.** 850 cm³ **11.** £120
6. £650 **9.** 25 cm **12.** 2825
7. £160 **10.** £80 000

Exercise 16E (p. 298)

1. 40 **3.** 78 **5.** £4500 **7.** £1800
2. £60 **4.** £350 **6.** 40 **8.** 355

Exercise 16F (p. 299)

1. £77 520
2. £13.69
3. $33\frac{1}{3}$%
4. £1485
5. £37.50

6. 42 504
7. a 70% **b** £32.50
8. a £180 **b** 150%
9. £35 500
10. a £70 **b** £8.75

Exercise 16G (p. 300)

1. £30 **2.** £731.25
3. a £20 **c** £26.40 **e** £425
      b £52.50 **d** £33.74 **f** £215.80
4. a 8.5% **b** 5.2% **6.** £250
5. £41.28 **7. a** £1000 **b** £12 500

Exercise 16H (p. 302)

1. a £42 **c** £103.88 **e** £143.99
      b £76.32 **d** £191.77 **f** £64.26
2. £69 984 **3.** £76 (nearest £)
4. a £4.90 **b** £5.10
5. 4650 (nearest 10)
6. David £51 840, Charles £15 360
7. a i £12 300 **ii** £6782 **b** 54.8%
8. a 135 cm **b** 109 cm
9. a £25 500 **b** £20 655
10. a £35 500 **b** £17 920
11. a £3880 **b** £4500
12. a 18 957 **b** 17 969
13. a 12 500 **b** 8000
14. a i 335 **ii** 280 **iii** 230
      b A:T, B:F, C:T
15. a 2 **b** 4 **c** 8
16. start of 2015 **17. a** 2 **b** 9
18. a 1.08P **c** $(1.08)^6 \times P$
      b $(1.08)^2 \times P$ **d** $(1.08)^n \times P$; £1080 (3 s.f.)

Exercise 16I (p. 307)

1. a 352 **2. a** 60% **3. a** £25
      b $\frac{1}{9}$ **b** 25% **b** £30
4. 432 **5.** 15%
6. a 7260 **b** 6600 **c** 6000

Exercise 16J (p. 307)

1. a £9.63 (nearest p) **b** £435.50
2. a 6.5% on £212 by 76 p
3. a £76.96 **b i** £156 **ii** £179.40
4. a £114.64 **b** £175.81
5. a 189
      b 172 (both to nearest whole number)
6. a £69 000 **b** £36 000

Summary 4

Revision Exercise 4.1 (p. 311)

1. a A(0, −3), B(2, 0), C(6, 6)
      b $y = 5 - 3x$
2. C
3. yes; angles equal; 4 : 3
4. $x = 5.4$, $y = 6$, $z = 4.8$
5. a towards Coldham
      b Amberley to Brickworth
      c Brickworth for 15 min
6. a $\widehat{B} = \widehat{D}$ and $\widehat{A} = \widehat{E}$
      b DE = 8 cm, CD = $6\frac{2}{3}$ cm

7. a $b = a + c$

b $x = \dfrac{2y + z}{3}$

c $c = 5(A - b)$

8. a $t = \dfrac{v - u}{5}$

b $y = \dfrac{w - x}{4}$

c $q = 9p^2$

11. a 0.6 m

12. a 6.28 cm (3 s.f.)

b $y = \dfrac{180x}{\pi r}$

9. a $b = \pm\sqrt{\dfrac{V}{a}}$

b $x = -b \pm \sqrt{c}$

c $x = p^2 - q$

d $x = \pm\sqrt{\dfrac{b}{ac}}$

10. a $k = \dfrac{v - lb}{a}$

b 7

b 42 cm

c 34.4° (3 s.f.)

Revision Exercise 4.2 (p. 314)

1. a $4(a + 3)$

b $x(x - 5)$

c $b^2(b - 3)$

2. a $(x + 2)(x + 9)$

b $(x - 2)(x - 4)$

c $(x - 5)^2$

3. a $(x + 3)(x - 5)$

b $(x + 4)(x - 2)$

c $(x + 3)(x + 6)$

d $(7 - x)(2 + x)$

4. a i $(a + b)(a - b)$

ii $(p + 2q)(p - 2q)$

iii $(4x + y)(4x - y)$

b i 3400

ii 39.82

iii 98.3

5. a $3(x^2 - 3)$

b $2(x + 2)(x + 4)$

c $p(9p - 1)$

d $3(x + 3)(x - 3)$

6. a £5092

b £22

7. a 3.56% on £250 by £1.03   **b** £6144

8. a £65

b £44

9. a £446.25

b £9415.93 (nearest p)

10. a £12.42

b £14.60

11. a 3

b £88 000

12. a 3407

b 1999

13. a $3a^2b^2(3b + 5a)$

b $(x + 12)(x - 5)$

Revision Exercise 4.3 (p. 315)

1. a $(0, 8)$ and $(-2, 0)$ **b** $y = 4x - 4$

2. a i £29.50

ii £84.60

iii $131

iv $42

b £1 = $1.56

3. $x = 9, y = 2, z = 5$ **4.** 16 cm

5. a $q = p - 5$

b $t = 3x$

c $x = yz$

d $x = p \pm \sqrt{q}$

6. a $c = \dfrac{b - a}{d}$

b 2

7. a $5(3 - x)$

b $(x - 5)(x + 3)$

c $(x - 3)(x - 7)$

d $2(x^2 + 2x + 4)$

8. a $(x - 3)(x - 4)$

b $(3 + a)(3 - a)$

c $(3 + x)(4 - x)$

d $(x - 2)(x - 4)$

9. a £220

b £69.80

10. a £24.50

b 4200 basic, 4895 de luxe; decreased by 740

Revision Exercise 4.4 (p. 317)

1. a i 3^{-4}

ii 10^{-3}

iii 2^{-4}

iv 5^{-3}

b i 0.0062

ii 2900

iii 6.4

c i $\frac{1}{6}$

ii $\frac{4}{9}$

iii $\frac{5}{17}$

iv $\frac{4}{5}$

2. a i $\dfrac{3ab}{c^2}$

ii $\dfrac{3b}{4(a - b)}$

iii $\dfrac{x}{3}$

iv $\dfrac{2t^2}{3s}$

b i 5.716×10^9

ii 7.404×10^9

3. a 6, 12, 20, 30, ..., 132   **b** $5(n - 1)$

4. a $a^2 - 3ab + 2b^2$

b $3x^2 + 7x + 2$

c $p^2 + 2pq + q^2$

5. a 2.4   **b** 1.375   **6. a** $\frac{1}{6}$ **b** $\frac{25}{36}$

7. a i $(4, 0)$ **ii** $(0, 8)$

b $(2.5, 3)$

c $y = 2 - 2x$

8. a $T = \dfrac{100I}{PR}$, 2

b i $s = \dfrac{v^2 - u^2}{2a}$

ii $x = p^2 - q$

9. a $x(x + 6)$

b $(x - 4)(x - 6)$

c $(x - 2)(x - 4)$

d $(p + 6)(p - 6)$

10. a £150

b £45

Revision Exercise 4.5 (p. 318)

1. a 34.7 cm

b i $x = 30$

ii $x = 18$

iii $x = \frac{15}{14}$

iv $y = 10$

v $x = 7$

vi $x = 5\frac{1}{3}$

2. 7

3. a $9xy - 3xz$

b $x^2 - 9x + 18$

c $7 + 20a - 3a^2$

d $16x^2 - 9$

4. a $5\frac{1}{4}$

b i $Q = \dfrac{70P}{11}$ **ii** $P = \dfrac{11Q}{70}$

5. a 60.75 cm

b 16.75 cm

c i 8.8 cm   **ii** 15.4 cm

6. b 9.85 cm   **c** 37.4 cm² (3 s.f.)   **d** 164 cm² (3 s.f.)

7.

8. yes; $\hat{A} = \hat{F}$, $\hat{B} = \hat{E}$;
DF = 22.32 cm

9. a i $b = \dfrac{2}{a}$

ii $q = \dfrac{p}{3r}$

iii $x = (p - q)^2$

iv $I = 5(A - P)$

v $x = \pm\sqrt{\dfrac{A}{4\pi}}$

vi $c = \frac{3}{2}(2a - b)$

b i $b = \dfrac{Z - ax}{y}$

ii 3

10. a $3t(1 - 2t)$

b $3(x + 4)(x - 1)$

c $(x - 6)(x + 2)$

d $(x + 4)^2$

Chapter 17

Exercise 17A (p. 321)

1. a no   **b** nothing   **c** no   **d** no

2. a 4, 2, 6   **b** 4, 4, 2

c mean and range together are better   **d** no

Exercise 17B (p. 326)

1. 8.03   **3.** 7.6 cm   **5.** 29.5 (3 s.f.)

2. 4.2   **4.** 50.5 p

6.

Defective screws	0–2	3–5	6–8	9–11
Frequency	10	7	2	1

; 3.1

7. a 195   **b** 25 min

c

Midclass value, t min	2.5	7.5	12.5	17.5	22.5
Frequency	25	35	100	25	10

d 11.5 min

8. a 1040   **b** They vary; no   **c** 1116

d

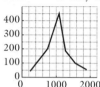

9. a

Time (min)	20	21	22	23	24	25	26	27	28	29	30
Frequency	2	5	4	2	6	4	2	1	1	2	1

b 23.9 min   **c** 10 min

d Derek doesn't take less time on average but his times are more reliable.

10. Mean between 8 p.m. and 9 p.m. is much higher (13 mph) than between 8 a.m. and 9 a.m., while the range is more than 3 times as much. Traffic moves far more freely in the evening.

11. a B has smaller fields of smaller area on average and none as large as the largest in A.

b A: 50, 24; B: 152, 12

c **i** 32.3   **ii** 30.2

d no

Exercise 17C (p. 331)

1. 8   **3.** 50–74

2. 21–30   **4.** $155 \leqslant h < 160$

5. a 25.75, 28

b 12; at least 10 had 32 or more

Exercise 17D (p. 332)

1. b 3.48   **c** 3

2. a 30.6 min   **b** 85   **c** 20–30 min

3. 141 miles

4. a 98   **b** 102   **c** $\frac{5}{102}$ **d** 0

e girls: mean £3, range £10, boys: mean £4.22, range £16

f The girls have less, on average, than the boys and the amounts the girls have are less widely spread than the amounts the boys have.

g £3.62

Chapter 18

Exercise 18B (p. 336)

1. a −0.8, 3.8   **c** −1.5, 4.5

b −1.7, 4.7   **d** 0.4, 2.6

2. a **i** −0.8, 4.8   **iii** −0.2, 4.2

ii 0.3, 3.7   **iv** −0.1, 4.1

b 2, the value repeats

c No; there is no value of x on the graph for which $y = 10$.

3. a **i** 0.7, 4.3   **ii** 0.2, 4.8   **iii** 1.4, 3.6

b No; the lowest point on the graph is $(2.5, -3.25)$, it does not go down to $y = -4$.

4. b −6.25 at $x = 1.5$ **c** −1, 4

d −1.9, 4.9; $x^2 - 3x - 9 = 0$

Exercise 18C (p. 339)

1. a 2.4   **b** −1.7

2. b 2

3. a **i** −2.9, −0.5, 3.4   **ii** −3.6, 1.1, 2.4

b **i** 0, ±3.2

ii −0.5, −2.9, 3.4

iii 1.2, −3.6, 2.4

c yes, only solution is −3.7.

4. a **i** 4   **ii** −5

b **i** 2.5, −2.5, 0   **ii** 0.3, −2.6, 2.3   **iii** 2.9

c 0.7, −2.7, 2; $x^3 - 6x + 4 = 0$

5. b **i** −0.9   **ii** 1.5

c **i** 1.7   **ii** 2.8   **iii** 3.6   **iv** 2.9

Exercise 18D (p. 342)

1. cannot divide by zero

2. a 0.4   **b** 0.4   **c** 5

d y gets larger very fast

e 2 lines of symmetry, rotational symmetry, order 2, about O

3. a missing values are: −0.67, −1, −2, 1, 0.67, 0.5

c cannot divide by zero

d **i** 0.8   **ii** −1.1

4. a $y = 1$ when $x = 12$ **b** 0.12

c approaching zero

5. a $y < 0.1$ and getting smaller

b no; if $y = \frac{1}{x}$ then $xy = 1$ and $x \times 0 \neq 1$

c no; $0 \times y \neq 1$

Exercise 18E (p. 344)

1. D   **8.**   **12.**

2. B

3. A

4. A

5. 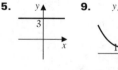   **9.**   **13.**

6. 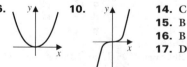   **10.**   **14.** C

15. B

16. B

17. D

7. 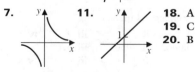   **11.**   **18.** A

19. C

20. B

Exercise 18F (p. 348)

1. a i 2.5   **ii** 0.8   **b** $k = 3$
2. a i 13 °C   **ii** 4 °C   **b** 3.6 min
  c There is a value for temperature when time is
    zero so the equation is not of the form $y = \dfrac{1}{x}$

3. a i 13 m   **iii** 1 second and 4 seconds
  ii 15.5 m   **iv** 5 seconds
  b A
4. a 30   **c** 16
  b 240   **d**

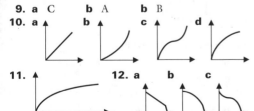

5. B   **6. a** C   **b** B

Exercise 18G (p. 351)

1. +ve increasing   **2.** +ve decreasing
3. +ve large, decreasing to C, then increasing
4. −ve increasing
5. +ve increasing to C, then constant
6. large +ve decreasing to zero, then −ve increasing

Exercise 18H (p. 352)

1. a decreases rapidly at first then more slowly as it
    reaches room temperature
  b falling very slowly
  c room temperature
2. a increase
  b B to C constant; C to D increasing more
    quickly
3. a i A to B   **ii** B to C   **d** D
  b maximum   **e** E
  c red; car stops
4. a balloon bursts
  b i A–B increasing   **ii** B–C constant
  c stopping to take breath
5. a Gita, 16 s   **c** Phyllis
  b ½ second   **d** 40 m
6. a 25 cm   **b** 10 cm   **c** 25 seconds
7. a room temperature   **b** increasing
  c The thermostat cuts in and out, keeping the
    temperature within a narrow range.
8. A
9. a C   **b** A   **b** B
10. a   **b**   **c**   **d**

11.   **12. a**   **b**   **c**

13.   **14.**

Chapter 19

Exercise 19A (p. 359)

1. b 37°   **c** 0.75   **5. b** 37°   **c** 0.75
2. b 37°   **c** 0.75   **6.** yes
3. b 37°   **c** 0.75   **7.** Â = 26.5°; 0.5; all equal
4. b 37°   **c** 0.75   **9. a** 0.6   **b** 0.8

Exercise 19B (p. 361)

1. a 0.364   **d** 4.70   **g** 1.33   **j** 5.67
  b 0.532   **e** 3.08   **h** 1
  c 0.781   **f** 0.649   **i** 1.66
2. 0.75, they are the same
3. a 0.277   **c** 0.202   **e** 0.0664
  b 0.568   **d** 1.74

Exercise 19C (p. 362)

1.   **3.**   **5.**

2.   **4.**   **6.**

Exercise 19D (p. 363)

1. a 5.64 cm   **b** 1.43 cm   **c** 5.81 cm
2. a 0.975 cm   **b** 14.1 cm   **c** 5.38 cm
3. a 7.77 cm   **b** 7.00 cm   **c** 3.12 cm
4. a 4.50 cm   **b** 16.9 cm   **c** 7.05 cm
5. a 6.43 cm   **b** 9.33 cm   **c** 6.24 cm
6. a 5.22 cm   **b** 17.8 cm
7. a 3.00 m   **b** 9.23 m

Exercise 19E (p. 365)

1. a 5.77 cm   **3. a** 3.68 cm   **5. a** 9.99 cm
  b 8.96 cm   **b** 4.18 cm   **b** 3.50 cm
2. a 4.60 cm   **4. a** 5.60 cm   **6. a** 14.1 cm
  b 6.64 cm   **b** 32.4 cm   **b** 17.9 cm

Exercise 19F (p. 367)

1. a 65.6°   **2. a** 31.0°   **3. a** 18.4°
  b 19.8°   **b** 38.7°   **b** 8.1°
  c 76.3°   **c** 26.6°   **c** 9.5°
  d 54.5°   **d** 35.0°   **d** 39.8°
  e 34.0°   **e** 8.5°   **e** 59.0°
  f 44.8°   **f** 51.3°   **f** 23.2°
  g 64.4°   **g** 20.6°   **g** 12.5°
  h 45°   **h** 66.0°   **h** 66.8°
    i 6.8°   **i** 24.0°
    j 67.4°   **j** 53.1°

Exercise 19G (p. 368)

1. a 42.0° b 50.2° c 33.7°
2. a 55.0° b 59.0° c 22.8°
3. a 33.7° b 36.9°
4. a 33.7° b 33.7°
5. a 31.8° b 47.7°
6. a 59.0° b 51.3°
7. a 73.3° b 30.3°

Exercise 19H (p. 370)

1. a 0.438 c 0.429 e 0.981
   b 0.995 d 0.603
2. a 56.5° d 44.7° g 33.8°
   b 24.4° e 69.7° h 21.1°
   c 39.7° f 59.2°

Exercise 19I (p. 371)

1. a 8.83 cm 4. a 1.07 cm 7. a 23.6°
   b 2.68 cm b 9.54 cm b 51.3°
2. a 6.22 cm 5. a 6.02 cm 8. a 23.6°
   b 2.63 cm b 4.85 cm b 30°
3. a 1.95 cm 6. a 44.4° 9. a 33.4°
   b 2.51 cm b 36.9° b 42.2°

Exercise 19J (p. 374)

1. a 0.515 c 0.998 e 0.498
   b 0.669 d 0.708
2. a 64.2° c 89.3° e 76.1°
   b 19.4° d 45.6°

Exercise 19K (p. 375)

1. a 8.48 cm b 2.68 cm
2. a 5.07 cm b 3.08 cm
3. a 3.75 cm b 3.22 cm
4. a 10.2 cm b 2.78 cm
5. a 53.1° b 60° c 68.0°
6. a 38.7° b 63.3° c 41.1°
7. a 34.3° b 56.5°

Exercise 19L (p. 377)

1. a tangent b sine c cosine
2. a tangent b cosine c sine
3. a tangent b cosine
4. a sine b sine
5. a tangent b cosine
6. a 51.3° b 61.0° c 49.5°
7. a 41.8° b 32.6° c 41.4°
8. a 55.6° b 35.3° c 31.3°
9. a 3.06 cm b 32.7 cm c 0.282 cm
10. a 1.09 cm b 320 cm c 2.37 cm
11. a 24.7 cm b 34.1 cm c 28.8 cm
12. a 44.4°, 45.6° b 4.50 cm c 12.2 cm
13. a 35.3 cm b 13.4 cm c 71.9°, 18.1°

Exercise 19M (p. 381)

1. a 4.13 cm b 4.67 cm c 8.72 cm
2. a 23.3 cm b 17.0 cm c 14.9 cm
3. a 24.6 cm b 22.9 cm c 10.8 cm

4. a 4.40 cm b 33.1 cm
5. a 14.9 cm b 42.6 cm
6. a 16.4 cm, 18.3 cm
   b 26.2°, 84.3 mm, 41.5 mm
7. a 65.7°, 13.9 cm, 6.30 cm
   b 17.6°, 51.5 cm, 16.3 cm
8. a 55.8°, 399 mm, 224 mm
   b 37.6°, 52.4°, 43.3 cm
   c 48.8°, 41.2°, 15.9 cm
9. a 38.0°, 52.0°, 79.2 cm
   b 65.6°, 17.2 cm, 18.9 cm
   c 31.6°, 22.3 cm, 26.1 cm
10. a 37.5°, 27.9 m, 45.9 m
   b 36.2°, 53.8°, 6.70 cm
   c 36.3°, 53.7°, 3.97 cm

Summary 5

Revision Exercise 5.1 (p. 385)

1. a 0–5 b 0–5 c 6.1
2. a 55 b 17 c 76.3 kg
   d

3. a 41 c 10–14
   b

Number of plants	Frequency	
0–4	4	10
5–9	16	
10–14	13	
15–19	8	

4. B
5. a i −0.2 and 5.2
      ii 0.7 and 4.3
      iii −0.9 and 5.9
   b no; highest value for y is 7.25
6. a decrease; no, attendances decreased faster as time passed
   b i constant attendance
      ii attendance increased at a constant rate
7. 14.0 cm 8. a 55.2° b 43.4°
9. a 32.0° b 36.6° c 39.5°
10. a 3.84 cm b 5.54 cm c 11.2 cm
11. a 15.5 feet b 75.5° 12. 73.1 kg
13. a y: 1, 2, 5, 10, 17, 26, 37, 50, 65
   b

   c 6.6

Revision Exercise 5.2 (p. 390)

1. a 48 b 18 min
   c

Middle value, t	1.5	4.5	7.5	10.5	13.5	16.5
Frequency	3	6	17	13	7	2

   d 8.81 minutes; midvalues used, not original data

2. a

Time (min)	15	16	17	18	19	20	21	22	23	24	25
Frequency	2	5	4	2	6	4	2	1	1	2	1

  b **i** 18.9 min   **ii** 10
  c Bob's average is about the same as George's,
    but his range is only half,
    i.e. George is sometimes much slower,
    other times much faster.

3. C

4. a B   **b** D   **c** C   **d** A

5. a $51.6°$ **b** 13.3 cm   **c** 21.4 cm

6. a 11.4 m   **b** 16.9 m

Revision Exercise 5.3 (p. 391)

1. a **i** 47 300 **ii** 0.0176   **b** 2
  c **i** $\frac{1}{8}$ **ii** $\frac{1}{16}$ **iii** 1 **iv** $\frac{4}{9}$
  d **i** p^4 **ii** x^9 **iii** p^2 **iv** a^{-5}

2. a $\frac{3}{5}$ **c** $\frac{9}{25}$ **d** $\frac{12}{25}$

3. a $n^2 + 4$ **b** **i** 1, 4, 7, 10
                    ii 2, 5, 10, 17
                    iii $\frac{2}{3}, \frac{3}{4}, \frac{4}{5}, \frac{5}{6}$

4. a $1\frac{1}{3}$ **b** $3\frac{1}{8}$ cm

5. a **i** £10.80 **ii** 200 miles   **b** 12

6. a **i**

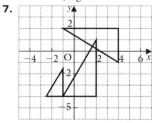

an estate agent or farmer

    ii 61 hectares

  b **i** $\frac{2}{3}$; 1 litres costs £0.67
    ii $-\frac{1}{10}$; tank decreases by $\frac{1}{10}$ litre for each km
        travelled
    iii 4.5; 1 gallon = 4.5 litres

7.

8. a **i** $a^2(1 - a)$ **iii** $(x + 4)(x + 6)$
    ii $(x - 7)(x + 3)$ **iv** $(x + y)(x - y)$
  b 70.8

  c **i** $\frac{3}{2y}$ **ii** $\frac{a}{(a + b)}$ **iii** 12 **iv** $\frac{2y}{x}$

Revision Exercise 5.4 (p. 394)

1. a $\frac{5}{12}$ **c** 15   **e** 5
  b $3\frac{1}{2}$ **d** 8   **f** 2

2. a 135 cm   **b** $1\frac{1}{4}$

3. a $4ab - 12ac$ **b** $x^2 - 4x - 12$
  c $4x^2 + 19x - 5$ **d** $25p^2 - 4q^2$

4. a 131 mm   **b** 32 mm

5. a **i** $u = 4v$ **iii** $t = \dfrac{b^2 - c^2}{2a}$
    ii $V = xy^2$ **iv** $c = \dfrac{b - 2a}{4}$
  b **i** $B = C(A - D)$ **ii** $\frac{9}{16}$

6. a £7550   **b** 55.6% (3 s.f.)

7. a 46   **d** 20 cm
  b 12.7 cm (3 s.f.) **e** $10 \leqslant h < 15$
  c

8. a $25.7°$ **b** 20.6 cm   **c** 47.5 cm

9. a £58.75   **b** 23.5%

10. a A
  b **i** slows down and stops
    ii increases speed and goes through lights at
        the increased steady speed
    iii slows down but increases to original speed
        to go through lights

11. a   **c**

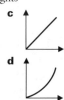

  b   **d**

INDEX